THE JUMBO BIBLE CROSSWORD COLLECTION

● Over 400 pages of challenging, fun Bible crosswords! ●

BARBOUR
PUBLISHING, INC.
Uhrichsville, Ohio

Published by Barbour Publishing, Inc.
   P.O. Box 719
   Uhrichsville, Ohio 44683
   http://www.barbourbooks.com

 Member of the
Evangelical Christian
Publishers Association

Printed in the United States of America.

BIBLE
CROSSWORD
COLLECTION #1

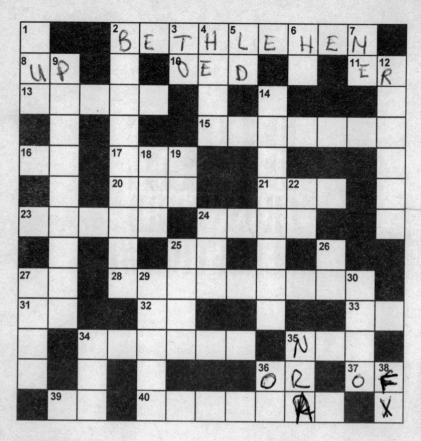

PUZZLE 1

ACROSS CLUES

2. _____ of Judea. (Matt. 2:1)
8. They rose _____ early. (Num. 14:40)
10. Oxford English Dictionary (abbr.).
11. Emergency Room (abbr.).
13. Melchisedec, king of _____. (Heb. 7:1)
15. Ahad called _____. (1 Kgs. 18:3)
16. This is the way, walk ye in _____. (Isa. 30:21)
17. That we may _____ and believe. (Mark 15:32)
20. For by _____ were all things created. (Col. 1:16)
21. The _____ appeareth, and the tender grass sheweth itself. (Prov. 27:25)
23. Temptress.
24. Decays.
25. _____ and Ma.
27. _____ the cross.

28. Who smote _____ the son of Jerubbesheth? (2 Sam. 11:21)
31. _____ it not written? (Mark 11:17)
32. _____ angel of the Lord. (Judg. 6:11)
33. Each (abbr.).
34. Saul of _____.
35. Ye seek me, _____. (John 6:26)
36. Either/ _____.
37. This was _____ of whom I spake. (John 1:15)
39. I in them, and thou in _____. (John 17:23)
40. Abraham took a wife, and her name was _____. (Gen. 25:1)

DOWN CLUES

1. Liquid of decay.
2. In the wilderness of _____. (Gen. 21:14)
3. _____ and fro.
4. David was one.
5. 450 (Roman).

6. Hello (informal).
7. Without _____ ye can do nothing. (John 15:5)
9. _____, and Medes. . . . (Acts 2:9)
12. Belonging to the son of Bani. (Neh. 3:17)
14. Rachel. . .called his name _____. (Gen. 30:8)
18. Masculine object (German).
19. Printer's measure.
22. _____ ye have. . .received Christ Jesus. (Col. 2:6)
24. A _____ caught in a thicket. (Gen. 22:13)
25. Sewing fasteners.
26. Before Christ (abbr.).
27. Olive and sunflower.
29. The son of Abinoam. (Judg. 4:6)
30. Sidon. . .and _____. (Gen. 10:15)
34. Open _____ door.
35. National Rifle Association (abbr.).
36. This _____ that.
38. For example (abbr.).

PUZZLE 2

Mary Ann Freeman

ACROSS CLUES

1. Zilpah's first son. (Gen. 30:11)
4. Exclamation said when making a mistake.
8. Doth the wild ass _____ when he hath grass? (Job 6:5)
12. I and my Father are _____. (John 10:30)
13. The truth shall make you _____. (John 8:32)
14. They put on him a purple _____. (John 19:2)
15. Deoxyribonucleic acid.
16. _____ my lambs. (John 21:15)
17. Poems intended to be sung.
18. Abram's wife. (Gen. 16:1)
20. For fear that.
22. The _____ of violence is in their hands. (Isa. 59:6)
24. Belonging to a Jericho woman. (Josh. 2:1)
28. All-terrain vehicle.
31. The mother of all living. (Gen. 3:20)
33. Abram's father. (Gen. 11:26)
34. Chemical (abbr.).
36. The rich man was _____. (Mark 10:22)
38. Uncommon.
39. Attempts.
41. And take away all thy _____. (Isa. 1:25)
43. Thirteenth letter of the Hebrew alphabet.
44. Before twilight.
46. Doth not your master _____ tribute? (Matt. 17:24)
48. Potato.
50. Neither hot nor cold.
54. Siamese.
57. Biblical liquid measure.
59. Sweetened lemon drink.
60. Very small amount.
61. Telephone _____ code.
62. National Education Association.
63. Sun at evening.
64. _____ not unto thine own understanding. (Prov. 3:5)
65. One of the twelve tribes. (Ex. 1:4)

DOWN CLUES

1. No other _____ before me. (Ex. 20:3)
2. Prophetess. (Luke 2:36)
3. As _____ children. (Eph. 5:1)
4. All members have not the same _____. (Rom. 12:4)
5. Mineral.
6. _____ an orange.
7. Passover feast.
8. Closer than a _____. (Prov. 18:24)
9. Thy _____ and thy staff. (Ps. 23:4)
10. Lincoln.
11. Yea.
19. Associate in Arts (abbr.).
21. _____ down on the right hand of God. (Heb. 10:12)
23. Televisions.
25. Biblical name for Syria.
26. John _____ witness of him. (John 1:15)
27. Noah's son. (Gen. 6:10)
28. New Testament book.
29. Through (informal).
30. Blood vessel.
32. Desired to _____ this passover. (Luke 22:15)

35. I know that _____ cometh. (John 4:25)

37. That he may _____ the tip of his finger. (Luke 16:24)

40. September (abbr.).

42. He rebuked David. (2 Sam. 12:1-12)

45. Son of Japheth. (1 Chron. 1:5)

47. Seek _____ first the kingdom of God. (Matt. 6:33)

49. Some would even _____ to die. (Rom. 5:7)

51. _____ of remorse.

52. Thought.

53. The _____ in Christ shall rise. (1 Thes. 4:16)

54. _____ the season to be jolly.

55. To cultivate.

56. Ma Bell.

58. Hot beverage.

PUZZLE 3

ACROSS CLUES

1. Daniel the _____. (Matt. 24:15)
7. _____ stilled the people. (Num. 13:30)
12. Lord, _____ long? (Isa. 6:11)
13. Iron _____.
14. Not live by bread _____. (Matt. 4:4)
15. _____ I my brother's keeper? (Gen. 4:9)
16. The family of _____. (1 Sam. 10:21)
17. Measure of weight.
18. A pharaoh.
20. Middle Atlantic state (abbr.).
22. _____ will we sing. (Ps. 21:13)
23. I am _____ the Father. (John 14:10)
24. How _____ it that ye have no faith (Mark 4:40)
25. Go up _____ Jerusalem. (Acts 25:9)
26. Old Testament (abbr.).
27. Saint (abbr.).
28. That it shall _____. (Acts 27:25)
29. Social Security (abbr.).
30. Yes (Spanish).
31. Samuel ran to _____. (1 Sam. 3:5)
33. He looked on the _____. (Num. 24:21)
36. Variation of *aeon.*
37. And the Lord shut him _____. (Gen. 7:16)
38. To scheme. (2 words)
40. Disc jockeys (abbr.).
42. _____ he is come. (John 4:25)
43. Long _____.

45. To the slaughter, like _____. (Jer. 51:40)
46. Christ _____ me. (1 Cor. 1:17)
48. Elimelch's wife. (Ruth 1:2)
50. Standard in golf.
51. Long, narrow fish.
53. Type of acid.
55. Nos.
56. Orderly.
57. Mine enemy and my _____ (sing.) (Ps. 27:2)

DOWN CLUES

1. A certain _____ besought him. (Luke 11:37)
2. Art thou a _____? (Acts 22:27)
3. Exclamation of pain.
4. Houses.
5. Periods of time.
6. Asian holiday.
7. _____ and Abel.
8. American League (abbr.).
9. _____ sat in the gate of Sodom. (Gen. 19:1)
10. Seth called his son's name _____. (Gen. 4:26)
11. Name Rachel called Benjamin. (Gen. 35:18)
19. _____ thou on my right hand. (Matt. 22:44)
21. _____ coat of many colors.
25. Number of lepers. (Luke 17:12)
27. All manner of _____. (Matt. 12:31)
28. The sons of Rachel; Joseph, and _____. (Gen. 35:24)
29. Put away (on a boat).
32. _____ ago.
33. Passest over the brook _____. (1 Kgs. 2:37)

8

34. Consider _____ in thine heart. (Deut. 4:39)
35. Let us not _____, as do others. (1 Thes. 5:6)
39. Was one _____ a prophetess. (Luke 2:36)
41. I will _____ all thy borders with frogs. (Ex. 8:2)
43. So be it.
44. The _____ true God. (John 17:3)
47. The _____ of life. (Rev. 22:2)
49. The _____ wherein Ishmael had cast...the dead. (Jer. 41:9)
52. Each (abbr.).
54. Egyptian god.

PUZZLE 4

ACROSS CLUES

2. Charge _____, and encourage him. (Deut. 3:28)
8. Terrorist.
9. Ye shall be _____ gods. (Gen. 3:5)
10. I _____ _____ pleasant bread. (Dan. 10:3; 2 words)
13. To _____ or not to _____.
14. Second book of the Bible.
16. Past.
18. He shall cry unto _____ (Ps. 89:26)
19. The Lord saved Hezekiah... from..._____. (2 Chron. 32:22)
24. Ascending up _____ Jerusalem.
25. I will let down the _____. (Luke 5:5)
26. _____ the Baptist.
28. First book of the Bible.
30. Rolled back the stone from the _____. (Matt. 28:2)
32. Yes (Spanish).
33. Buddy.

35. O.T. books of the Bible.
37. A grain often used for cereal.
40. I _____ that I _____.
42. O foolish _____. (Gal. 3:1)
45. _____ Lord and _____ God.
46. Made himself of _____ reputation. (Phil. 2:7)
47. So be it.
48. These are the three _____ of Noah. (Gen. 9:19)

DOWN CLUES

1. Long _____.
2. A son of Issachar. (Gen. 46:13)
3. They shall be _____ flesh. (Gen. 2:24)
4. Minor prophet.
5. We.
6. Take up thy _____. (Matt. 9:6)
7. The wringing of the _____ bringeth blood (Prov. 30:33)
10. Implement for cutting down trees.
11. Organized travel.
12. Fourth book of the Bible.
15. Postscript (abbr.).

16. _____ angel of the Lord. (Luke 1:11)
17. Ocean (abbr.).
20. Behold, a man of _____. (Acts 8:27)
21. Prefix for *not*.
22. Tenth book of the New Testament.
23. That I am _____ the Father. (John 14:10)
26. A son of Leah. (Gen. 35:23)
27. Last book of the Bible (abbr.).
29. _____ no more. (John 5:14)
31. Egyptian sun god.
34. Rich soil.
36. Belonging to Sam.
38. They... _____ the sacrifices of the dead. (Ps. 106:28)
39. A metal.
41. _____ name is Legion. (Mark 5:9)
42. _____ thy way; thy son liveth. (John 4:50)
43. Note on the scale.
44. Yet _____ as by fire. (1 Cor. 3:15)

PUZZLE 5

Mary Ann Freeman

ACROSS CLUES

1. Touched the _____ . (Matt. 9:20)
4. I know in _____. (1 Cor. 13:12)
8. Sendeth _____ on the just. (Matt. 5:45)
12. The serpent beguiled _____. (2 Cor. 11:3)
13. _____ despised his birthright. (Gen. 25:34)
14. Woe to them that are at _____ in Zion (Amos 6:1)
15. _____ as a sheep to the slaughter. (Acts 8:32)
16. I will give you _____. (Matt. 11:28)
17. As the Lord _____. (Josh. 11:9)
18. I _____ toward the mark. (Phil. 3:14)
20. Now abideth faith, _____, charity. (1 Cor. 13:13)
22. Your life is _____ with Christ in God. (Col. 3:3)
24. This is the _____ of John. (John 1:19)
28. They called for Jesus' death.
31. All things _____ possible. (Mark 9:23)
33. Where Joshua and all Israel stoned Achan. (Josh. 7:24-25)
34. A tenth of an ephah. (Ex. 16:36)
36. Verily I say unto _____.
38. Say ye unto your brethren, _____. (Hos. 2:1)
39. Moses' brother. (Ex. 4:14)
41. National Security Council (abbr.).
43. Labor Day month (abbr.).
44. How Samuel's sons were influenced. (1 Sam. 8:3)
46. _____ hath not seen. (1 Cor. 2:9)

48. Ahab served _____ a little. (2 Kgs. 10:18)
50. If thy _____ eye offend thee. (Matt. 5:29)
54. Run with patience the _____. (Heb. 12:1)
57. I am the true _____. (John 15:1)
59. Japanese drama.
60. The twelfth month. (Es. 3:7)
61. Seared with a hot _____. (1 Tim. 4:2)
62. Solomon's navy brought him this animal. (1 Kgs. 10:22)
63. The son of _____. (Mark 6:3)
64. _____ any of you. (1 Cor. 6:1)
65. Were there not _____ cleansed? (Luke 17:17)

DOWN CLUES

1. _____ thou mine unbelief. (Mark 9:24)
2. Sing of the mercies of the Lord for _____. (Ps. 89:1)
3. Darius' nationality. (Dan. 11:1)
4. Cyrus king of _____. (2 Chron. 36:23)
5. Indicates an enzyme.
6. Be not _____ with thy mouth. (Ec. 5:2)
7. Private instructor.
8. Isaac's wife. (Rom. 9:10)
9. Auto club.
10. Independent School District (abbr.).
11. Indicates maiden name.
19. Be quiet!
21. Green vegetable.
23. O ye _____ bones. (Eze. 37:4)
25. Electrical units.
26. Bear witness also at _____. (Acts 23:11)
27. To shed drops.
28. Ruth left this country. (Ruth 1:22)

29. One of the sons of Eliphaz. (Gen. 36:11)
30. One of the sons of Zophah. (1 Chron. 7:36)
32. Long time.
35. Thought it not _____ to be equal with God. (Phil. 2:6)
37. Them which despitefully _____ you. (Matt. 5:44)
40. National Education Association (abbr.).
42. They found a man of _____. (Matt. 27:32)
45. Jesse's youngest son. (1 Sam. 17:14)
47. East Indies (abbr.).
49. Italian money.
51. Which strain at a _____. (Matt. 23:24)
52. The _____ of glory. (Col. 1:27)
53. _____ that which is in part shall be done away. (1 Cor. 13:10)
54. Abraham went and took the _____. (Gen. 22:13)
55. American Dental Association (abbr.).
56. Automobile.
58. Neither cold _____ hot. (Rev. 3:16)

PUZZLE 6

David Greenlee

ACROSS CLUES

1. I _____ (name of God).
4. Father.
6. A deity or idol.
9. Fruit of the Spirit. (Gal. 5:22)
13. Satan went _____ and fro. (Job 1:7)
14. Small, humanlike mythical being.
15. Prefix of negation.
16. _____ from God the Father. (Gal. 1:3)
18. Moses' second book (abbr.).
19. _____, every one that thirsteth (Isa. 55:1)
20. _____ fell from Saul's eyes. (Acts 9:18)
23. Peter wrote _____ the scattered Jews. (1 Pet. 1:1)
24. I will...have mercy on _____. (Jer. 33:26)
25. Indefinite singular article.

26. Hiram's navy brought this animal to Solomon. (1 Kgs. 10:22)
27. Traveled with Rebekah. (Gen. 24:59)
29. Ancient city.
31. The Spirit descended in this form. (Matt. 3:16)
33. This animal spoke to Balaam. (Num. 22:28)
34. In him is _____ darkness. (1 John 1:5)
35. Used to kill Stephen. (Acts 7:58)
37. Pilate found no _____ of death in Jesus. (Luke 23:22)
39. Relationship of Martha and Mary to Lazarus. (John 11:1)
41. _____ his money. (Gen. 42:27)
42. Built the ark. (Luke 17:27)
45. Peleth's son. (Num. 16:1)
47. Year of the Lord (Latin abbr.).
48. Ye shall be _____ gods. (Gen. 3:5)
49. Love thy _____. (Matt. 5:43)

DOWN CLUES

1. Albert (short form).
2. Something small in the eye.
3. King of Bashan. (Num. 21:33)
4. King of Assyria. (2 Kgs. 15:19)
5. Set your _____ on the things above. (Col. 3:2, plural)
6. Fruit of the Spirit. (Gal. 5:22)
7. Gold (Spanish).
8. Eats.
10. A just and perfect man. (Gen. 6:9)
11. The pure in heart...shall _____ God. (Matt. 5:8)
12. Fruit of the Spirit. (Gal. 5:22)
16. Sound in faith, charity, and _____. (Titus 2:2)
1. Jesus was moved with _____. (Matt. 9:36)
21. _____, Lord God! (Jer. 4:10)
22. Ostrichlike bird.
25. Donkey.
26. Alabama (abbr.).
28. Brought food to Elijah. (1 Kgs. 17:6)
30. My soul _____ in the Lord. (Ps. 34:2)
31. It is lawful to _____ well. (Matt. 12:12)
32. Rebekah's face covering. (Gen. 24:65, modern spelling)
36. Golf ball supporter.
38. Opposite of down.
40. Lion's call. (1 Pet. 5:8)
43. Name of an altar. (Josh. 22:34)
44. See 3 down.
45. 21-verse prophet (abbr.).
46. If we say we have _____ sin. (1 John 1:8)

PUZZLE 7
Diana Rowland

ACROSS CLUES

1. Now the Lord said unto _____. (Gen. 12:1)
6. Are not _____ and Pharpar rivers of Damascus? (2 Kgs. 5:12)
11. Abraham... _____ the wood. (Gen. 22:3)
12. Athenian woman who believed. (Acts 17:34)
15. In charge of King Ahasuerus' women. (Es. 2:3)
16. The Lord sent him to meet Moses in the wilderness. (Ex. 4:27)
17. Infant's first word for *Daddy*.
18. Joseph's wife. (Gen. 41:45)
20. The works that are done _____ the sun. (Ec. 1:14)
22. I am, you are, he_____.
23. Dialect for *get*.
24. Eli heard the noise of the _____. (1 Sam. 4:14)
25. Joshua sent men from Jericho to _____. (Josh. 7:2)
26. Descendants of Eri. (Num. 26:16)
28. Sarah shall bear unto thee _____ this set time. (Gen. 17:21)
29. Not bow down thyself to them, _____ serve them. (Ex. 20:5)
31. I _____ the marathon.
32. Place of 12 wells of water. (Ex. 15:27)
34. _____ ye therefore. (Matt. 28:19)
35. The sons of Aaron, took either of them his _____. (Lev. 10:1)
37. They went forth _____ go. (Gen. 12:5)
38. King of Greek gods.
40. Cut off his right _____. (Luke 22:50)
41. God said, _____ shall not eat of every tree. (Gen. 3:1)
42. Bright _____.
44. Strong people set in battle _____. (Joel 2:5)
46. And, _____, the angel of the Lord came. (Luke 2:9)
47. Melts.
49. Upon the great _____ of their right feet. (Lev. 8:24)
52. For it is the _____ of _____ flesh. (Lev. 17:14; 2 words)
54. Ahian, and Schechem, and _____. (1 Chron. 7:19)
55. Led him away to _____ first. (John 18:13)
56. An _____ ___ the hole (2 words).

DOWN CLUES

1. Gallio was the deputy of _____. (Acts 18:12)
2. Thou shalt be a _____. (Gen. 12:2)
3. Why do the heathen _____? (Ps. 2:1)
4. The Lord is the _____ of all such. (1 Thes. 4:6)
5. _____, myself, and I.
6. And _____ bare Jabal. (Gen. 4:20)
7. Candy or ice cream _____.
8. Loves.
9. Mary Poppins was one.
10. Pass over through _____. (Deut. 2:18)
13. Joseph's brothers didn't know his _____.
14. "Hey, _____." Beetle Bailey's call.
16. Dresses (verb).
19. The fowl of the _____. (Gen. 1:26)
21. The sun _____ of Ahaz. (Isa. 38:8)

24. And the _____ of pure gold. (1 Kgs. 7:50)

27. You get this at a beach.

30. Leak out slowly.

32. Flighty, capricious.

33. _____, Larry, and Curly.

35. The tents of _____ in affliction. (Hab. 3:7)

36. Give _____ to his commandments. (Ex. 15:26)

39. Hast thou _____ of the tree? (Gen. 3:11)

42. So that it went _____ with Moses. (Ps. 106:32)

43. The noise of them that sing _____ ___ hear. (Ex. 32:18; 2 words)

44. Pointed tools for piercing holes.

45. Broken the bands of your _____. (Lev. 26:13)

48. Order ___ _____ carte (2 words).

50. Benjamin's son. (Gen. 46:21)

51. Cleanseth us from all _____. (1 John 1:7)

53. Do, Re, Mi, _____.

54. Syllable to sing when you don't know the words.

PUZZLE 8
Mary Ann Freeman

ACROSS CLUES

1. Pick up your _____.
   (John 5:8 NIV)
4. Go _____ to thy friends.
   (Mark 5:19)
8. Mary hath chosen that good
   _____. (Luke 10:42)
12. Many _____ called.
    (Matt. 22:14)
13. A garden eastward in _____.
    (Gen. 2:8)
14. The Eranites came from _____.
    (Num. 26:36)
15. Likened unto _____ virgins.
    (Matt. 25:1)
16. Part of a necklace.
17. The veil...was _____ in twain.
    (Matt. 27:51)
18. _____ Tots (brand name).
20. Turn and _____. (Isa. 22:18)
22. For the sky is _____. (Matt. 16:2)
24. The third day he shall be _____
    again. (Matt. 17:23)
28. Who Matthew would work for
    today.
31. Harder to be _____ than a strong
    city. (Prov. 18:19)
33. The Lord added to the church
    _____. (Acts 2:47)
34. Lament.
36. My _____ shall supply.
    (Phil. 4:19)
38. Thy _____ is as the tower of
    Lebanon. (Song of Sol. 7:4)
39. Scourge a man that is a _____?
    (Acts 22:25)
41. In the beginning _____ the
    Word. (John 1:1)
43. Nickname for Edward.
44. That I may _____ unto you.
    (Rom. 1:11)

46. Your yea be yea; and your
    _____. (Jam. 5:12)
48. Call me not Naomi, call me
    _____. (Ruth 1:20)
50. Goodness and _____. (Ps. 23:6)
54. In _____ was there a voice
    heard. (Matt. 2:18)
57. _____ was a cunning hunter.
    (Gen. 25:27)
59. International Labor Organization
    (abbr.).
60. Worthy to _____ the book.
    (Rev. 5:2)
61. Ireland.
62. Country northeast of India
    (abbr.).
63. Belonging to Rachel's youngest
    son (nickname). (Gen. 35:18)
64. _____, why persecutest thou me?
    (Acts 9:4)
65. The light of the body is the
    _____. (Matt. 6:22)

DOWN CLUES

1. Gospel name (abbr.).
2. Length times width.
3. Enlarge the place of thy _____.
   (Isa. 54:2)
4. Nurse of the _____ women.
   (Ex. 2:7)
5. Poem.
6. Strong _____ belongeth to them.
   (Heb. 5:14)
7. A familiar spirit at _____.
   (1 Sam. 28:7)
8. Cyrus the _____. (Dan. 6:28)
9. Ye _____ the branches.
   (John 15:5)
10. Esau _____ to meet him.
    (Gen. 33:4)
11. Explosive.
19. A son of Judah. (Num. 26:19)
21. He was _____. (Mark 10:22)
23. A living _____ is better than a
    dead lion. (Ec. 9:4)
25. I lay in _____. (1 Pet. 2:6)

26. Children, or _____ I die. (Gen. 30:1)
27. Bring rams' skins _____ red. (Ex. 25:5)
28. Father of Omri. (1 Chron. 9:4)
29. No _____ for them. (Luke 2:7)
30. Corn mush.
32. _____ is the day of salvation (2 Cor. 6:2)
35. Belonging to the captain of the king of Syria. (2 Kgs. 5:1)
37. Bilhah's first son. (Gen. 30:5-6)
40. National Rifle Association (abbr.).
42. Moses and _____ stood before me. (Jer. 15:1)

45. All the _____ of the field. (Isa. 55:12)
47. All _____ people. (Ps. 47:1)
49. They which dwelt in _____ heard the word. (Acts 19:10)
51. The harvest of the earth is _____. (Rev. 14:15)
52. Hath not the potter power over the _____? (Rom. 9:21)
53. My _____ is easy. (Matt. 11:30)
54. Will a man _____ God? (Mal. 3:8)
55. To mimic.
56. Fishers of _____. (Mark 1:17)
58. Islands east of Indonesia.

PUZZLE 9

Diana Rowland

ACROSS CLUES

1. I will raise unto David a righteous _____. (Jer. 23:5)
7. If any be a _____ of the word. (Jam. 1:23)
13. An ocean-edge lake.
14. _____ for thy life. (Gen. 19:17)
15. Ivory and _____. (Ezek. 27:15)
16. Of _____ shall there be _____ like weight. (Ex. 30:34; 2 words)
17. That I might not _____ against thee. (Ps. 119:11)
18. Who walk in the _____ of the Lord. (Ps. 119:1)
21. Pay _____ view.
22. Temporary duty (abbr.).
23. Could not drink of the waters of _____. (Ex. 15:23)
25. And I will walk _____ liberty. (Ps. 119:45)
27. Accompanied him into Asia _____ of Berea. (Acts 20:4)
29. Delayed not _____ keep thy commandments. (Ps. 119:60)
30. Thy law _____ my delight. (Ps. 119:77)
32. _____ Naomi's husband died. (Ruth 1:3)
34. And _____ them, and _____ them down with ease. (Judg. 20:43; 2 words)
36. Halah, and Habor, and _____. (1 Chron. 5:26)
37. _____ Jerusalem...as a _____ doth gather. (Luke 13:34; 2 words)
38. And Peleg lived after he begat _____. (Gen. 11:19)
41. _____, and Shema, and Moladah. (Josh. 15:26)
42. Nickname for Edward.
43. _____ and feather.
44. They assigned _____ in the wilderness. (Josh. 20:8)
46. Three wise men of Christmas.
47. Hear _____ Israel: . . .to _____ in . . ._____ shalt thou drive them out. (Deut. 9:1, 3; 3 words)
48. I shall keep _____ unto the end. (Ps. 119:33)
50. A little _____ in _____ cruse. (1 Kgs. 17:12; 2 words)
51. The region of _____; ...daughter of Solomon _____ wife. (1 Kgs. 4:11; 2 words)
52. They also do _____ iniquity. (Ps. 119:3)
53. And for our little _____. (Ezra 8:21)

DOWN CLUES

1. Hallowed.
2. Furious.
3. And being in an _____ he prayed. (Luke 22:44)
4. Prefix meaning "not."
5. Shy.
6. Head nurse (abbr.).
7. And _____ heard me. (Ps. 120:1)
8. East-southeast (abbr.).
9. Not a hat, but _____ baseball _____ (2 words).
10. The _____ is not to the swift. (Ec. 9:11)
11. Caleb took unto him _____. (1 Chron. 2:19)
12. Rural Electrification Administration (abbr.).
18. Deborah...the wife of _____(h). (Judg. 4:4)
19. Geshur, and _____, with _____ towns. (1 Chron. 2:23; 2 words)
20. And _____ the whole face of the ground. (Gen. 2:6)

23. The snail, and the _____.
   (Lev. 11:30)
24. Eliab the son of _____.
   (Num. 2:7)
26. _____ day.
27. Child's TV program.
28. Bright color.
30. Eli's grandson. (1 Sam. 4:21)
31. Whither shall I cause my _____
   to _____? (2 Sam. 13:13;
   2 words)
33. A _____ man had two sons,
   (Luke 15:11)

35. Not come ____ _____ upon mine
   head. (Judg. 16:17; 2 words).
39. Doth the _____ mount up?
   (Job 39:27)
40. That had been the wife of _____.
   (Matt. 1:6)
45. Kanga's child.
46. Sound made by a cow.
48. Thy word have I had _____ my
   heart. (Ps. 119:11)
49. Make me _____ understand.
   (Ps. 119:27)

PUZZLE 10

ACROSS CLUES

1. To carry something.
4. Call thy land _____ ah (Isa. 62:4)
8. Shish_____ob.
10. Seen his star in the _____.
    (Matt. 2:2)
11. Him only shalt thou _____.
    (Matt. 4:10)
13. To go on a _____.
14. Also.
15. Thy word... I will _____ it.
    (Ps. 119:105-106)
18. Anna (var.).
19. Just a little bit.
20. Samuel ran unto _____.
    (1 Sam. 3:5)
21. Printer's measure.
23. That my joy might _____ in you.
    (John 15:11)
25. Gives medicine to.
27. In the country of _____.
    (1 Kgs. 4:19)
29. Praises.
31. A little while, and ye shall not
    _____ me. (John 16:16)
32. To tie a rope off.
33. As he _____ pure. (1 John 3:3)
34. Not B.C.
35. They _____ the ship aground.
    (Acts 27:41)
36. To exist.
38. Give _____, all ye inhabitants.
    (Joel 1:2)
39. Parent Teacher Association
    (abbr.).
40. A two year college degree.
41. Medical specialty (abbr.).
43. To rest.

45. Better...he were _____ into the
    sea. (Mark 9:42)
46. Or the _____, be not darkened.
    (Ec. 12:2)
47. I have fed you with _____.
    (1 Cor. 3:2)
48. Professional engineer (abbr.).

DOWN CLUES

1. To sit or ___ _____. (2 words)
2. For there are set _____ of
   judgment. (Ps. 122:5)
3. Mommy (var.).
4. Thou shalt not _____ false
   witness. (Ex. 20:16)
5. What cannibals do.
6. Teach Judah the _____ of the
   bow. (2 Sam. 1:18)
7. Light (abbr.).
8. When I _____ silence. (Ps. 32:3)
9. Or touch the _____. (Ex. 19:12)
12. Length of time.
13. To perform something.
16. Cut off his right _____.
    (Luke 22:50)
17. Lord of lords, and _____ of kings.
    (Rev. 17:14)
22. Cast the _____ on the right side
    of the ship. (John 21:6)
24. When fowls came Abram drove
    them _____ (Gen. 15:11)
26. Ephlal begat _____.
    (1 Chron. 2:37)
27. Office of Strategic Services
    (abbr.).
28. _____ men that were lepers.
    (Luke 17:12)
29. Thy word is a _____ unto my
    feet. (Ps. 119:105)
30. That we may _____ with him.
    (John 11:16)

31. Jesus _____.
32. So shall thy _____ be filled. (Prov. 3:10)
35. Egyptian sun god.
36. Rolled _____ the stone. (Matt. 28:2)

37. Jesus also suffered without the _____. (Heb. 13:12)
38. Estimated Time of Arrival (abbr.).
40. Snake.
42. New Testament (abbr.).
44. Not A.M.

PUZZLE 11

ACROSS CLUES

1. Hannah's son. (1 Sam. 1:20)
5. For _____ persecuted they the prophets. (Matt. 5:12)
7. Spirit of the Lord came up _____ David. (1 Sam. 16:13)
8. John also was baptizing in _____ near to Salim. (John 3:23)
10. The promise is ... to all that are _____ off. (Acts 2:39)
12. An explosive.
13. The _____ of God. (Ps. 46:4)
15. A great _____ dragon. (Rev. 12:3)
17. Whose son is _____? (Matt. 22:42)
18. How long is it _____ since this came unto him? (Mark 9:21)
19. Either/_____.
21. Hated.
23. A little bear.
25. _____ it not written? (Mark 11:17)
27. I have never _____ any thing common. (Acts 10:14)
30. That they might have life more _____. (John 10:10)
34. To be a certain place.
35. The director _____ the play.
36. A carnivore _____ meat.
39. Printer's measure.
41. Call for the elders of the _____. (Jam. 5:14)
45. A torn-up piece of material.
48. The Thin Man's wife (Nick and _____).
50. In _____ was there a voice heard. (Matt. 2:18)
51. Poetic for *before*.
52. Walked.
53. I am (contraction).
54. _____ them that love us in the faith. (Titus 3:15)

DOWN CLUES

1. Belonging to Adam's son.
2. English princess.
3. A witty saying.
4. United Nations (abbr.).
5. Take no thought...what ye shall _____. (Luke 12:11)
6. A man _____ God.
7. Metal from mining.
9. He that is _____ days old. (Gen. 17:12)
11. To capture a lawbreaker.
13. A yellow car in New York City.
14. Also.
16. Authority to _____ these things. (Mark 11:28)
19. Firstlings of thy herds _____ of thy flock. (Deut. 12:17)
20. _____ not a servant unto his master. (Prov. 30:10)
21. Now _____ faith, hope, charity. (1 Cor. 13:13)
22. A spool of film.
24. Industrious insects.
26. He was _____ at that saying. (Mark 10:22)
28. Yes (nautical).
29. Sat down to _____ and to drink. (Ex. 32:6)
30. Slight variation in speech patterns.
31. Sheep's sound.
32. New Testament (abbr.).
33. _____ have and _____ hold.
37. _____ with thine adversary quickly. (Matt. 5:25)

38. Type of train.
40. Neither/_____.
41. A heel.
42. Bezaleel the son of _____.
    (Ex. 38:22)
43. 900 in Roman numerals.

44. A witch is an old _____.
46. He is, they _____.
47. And so _____ them up out of the
    land. (Ex. 1:10)
49. Rosemary (nickname).

PUZZLE 12

ACROSS CLUES

1. Los Angeles (abbr.).
3. Paul came to _____. (Acts 18:19)
10. National Basketball Association (abbr.).
12. To make joyful.
13. 3.14159265.
15. Tool for weeding.
17. This is the way, walk ye in _____. (Isa. 30:21)
18. Even _____ Christ forgave you. (Col. 3:13)
19. They...travelled as far as..._____. (Acts 11:19)
21. Ehud the son of _____. (Judg. 3:15)
22. Distress signal.
24. _____ not.
25. Where is the king of..._____? (2 Kgs. 19:13)
26. Ready...also to _____ at Jerusalem. (Acts 21:13)
28. Cast _____ between me and Jonathan. (1 Sam. 14:42)

30. Catholic service.
31. Over the brook _____. (John 18:1)
32. Jacob called Rachel and _____. (Gen. 31:4)
34. Mistreat.
37. You (biblical).
38. _____ of the Chaldees. (Gen. 15:7)
40. Intending after _____ to bring him forth. (Acts 12:4)
42. _____ came out to meet Barak. (Judg. 4:22)
43. Holland cheese.
44. God _____ loved the world. (John 3:16)
45. An unruly crowd.

DOWN CLUES

2. Unknown author (abbr.).
3. Each (abbr.).
4. Art thou _____ that should come? (Matt. 11:3)
5. _____ and Semachiah were strong men. (1 Chron. 26:7)
6. Jesus...wearied..._____ thus on the well. (John 4:6)
7. Western state (abbr.).

8. All flesh shall _____. (Luke 3:6)
9. A relaxing pool.
11. Now Philip was of _____. (John 1:44)
14. Belonging to Abraham's son.
15. _____ is the father of Canaan. (Gen. 9:18)
16. A person may have many _____ in his life.
20. We would call Samson a _____.
21. Shall Christ come out of _____? (John 7:41)
23. Exclamation.
24. Porcius _____. (Acts 24:27)
25. To make part of a group.
26. Belonging to the man who did not fear the lions.
27. Exists.
29. Used to carry other objects.
30. Mother.
33. Belonging to Canaan's son. (Gen. 10:15)
35. South America (abbr.).
36. Out of the _____ of Jesse. (Isa. 11:1)
39. Take...a _____ for a burnt offering. (Lev. 9:2)
41. Adam's _____.
42. *Yes* in German.

PUZZLE 13

ACROSS CLUES

1. Forces.
7. The sword of _____. (Judg. 7:14)
12. An horn of _____ for us. (Luke 1:69)
14. But _____ mightier than I cometh. (Luke 3:16)
15. Consumed.
16. Nor hear your _____. (Matt. 10:14)
17. He is cast into a _____. (Job 18:8)
18. Interational Cooperative Alliance (abbr.).
19. Standing Room Only (abbr.).
20. A disease of the lungs (abbr.).
22. Wind direction.
23. Exclamation of satisfaction.
25. To impose a necessary accompaniment or result.
26. Batters.
29. Negative.
30. Either/ _____.
31. Lamech...begat _____. (Gen. 5:30)
32. Saint (abbr.).
33. A large long-haired Asian animal.
34. The kingdom of _____ in Bashan. (Josh. 13:31)
35. To take _____.
37. Oriental cooking pans.
38. Very wet dirt.
39. I _____ no pleasant bread. (Dan. 10:3)
40. Left Tackle (abbr.).
41. Shalt thou find no _____. (Deut. 28:65)
43. _____, I come to do thy will. (Heb. 10:7)
44. Hairy Southern vegetable.
46. Roman numeral for 550.
47. Lest any of them should _____ out. (Acts 27:42)
49. For I trust _____ _____ you. (Rom. 15:24; 2 words)
50. Lay not this _____ to their charge. (Acts 7:60)
52. In the middle of.
53. Emergency Room (abbr.).
54. Throws.
55. Made...the sea, and all that in them _____. (Acts 4:24)
56. _____ Abram departed. (Gen. 12:4)

DOWN CLUES

1. A prophet.
2. Identical.
3. Request.
4. Electron volt (abbr.).
5. Abraham...kept...my statutes and my _____. (Gen. 26:5)
6. A person who saves things.
7. They were both righteous before _____. (Luke 1:6)
8. Continuing _____ in prayer. (Rom. 12:12)
9. Long period of time.
10. I have commanded my sanctified _____. (Isa. 13:3)
11. NBC, CBS, ABC.
13. Fill his skin with barbed _____. (Job 41:7)
21. Having to do with a natural science (prefix).
24. Idols.
27. Christ went up _____ Jerusalem.
28. The son of Gera. (Judg. 3:15)
30. A strong wood comes from these.
32. Supersonic Transport (abbr.).

33. Part of an egg (plural).
34. Belonging to the son of Ephlal. (1 Chron. 2:37)
36. Belonging to Ruth's mother-in-law. (Ruth 1:2)
38. Used instead of *Miss* today.
42. _____ _____ lamp (2 words).
43. Citrus fruit.

44. Expression of regret after a mistake.
45. Having to do with airplanes or space.
48. God _____ with the lad. (Gen. 21:20)
51. Yes or _____.

PUZZLE 14

ACROSS CLUES

1. Jonathan _____ up upon his hands. (1 Sam. 14:13)
5. Automobile.
8. The Philistines took the ark...to _____. (1 Sam. 5:1)
11. Belonging to the son of Jephunneh. (Num. 13:6)
14. Lizard, snail, and _____ are unclean. (Lev. 11:30)
15. Much _____ about nothing.
16. He is up _____ _____ good (2 words).
17. Printer's measure.
18. Sea bird.
21. Prefix meaning into.
23. Mother.
25. Thou hast followed _____. (1 Kgs. 18:18)
27. For example.
28. Duty every soldier hates.
29. Take thy neighbour's raiment _____ pledge. (Ex. 22:26)
30. National Football League (abbr.).
32. Good _____ are not everything.
35. Bela the son of _____. (Gen. 36:32)
37. Hello.
38. Fe, _____ Fo, Fum.
39. To exist.
41. The strong hold of _____. (2 Sam. 24:7)
43. To offer a sacrifice unto_____ their god. (Judg. 16:23)
46. What holds up a golf ball.
47. To surprise someone.
49. I am (contr.).
50. There was a marriage in _____ of Galilee. (John 2:1)
52. He killed Goliath.
53. A meat offering baken in a _____. (Lev. 2:5)
54. Ancient wisdom.
55. Rulers of _____. (Ex. 18:21)

DOWN CLUES

2. I _____ in the way of righteousness. (Prov. 8:20)
3. Curley and _____.
4. Emergency Medical Service (abbr.).
5. Them which are of the house of _____. (1 Cor. 1:11)
6. A sweetened fruit drink.
7. Rosemary (abbr.).
8. Thy father was an _____. (Ezek. 16:3)
9. This is my beloved _____. (Matt. 3:17)
10. Spoken of by _____ the prophet. (Matt. 24:15)
11. The excellency of _____ and Sharon. (Isa. 35:2)
12. _____ sat in the gate of Sodom. (Gen. 19:1)
13. Belonging to the son of Abinoam. (Judg. 4:6)
19. Ebenezer (abbr.).
20. Just a little rest.
22. Prefix meaning *not*.
24. Lost three days _____. (1 Sam. 9:20)
26. What a cow says.
31. Fabulous.
33. _____ _____ of little faith. (Matt. 6:3; 2 words, var.)
34. The king carried the people captive to _____. (2 Kgs. 16:9)
35. Said Jehu to _____ his captain. (2 Kgs. 9:25)

36. Joseph and Mary looked for a
    _____ _____ an inn. (Luke 2:7;
    2 words)
40. Belonging to Gaal's father.
    (Judg. 9:30)
41. Son of Ishmael. (Gen. 25:13, 15)
42. Joshua built an altar in mount
    _____. (Josh. 8:30)

44. Moses gave unto..._____...the
    kingdom of Sihon. (Num. 32:33)
45. Part of a cathedral.
46. Given for good service.
48. Ye rebelled...in the desert of
    _____. (Num. 27:14)
51. Not *yes*.

PUZZLE 15

ACROSS CLUES

1. Having to do with the Bible.
9. There _____ none good but one. (Mark 10:18)
11. The _____ of March.
12. _____ the money.
13. To utilize.
14. 1,400 in Roman numerals.
15. To drift off to sleep.
16. Your children...received _____ correction. (Jer. 2:30)
17. Old Testament (abbr.).
19. Whom the Father will _____ in my name. (John 14:26)
22. They _____ go the man. (Judg. 1:25)
25. Art not thou a _____? (2 Sam. 15:27)
26. One of the Great Lakes.
27. They came to him from _____ quarter. (Mark 1:45)
29. Paul, a _____ of Jesus Christ. (Rom. 1:1)
30. To raise a child, or to _____ a child.
31. Sound of satisfaction.
32. Manuscript (abbr.).
33. Dad.
35. The harvest is the _____ of the world. (Matt. 13:39)
36. _____ Abram departed. (Gen. 12:4)
37. The one who gets to the finish line first _____ the prize.
39. Alternating Current (abbr.).
41. Israel assembled together at _____. (Josh. 18:1)
42. Policeman's Benevolent Association (abbr.).
43. A tall, flightless bird.
44. Talk-show host.
45. I will come down and _____ with thee. (Num. 11:17)
46. Hear my _____, O God. (Ps. 61:1)
48. They filled them _____ to the brim. (John 2:7)
50. Ye shall not _____ me hence forth. (Matt. 23:39)
51. To _____ away our sins. (1 John 3:5)
52. A crown of twelve _____. (Rev. 12:1)

DOWN CLUES

1. Less complex.
2. Centers for Disease Control (abbr.).
3. God led them by the way of the _____ sea. (Ex. 13:18)
4. God _____ a Spirit. (John 4:24)
5. Also.
6. Does, then _____.
7. I took the little book, and _____ it up. (Rev. 10:10)
8. And, _____, the heavens were opened. (Matt. 3:16)
9. God _____ my strength and power. (2 Sam. 22:33)
10. And _____ rain on the just and on the unjust. (Matt. 5:45)
15. Someone who can't mind his or her own business is _____.
18. "Star _____."
19. Fives, sixes, and _____.
20. Equal Rights Amendment (abbr.).
21. _____, Pinta, and Santa Maria.
23. Adam's wife.
24. Go, _____, go!
28. Railroads (abbr.).

33. I will even make the _____ for fire great. (Ezek. 24:9)
34. Most-quoted author in the world.
36. He made the pure incense of _____ spices. (Ex. 37:29)
37. Clever coyote's name.
38. All the people shall _____. (Josh. 6:5)
39. For God is _____ to make him stand. (Rom. 14:4)

40. They baked unleavened _____ of the dough. (Ex. 12:39)
41. He made him to _____ honey out of the rock. (Deut. 32:13)
42. As the flower of the grass he shall _____ away. (Jam. 1:10)
47. About (abbr.).
49. Dad.

PUZZLE 16

ACROSS CLUES

1. Hid from _____ and from generations. (Col. 1:26)
5. _____ is your reward in heaven. (Matt. 5:12)
10. The _____ shall come and take our place. (John 11:48)
12. I will not _____ to speak of any thing. (Rom. 15:18)
14. For example.
15. Missouri.
16. _____ thy son, he shall build my house. (1 Chron. 28:6)
17. David...feigned himself _____. (1 Sam. 21:12,13)
18. _____ I my brother's keeper? (Gen. 4:9)
19. The power of _____. (Es. 1:3)
21. As _____ obeyed Abraham. (1 Pet. 3:6; alt. spelling)
24. How can these things _____? (John 3:9)
25. Truth _____ Consequences.
26. Ambush between Beth-el and _____. (Josh. 8:12)
27. All sailors can tie a _____.
29. An authoritative standard.
31. Into captivity unto _____. (Amos 1:5)
32. Where are the gods of...Hena and _____? (2 Kgs. 18:34)
33. Amos, the son of _____. (Luke 3:25)
35. A middle point between extremes.
36. A unit of dry measure.
38. Above-ground subway.
39. _____ and Bartholomew. (Matt. 10:3)

40. _____, Tekel, Upharsin. (Dan. 5:25)
43. Let us _____ over unto the other side. (Luke 8:22)
44. These _____ght Milcah did bear to Nahor. (Gen. 22:23)
46. Prefix having to do with the earth.
47. I write not these things to _____ you. (1 Cor. 4:14)
51. Simeon that was called _____. (Acts 13:1)
52. In the top of the rock _____. (Judg. 15:8)

DOWN CLUES

1. Height times width.
2. _____ and Magog. (Rev. 20:8)
3. Typesetter's measure.
4. But a certain _____. (Luke 10:33)
6. City in Brazil.
7. Why make ye this _____, and weep? (Mark 5:39)
8. Absalom's sister. (2 Sam. 13:1)
9. As a _____ gathereth her chickens. (Matt. 23:37)
11. Drifts off to sleep.
13. Rome (Ital.).
16. The excellency of Carmel and _____. (Isa. 35:2)
17. Pray ye to the Lord for _____. (Acts 8:24)
19. Jacob called the name of the place _____. (Gen. 32:30)
20. A free electron.
21. Hannah...bare a son, ...called ..._____. (1 Sam. 1:20)
22. They fled before the men of _____. (Josh. 7:4)
23. Speed it up!
24. Book (abbr.).
28. Eggs.

30. Whitewater.
34. 1, 101 in Roman numerals.
35. What the hand wrote on the wall. (Dan. 5:25)
37. Kitchen Police (abbr.).
39. Balak brought Balaam unto the top of _____. (Num. 23:28)
41. In the white of an _____. (Job 6:6)

42. Formerly.
43. Jewel.
45. I am glorified _____ them. (John 17:10)
48. Cursed is _____ that curseth thee. (Num. 24:9)
49. But also to die _____ Jerusalem. (Acts 21:13)
50. Mom.

PUZZLE 17

ACROSS CLUES

1. Expression of satisfaction.
3. Stayed.
8. God heard the voice of the _____. (Gen. 21:17)
9. A prohibition.
10. Mom.
11. One _____ the other.
12. Joseph...entered into his _____. (Gen. 43:30)
15. The child Jesus tarried _____. (Luke 2:43)
18. Drink originally from China.
19. Compass direction.
20. _____ not this folly. (Judg. 19:23)
22. The people sin against _____ Lord. (1 Sam. 14:33)
23. As they that must give _____. (Heb. 13:17)
26. _____ and good. (Gen. 41:5)
27. And they did eat of the _____ corn. (Josh. 5:11)
28. I am (contraction).

32. Set your _____ on things above. (Col. 3:2)
36. Let not the sun _____ down on your wrath. (Eph. 4:26)
37. Deliver thyself as a _____ from the...hunter. (Prov. 6:5)
38. Ribonucleic acid.
39. 2,000 pounds.
40. Larry, Curley, and _____.
42. Their _____ hath been to feed cattle. (Gen. 46:32)
44. That all men through him might _____. (John 1:7)
46. What a boat needs if it has no motor.
47. Estimated Time of Arrival (abbr.).
48. Of your daily _____. (Ex. 5:19)
49. Added to a word to make it an adverb.

DOWN CLUES

1. Rabbits.
2. Not *B.C.*
3. The _____ of their joy. (2 Cor. 8:2)
4. What a sheep says.
5. Incorporated (abbr.).
6. English noblewoman.
7. 3 measures of _____ for a penny. (Rev. 6:6)
8. Part of the ear or brain.
10. He walked with _____. (Mal. 2:6)
13. In a certain place.
14. When kings go forth to _____. (2 Sam. 11:1)
16. Ye therefore _____ them not. (John 8:47)
17. A place to tie a boat.
21. He that is of _____ heareth. (John 8:47)
24. There had been _____ rain. (1 Kgs. 17:7)
25. Hello!
29. Former Chinese leader.
30. Take ye a kid of the _____ for a sin offering. (Lev. 9:3)
31. Full of dead men's _____. (Matt. 23:27)
33. Guy, pal, a good _____.
34. All the _____ of the field are withered. (Joel 1:12)
35. Not out.
36. Reverence and _____ fear. (Heb. 12:28)
37. They put on Jesus a scarlet _____. (Matt. 27:28)
39. Take it by the _____. (Ex. 4:4)
40. Martha...went and _____ him. (John 11:20)
41. Eggs.
43. Egyptian god.
45. "Entertainment Tonight" (abbr.).

PUZZLE 18

Diana Rowland

ACROSS CLUES

1. Son of God.
6. The book of the generation of Jesus _____. (Matt. 1:1)
12. Nebuzar-_____, captain of the guard, _____ servant. (2 Kgs. 25:8; 2 words)
13. Thou mayest prosper and be in _____. (3 John 2)
14. And flee into _____. (Matt. 2:13)
15. Published throughout all his _____. (Es. 1:20)
16. Behold, there came a _____. (Matt. 8:2)
17. I have given _____ unto the children of Lot. (Deut. 2:9)
18. Knockout (abbr.).
19. _____, the chamberlain of the city. (Rom. 16:23)
22. Blessed are the pure _____ heart. (Matt. 5:8)
23. _____ it is not _____. (Acts 22:22; 2 words)
25. If ye then, _____ evil. (Matt. 7:11)
27. Did _____ _____ lightness?... that with ___. (2 Cor. 1:17; 3 words)
28. Put off all these; _____, wrath. (Col. 3:8)
30. Party after a wedding.
33. Do, _____, Mi.
34. In the very _____. _____ Moses...us, _____. (John 8:4,5; 3 words)
36. The sons of Caleb, _____, Elah, and Naam. (1 Chron. 4:15)
37. Day after Monday (abbr.).
38. By faith, _____, being warned of God. (Heb. 11:7)
41. City that is _____ on a hill. (Matt. 5:14)
42. And when the _____ heard it. (Matt. 20:24)
43. Whosoever shall _____ me before men. (Matt. 10:33)
44. They did all _____. (Matt. 14:20)
47. As a _____ lappeth. (Judg. 7:5)
49. The son of _____. (Luke 3:36)
50. Let your light _____ shine. (Matt. 5:16)
51. They may appear unto men _____ fast. (Matt. 6:16)
52. Registered Nurse (abbr.).

DOWN CLUES

1. _____ went out to meet Sisera. (Judg. 4:18)
2. Fall by the _____ of the sword. (Luke 21:24)
3. But I _____ unto you...use you, and _____ you. (Matt. 5:44; 2 words)
4. My substance, yet being _____. (Ps. 139:16)
5. And _____ upon it...his _____ white as snow. (Matt. 28:2,3; 2 words)
6. Every _____ had two faces. (Ezek. 41:18)
7. Touched the _____ of his garment. Matt. 9:20)
8. Hit sharply.
9. _____ fear my lord...your faces worse _____. (Dan. 1:10; 2 words)
10. Weakness of God is _____ than men. (1 Cor. 1:25)
11. Blessed are _____ merciful. (Matt. 5:7)

17. Heaven is _____ hand.
    (Matt. 3:2)
20. If my _____ hath turned _____ of
    the way. (Job 31:7; 2 words,
    reverse order)
21. _____(h) Zidon: for the _____
    hath spoken. (Isa. 23:4; reversed)
23. Fe, _____, Fo, Fum.
24. For _____ lamps _____ gone out.
    (Matt. 25:8; 2 words)
26. Brought him to an _____., _____.
    (Luke 10:34; 2 words)
29. Do, _____, Mi.
31. Wool fabric.
32. Groweth of _____ own...shalt

_____ reap. (Lev. 25:5; 2 words)
35. As the _____ of the feet.
    (Dan. 2:42)
36. Theirs _____ the kingdom of
    heaven. (Matt. 5:3)
39. _____, Eshcol, and Mamre.
    (Gen. 14:24)
40. And when they had sung an
    _____. (Matt. 26:30)
45. Ye shall be _____ gods.
    (Gen. 3:5)
46. Think not that I am come _____
    destroy the law. (Matt. 5:17)
48. _____ and search diligently.
    (Matt. 2:8)

PUZZLE 19

ACROSS CLUES

1. Works, which were _____ in you. (Matt. 11:21)
5. Him and _____.
8. Kimberly (nickname).
10. This...sinful _____. (Mark 8:38)
12. Her countenance was no more _____. (1 Sam. 1:18)
13. Set it up there under an _____. (Josh. 24:26)
14. Whose waters cast up mire and _____. (Isa. 57:20)
17. Emergency Medical Technician (abbr.).
18. _____ and mercy shall follow me. (Ps. 23:6)
20. Shed _____ blood. (Gen. 37:22)
21. There shall be _____ poor among you. (Deut. 15:4)
22. Ye have _____ portion...in Jerusalem. (Neh. 2:20)
25. Audiovisual (abbr.).
26. Large tree, largely destroyed by blight.

28. Though now ye _____ him not. (1 Pet. 1:8)
29. From my youth _____. (Luke 18:21)
30. They that handle the _____. (Judg. 5:14)
31. Love is the _____ of the law. (Rom. 13:10)
36. Not out.
37. Support group for those who quit drinking.
38. Prefix meaning *new*.
39. Coming to him and _____ him vinegar. (Luke 23:36)
43. I...quieted myself, as a child, _____ _____ weaned child. (Ps. 131:2; 2 words)
44. Actual.
45. Saint (abbr.).
46. Tenant farmer in the Middle Ages.
47. Esau _____ Jacob. (Gen. 27:41)

DOWN CLUES

2. Bashan was ruled by king _____. (Deut. 3:1)
3. Bring the offering...of the _____ wine. (Neh. 10:39)
4. Printer's measure.
5. See that ye _____ the matter. (2 Chron. 24:5)
6. Estimated Time of Arrival (abbr.).
7. Jumps on his horse and _____.
8. Something a sailor is good at.
9. Maketh (mod.).
11. Go on before _____. (1 Sam. 25:19)
14. He that is mighty hath _____ ... great things. (Luke 1:49)
15. Set...the _____...in the house of God. (2 Chron. 33:7)
16. Registered Nurse (abbr.).
18. Ye shall be brought before _____ and kings. (Matt. 10:18)
19. Ship's cry of distress.
20. To sleep for a little while.
23. Stretching forth thine hand to _____. (Acts 4:30)
24. In thy presence is _____ of joy. (Ps. 16:11)
27. Tooth.
32. The unfeigned _____ that is in thee. (2 Tim. 1:5)
33. But if we walk in the _____. (1 John 1:7)
34. "Are you coming?"
   "_____ _____ minute" (2 words).
35. He shall set the _____ on the left. (Matt. 25:33)
40. Charge for professional services.
41. To be with Christ; which is _____ better. (Phil. 1:23)
42. Small imaginary being.

PUZZLE 20

ACROSS CLUES

1. Johoiada was leader of the _____. (1 Chron. 12:27)
7. A serviceman who did not return from war may be one of these.
9. To forbid.
10. Learn to _____ well. (Isa. 1:17)
11. Abraham would be called this today.
13. Remember what _____ did. (Deut. 25:17)
16. A wise guy.
18. Speak unto...Israel, that they _____ forward. (Ex. 14:15)
20. He will _____ a wild man. (Gen. 16:12)
21. Familiar form of *you* in German.
22. _____ the son of Ner. (2 Sam. 3:25)
23. Parts of a play.

42

25. Sons of Zeruiah, Joab, Abishai, and _____. (2 Sam. 2:18)
27. Saint (abbr.).
28. Extol him...by his name _____. (Ps. 68:4)
29. Compass direction.
31. All the _____ and strangers. (Acts 17:21)
34. Judah and _____. (Jer. 9:26)
36. For example (abbr.).
37. Thou shalt not..._____. (Lev. 19:13)
39. Elevation (abbr.).
41. The name thereof is called_____. (Ezek. 20:29)
44. _____ and Caiaphas being high priests. (Luke 3:2)
46. Captains over _____. (Deut. 1:15)
47. 1,001 in Roman numerals.
48. Carried them captive to _____. (2 Kgs. 15:29)
49. From _____ to Beer-sheba. (Judg. 20:1)

DOWN CLUES

1. Belonging to Nabal's wife (1 Sam. 25:3)
2. Antiaircraft (abbr.).
3. Ribonucleic acid (abbr.).
4. Not working.
5. Upon the great _____ of their right foot. (Ex. 29:20)

6. South America (abbr.).
7. The sound a kitten makes.
8. A decree from Caesar _____. (Luke 2:1)
12. The beginning of his kingdom was _____. (Gen. 10:10)
14. Sarah died...and _____ came to mourn. (Gen. 23:2)
15. King Saul's father. (1 Sam. 10:21)
17. Fruit drinks.
19. Obstetrician (abbr.).
24. Chemical Engineer (abbr.).
26. And Leah...called his name _____. (Gen. 30:13)
30. _____ are labourers together with God. (1 Cor. 3:9)
32. _____, id, superego.
33. The young men of _____. (Ezek. 30:17)
35. Made silver shrines for _____. (Acts 19:24)
38. Passing through the valley of _____. (Ps. 84:6)
40. An Eastern monk.
41. To _____ or not to be.
42. Manuscripts (abbr.).
43. The _____ is withered away. (Isa. 15:6)
45. Which taketh away the _____ of the world. (John 1:29)
46. Their cry came up _____ God. (Ex. 2:23)

PUZZLE 21

ACROSS CLUES

1. Let him deny _____ and take up his cross. (Mark 8:34)
6. _____ Lincoln.
9. Spirit of the Lord came up_____ David. (1 Sam. 16:13)
10. Being exceedingly _____ against them. (Acts 26:11)
12. We.
13. _____, and also our fathers. (Gen. 46:34)
14. Tower, whose _____ may reach unto heaven. (Gen. 11:4)
16. Defeats.
22. Environmental Protection Agency (abbr.).
23. To and _____.
24. The _____ was upon the earth forty days. (Gen. 7:12)
28. Take the widow's ox for a _____. (Job 24:3)
30. Tool for weeding.
31. Mary anointed the Lord with _____. (John 11:2)
33. God gave them up unto _____ affections. (Rom. 1:26)
35. New Testament (abbr.).
36. United States (abbr.).
37. Mary _____ Joseph.
38. And thine _____ as the grass of the earth. (Job 5:25)
41. Is able to.
43. Is the correct size.
44. Hereafter ye shall _____ heaven open. (John 1:51)
46. A grain.
47. As he is Christ's, even _____ are we Christ's. (2 Cor. 10:7)
48. Pound (abbr.).

50. Mother.
51. Yea.
52. Teach us to _____ our days. (Ps. 90:12)

DOWN CLUES

1. A prophet is not without _____. (Matt. 13:57)
2. Not out.
3. O thou _____, go. (Amos 7:12)
4. 950 in Roman numerals.
5. Do, re, me, _____.
7. Unclean animal. (Deut. 14:18)
8. It _____ not good (Gen. 2:18)
11. And to _____ is gain. (Phil. 1:21)
12. Jesus went _____ to Jerusalem.
13. For _____ are his workmanship. (Eph. 2:10)
15. Remember all thy _____. (Ps. 20:3)
17. Christian Era (abbr.).
18. The Lord heard...and looked on ...our _____. (Deut. 26:7)
19. Sickness (French).
20. He was _____ at that saying. (Mark 10:22)
21. One of the king's most _____ princess. (Es. 6:9)
25. What every director hopes for.
26. Charged particle.
27. Cast the _____ on the right side. (John 21:6)
29. Be not among...riotous _____ of flesh. (Prov. 23:20)
31. _____ top of that....
32. Something worn to warm the ears or hands.
33. A form of car.
34. 450 in Roman numerals.
38. I have commanded my sanctified _____. (Isa. 13:3)

39. Physical therapy (abbr.).
40. A group of people working for a common cause.
41. Hear, O Lord, when I _____. (Ps. 27:7)
42. *Yes,* in the navy.
45. Printer's measure.
48. Pound (abbr.).
49. To exist.

PUZZLE 22

ACROSS CLUES

1. Like a flying _____. (Rev. 4:7)
6. Boards of fir trees of _____. (Ezek. 27:5)
11. Treatise have I made, _____, _____, _____ all that Jesus began. (Acts 1:1; 3 words)
14. Ye shall be witnesses unto _____. (Acts 1:8)
15. Descended to the stone of _____. (Josh. 18:17)
16. Peter and John about to _____ into the temple. (Acts 3:3)
17. Took a wife _____...whose_____ was Tamar. (Gen. 38:6; 2 words)
19. California (abbr.).
21. I will punish _____ in Babylon. (Jer. 51:44)
22. Animal that sounds like *new*.
23. Earth shall _____ to an fro. (Isa. 24:20)
25. Close relative to reindeer.
26. Alcoholics Anonymous (abbr.).
27. Why look ye _____ earnestly on us? (Acts 3:12)
29. To _____ away disciples. (Acts 20:30)
31. It _____ not for you to know. (Acts 1:7)
32. The son of Jair slew _____. (1 Chron. 20:5)
35. _____, Judah's firstborn...and the Lord slew _____. (Gen. 38:7; 2 words)
37. Shilshah, and Ithran, and _____. (1 Chron. 7:37)
39. Ye _____ of Galilee. (Acts 1:11)
40. Adam was first formed, then _____. (1 Tim. 2:13)
42. _____ it, rase it. (Ps. 137:7)
44. The troops of _____ looked. (Job 6:19)
47. _____ boweth down, Nebo stoopeth. (Isa. 46:1)
48. An odour of a sweet _____. (Phil. 4:18)
50. And in the _____ sea. (Acts 7:36)
51. Until _____ offering should be offered. (Acts 21:26)
52. _____, the son of Azariah. (Ezra 7:3)
54. North American (abbr.).
55. The _____ said unto me...I have given _____ unto the children of Lot. (Deut. 2:9; 2 words)
57. _____, and Ramah, and Hazor. (Josh. 19:36)
59. Could ye not watch with ___ ___ hour? (Matt. 26:40; 2 words)
60. People of an ancient Asian country.

DOWN CLUES

1. As many as were ordained to _____ life believed. (Acts 13:48)
2. Saying, _____ thou that destroyest the temple. (Mark 15:29)
3. From _____ to Rimmon. (Zech. 14:10)
4. Machine for weaving.
5. The sons of Midian; Ephah, and _____. (Gen. 25:4)
6. Desire the _____ milk of the word. (1 Pet. 2:2)
7. Erected an altar, and called it _____-elohe-Israel. (Gen. 33:20)
8. Name unknown (abbr.).
9. This _____ that which was spoken. (Acts 2:16)
10. Barzillai the Gileadite of _____. (2 Sam. 17:27)
11. I am Alpha and _____. (Rev. 1:8)
12. _____, ha. (Job 39:25)
13. Bringing sick _____. (Acts 5:16)
18. Name unknown (abbr.).
20. Sound an _____. (Joel 2:1)
21. Why should it _____ thought a thing incredible? (Acts 26:8)
24. Called the altar _____. (Josh. 22:34)
27. And _____ opened her eyes. (Acts 9:40)

28. Two _____ for one _____.
    (Ex. 16:22; 2 words.)
30. I _____ my glittering sword.
    (Deut. 32:41)
33. _____ offered unto God a more
    excellent sacrifice. (Heb. 11:4)
34. Duke _____. These _____ the
    dukes of Edom. (1 Chron. 1:54;
    2 words)
36. Went _____ unto her...called his
    name _____. (Gen. 38:2,3;
    2 words)
38. Of the tribe of _____. (Rev. 7:6)
40. An altar...in mount_____.
    (Josh. 8:30)
41. The cruel _____ of asps.
    (Deut. 32:33)

43. Bath-sheba, the daughter of
    _____. (2 Sam. 11:3)
45. Parted them to all _____, _____
    every man had need. (Acts 2:45;
    2 words)
46. _____ bare to Esau Eliphaz.
    (Gen. 36:4)
49. Ye _____ men with burdens.
    (Luke 11:46)
52. Why make ye this _____?
    (Mark 5:39)
53. When the angels _____ left them
    ... (Luke 2:15 NIV)
56. Do ____ Me
58. Take it from _____.

47

PUZZLE 23

ACROSS CLUES

2. Behold, it _____ very good. (Gen. 1:31)
4. Thou and thy house shall be _____. (Acts 11:14)
9. Sound of sudden enlightenment.
11. Long-legged bird.
12. Before (poetic).
14. West African river.
16. The beast...shall make _____ against them. (Rev. 11:7)
17. Peels.
21. Intravenous (abbr.).
23. My _____ ye shall keep. (Ex. 31:13)
24. Yes (Russian).
26. Love worketh no _____ to his neighbour. (Rom. 13:10)
28. She bound the _____ line in the window. (Josh. 2:21)
32. A type of star.
35. _____ ye drink of the cup that I drink of? (Mark 10:38)
36. _____ them through thy truth. (John 17:17)
40. To _____ at liberty them that are bruised. (Luke 4:18)
41. The price set by a professional person.
42. _____ and fro.
43. I have sinned...and in thy _____. (Luke 15:21)
46. Them also which _____ in Jesus. (1 Thes. 4:14)
49. Israel...had made a great _____. (Judg. 21:5)
51. Elevated trains.
52. God be merciful to me a _____. (Luke 18:13)
53. They had a few _____ fishes. (Mark 8:7)

DOWN CLUES

1. A prohibition.
2. Every one that passeth by shall _____ his head. (Jer. 18:16)
3. The pen of the _____ is in vain. (Jer. 8:8)
4. Gird thyself, and bind on thy _____. (Acts 12:8)
5. Sent _____ angel and brought us out of Egypt. (Num. 20:16)
6. _____ certain of the church. (Acts 12:1)
7. God give thee of the _____ of heaven. (Gen. 27:28)
8. O thou wicked _____. (Matt. 18:32)
10. Let _____ that readeth understand. (Mark 13:14)
13. A sudden attack.
15. Equal Rights Amendment (abbr.).
18. New Brunswick (abbr.).
19. Saint (abbr.).
20. There _____ none good but one. (Mark 10:18)
22. Use not _____ repetitions. (Matt. 6:7)
23. Thou art the God of my _____. (Ps. 25:5)
25. The revenger of blood...shall _____ the murderer. (Num. 35:19)
27. Doesn't win.
29. Sidewalk _____.
30. Royal Canadian (abbr.).
31. Printer's measure.
33. I will be _____ enemy unto thine enemies. (Ex. 23:22)
34. How is _____ that ye are come so soon? (Ex. 2:18)

37. _____ now I have found favour in thy sight. (Gen. 18:3)
38. Yea.
39. The _____ of the mountains seen. (Gen. 8:5)
42. _____ John what things ye have seen. (Luke 7:22)

44. Tool for weeding.
45. _____ and feathers.
47. Snake-like fish.
48. This _____ the way. (Isa. 30:21)
50. High School (abbr.).

PUZZLE 24

ACROSS CLUES

1. They delivered him to _____ _____ the governor. (Matt. 27:2; 2 words)
11. Despise not _____ of these little ones. (Matt. 18:10)
12. Standing Room Only (abbr.).
13. Unknown writer (abbr.).
14. Ye shall be _____ gods. (Gen. 3:5)
16. _____ Francisco.
18. Come from God, and went _____ God. (John 13:3)
19. To hold onto something with your hands.
21. Fathers (Span.).
23. Lower case (abbr.).
24. Missouri (abbr.).
25. Thus.
26. For mine eyes have seen thy _____. (Luke 2:30)
29. I will let down the _____. (Luke 5:5)
32. A high standard.
33. His raiment white as _____. (Matt. 28:3)
35. There was _____ strength in him. (1 Sam. 28:20)
36. Cleanest, best arranged, coolest.
38. With many other _____ did he testify. (Acts 2:40)
40. Thou didst _____ upon thine horses. (Hab. 3:8)
41. A group of singers or part of a song.
42. _____ Domini.
44. The multitude _____ him to Pilate. (Luke 23:1)
45. In regard to (abbr.).

46. He cleaveth my _____(s) asunder. (Job 16:13)
47. The angel rolled the stone from the _____. (Matt. 28:2)
48. In between, in the midst of.
49. 2,000 pounds.
50. Let there _____ light. (Gen. 1:3)
51. _____ _____ order. (2 Chron. 29:35; 2 words)
52. I _____ to prepare a place for you. (John 14:2)
53. Fish eggs.
54. The asses that were lost three days _____. (1 Sam. 9:20)

DOWN CLUES

1. Dad.
2. Pilate wrote a title, and put it _____ the cross. (John 19:19)
3. Ye know that summer is _____. (Mark 13:28)
4. Jesus _____ the Savior.
5. _____ of the Chaldees. (Gen. 15:7)
6. _____ Abram departed. (Gen. 12:4)
7. The fame of David went into all _____. (1 Chron. 14:17)
8. Sent _____ angel. (Num. 20:16)
9. To carry something.
10. Seth called his son's name _____. (Gen. 4:26)
15. Neither is there _____ in any other. (Acts 4:12)
16. Knife, fork, _____.
17. Support group for alcoholics.
19. A level in school.
20. Climbed.
22. Ronald (nickname).
24. Went up a _____ from the earth. (Gen. 2:6)

26. Lay not this _____ to their charge. (Acts 7:60)
27. A wise man will hear and increase _____. (Prov. 1:5)
28. In no specific place.
30. The fear of the Lord is clean, _____ for ever. (Ps. 19:9)
31. The ship was now..._____ with waves. (Matt. 14:24)
34. Abraham took the _____, ...and laid   it upon Isaac. (Gen. 22:6)
37. One who sends.
39. Railroad (abbr.).
41. Near.
42. _____ and crafts.
43. New (prefix).
48. Missing in Action (abbr.).

PUZZLE 25

ACROSS CLUES

1. The fear of the Lord is the beginning of _____. (Prov. 1:7)
8. _____ the kine to the cart. (1 Sam. 6:7)
11. _____ Domini.
12. To use oars (2 words).
14. I shall be a _____ for ever. (Isa. 47:7)
16. In all the region of _____. (1 Kgs. 4:11)
18. Tasted the water that was made _____. (John 2:9)
20. Registered Nurse (abbr.).
21. Pierced themselves through with many _____. (1 Tim. 6:10)
24. Keepers at _____. (Titus 2:5)
25. David did _____ the shew bread. (Matt. 12:4)
26. Los Angeles (abbr.).
27. The end is not _____ and by. (Luke 21:9)
29. "Entertainment Tonight's" popular name.
30. The mouth of the righteous speaketh _____. (Ps. 37:30)
31. Shem, _____ and Japheth. (Gen. 5:32)
33. To forbid something.
34. He will hate the _____, and love the other. (Matt. 6:24)
35. Exclamation of satisfaction.
36. And _____ not his sisters here with us? (Mark 6:3)
39. Charged particle.
41. Did all eat the same _____ meat. (1 Cor. 10:3)
45. Gathered the good but cast the _____ away. (Matt. 13:48)
46. He was _____ at that saying. (Mark 10:22)
47. 2,000 pounds.
48. Tax department (abbr.).
49. Neither _____ there any rock like our God. (1 Sam. 2:2)
50. Detached Service (abbr.).
51. This is my beloved _____. (Matt. 3:17)
52. Universally (prefix).

DOWN CLUES

2. Sportsmen's group (abbr.).
3. The Lord...will prosper thy _____. (Gen. 24:40)
4. _____, M, _____ (2 words).
5. In the _____ of this world. (Matt. 13:40)
6. Opened the prison _____. (Acts 5:19)
7. Eastern time (abbr.).
8. Shout unto God with the voice of _____. (Ps. 47:1)
9. Charged particle.
10. He chose David...from following the _____. (Ps. 78:70,71)
13. Expression of pain.
15. Thrust through with a _____. (Heb. 12:20)
17. Symbol for radon.
19. Continue in faith...and _____. (1 Tim. 2:15)
21. The Greeks _____ after wisdom. (1 Cor. 1:22)
22. A grain.
23. Of whom the world _____ not worthy. (Heb. 11:38)
24. When they had sung an _____. (Matt. 26:30)
27. What a ghost says.
28. A Pharisee might say: "I _____ _____ " (2 words).

30. The beast shall make _____ against them. (Rev. 11:7)

32. Alcoholics Anonymous (abbr.).

33. The centurion loosed Paul from his _____. (Acts 22:30)

37. Offers to buy at auction.

38. Joshua the son of _____. (Josh. 1:1)

39. Ibidem (abbr.).

40. Wherein shall go no galley with _____. (Isa. 33:21)

42. Look upon mine affliction and my _____. (Ps. 25:18)

43. Impersonal pronoun.

44. The unclean spirit had _____ him. (Mark 1:26)

PUZZLE 26

ACROSS CLUES

1. Belonging to a minor prophet.
7. Belonging to the son of Issachar. (Gen. 46:13)
9. I'm _____ the end of my rope.
10. Each (abbr.).
11. The beloved disciple.
13. Spoken of by _____ the prophet. (Matt. 24:15)
16. Abbreviation meaning "all right"
17. Though they have _____ chariots. (Josh. 17:18)
20. Woodworking tool.
21. Cupbearer to the king. (Neh. 1:1,11)
23. Styling _____ for the hair.
24. _____ is the father of Canaan. (Gen. 9:18)
26. Negative.
27. They set the ark...upon a new _____. (2 Sam. 6:3)
30. _____ lamented for Josiah. (2 Chron. 35:25)

34. _____ of the Chaldees. (Gen. 15:7)
35. And _____ shall rule over thee. (Gen. 3:16)
36. Type of armament.
37. "I _____ that test!"
40. _____ have and to hold.
41. 28th book of the Bible.
43. Belonging to a man of mount Ephraim. (Judg. 17:1)
45. Compass direction.
46. He dwelleth in _____. (John 6:56)
48. Tyrone (abbr.).
50. "_____ top of old Smokey."
51. Pharaoh's daughter called his name _____. (Ex. 2:10)
52. Before the Israelites had kings, they had _____.

DOWN CLUES

2. Written in the _____ of the prophets. (Acts 7:42)
3. He had the gift of interpreting dreams.
4. A word...in due season, how good is _____! (Prov. 15:23)
5. Where is _____ that is born King of the Jews? (Matt. 2:2)
6. Why is thy countenance _____? (Neh. 2:2)
7. Prophet to Nineveh.
8. Part of a shoe.
11. The patience of _____.
12. The name of Samuel's firstborn was _____. (1 Sam. 8:2)
14. _____, ego, superego.
15. Seraiah, Jeremiah, _____. (Neh. 12:1)
18. Blood factor.
19. Southwestern state (abbr.).
21. Compass direction.
22. As my servant _____ hath walked naked. (Isa. 20:3)
23. _____ in peace. (Luke 7:50)
25. Barnabas took _____, and sailed to Cyprus. (Acts 15:39)
26. 34th book of the Bible.
27. 900 in Roman numerals.
28. Radar beacon.
29. Solomon was not arrayed like one of _____. (Matt. 6:29)
31. For example.
32. Boaz begat Obed of _____. (Matt. 1:5)
33. Seth called his son's name _____. (Gen. 4:26)
38. Defensive End (abbr.).
39. _____ of the Apostles.
42. Prophet who was a herdsman of Tekoa.
44. Yes (nautical).
47. Printer's measure.
49. Middle Atlantic state (abbr.).

PUZZLE 27

ACROSS CLUES

1. Charity suffereth long, and is _____. (1 Cor. 13:4)
5. They have spread a _____ by the wayside. (Ps. 140:5)
7. Gather the wheat into my _____. (Matt. 13:30)
11. A thought or concept.
12. I will set him _____ high. (Ps. 91:14)
13. Having to do with life science (prefix).
14. Compass direction.
15. Glory to God in _____ highest.
16. How long shall I _____ with you? (Mark 9:19)
18. British word for bathroom.
19. Some would even _____ to die. (Rom. 5:7)
21. _____, _____, C.
22. _____, and it shall be given you. (Matt. 7:7)
24. _____, Father. (Mark 14:36)
27. And did all _____ the same spiritual meat. (1 Cor. 10:3)
29. Behold, the _____ wept. (Ex. 2:6)
30. And his _____ went throughout all Syria. (Matt. 4:24)
33. Decimeter (abbr.).
35. Calls for someone in a public place.
36. Far _____ all principality, and power. (Eph. 1:21)
38. The veil of the temple was _____ in twain. (Matt. 27:51)
40. Nancy (abbr.).
41. _____ angel of the Lord.
42. _____ and walk? (Matt. 9:5)
44. Before Christ (abbr.).

45. He is _____; yet is he clean. (Lev. 13:40)
49. Gets up in the morning.
50. All that handle the _____. (Ezek. 27:29)
52. Side away from the wind.
53. One of the Three Stooges.
54. A type of deer.
55. The father shall be divided against the _____. (Luke 12:53)
56. Saint (abbr.).
57. But also _____ die at Jerusalem. (Acts 21:13)
58. His _____ was cleansed. (Matt. 8:3)

DOWN CLUES

1. Boaz was of the _____ of Elimelech. (Ruth 3:2)
2. "I've got a great _____!"
3. Compass direction.
4. Sweet fruit grown on palm trees.
5. Christmas.
6. Inhabitants of_____dor. (Josh. 17:11)
8. No man...was _____ to open the book. (Rev. 5:3)
9. City in Brazil.
10. About _____...there shone great light round me. (Acts 22:6)
16. Find the _____ wrapped in swaddling clothes. (Luke 2:12)
17. One type of tide.
20. A type of vermin.
23. Kilobytes (abbr.).
24. He is _____ also to save. (Heb. 7:25)
25. When he saw Jesus _____ off, he ran. (Mark 5:6)
26. So be it.

56

28. _____ I my brother's keeper? (Gen. 4:9)
31. Die in the flower of their _____. (1 Sam. 2:33)
32. Eastern Standard Time (abbr.).
34. And _____ him that is high. (Ezek. 21:26)
36. Pay tithe of mint, _____ and cummin. (Matt. 23:23)
37. I have commanded my sanctified _____. (Isa. 13:3)
39. They went their ways, one to his _____ (plural). (Matt. 22:5)
41. If I knew you were coming, I'd have baked _____ (2 words).
43. They that count it pleasure to _____. (2 Pet. 2:13)
44. The fire causeth the waters to _____. (Isa. 64:2)
46. Who loveth God love his brother _____. (1 John 4:21)
47. Several popes sharing one name.
48. Lest ye _____ your God. (Josh. 24:27)
51. To knock on a door; form of music.

PUZZLE 28

ACROSS CLUES

2. Kilogram (abbr.).
4. Not very often.
10. Computer communication.
12. Joshua...left nothing _____. (Josh. 11:15)
13. _____ each his own.
14. Their cry came up un_____ God. (Ex. 2:23)
15. New Testament (abbr.).
16. Egyptian sun god.
18. Royal Canadian (abbr.).
20. Not *A.D.*
21. The..._____ that came out of Egypt ...died. (Josh. 5:4)
24. Live in _____. (2 Cor. 13:11)
27. _____ our eye hath seen it. (Ps. 35:21)
28. Deutsche mark (abbr.).
29. The cup was found in Benjamin's _____. (Gen. 44:12)
30. Our _____ is near. (Lam. 4:18)
32. Shem, _____ and Japheth. (Gen. 5:32)
33. Saul...fought against...Moab and ..._____. (1 Sam. 14:47)
36. Takes care of a bill.
38. _____ la la la la.
39. The _____ of that house was great. (Luke 6:49)
40. So be it.
42. Led us through a land...of _____. (Jer. 2:6)
43. "Kukla, Fran, and _____."
46. Energy, vim, vigor.
47. Lung disease.
49. They _____ hands on the apostles. (Acts 4:3)

50. Behold...the _____ and it shineth not. (Job 25:5)
51. As he thinketh in his heart, _____ is he. (Prov. 23:7)
52. A long period of time.
53. He saith among the trumpets, _____. (Job 39:25)
54. Heareth...and _____ with joy receiveth it. (Matt. 13:20)
56. I am a..._____ of the Gentiles. (1 Tim. 2:7)
57. As _____ that mourneth for his mother. (Ps. 35:14)

DOWN CLUES

1. Cornelius _____ him, and fell down. (Acts 10:25)
2. Baby fox.
3. The earth is a _____.
4. I saw an angel standing in the _____. (Rev. 19:17)
5. Inner, within (prefix).
6. 450 in Roman numerals.
7. Who rejoice to _____ evil. (Prov. 2:14)
8. Cherubims stretch wings _____ high. (Ex. 25:20)
9. Being nothing more than.
11. Jacob loved Rachel _____ than Leah. (Gen. 29:30)
17. The cruel venom of _____. (Deut. 32:33)
19. A person who carries another's clubs.
21. _____ straight the way of the Lord. (John 1:23)
22. _____, thou that destroyest the temple. (Mark 15:29)
23. The arrangement of items.
24. Wizards that _____, and that mutter. (Isa. 8:19)

58

25. 900 in Roman numerals.
26. _____ sought to destroy all the Jews. (Es. 3:6)
29. Is the young man Absalom _____? (2 Sam. 18:29)
31. North America (abbr.).
34. One drop of water.
35. Sprinkles lightly on something.
37. He hath _____ in his heart. (Ps. 10:6)
41. He dwelleth in _____. (John 6:56)
42. I will not with ink and _____ write unto thee. (3 John 13)

43. Bravo (Span.).
44. Citizen of an Asian country.
45. Pieces of material shed during washing or drying.
46. Corn_____.
48. _____ of my bones, and flesh of my flesh. (Gen. 2:23)
50. Brand of computer (abbr.).
53. Sound made when laughing.
55. Negative.

PUZZLE 29

ACROSS CLUES

2. Are not two _____ sold for a farthing? (Matt. 10:29)
9. Thou couldest have no power _____ all. (John 19:11)
11. New Testament (abbr.).
13. To give off.
14. God _____ loved the world. (John 3:16)
15. They have _____ rest day nor night. (Rev. 14:11)
16. Sun, _____ or stars. (Ec. 12:2)
18. They shall beat their _____ into plowshares. (Isa. 2:4)
20. A long period of time.
21. Fellow (British).
22. The centurion's servant was ready _____ die. (Luke 7:2)
23. Mother.
24. "When I go to the mall, _____ _____." (2 words)
27. _____...in the field. (Luke 2:8)
31. It _____ not for you to know the times. (Acts 1:7)
33. _____ the furnace. (Dan. 3:19)
34. Samuel ran to _____. (1 Sam. 3:5)
35. Isn't (ungrammatical but popular).
36. God said to Adam, Where _____ thou? (Gen. 3:9)
37. A person from the British Isles is sometimes called this.
38. Took counsel _____ slay the apostles. (Acts 5:33)
39. Recreational Vehicle (abbr.).
40. Render therefore to all their _____: tribute. (Rom. 13:7)
41. Electrical Engineer (abbr.).
42. Take thou unto thee an iron _____. (Ezek. 4:3)

44. As the morning _____ upon the mountains. (Joel 2:2)
46. Compass direction.
47. I make thy _____s thy footstool. (Acts 2:35)
50. I will...build again the _____ of David. (Acts 15:16)
53. A fall-blooming flower.
54. As my beloved _____ I warn you. (1 Cor. 4:14)

DOWN CLUES

1. Needs that are unsatisfied are _____.
3. I will not with ink and _____ write to thee. (3 John 13)
4. When I am weak, then _____ I strong. (2 Cor. 12:10)
5. He was very sorrowful: for he was very _____. (Luke 18:23)
6. Right (abbr.).
7. Compass direction.
8. Thou shalt have no more _____s. (Micah 5:12)
9. Surely goodness _____ mercy shall follow me. (Ps. 23:6)
10. He will...turn and _____ thee like a ball. (Isa. 22:18)
12. Also.
17. I meditate _____ all thy works. (Ps. 143:5)
18. Jesus was led up of the _____. (Matt. 4:1)
19. Shortened form of the word *kangaroo*.
21. A small hat.
23. Abigail _____ David and his men. (1 Sam. 25:20)
25. South Dakota (abbr.).
26. A liquid measure.
27. On my _____ I will pour out of my Spirit. (Acts 2:18)

28. Fedora, Stetson, or derby.
29. It is good for us to be _____. (Matt. 17:4)
30. Belonging to Samuel's teacher.
32. Jesus _____ _____ to read in the synagogue. (Luke 4:16; 2 words)
33. Praise the Lord with _____. (Ps. 33:2)
37. An item placed between other items to keep them apart.

41. Several film _____ have been made from the Bible.
43. _____ and clean.
45. Doth not _____ nature itself teach you? (1 Cor. 11:14)
48. Either/_____.
49. Prefix meaning "inner."
51. To _____ or not to be.
52. And _____, the heavens were opened. (Matt. 3:16)

PUZZLE 30

ACROSS CLUES

1. God be _____ to me a sinner. (Luke 18:13)
7. A female horse of breeding age.
11. For example.
12. Alternating Current (abbr.).
13. _____ be ye holy. (1 Pet. 1:15)
14. According to my _____est expectation and hope. (Phil. 1:20)
15. Wide is the _____. (Matt. 7:13)
17. Belonging to the son of Ner. (2 Sam. 3:25)
18. Social Security (abbr.).
20. We desire _____ hear...what thou thinkest. (Acts 28:22)
23. The month of _____ (Ex. 13:4)
25. _____ with hr suburbs. (1 Chron. 6:70)
26. A red root vegetable.
29. For we have heard...what ye did unto..._____. (Josh. 2:10)
31. The Lord _____ Eglon...against Israel. (Judg. 3:12)

35. Tell me, art thou a _____? (Acts 22:27)
37. Haran begat _____. (Gen. 11:27)
39. I will take away all thy _____. (Isa. 1:25)
41. Type of acid.
42. _____ King of Bashan. (1 Kgs. 4:19)
43. Joshua...gave _____...Hebron. (Josh. 14:13)
45. _____ the kine to the cart. (1 Sam. 6:7)
47. Another word for *bill*.
49. A train that runs above street level.
50. Volumes (abbr.).
53. Many _____ and troubles shall befall them. (Deut. 31:17)
55. _____ shall a man leave his father and mother. (Gen. 2:24)

DOWN CLUES

1. He dwelleth in _____. (John 6:56)
2. As the partridge sitteth on _____. (Jer. 17:11)
3. A feline.
4. Blackish by reason of the _____. (Job 6:16)
5. United States of America (abbr.).
6. A high return in tennis.
7. There shall _____ you _____ man. (Mark 14:13; 2 words)
8. Moses' brother. (Ex. 4:14)

9. Railroads (abbr.).
10. Printer's measure.
16. Leah...called his name _____. (Gen. 30:13)
19. Nabal's wife was _____. (1 Sam. 25:3)
21. Tempted like as we _____, yet without sin. (Heb. 4:15)
22. I saw _____ hanged in an oak. (2 Sam. 18:10)
24. Bohemia (abbr.).
27. Hero of a popular child's science-fiction movie.
28. One of the Kennedy family sons.
30. Ehud's father. (Judg. 3:15)
32. Nominative (abbr.).
33. To give off.
34. Spoken of by _____ the prophet. (Matt. 24:15)
36. Christmases.
38. _____ King of Bashan. (1 Kgs. 4:19)
39. Crumbs which fell from the rich man's _____. (Luke 16:21)
40. When he draweth him into his _____. (Ps. 10:9)
44. Bachelor of Arts (abbr.).
46. Adam and _____.
48. A swarm of _____s in the carcase of the lion. (Judg. 14:8)
51. Either/_____.
52. San Francisco (abbr.).
54. _____ is finished. (John 19:30)

PUZZLE 31

ACROSS CLUES

1. He laid each _____ one against another. (Gen. 15:10)
4. _____ for the multitude of Egypt. (Ezek. 32:18)
8. _____ are of God. (1 John 4:6)
10. Bachelor of Arts (abbr.).
11. And the Jews' _____ was at hand. (John 2:13)
13. _____, when camest thou hither? (John 6:25)
16. Right (abbr.).
17. They fled before the men of _____. (Josh. 7:4)
18. Neither _____ there salvation in any other. (Acts 4:12)
19. Left Tackle (abbr.).
21. Bring him _____ unto Felix. (Acts 23:24)
23. The number of the army of the _____ were. (Rev. 9:16)
27. The hour cometh, and _____ is. (John 4:23)
28. Jesus began to be _____ amazed and heavy. (Mark 14:33)
29. _____ in their hands. (Rev. 7:9)
31. Why _____ ye that which is not lawful to do? (Luke 6:2)
32. 400 in Roman numerals.
33. The swallow hath found...a _____ for herself. (Ps. 84:3)
34. Why make ye this _____, and weep? (Mark 5:39)
36. _____ doth he yet find fault? (Rom. 9:19)
37. Let it be _____ with the dew of heaven. (Dan. 4:15)
38. Unknown author (abbr.).

40. Let us _____ with patience the race before us. (Heb. 12:1)
41. To satisfy hunger or thirst.
44. He went before, ascending up to _____. (Luke 19:28)
47. Enemies and my _____ s came upon me. (Ps. 27:2)
48. 2 in Roman numerals.
49. I have many things to _____ to judge of you. (John 8:26)
50. They went their ways, one to his _____. (Matt. 22:5)
51. There shall not be left one _____ upon another. (Matt. 24:2)
52. His enemy...sowed _____ among the wheat. (Matt. 13:25)

DOWN CLUES

1. Lord, save us, we _____. (Matt. 8:25)
2. A type of tide.
3. Many different wires make up a _____.
4. The beast...shall make _____ against them. (Rev. 11:7)
5. Fall-blooming flower.
6. There _____ not one of them left. (2 Sam. 13:30)
7. A lad here which hath five barley _____. (John 6:9)
8. Why could not _____ cast him out? (Mark 9:28)
9. Unit of work.
12. 6 in Roman numerals.
14. _____ did what was right. (1 Kgs. 15:11)
15. Hold _____!
20. Goodness and _____. (Ps. 23:6)
22. On our solemn _____ day. (Ps. 81:3)
23. What the people yelled to the son of David. (Matt. 21:9)

64

24. Expression of pain.
25. Missouri (abbr.).
26. Nickname for Edward.
27. New Mexico (abbr.).
29. Pet _____.
30. Left Tackle (abbr.).
31. Animal that is called an ass in the Bible.
33. Compass direction.
35. Learn to _____ well. (Isa. 1:17)
36. There _____ a great earthquake. (Matt. 28:2)
38. Australia (abbr.).

39. Any among you _____ (singular verb form) to be religious. (Jam. 1:16)
40. They were the _____ of him. (2 Chron. 28:23)
42. Having seen the promises _____ off. (Heb. 11:13)
43. He _____ his hair out.
44. Jesse (abbr.).
45. City in Brazil.
46. Lay not thine hand upon the _____. (Gen. 22:12)
50. Name of a musical note.

PUZZLE 32

ACROSS CLUES

2. He calleth together his friends and _____. (Luke 15:6)
10. His kingdom was lifted up _____ high. (1 Chron. 14:2)
11. Loosen, free from bonds.
12. North America (abbr.).
13. Vermont (abbr.).
14. Doctor (abbr.).
16. Buddy, friend, _____.
17. Your _____ is come abroad. (Rom. 16:19)
18. The state of wearing a robe.
19. A type of grain (singular).
21. Expression of pain.
22. Four and twenty blackbirds baked in a _____.
23. Cain brought...an _____ unto the Lord. (Gen. 4:3)
27. Ye have put off the _____ man. (Col. 3:9)
28. 2,000 in Roman numerals.
29. Disk Operating System (abbr.).
30. Prefix meaning "before."
33. Either/_____.
34. They...weave the spider's _____. (Isa. 59:5)
35. _____-ta ("good-bye" in baby talk).
36. Who am also a _____ of the glory. (1 Pet. 5:1)
38. Mice that _____ the land. (1 Sam. 6:5)
39. Prefix meaning very small.
40. An island in eastern Indonesia.
42. In the _____ of one Tyrannus. (Acts 19:9)
43. Ye shall be _____ from your enemies. (Num. 10:9)
44. A brand of sneakers (singular).
45. Whose _____ I am not worthy to bear. (Matt. 3:11)

DOWN CLUES

1. Go to the _____, thou sluggard. (Prov. 6:6)
2. For he was _____ with us. (Acts 1:17)
3. When forty days...were _____ he hungered. (Luke 4:2)
4. This is the way, walk ye in _____. (Isa. 30:21)
5. "Get in" (colloquial).
6. Whose son is _____? (Matt. 22:42)
7. Eat straw like the _____. (Isa. 11:7)
8. Ribonucleic acid (abbr.).
9. _____ them that have the rule over you. (Heb. 13:24)
10. I have _____ the world. (John 16:33)
15. He _____ who should betray him. (John 13:11)
16. A _____ prepared for the Lord. (Luke 1:17)
17. Obstetrical (abbr.).
20. _____ed him in the killing of his brethren. (Judg. 9:24)
21. _____ the King of Bashan. (Num. 21:33)
24. Frequency Modulation (abbr.).
25. Because they had no _____ they withered away. (Matt. 13:6)
26. Belonging to God's chosen nation.
27. Globe.
30. Lord, save us: we _____. (Matt. 8:25)
31. Though _____ should rise against me. (Ps. 27:3)
32. A hidden supply of stores.

34. They are _____ with the showers of the mountains. (Job 24:8)
35. The _____ of the field. (Matt. 13:36)
36. The ravens of the valley shall _____ it out. (Prov. 30:17)
37. Medieval churches had a _____ screen at the entrance of the chancel.
38. To take from one place to another.
39. Postscript (abbr.).
41. Former Chinese leader.

PUZZLE 33

ACROSS CLUES

1. The name of the second river is _____. (Gen. 2:13)
6. If it please the king...send me unto _____. (Neh. 2:5)
10. Registered Nurses (abbr.).
11. *River*, in Spanish.
13. Why make ye this _____? (Mark 5:39)
14. He that doeth good is _____ God. (3 John 11)
15. _____, the abominaiton of the children.. (1 Kgs. 11:7)
16. A sorcerer...whose name was _____-Jesus. (Acts 13:6)
17. Eithers/_____.
19. Captains over _____. (Deut. 1:15)
21. I in them, and thou in _____. (John 17:23)
22. The _____ became David's servants. (2 Sam. 8:2)
24. God _____ my strength and power. (2 Sam. 22:33)
26. New Mexico (abbr.).
28. Immigration and Naturalization Service (abbr.).
30. A boy named Stuart is probably called _____.
31. Jonah rose up to flee unto _____. (Jonah 1:3)
34. Town in central England with a famous school.
36. _____ not ten cleansed? (Luke 17:17)
38. Rebekah's brother. (Gen. 24:29)
39. Used for sending greetings on holidays.
40. Geber...in the country of _____. (1 Kgs. 4:19)

42. Do unto them as unto the _____; as to Sisera. (Ps. 83:9)
47. To _____ or not to be.
48. Eggs (Latin).
49. _____ king of Tyre. (2 Sam. 5:11)
50. The way of an eagle in the _____. (Prov. 30:19)
51. Moab shall howl over _____. (Isa. 15:2)
52. To forbid something is to _____ it.
53. A slight coloration.

DOWN CLUES

1. He that hath the bride is the bride_____. (John 3:29)
2. The porch that was _____ the _____ of the house. (2 Chron. 3:4; 2 words)
3. High School (abbr.).
4. Elimelech's wife was _____. (Ruth 1:2)
5. Left I thee in_____. (Tit. 1:5)
6. Mary the mother of_____. (Acts 12:12)
7. A little _____ will do you.
8. _____ gave names to all cattle and ...fowl of the air. (Gen. 2:20)
9. Belonging to a certain mountain. (Ex. 3:1)
12. Decorates a cake.
18. Hannah...called his name _____. (1 Sam. 1:20)
20. *Yes,* in Spanish.
23. What is stronger _____ _____ lion? (Judg. 14:18; 2 words)
25. The captain of Jabin's host was _____. (Judg. 4:2)
27. Jacob came to Shalem, a city of _____. (Gen. 33:18)
29. New Hampshire (abbr.).
30. _____ built the house and finished it. (1 Kgs. 6:14)

31. Sanballat...and..._____ heard. (Neh. 2:10)
32. Compass direction.
33. Irish Republican Army (abbr.).
35. _____-ta.
37. To state something with confidence.
41. Such as I have _____ I thee. (Acts 3:6)

43. A small amount.
44. Part of a pen.
45. Individual Retirement Account (abbr.).
46. To cure a skin.
47. Place for storing grain or other small items.
50. _____ is spoiled. (Jer. 49:3)

PUZZLE 34

ACROSS CLUES

1. _____ angel of the Lord. (Judg. 6:11)
3. He _____ the number of the stars. (Ps. 147:4)
7. This is the way, walk ye in _____. (Isa. 30:21)
9. What have I _____ _____ any more with idols? (Hos. 14:8; 2 words)
11. Eli...sat up_____ _____ seat. (1 Sam. 1:9; 2 words)
12. It is _____ of the twelve. (Mark 14:20)
13. Prefix meaning "within."
14. Each (abbr.).
15. Gold is often formed into a _____.
17. Paul..._____ God, and took courage. (Acts 28:15)
20. Filled them _____ to the brim. (John 2:7)
22. When the sun waxed _____. (Ex. 16:21)

23. They took him, and brought him unto _____pagus. (Acts 17:19)
25. To hurry somewhere.
28. Woman's name.
29. Plural of Pi.
31. _____ wine is better. (Luke 5:39)
32. The mediator of the new _____. (Heb. 9:15)
35. *The Cat in the* _____.
36. _____ two walk together, except they be agreed? (Amos 3:3)
37. *Yes* in Spanish.
39. Bind the _____ of thine head upon thee. (Ezek. 24:17)
40. _____ panteth my soul. (Ps. 42:1)
41. Poisonous snake. (Deut. 32:33)
43. Exacted...of _____ man fifty shekels. (2 Kgs. 15:20)
45. A manifest _____ of the righteous judgment. (2 Thes. 1:5)
47. God _____ high.
49. Learn to _____ well. (Isa. 1:17)
51. Regarding.
52. In her mouth was an _____ leaf. (Gen. 8:11)
54. A crown of _____. (Matt. 27:29)
55. Sin which doth so easily _____ us. (Heb. 12:1)

DOWN CLUES

1. I _____ no pleasant bread. (Dan. 10:3)
2. There is _____ like unto thee, O Lord. (Jer. 10:6)
3. Trouble is like a broken _____. (Prov. 25:19)
4. For the _____ which is lent to the Lord. (1 Sam. 2:20)
5. Printer's measure.
6. Will build again the _____ of David. (Acts 15:16)
7. That I am _____ the Father. (John 14:10)
8. Ye are not come unto...darkness and _____. (Heb. 12:18)
10. Doctor of Divinity (abbr.).
12. One _____ the other.
14. _____ such things as are set before you. (Luke 10:8)
16. A summer fruit drink.
18. _____, ho, ho.
19. German philosopher.
21. Satan...bound...a _____ years. (Rev. 20:2)
24. I will _____ my mouth in parables. (Matt. 13:35)
26. Prefix meaning "not"
27. Asner, Wynne, Bradley.
28. To the back of a ship.
30. Hosanna _____ the highest. (Matt. 21:9)
32. My little finger shall be _____. (1 Kgs. 12:10)
33. Cut off his right _____. (Luke 22:50)
34. Mom.
38. It _____ his angel. (Acts 12:15)
40. To push and _____.
42. Physical Therapy (abbr.).
44. He is _____ also to save. (Heb. 7:25)
46. *Gold* in Spanish.
48. Drew the _____ to land. (John 21:11)
50. Old Testament (abbr.).
52. Obstetrician (abbr.).
53. How good _____ it! (Prov. 15:23)

PUZZLE 35

ACROSS CLUES

1. I am from _____. (John 7:29)
4. _____, thou that destroyest the temple. (Mark 15:29)
6. He shewed himself _____. (Acts 1:3)
10. To goad.
12. Local area network (abbr.).
13. Have mercy on _____. (Matt. 15:22)
15. He giveth meat in _____. (Job 36:31)
17. Abram said unto Lot, Let there _____ strife. (Gen. 13:8; 2 words)
19. Royal Canadian (abbr.).
20. Missing in Action (abbr.).
23. Registered nurse (abbr.).
24. Strain at a gnat, and swallow a _____. (Matt. 23:24)
26. 1,100 in Roman numerals.
27. The _____ a Pharisee, the other a publican. (Luke 18:10)
29. _____ the King of Bashan. (Num. 21:33)
31. Now _____ faith, hope, charity. (1 Cor. 13:13)
33. The price of wisdom is _____ rubies. (Job 28:18)
34. They _____ Jesus to the brow of the hill. (Luke 4:29)
35. Be not _____. (Matt. 14:27)
37. In a certain place.
38. The tower of _____. (Gen. 11:9)
42. Bringing sick f_____s. (Acts 5:16)
43. Mom.
44. For many be _____. (Matt. 20:16)
45. The falling tide.
48. It is (contraction).

5. They shall _____ as lions' whelps. Jer. 51:38)
52. Demonstrated.
53. Horse's strut. (Nah. 3:2)

DOWN CLUES

2. Out of _____ are the issues of life. (Prov. 4:23)
3. What _____ these seven ewe lambs? (Gen. 21:29)
4. Arizona State University (abbr.).
5. As a _____ gathereth her chickens. (Matt. 23:37)
6. Trumpets to cry _____ (2 Chron. 13:12)
7. They shall hold the..._____. (Jer. 50:42)
8. Incorporated (abbr.).
9. Dorothy's aunt.
11. A faithful man shall _____ with blessings. (Prov. 28:20)
14. The love of God is shed _____ in our hearts. (Rom. 5:5)
16. Printer's measure.
18. _____able.
21. I am (contraction).
22. For this is _____ in the sight of God. (1 Tim. 2:3)
25. Divided into sections, such as the brain, the ear.
27. Thou didst eat fine flour, honey, and _____. (Ezek. 16:13)
28. Electrical Engineer (abbr.).
30. He that is of _____ heareth. (John 8:47)
32. _____ feared John. (Mark 6:20)
33. Whether they both shall be _____ good. (Ec. 11:6)
35. That which I do I _____ not. (Rom. 7:15)
36. American League (abbr.).

72

37. Whom do men say that I the Son of man _____? (Matt. 16:13)
39. Praise him for his mighty _____. (Ps. 150:2)
40. To smash, or a wild party.
41. Elevation (abbr.).
46. Even a fruitful bough _____ well. (Gen. 49:22; 2 words)
47. Benjamin's nickname.
49. All these things I kept from my youth _____. (Luke 18:21)
51. Lower case (abbr.).

PUZZLE 36

ACROSS CLUES

1. River in northern Italy.
3. Before Christ (abbr.).
5. The _____ of the loaves. (Mark 6:52)
10. _____ unto God thanksgiving. (Ps. 50:14)
11. Glory be to God _____ high.
12. Musical note.
13. _____ it be of God, ye cannot overthrow it. (Acts 5:39)
14. To patch a hole in a sock.
16. The lowest point.
17. The _____ of Jesus was there. (John 2:1)
19. Have mercy _____ me. (Matt. 15:22)
22. To hurry away.
23. _____meal; a cereal.
25. Let all the _____ be gathered together. (Isa. 43:9)
28. The quick and the _____. (1 Pet. 4:5)
30. Let your moderation be known unto all _____. (Phil. 4:5)
32. A type of bomb.
34. In order; picked up.
35. They shall walk every one in his _____. (Joel 2:8)
37. Senior (abbr.).
38. _____, so would we have it. (Ps. 35:25)
39. Bachelor of Science (abbr.).
40. Television (abbr.).
42. Paul stood on the _____s, and beckoned. (Acts 21:40)
44. That they may be one, as we _____. (John 17:11)
45. Ye shall be _____ gods. (Gen. 3:5)

47. The fruit of righteousness is sown in _____. (Jam. 3:18)
49. 3.14159265.
50. A wise man.
53. Persia is now known as _____.
54. The time is now _____. (Matt. 14:15)
55. Who rejoice to _____ evil. (Prov. 2:14)
56. God led them by the way of the _____ Sea. (Ex. 13:18)

DOWN CLUES

1. The _____ of asps is under their lips. (Rom. 3:13)
2. Not on.
3. I have made my _____ in the darkness. (Job 17:13)
4. To study for a test at the last minute.
5. There are 12 in a year.
6. I am _____ the Father. (John 14:10)
7. The promise is to all that are _____ off. (Acts 2:39)
8. A man who is a heel is called a _____.
9. Give _____ to my words, O Lord. (Ps. 5:1)
15. Nickname for Rosemary.
16. I am rich, and...have _____ of nothing. (Rev. 3:17)
18. Hello!
20. Whose _____ are in the book of life. (Phil. 4:3)
21. To give clues.
23. If a man swear an _____. (Num. 30:2)
24. Why make ye this _____, and weep? (Mark 5:39)
26. Began to wash his feet with _____. (Luke 7:38)
27. Say _____ to any man. (Mark 1:44)
29. Ingests.

74

31. When the sun was _____.
    (Matt. 13:6)
33. In him we live, and _____.
    (Acts 17:28)
36. He is _____ also to save.
    (Heb. 7:25)
38. Support group for problem
    drinkers.
40. Power to _____ on scorpions.
    (Luke 10:19)
41. A little rest.

43. He will turn and _____ thee like a
    ball. (Isa. 22:18)
44. Men within...an half _____ of land.
    (1 Sam. 14:14)
46. To drink slowly.
48. The way of an eagle in the _____.
    (Prov. 30:19)
51. Evil to him that was _____ peace.
    (Ps. 7:4)
52. Children of Gad called the altar
    _____. (Josh. 22:34)

PUZZLE 37

ACROSS CLUES

1. Omri...did _____ than all before him. (1 Kgs. 16:25)
5. Fools die for _____ of wisdom. (Prov. 10:21)
8. _____ are his people. (Ps. 100:3)
10. Tempted like as we _____. (Heb. 4:15)
11. Migratory birds.
13. Shortened form of a place to wash up.
14. The _____ of sin is death (Rom. 6:23)
15. The women _____ hangings for the grove. (2 Kgs. 23:7)
16. Compass direction.
18. *Anno Domini* (abbr.).
19. He that _____eth is like a wave of the sea. (Jam. 1:6)
20. One way to move a boat.
21. Desert places with water and vegetation.
22. Let us _____ and be sober. (2 Thes. 5:6)
24. If he _____ _____ lamb. (Lev. 3:7; 2 words)
27. Children of Gad called the altar _____. (Josh. 22:34)
29. Is not her younger sister _____ than she? (Judg. 15:2)
30. Your wives shall be _____. (Ex. 22:24)
33. Railroad (abbr.).
34. _____ I go unto him that sent me. (John 7:33)
36. Thy _____ goats have not cast their young. (Gen. 31:38)
37. I Daniel was mourning three full _____. (Dan. 10:2)
39. The Lord is with thee, thou mighty _____. (Judg. 6:12)
40. Vietnamese new year celebration.
41. If he gain the _____ world. (Matt. 16:26)
43. Love thy neighbour _____ thyself. (Matt. 19:19)
44. Egyptian sun god.
45. The path of virtuous conduct in Confucianism.
46. A highly prized game fish.
49. Where David and his men were _____ to haunt. (1 Sam. 30:31)
50. New Testament (abbr.).

DOWN CLUES

1. Cautions.
2. Northwest state (abbr.).
3. Symbol for rhenium.
4. Goodness gracious!
5. Blessed are ye that _____ now. (Luke 6:21)
6. Biblical word for *donkey*.
7. Compass direction.
8. The ship was covered with the _____. (Matt. 8:24)
9. Christ abideth for _____. (John 12:34)
12. For example (abbr.).
13. The _____ of the Father is not in him. (1 John 2:15)
14. Equipment used to help patients move around.
15. Have _____ their robes and made them white. (Rev. 7:14)
17. Mightest war a good _____. (1 Tim. 1:18)
19. Women's Army Corps (abbr.).
21. Old Testament (abbr.).
22. A growth on the skin.
23. Strong bulls of Bashan have _____ (singular verb form) me. (Ps. 22:12)

24. He that is _____ God heareth. (John 8:47)
25. It rained _____ and brimstone. (Luke 17:29)
26. Regarding (abbr.).
28. Does (biblical variation).
30. I rejoiced because my _____ was great. (Job 31:25)
31. Set cherubims within the _____ house. (1 Kgs. 6:27)
32. Except a corn of _____ fall into the ground. (John 12:24)
35. Health Maintenance Organization (abbr.).
37. And _____ not a little comforted. (Acts 20:12)
38. And the _____, and the pelican. (Lev. 11:18)
42. Not cold.
45. A preposition.
47. The head of Elisha...stand _____ him this day. (2 Kgs. 6:31)
48. Utah (abbr.).

PUZZLE 38

ACROSS CLUES

1. Outer covering of a fruit or seed.
4. Thou and all thy _____ shall be saved. (Acts 11:14)
8. Mom.
10. A vessel...meet for the master's _____. (2 Tim. 2:21)
11. Made upon the _____ of the robe. (Ex. 39:24)
12. That the _____ men be sober, grave, temperate. (Titus 2:2)
14. _____ thee hence, Satan. (Matt. 4:10)
15. To make a mistake.
16. Ear_____.
17. Suffix used to make a comparative word.
18. Let his _____ be desolate. (Acts 1:20)
20. Felines.
21. National Hockey League (abbr.).
23. The men went up and viewed _____. (Josh. 7:2)
24. There is none other but _____. (Mark 12:32)
26. We have seen his _____ in the east. (Matt. 2:2)
28. _____ be thy name. (Matt. 6:9)
31. Pound (abbr.).
32. Woes, troubles.
33. Behold, it _____ very good. (Gen. 1:31)
34. Sound a cat makes.
36. New York City baseball team.
37. _____ thee, escape thither. (Gen. 19:22)
38. Standing Room Only (abbr.).
39. A period of time.

41. _____ hath washed my feet with tears. (Luke 7:44)
43. Negative.
45. It is a _____ thing that the king requireth. (Dan. 2:11)
46. Children of Gad called the altar _____. (Josh. 22:34)
47. A group of people working together for a common goal.
49. _____, ego, superego.
50. That they may be one, as we _____. (John 17:11)
51. Your children...received _____ correction. (Jer. 2:30)
52. My covenant shall _____ fast with him. (Ps. 89:28)
53. _____ angel of the Lord.

DOWN CLUES

1. Very big.
2. One who uses.
3. _____ me not wander from thy commandments. (Ps. 119:10)
4. Ye tithe...all manner of _____. (Luke 11:42)
5. Athaliah, daughter of _____. (2 Kgs. 8:26)
6. We.
7. Belonging to our planet.
8. Note sent as a reminder.
9. *Anno Domini* (abbr.).
11. _____ the furnace. (Dan. 3:19)
13. Ye would not have condemned the _____. (Matt. 12:7)
16. _____ is a lion's whelp. (Deut. 33:22)
18. I will rain...great _____. (Ezek. 38:22)
19. Neither/_____.
20. One who calls.
22. 22nd letter of Greek alphabet.

24. I will not be an _____. (Isa. 3:7)
25. Eddie, Teddy, Edward.
27. A pain in the neck (2 words).
29. Do not your _____ before men. (Matt. 6:1)
30. World War (abbr.).
34. _____ and Pa.
35. One who cultivates a garden.
37. Is anything too _____ for the Lord? (Gen. 18:14)
40. A sneak attack.
42. _____ that were lepers. (Luke 17:12)
44. One type of grain.
48. Master of Arts (abbr.).
50. _____ angel.

PUZZLE 39

Diana Rowland

ACROSS CLUES

1. Central Intelligence Agency (abbr.).
4. _____, every one. (Isa. 55:1)
6. Greet them that _____. (Rom. 16:11)
8. The _____ shall overflow. (Joel 2:24)
9. _____ children, then heirs. (Rom. 8:17)
10. Great, terrific.
13. _____ I am the apostle. (Rom. 11:13)
14. Wretched man that I _____! (Rom. 7:24)
16. _____ Shemaiah; _____, and Rephael. (1 Chron. 26:7; 2 words)
18. _____ servant of the church. (Rom. 16:1; 2 words)
20. Bare _____ son..._____. (Gen. 38:4; 2 words)
22. Nickname for Ronald.
23. _____, and iron, _____ lead, _____ the midst. (Ezek. 22:18; 3 words)
25. Shall come to _____. (Rom. 9:26)
26. _____; _____ he smelleth..._____ the captains. (Job 39:25; 3 words)
27. _____, and Hushim, _____ sons of Aher. (1 Chron. 7:12; 2 words)
28. Joram went over to _____. (2 Kgs. 8:21)
29. Cappadocia, _____. (1 Pet. 1:1)
30. _____ of his Son. (Rom. 8:29)
32. _____ toward...valley of _____. (Josh. 15:7; 2 words)
35. The _____ of thine head. (Ezek. 24:17)
36. Jesus...saying _____, _____.
(Mark 15:34; 2 words.)
37. And _____ it up. (Rev. 10:10)
38. Said the king to _____. (2 Sam. 20:4)
39. Lyric poem of strong feeling.
40. _____: the same is _____ father. (Gen. 19:38; 2 words, var.)
43. Long Island (abbr.).
44. _____ God, _____ me up on high. (Ps. 69:29; 2 words)
45. Pouring in _____. (Luke 10:34)
46. Have _____ among the pots. (Ps. 68:13)
48. Shall _____ to reign. (Rom. 15:12)
49. The _____ were not smitten. (Ex. 9:32)
50. When he had found a young _____. (John 12:14)

DOWN CLUES

1. Iron, _____, and calamus. (Ezek. 27:19)
2. But what saith _____? (Rom. 10:8)
3. _____ did that which was right. (1 Kgs. 15:11)
4. Hello.
5. _____ God: _____ them which fell..._____ thou continue. (Rom. 11:22; 3 words)
6. _____ the children of the promise are counted. (Rom. 9:8)
7. _____, we heard of it at _____. (Ps. 132:6; 2 words, reversed)
8. Your _____ is spoken of. (Rom. 1:8)
10. The image of his _____. (Rom. 8:29)
11. Adam, Sheth, _____. (1 Chron. 1:1)
12. Wash, _____, and dry.
15. _____, so that he _____. (Ex. 21:12; 2 words)

17. _____ is in his hand. (Luke 3:17)
19. _____ ringleader of the sect of the _____. (Acts 24:5; 2 words)
21. Smell.
24. _____ old man...child of his old _____. (Gen. 44:20; 2 words.)
25. Bought with a _____. (1 Cor. 6:20)
27. _____ the son of Amoz. (Isa. 1:1)
29. Called to be an _____. (Rom. 1:1)
30. As _____ live...as _____ is among the mountains. (Jer. 46:18; 2 words)
31. Threw in two _____...Verily _____ say. (Mark 12:42,43; 2 words)
32. Banks of _____...near where

_____..._____ was afraid. (Dan. 8:16,17; 3 words)
33. Slang for *lots and lots*.
34. Barley and the _____ _____. (Isa. 28:25; 2 words)
36. Sons of _____ the father of Sychem. (Acts 7:16)
38. I _____ THAT I AM. (Ex. 3:14)
41. _____ the sacrifices of the dead. (Ps. 106:28)
42. God of Beth-_____...vowedst _____ vow. (Gen. 31:13; 2 words)
47. There _____ no power but of God. (Rom. 13:1)

PUZZLE 40

Mary Ann Freeman

ACROSS CLUES

1. Primate.
4. Every perfect gift is from _____. (Jam. 1:17)
9. Fruit of the Spirit. (Gal. 5:22)
12. Another fruit of the Spirit. (Gal. 5:22)
15. _____ of the Chaldees. (Gen. 15:7)
16. South American mountains.
17. What a pregnant woman does.
19. Sacred image.
20. Poem.
21. Wesley (nickname).
22. Behold, I will do a _____ thing. (Isa. 43:19)
23. As a _____ adorneth herself with jewels. (Isa. 61:10)
25. The priest shall _____ his finger in the blood. (Lev. 4:6)
27. The _____ of knowledge. (Gen. 2:17)
28. Digging tool.

30. _____ _____ of God. (1 John 4:7; 2 words)
33. Sarai was _____; she had no child. (Gen. 11:30)
34. Son of Shemidah. (1 Chron. 7:19)
35. In royal apparel of _____. (Es. 8:15)
36. Missing in Action (abbr.).
37. The elder unto the wellbeloved _____. (3 John 1)
39. Chlorine, caron (symbol).
42. Put off...the _____ man. (Eph. 4:22)
44. Soviet Socialist Republic (abbr.).
45. Fire causeth the waters to _____. (Isa. 64:2)
46. The daughter of Solomon. (1 Kgs. 4:15)
48. Major artery.
49. Not (prefix).
50. Study of places.
52. Compass direction.
53. Ruth's sister-in-law. (Ruth 1:4)
54. Socioeconomic status (abbr.).

DOWN CLUES

1. _____ I say, Rejoice. (Phil. 4:4)
2. British coin.
3. He shall surely _____ her to be his wife. (Ex. 22:16)
4. Einstein and Gore.
5. _____ ye transformed. (Rom. 12:2)
6. For a righteous man will _____ _____. (Rom. 5:7; 2 words)
7. Heal me; for my bones are _____. (Ps. 6:2)
8. Extrasensory perception (abbr.).
10. Ye make clean the _____ of the cup. (Matt. 23:25)
11. Years (abbr.).
13. Red dragon, having seven heads and _____ horns. (Rev. 12:3)
14. A time to rend, and a time to _____. (Ec. 3:7)
18. So Hiram gave Solomon _____ trees. (1 Kgs. 5:10)
20. Minerals.
23. _____ ye all the tithes. (Mal. 3:10)
24. His hands were hairy, as..._____ hands. (Gen. 27:23)
26. My tongue is the _____ of a ready writer. (Ps. 45:1)
27. Late-afternoon meal.
29. Before (prefix).
30. Book written by Jeremiah (abbr.).
31. Buckeyes.
32. Seven _____ full of the seven last plagues. (Rev. 21:9)
33. Cloud or confuse.
35. A _____ must be blameless. (1 Tim. 3:2)
38. Fall flower.
39. Military subdivisions.
40. Flexible.
41. Loams.
43. Decimeter (abbr.).
45. Feather scarf.
46. Ride a yellow one to school.
47. Cornelius said, Four days _____. (Acts 10:30)
48. Argon, hydrogen (symbol).
51. Peach tree state (abbr.).

PUZZLE 41

Diana Rowland

ACROSS CLUES

1. _____ the son of Amoz. (Isa. 1:1)
7. _____ doth now know. (Isa. 1:3)
13. Jesus loved _____. (John 11:5)
14. Thus did _____; according _____. (Gen. 6:22; 2 words)
15. Albert (nickname).
16. Samuel (nickname).
17. Popular type of vehicle.
18. Informal greeting.
19. The going up to _____. (2 Kgs. 9:27)
21. Hadarezer king of _____. (1 Chron. 18:3)
23. Brought him to an _____. (Luke 10:34)
24. Beth-lehem, and _____, and Tekoa. (2 Chron. 11:6)
26. Though they be _____ like crimson. (Isa. 1:18)
27. _____ is desolate, _____ overthrown. (Isa. 1:7; 2 words)
28. The _____ great with young. (Ps. 78:71)
30. _____ shall be rooted up. (Zeph. 2:4)
32. Tomorrow we shall _____. (Isa. 22:13)
34. Kanga's baby son.
35. _____ happeneth to them all. (Ec. 2:14)
37. The _____ are a people not strong. (Prov. 30:25)
40. Seth lived after be begat _____. (Gen. 5:7)
41. Give ye _____, and hear. (Isa. 28:23)
44. Heber...the son of _____. (Luke 3:35)
46. Eat not of it _____. (Ex. 12:9)
47. Arcturus, _____. (Job 9:9)
49. _____ boweth down. (Isa. 46:1)
50. A familiar spirit at _____-dor. (1 Sam. 28:7)
51. Anna (nickname).
52. Chief Executive Officer (abbr.).
54. Warrant Officer.
55. How should one _____ _____ thousand. (Deut. 32:30; 2 words)
57. _____ with her suburbs. (Josh. 21:32)
59. As _____ was about to _____ into Syria. (Acts 20:3; 2 words)
60. _____ rose up before _____ could know another. (Ruth 3:14; 2 words)

DOWN CLUES

1. A graven _____. (Isa. 44:9)
2. _____ every saint in Christ Jesus. (Phil. 4:21)
3. _____ of Moab is laid waste. (Isa. 15:1)
4. Groweth of _____ own accord. (Lev. 25:5)
5. _____ said, I will not ask. (Isa. 7:12)
6. _____ the father of Shechem. (Josh. 24:32)
7. One who invades.
8. _____, _____ would we have it. (Ps. 35:25; 2 words; reverse order)
9. And _____ unto him. (Dan. 8:6)
10. _____ sinful nation. (Isa. 1:4)
11. Zereth, and Jezoar, and _____. (1 Chron. 4:7)
12. Loose the _____ of kings. (Isa. 45:1)
20. _____ flesh appeareth in him. (Lev. 13:14)
22. It shall _____ eaten up. (Isa. 5:5)
23. _____ shall come to pass..._____ ye children. (Isa. 27:12; 2 words)
25. Stir up the _____. (Isa. 13:17)

1	2	3	4	5	6		7	8	9	10	11	12
13							14					
15			16				17				18	
19		20		21		22				23		
24			25		26				27			
	28			29			30	31				
		32		33		34						
	35	36						37		38	39	
40				41	42	43		44				45
46				47			48		49			
50			51			52		53		54		
55		56				57			58			
59						60						

27. His skin with barbed _____?· (Job 41:7)
29. Bare the _____ of many. (Isa. 53:12)
31. Pekod, and Shoa, and _____. (Ezek. 23:23)
33. An _____ excellency. (Isa. 60:15)
35. Five _____ goats... Ahira the son of _____. (Num. 7:83; 2 words); reverse order)
36. Vow a _____ unto the Lord. (Isa. 19:21)
38. Pull-_____ to open a can of soda.
39. He _____ _____ Egyptian. (2 Sam. 23:21; 2 words)

40. _____, and Accad. (Gen. 10:10)
42. Bethel and _____. (Ezra 2:28)
43. Clefts of the _____. (Isa. 2:21)
45. I was left _____. (Isa. 49:21)
47. _____ shall say, _____ am the Lord's. (Isa. 44:5; 2 words)
48. Remmon-methoar to _____. (Josh. 19:13)
51. Which _____ the king had made. (Jer. 41:9)
53. Source of minerals.
56. Shall be _____ an hiding place. (Isa. 32:2)
58. Nor the churl said _____ be bountiful. (Isa. 32:5)

PUZZLE 42

Diana Rowland

ACROSS CLUES

1. The _____ of life. (1 John 1:1)
5. There is a _____ here. (John 6:9)
8. The month of _____. (Deut. 16:1)
12. Roboam begat _____. (Matt. 1:7)
13. Naaman, _____, and Rosh. (Gen. 46:21)
14. Woman's title equal to a "sir."
15. Sky is _____ ...but can ye _____. (Matt. 16:3; 2 words)
17. Cut down, O _____. (Jer. 48:2)
19. Fountain both _____ salt water and fresh. (Jam. 3:12)
20. Maketh the seven stars and _____. (Amos 5:8)
21. Unto you, young _____. (1 John 2:13)
22. Not weary in well _____. (2 Thes. 3:13)
24. Timothy (nickname).
26. Escaped the _____ of the sword. (Heb. 11:34)
28. A _____ person. (Prov. 6:12)
30. The flower of her _____. (1 Cor. 7:36)
33. As a _____ gathereth. (Matt. 23:37)
34. Thou barren that _____ not. (Gal. 4:27)
38. Bakbukiah and _____. (Neh. 12:9)
42. Receiving the _____ of your faith. (1 Pet. 1:9)
43. Will also _____ up us by his own power. (1 Cor. 6:14)
46. Neither did we _____ any man's bread. (2 Thes. 3:8)
47. Was _____ an Ahohite. (1 Chron. 27:4)
49. Elihoreph and _____. (1 Kgs. 4:3)

51. Abimelech king of _____ sent...for she is _____ man's wife. (Gen. 20:2,3; 2 words)
52. Sons also of Jediael; _____. (1 Chron. 7:10)
54. Not _____ all to come _____. (1 Cor. 16:12; 2 words)
55. _____ thou on my right hand. (Acts 2:34)
57. _____ Ephesus, and _____ the faithful. (Eph. 1:1; 2 words)
58. _____, let _____ escape thither. (Gen. 19:20; 2 words)
59. _____ an Ithrite. (2 Sam. 23:38)
60. _____ said, _____ that _____ had wings. (Ps. 55:6; 3 words)

DOWN CLUES

1. Ye fight and _____. (Jam. 4:2)
2. Sara _____ Abraham. (1 Pet. 3:6)
3. Man _____ upon a red horse. (Zech. 1:8)
4. Breed of dog: Great _____.
5. _____ us _____ good unto all men. (Gal. 6:10; 2 words)
6. _____, thou that destroyest the temple. (Mark 15:29)
7. Kinah, and _____. (Josh. 15:22)
8. The son of _____. (Luke 3:28)
9. From _____ in the valley. (Num. 21:20)
10. _____ have ...think of _____...didst receive _____. (1 Cor. 4:6,7; 3 words)
11. Zechariah, _____. (1 Chron. 15:18)
16. _____ commandment. (1 John 2:7)
18. To fight with words.
21. Profitable to thee and to _____. (Philemon 11)
23. Abideth _____ him sinneth not. (1 John 3:6)
25. _____ little children. (1 John 3:18)

27. _____ shall say. (1 Cor. 12:16)
29. African antelope or wildebeest.
31. Isaac dwelt in _____. (Gen. 26:6)
32. _____ is very bold... _____ was found. (Rom. 10:20; 2 words)
34. Not _____ ashamed before him. (1 John 2:28)
35. Them that rejoice _____. (Isa. 24:8)
36. King Rehoboam sent _____. (1 Kgs. 12:18)
37. Fa, So, La, _____.
39. To Remmonmethoar _____. (Josh. 19:13; 2 words; reverse order)

40. And _____ his son. (1 Chron. 6:26)
41. _____ is the Spirit . (1 John 5:6)
44. Havilah, and _____. (1 Chron. 1:9)
45. Naaman, _____. (Gen. 46:21)
48. For example, July 1, 1994.
50. _____ the Ahohite. (1 Chron. 11:29)
51. General Accounting Office (abbr.).
53. _____ ...and _____ will write. (Rev. 3:12; 2 words)
56. The children of _____. (1 Chron. 7:12)

87

PUZZLE 43

Janet Adkins

ACROSS CLUES

1. Am I in God's _____? (Gen. 30:2)
5. They say he has a _____. (Matt. 11:18 NIV)
10. Consumes.
11. By a mighty hand, and by a stretched out _____. (Deut. 4:34)
14. Lion's headdress.
15. By way of.
16. Alaskan native.
18. Department of Economic Affairs (abbr.).
19. Building addition.
20. I will _____ him up at the last day. (John 6:40)
21. People that do _____ in their heart. (Ps. 95:10)
22. They follow "M"s.
23. Naval vessel designation.
24. Goes up.
29. Alternate spelling of *Baal*.
30. Sanballat invited Nehemiah to the plain of _____. (Neh. 6:2)

31. Thickness or layer.
32. _____ my statutes, and do them. (Ezek. 37:24)
35. And _____ shall judge the world. (Ps. 9:8)
37. Add _____ your faith virtue. (2 Pet. 1:5)
38. Commercial message.
39. News agency.
41. Spanish cheer.
43. I will make thee a _____ nation. (Gen. 12:2)
47. *Much _____ About Nothing.*
48. Cleaning tool.
49. Classifies.
50. Gay Pa_____.
51. Long, exciting adventure tale.
53. They compassed me about like _____(s). (Ps. 118:12)
54. An atlas is a book of _____.
55. There remaineth a _____ (plural). (Heb. 4:9)
56. _____p_____ Dumpty sat on a wall.

DOWN CLUES

1. John to the _____ churches... in Asia. (Rev. 1:4)
2. His _____(s) drew the third part of the stars. (Rev. 12:4)
3. And others (Latin).
4. Like.
6. Printer's measure.
7. Thou hast _____ him a little lower than the angels. (Ps. 8:5)
8. Dollar bills.
9. Approaches.
11. In this manner.
12. Real estate investment (abbr.).
13. He heard _____ick and dancing. (Luke 15:25)
16. _____(s) of the Covenant.
17. Began the golf game.
24. Great amount (2 words)
25. Type of lettuce.
26. Compass direction.
27. Neither/_____.
28. Went rapidly.
33. Mires.
34. Large tubs.
35. Ancient author.
36. Run away to wed.
39. Able, skillful.
40. The art of poetry.
42. American Anglican church: _____copal.
44. Will a man _____ God? (Mal. 3:8)
45. Before (poetic).
46. Did eat.
47. Kemuel the father of _____. (Gen. 22:21)
52. Court (abbr.).
54. Invent to themselves instruments of _____sick. (Amos 6:5)

PUZZLE 44

Janet Adkins

ACROSS CLUES

1. Poetic foot.
5. I looked through my ____ment. (Prov. 7:6)
9. Shall be in _____ of the judgment. (Matt. 5:21)
11. Thou hast _____d all things. (Rev. 4:11)
14. By me if any man _____ in. (John 10:9)
16. Alma _____.
17. Indefinite article.
18. Belonging to the talking horse.
20. Continent (abbr.).
21. Baby's first word.
22. Shade tree.
24. Let us make man in our _____ge. (Gen. 1:26)
27. Poet Eliot's initials.
28. The shortest month.
29. He who now letteth will _____. (2 Thes. 2:7)
30. Quiet, please.
32. Effectual _____ prayer. (Jam. 5:16)
33. Alabama (abbr.).
35. When they... had gone six _____s. (2 Sam. 6:13)
37. In _____ was there a voice heard. (Matt. 2:18)
39. Form of *Alex*.
40. Part of a list.
41. The Lord hath _____ the kingdom. (1 Sam. 15:28)
42. Adam called his wife's name _____. (Gen. 3:20)
44. Neither shall ye break a _____ thereof. (Ex. 12:46)
45. Day of the week (abbr.).
47. The Lord God is a _____ and shield. (Ps. 84:11)
48. Belonging to Sarai's husband.
50. Belonging to Cephas.
51. "Strength" or "strong one." (Heb.)
52. In Isaac shall thy _____ be called. (Gen. 21:12)

DOWN CLUES

1. Money earned on account (abbr.).
2. He is of _____, ask him. (John 9:21)
3. Sea (French).
4. One in a monastery (abbr.).
5. Medicine measure.
6. _____ yourselves likewise. (1 Pet. 4:1)
7. The wicked are like the troubled _____. (Isa. 5:20)
8. Ye shall _____ no manner of blood. (Lev. 7:26)
9. Quickened who were _____ in trespasses, and sins. (Eph. 2:1)
10. There was one _____, a prophetess. (Luke 2:36)
12. The father of such as dwell in _____s. (Gen. 4:20)
13. Historical periods.
15. Savings document.
18. Paul, called unto him the disciples, and _____d them. (Acts 20:1)
19. Let the woman learn in _____. (1 Tim. 2:11)
22. The _____ fervent prayer. (Jam. 5:16)
23. Southern general.
25. Not with eyeservice, as _____pleasers. (Eph. 6:6)
26. Characteristic.
30. To practice boxing.

90

31. Lest he _____ thee to the judge. (Luke 12:58)
33. To whom be glory for ever, ____. (Rom. 11:36)
34. Jonathan...had a son..._____ of his feet. (2 Sam. 4:4)
36. Midpoint (British var.).

38. Will never be _____ for by sacrifice. (1 Sam. 3:14 NIV)
43. Roman numeral for 6.
46. Printer's measure.
47. We shall _____ him as he is. (1 John 3:2)
49. Naval vessel insignia.
50. Thought added to a letter.

PUZZLE 45

Janet Adkins

ACROSS CLUES

1. Rather give _____ (s). (Luke 11:41)
4. Crustacean.
8. Like a _____ planted by the rivers. (Ps. 1:3)
12. Roman numeral 52.
13. Samuel answered, _____ am I. (1 Sam. 3:4)
14. Saul came after the _____. (1 Sam. 11:5)
15. Who will have all _____ to be saved. (1 Tim. 2:4)
16. Grain.
17. How _____ (ble) are thy tabernacles. (Ps. 84:1)
18. He shall give his _____ charge over thee. (Ps. 91:11)
20. Meekness, _____ ance. (Gal. 5:23)
22. New (prefix).
23. Mouths.
24. A cave.
27. The flesh of the child waxed _____. (2 Kgs. 4:34; comparative)
31. _____ not two sparrows sold. (Matt. 10:29)
32. Eggs (Latin).
33. But seek not _____. (Amos 5:5)
37. The vision of _____ the son of Amoz. (Isa. 1:1)
40. Before (poetic).
41. And _____ brought forth her firstborn son. (Luke 2:7)
42. Of _____ many books there is no end. (Ec. 12:12)
45. Sons of _____; Joseph and Benjamin. (Gen. 35:24)
49. Belonging to Hezekiah's mother. (2 Kgs. 18:1,2)
50. Kemuel the father of _____. (Gen. 22:21)
52. Short for Abraham.
53. Is not (slang).
54. To be prolific.
55. The 23rd letter of the Hebrew alphabet.
56. Loiters behind.
57. Good woman's name.
58. The sons of _____ were sons of Belial. (1 Sam. 2:12)

DOWN CLUES

1. _____ Mater.
2. Property right.
3. Chinese dynasty.
4. He was moved with _____ against him. (Dan. 8:7)
5. Let us _____ together. (Isa. 1:18)
6. Nathan said to David, thou _____ the man. (2 Sam. 12:7)
7. Though I _____ all my goods to feed the poor. (1 Cor. 13:3)
8. Absalom had a fair sister whose name was _____. (2 Sam. 13:1; alt. spelling)
9. Star of your god _____ han. (Acts 7:43)
10. Great Lake.
11. Southward were Kabzeel, and _____. (Josh. 15:21; alt. spelling).
19. Compass direction.
21. Historical period.
24. The fourth part of a _____ of dove's dung. (2 Kgs. 6:25)
25. Form of *to be*.
26. Former serviceman.
28. Me (French).
29. Madame Peron.
30. Stadium cheer.
34. Robberies (slang).

1	2	3		4	5	6	7		8	9	10	11
12				13					14			
15				16					17			
18			19				20	21				
			22				23					
24	25	26					27			28	29	30
31										32		
33			34	35	36		37	38	39			
			40				41					
42	43	44					45			46	47	48
49				50	51					52		
53				54						55		
56				57						58		

35. Sea eagle.
36. Ambassador.
37. Hear, O _____. (Deut. 6:4)
38. Bezer, and Hod, and _____.
    (1 Chron. 7:37)
39. Atomic Energy Commission
    (abbr.).
42. Out to the south side to _____eh.
    (Josh. 15:3)

43. Solomon thrust out _____ thar.
    (1 Kgs. 2:27)
44. _____ of kings. (Rev. 17:14)
46. They that _____ the righteous.
    (Ps. 34:21)
47. I command you this day in mount
    _____. (Deut. 27:4)
48. Jacob's third son by Leah.
    (Gen. 29:34)
51. Peleg...begat _____. (Gen. 11:18)

PUZZLE 46

Pamela Jensen

ACROSS CLUES

1. _____ and honour are her clothing. (Prov. 31:25)
8. And _____ gave names to all. (Gen. 2:20)
12. United States of America (abbr.).
13. Save the beast that _____ _____ upon. (Neh. 2:12; 2 words)
15. Casteth forth his _____ like morsels. (Ps. 147:17)
16. He must _____ his own family well. (1 Tim. 3:4 NIV)
18. I will _____ in the house of the Lord. (Ps. 23:6)
20. Mister (abbr.).
21. Blessed be the Lord God of _____. (Gen. 9:26)
23. *Id est* (abbr.).
24. Each (abbr.).
25. _____ shall be _____ for the congregation. (Num. 19:9; 2 words)
27. Greater love hath no _____. (John 15:13)
28. I will give you _____ in due season. (Lev. 26:4)
31. Mom.
32. There should be time _____ longer. (Rev. 10:6)
33. _____ forth.
34. He shall eat at my _____. (2 Sam. 9:11)
38. Second letter in the Greek alphabet.
40. Roebuck, and the fallow _____. (Deut. 14:5)
41. And _____ did that which was right. (1 Kgs. 15:11)

43. _____ and his wife hid themselves. (Gen. 3:8)
44. Internal Revenue Service (abbr.).
45. Passed through the _____ Sea. (Heb. 11:29)
46. Id, _____ superego.
47. Bass horn.
50. Is the seed yet in the _____? (Hag. 2:19)
53. They lightened the _____. (Acts 27:38)
55. _____ apple.
56. The _____ of violence is in their hands. (Isa. 59:6)
58. To _____ with oil.
60. To _____.
61. _____ _____ are created equal. (2 words)
62. Atomic Energy Commission (abbr.).

DOWN CLUES

1. As snow in _____. (Prov. 26:1)
2. Former emperor of Russia.
3. He _____ to meet them. (Gen. 18:2)
4. In my prayers _____ and day. (2 Tim. 1:3)
5. Canst thou speak _____? (Acts 21:37)
6. Ye shall observe _____ do. (Deut. 12:1)
7. Hand, head (abbr.).
9. Thou shalt surely _____. (Gen. 2:17)
10. He wrapped it in _____ _____ linen cloth. (Matt. 27:59; 2 words)
11. A dark pigmented cancer.
14. To delete.
17. There is _____ _____ not unto death. (1 John 5:17; 2 words)
19. _____ will shew the interpretation. (Dan. 2:4)

22. For the body is not one _____. (1 Cor. 12:14)
26. All the coasts of _____? (Joel 3:4)
29. And the _____ arose. (Job 29:8)
30. Ninth letter in the Greek alphabet.
35. *Good-bye* in Spanish.
36. Emergency Room (abbr.).
37. International Atomic Energy Agency (abbr.).
38. A tree of tropical Africa.
39. People shall answer and say _____. (Deut. 27:15)
42. South Dakota (abbr.).
45. Symbol for rubidium.
48. I set my king _____ my holy hill. (Ps. 2:6)
49. _____ the seventh day. (Gen. 2:2)
51. An expert.
52. Route (abbr.).
54. _____ is the father of Caanan. (Gen. 9:18)
55. I _____ no pleasant bread. (Dan. 10:3)
57. Symbol for aluminum.
59. Symbol for sodium.

PUZZLE 47

Janet Hopper
(NIV)

ACROSS CLUES

1. Sermon on the _____. (Matt. 5-7)
5. Barabbas was in prison for insurrection and this. (Luke 23:19)
9. Old Testament priest and book.
10. Hill made of sand.
12. *Beersheba* means "well of the _____." (Gen. 21:31)
14. The Lord will do this to Zion. (Isa. 51:3)
16. The Sovereign Lord will _____ his anger on Israel. (Ezek. 7:3)
18. O taste and _____ that the Lord is good. (Ps. 34:8)
19. Master of Education (abbr.).
20. A, B, C, _____, _____.
21. What the risen Jesus did with broiled fish. (Luke 24:43)
22. Mister (abbr.).
23. I will not _____ you as orphans. (John 14:18)
25. Annum (abbr.).

26. Where lions lie down. (Ps. 104:22)
29. Radium (abbr.).
30. Nehemiah prayed before the God of _____. (Neh. 1:4)
33. One of Noah's sons. (Gen. 6:10)
34. J, _____, _____.
35. Slang for *simple*.
36. Little Jack Horner's pastry.
37. A half shekel was given to _____ for one's life. (Ex. 30:15)
38. A servant for life had an awl put through this. (Deut. 15:17)
40. District Superintendent (abbr.).
42. The apostles were unschooled, _____ men. (Acts 4:13)
44. Jesus' garment did not have one of these. (John 19:23)
46. I _____ WHO I AM. (Ex. 3:14)
47. Expression of mild sympathy.
48. Is the Lord's _____ too short?
49. Boaz told his men not to do this to Ruth. (Ruth 2:15)

DOWN CLUES

1. Come to _____, all you who are weary. (Matt. 11:28)
2. Layer of the atmosphere.
3. Mountains in Asia.
4. Nickname for Nathan.
5. You expected _____, but see, it turned out to be little. (Hag. 1:9)
6. *One* in Spain.
7. Type of place where 5,000 were fed. (Mark 6:35)
8. One of the kinds of love.
11. Believers receive this kind of life.
13. Son of Rehob. (2 Sam. 8:3)
15. Others _____, He seems to be advocating foreign gods. (Acts 17:18)
16. An inheritance of Asher. (Josh. 19:30)
17. Number of Sceva's sons. (Acts 19:14)
24. _____ Gedi. (1 Sam. 24:1)
27. An inheritance of Issachar. (Josh. 19:19)
28. Paul appealed to him. (Acts 25:25)
31. Jewish Queen of Persia.
32. This of the wicked is like that of a snake. (Ps. 58:4)
38. Zacchaeus sat on one of these. (Luke 19)
39. Bachelor of Arts (abbr.).
41. The people of Rabbah labored with these. (1 Chron. 20:3)
43. Starting a quarrel is like breaching one of these. (Prov. 17:14)
44. Salvation Army (abbr.).
45. I _____ the light of the world. (John 8:12)
47. _____ a hen gathers her chicks. (Matt. 23:37)

PUZZLE 48

Lee Esch

ACROSS CLUES

1. A son of Jacob. (Gen. 30:11)
4. King or emperor.
8. Opened slightly.
12. 52 in Roman numerals.
13. Southern vegetable.
14. Thy will be _____. (Matt. 6:10)
15. _____ him as a brother. (2 Thes. 3:15)
17. A son of Seth. (Gen. 4:26)
18. Wonders and mighty _____. (2 Cor. 12:12)
19. Take, _____: this is my body. (1 Cor. 11:24)
21. Go to the _____, thou sluggard. (Prov. 6:6)
22. If a man _____ a pit. (Ex. 21:33)
24. Pants' support.
26. Because Judas had the _____. (John 13:29)
29. Abraham's nephew. (Gen. 11:27)
31. A prophet of Judah.
34. My God. (Mark 15:34)
36. Daniel was in one. (Dan. 6:16)
38. Foundation.
39. That which I do I _____ not. (Rom. 7:15)
41. Cain lived here. (Gen. 4:16)
43. Peter and John used one in their work.
44. Combat between two persons.
46. A brother offended is harder to be _____ than a strong city. (Prov. 18:19)
48. Kind of tree.
50. Paper sack.
52. She answered the door when Peter knocked. (Acts 12:13)
56. Red and Dead.
58. To bind up the brokenhearted, to _____ liberty. (Isa. 61:1)
60. Cover (a road).
61. Abraham's wife, _____. (1 Pet. 3:6)
62. Hot or cold drink.
63. Simmer or boil slowly.
64. Falls away or declines.
65. Standard (abbr.).

DOWN CLUES

1. We will rejoice and be _____ in it. (Ps. 118:24)
2. Assistant.
3. Ten cent coin.
4. A common childhood illness, _____itis.
5. Slide on snow.
6. Funeral vehicle, he_____.
7. She hid the spies sent out by Joshua. (Josh. 2:1)
8. A sweetened beverage.
9. A son of king Saul. (1 Sam. 13:16)
10. He that heareth the word, and _____ with joy receiveth it. (Matt. 13:20)
11. I will give you _____. (Matt. 11:28)
16. Unusual.
20. The _____ Commandments.
23. The Supreme Being.
25. Experiment room (abbr.).
26. Nickname for Beatrice.
27. Come unto me, _____ ye that labour. (Matt. 11:28)
28. Silver and _____ _____ I none. (Acts 3:6; 2 words)
30. _____ little Indians.
32. _____ not liberty for an occasion to the flesh. (Gal. 5:13)
33. His servants _____ him and told him. (John 4:51)

35. Debt note (abbr.).
37. _____ I know in part. (1 Cor. 13:12)
40. Spider's home.
42. A seamstress who was brought back to life. (Acts 9)
45. Slip gradually, drift into.
47. National Hockey League (abbr.).
48. The poison of _____ is under their lips (Rom. 3:13)

49. Make a mercy _____ of pure gold. (Ex. 25:17)
51. Snatch.
53. Grain (plural).
54. Eating plan.
55. Will _____ _____ rob God? (Mal. 3:8; 2 words)
57. Stitch.
59. Sphere.

PUZZLE 49

Lee Esch

ACROSS CLUES

1. Thou _____ the Christ. (Matt. 16:16)
4. Ruler of old Russia.
8. He _____ unto his own. (John 1:11)
12. _____ Dolorosa, Jesus' route to Golgotha.
13. A Midwest state.
14. His ears are _____ unto their prayers. (1 Pet. 3:12)
15. New Testament letters.
17. In the beginning was the _____. (John 1:1)
18. A word peculiar to the book of Psalms.
19. Morning dampness.
21. A ship's distress call.
22. Ye have made it a _____ of thieves. (Matt. 21:13)
24. Quench all the fiery _____s. (Eph. 6:16)
26. Opposite of on.
29. He that hath the _____ hath life. (1 John 5:12)
31. In the days when the judges _____. (Ruth 1:1)
34. A distinctive quality that characterizes a person.
36. Abraham caught one in the thicket. (Gen. 22:13)
38. _____ ye one another's burdens. (Gal. 6:2)
39. _____, and it shall be opened. (Matt. 7:7)
41. Whether it be good or _____. (2 Cor. 5:10)
43. Pig pen.

44. _____ the Lord in the air. (1 Thes. 4:17)
46. Drew the_____ to the land full of great fishes. (John 21:11)
48. A form of "to be."
50. Puppy's bark.
52. The _____ of one crying the wilderness. (John 1:23)
56. Rant.
58. In that hour Jesus _____ in Spirit. (Luke 10:21)
60. Similar.
61. Jacob's brother. (Gen. 25:26)
62. Adam's helpmeet.
63. Kept in one's grasp.
64. Separate systematically.
65. A tribe of Israel.

DOWN CLUES

1. Thoroughfares (abbr.).
2. The harvest of the earth is _____. (Rev. 14:15)
3. Does the dog wag the _____, or does the _____ wag the dog?
4. A tenth part (plural).
5. Sun (Spanish).
6. Filled with reverence.
7. Demolished.
8. Bovine.
9. The chosen twelve.
10. Israel's enemies converged at _____m. (Josh. 11:7)
11. All the _____ of the earth. (Isa. 45:22)
16. Sorrowful.
20. Battle.
23. Neither purse, _____ scrip. (Luke 10:4)
25. "_____ my back, please."
26. King Saul was buried beneath one of these trees. (1 Chron. 10:12)

27. Enjoyment.
28. Deliver us _____ _____.
    (Matt. 6:13; 2 words)
30. Catch.
32. "_____ your vegetables."
33. Arid.
35. Expert.
37. _____ shall not live by bread alone.
    (Matt. 4:4)
40. Lock's companion.
42. Dwelling at Jerusalem Jews, _____
    men. (Acts 2:5)

45. The _____ are gathered and burned
    in the fire. (Matt. 13:40)
47. They _____ l not. (Matt. 6:28)
48. Abraham's wife, S_____.
49. Gather leaves.
51. Mexican coin.
53. Frozen over.
54. This priest had seven sons, S_____.
    (Acts 19:14)
55. Adam's home.
57. Cease.
59. Glass container.

PUZZLE 50

Evelyn Boyington

ACROSS CLUES

1. Grisled and _____ horses. (Zech. 6:3)
4. They removed from _____. (Num. 33:28)
9. The _____ that is in the land of Assyria. (Isa. 7:18)
12. Villages in the plain of _____. (Neh. 6:2)
13. My son was dead, and is _____ again. (Luke 15:24)
14. Rodent.
15. David...escaped to the cave _____. (1 Sam. 22:1)
17. _____ the son of Enan. (Num. 1:15)
19. Two _____ more hereafter. (Rev. 9:12)
20. _____ with zeal as a cloke. (Isa. 59:17)
21. Insensitive.
23. Lowest speed.
26. The _____, he is unclean unto you. (Lev. 11:6)
27. What _____ have ye? (Luke 6:32)
28. I am _____. (Isa. 41:4)
29. Assistance.
30. _____ that seek me early shall find me. (Prov. 8:17)
31. Whose _____ is in his hand. (Matt. 3:12)
32. _____, the son of Peleth. (Num. 16:1)
33. The _____ hear his voice. (John 10:3)
34. A sect.
35. Methods.
37. He _____ them all. (Ps. 147:4 NKJV)
38. _____ his garments. (2 Sam. 13:31)
39. The wicked man travaileth with _____. (Job 15:20)
40. Sharpen every man his _____. (1 Sam. 13:20)
42. Not in the _____ of the letter. (Rom. 7:6)
45. Took _____ by the hand. (Matt. 9:25)
46. There were _____ besides unto them. (Jer. 36:32)
48. A wave of the _____. (Jam. 1:6)
49. One little _____ lamb. (2 Sam. 12:3)
50. Son, go work _____. (Matt. 21:28)
51. God _____ them in the firmament. (Gen. 1:17)

DOWN CLUES

1. A snake.
2. _____ yet I say unto you. (Matt. 6:29)
3. Given me to _____. (Eph. 3:2)
4. Idle _____. (Luke 24:11)
5. _____, that great city Babylon! (Rev. 18:10)
6. Edge.
7. St.
8. _____ _____ on the land. (Mark 6:47; 2 words)
9. A _____ adorneth herself. (Isa. 61:10)
10. Eye, _____ nose, and throat dr.
11. Greek letter.
16. He that findeth his life shall _____ it. (Matt. 10:39)
18. Doth the _____ fly by thy wisdom? (Job 39:26)
20. A fastener.
21. Confusion.
22. In a very _____ day. (Prov. 27:15)
23. Put off thy _____. (Ex. 3:5)

24. I _____ not want. (Ps. 23:1)
25. A plain man, dwelling in _____. (Gen. 25:27)
27. A short essay.
30. Wash their hands and their feet _____. (Ex. 30:19)
31. Let the sea roar, and the _____ thereof. (Ps. 96:11)
33. His _____ in the east. (Matt. 2:2)
34. She conceived, and bare _____. (Gen. 4:1)
36. They look and _____ upon me. (Ps. 22:17)
37. Golfer's aide.

39. Between _____ and _____. (Deut. 17:8)
40. _____ shall bring forth a son. (Matt. 1:21)
41. _____ thee two tables of stone. (Ex. 34:1)
42. The _____ number of them. (Num. 3:48)
43. Thou shalt _____ greater things. (John 1:50)
44. The people _____ down to eat. (Ex. 32:6)
47. "I _____." (Wedding)

ANSWERS

PUZZLE 1

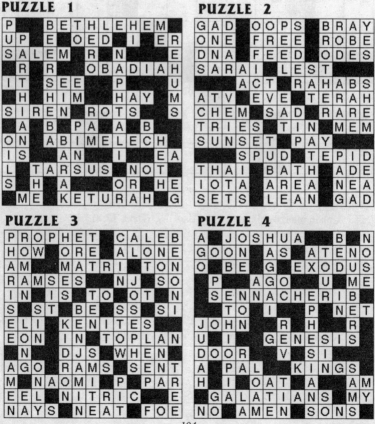

P		B	E	T	H	L	E	H	E	M
U	P		E		O	E	D		I		E	R
S	A	L	E	M		R		N		E
	R		R		O	B	A	D	I	A	H
I	T		S	E	E		P		U
	H		H	I	M		H	A	Y		M
S	I	R	E	N		R	O	T	S		S
	A		B		P	A		A		B
O	N		A	B	I	M	E	L	E	C	H
I	S		A	N		I		E	A
L		T	A	R	S	U	S		N	O	T
S		H		A		O	R		H	E
	M	E		K	E	T	U	R	A	H		G

PUZZLE 2

G	A	D		O	O	P	S		B	R	A	Y
O	N	E		F	R	E	E		R	O	B	E
D	N	A		F	E	E	D		O	D	E	S
S	A	R	A	I		L	E	S	T
		A	C	T		R	A	H	A	B	S
A	T	V		E	V	E		T	E	R	A	H
C	H	E	M		S	A	D		R	A	R	E
T	R	I	E	S		T	I	N		M	E	M
S	U	N	S	E	T		P	A	Y
	S	P	U	D		T	E	P	I	D
T	H	A	I		B	A	T	H		A	D	E
I	O	T	A		A	R	E	A		N	E	A
S	E	T	S		L	E	A	N		G	A	D

PUZZLE 3

P	R	O	P	H	E	T		C	A	L	E	B
H	O	W		O	R	E		A	L	O	N	E
A	M		M	A	T	R	I		T	O	N
R	A	M	S	E	S		N	J		S	O
I	N		I	S		T	O		O	T		N
S		S	T		B	E		S	S		S	I
E	L	I		K	E	N	I	T	E	S
E	O	N		I	N		T	O	P	L	A	N
	N		D	J	S		W	H	E	N
A	G	O		R	A	M	S		S	E	N	T
M		N	A	O	M	I		P		P	A	R
E	E	L		N	I	T	R	I	C		E
N	A	Y	S		N	E	A	T		F	O	E

PUZZLE 4

A		J	O	S	H	U	A		B		N
G	O	O	N		A	S		A	T	E	N	O
O		B	E		G		E	X	O	D	U	S
	P		A	G	O		U		M	E
	S	E	N	N	A	C	H	E	R	I	B
	T	O		I		P		N	E	T
J	O	H	N		R		H		R
U		I		G	E	N	E	S	I	S
D	O	O	R		V		S	I
A		P	A	L		K	I	N	G	S
H		I		O	A	T		A		A	M
	G	A	L	A	T	I	A	N	S		M	Y
N	O		A	M	E	N		S	O	N	S

104

PUZZLE 5

```
HEM PART RAIN
EVE ESAU EASE
LED REST BADE
PRESS HOPE
    HID RECORD
MOB ARE ACHOR
OMER YOU AMMI
AARON NSC SEP
BRIBED EYE
    BAAL RIGHT
RACE VINE NOH
ADAR IRON APE
MARY DARE TEN
```

PUZZLE 6

```
AM O PA GOD
LONGSUFFERING
 TO ELF NON O
PEACE E T EXO
A HO SCALES D
TO M THEM AN
I APE I NURSE
EBLA DOVE ASS
NO STONES V S
CAUSE SISTER
ESPIED L NOE
 TO O O ON AD
AS NEIGHBOUR
```

PUZZLE 7

```
ABRAM ABANA
CLAVE DAMARIS
HEGE AARON DA
ASENATH UNDER
IS GIT CRYING
AI ERITES AT
 NOR RAN ELIM
 GO CENSER TO
 ZEUS EAR YE
IDEAS ARRAY
LO THAWS TOES
LIFEALL LIKHI
 ANNAS ACEIN
```

PUZZLE 8

```
MAT HOME PART
ARE EDEN ERAN
TEN BEAD RENT
TATER TOSS
    RED RAISED
IRS WON DAILY
MOAN GOD NOSE
ROMAN WAS NED
IMPART NAY
    MARA MERCY
RAMA ESAU ILO
OPEN EIRE PAK
BENS SAUL EYE
```

PUZZLE 9

```
BRANCH HEARER
LAGOON ESCAPE
EBONY EACHA
SIN LAW PER
TDY MARAH AT
 SOPATER TO
IS ELIMELECH
CHASEDTRODE
HARA OHEN REU
AMAM TED TAR
BEZER MAGI
OGOSO IT OILA
DORTO NO ONES
```

PUZZLE 10

```
TOTE M BEUL
O H KAB EAST
SERVE O DATE
TOO PERFORM K
ANN TAD ELI
N EN REMAIN N
DOSES R W OG
 B T T LAUDS
SEE BELAY IS
AD RAN M BE G
V EAR PTA AA
ENT NAP CAST
STARS MILK PE
```

PUZZLE 11

```
S A M U E L     S O   O N
E N O N     E   A F A R
T N T     C I T Y   R E D
H E       A G O   O R   O
S   A   A B H O R R E D
  C U B   T   E   S   A
  C   I S     E A T E N
A B U N D A N T L Y   A T
C A S T E D   O   E A T S
C   E   T   T     G
E N   C H U R C H   R A G
N O R A   R A M A   E R E
T R O D   I M   G R E E T
```

PUZZLE 12

```
L A   E P H E S U S   S
  N B A   E L A T E   P I
H O E   J   I T   E   A S
A N T I O C H     H     A
M   H   B   U     G E R A
    S O S       F E A R
I V A H   D I E   L O T S
N   I   M A S S   I   R
C E D R O N   T   L E A H
L   A   M I S U S E   Y E
U R   R   E A S T E R   T
D   J A E L     E   I   H
E D A M   S O   M O B   S
```

PUZZLE 13

```
I M P E L S   G I D E O N
S A L V A T I O N   O N E
A T E   W O R D S   N E T
I C A   S R O   T B   S W
A H   S   E N T A I L   O
H I T T E R S   N O   O R
  N O A H     S T   Y A K
O G   T U R N S   W O K S
B   M U D   A T E   L T
E A S E   L O   O K R A
D L   S W I M   T O S E E
S I N   A M I D   P   E R
  T O S S E S   I S   S O
```

PUZZLE 14

```
C L I M B E D     C A R
  E   O   M   A S H D O D
C A L E B S   M O L E   A
A D O   A   T O N O   E N
R   T E R N   R   E N   I
M A   B A A L I M   O   E
E G     K P   T O   N F L
L O O K S   B E O R   A
    H I   F I     O   B E
  T Y R E   D A G O N   B
T E E   B   K   A M A Z E
I M   C A N A   D A V I D
P A N   L O R E   T E N S
```

PUZZLE 15

```
S C R I P T U R A L   I S
I D E S   O N   T O U S E
M C D   N O D   E       N
P   N O   O T   S E N D
L E T   S E E R   E R I E
E V E R Y   S E R V A N T
R E A R     K   E   A H
    M S   P A   E N D
S O   W I N S   S   A C
W   S H I L O H     P B A
E M U   L E N O   T A L K
E   C R Y     U P   S E E
T A K E     S T A R S   S
```

PUZZLE 16

```
A G E S     G R E A T   H
R O M A N S   I   D A R E
E G   M O   S O L O M O N
A   M A D   H     A M
  P E R S I A   S A R A H
B E   I   O R   A I     U
K N O T   N O R M   K I R
  I V A H   N A U M     R
M E A N     P E C K     Y
E L     P H I L I P
N   M E N E   D     G O
E I   G E O   S H A M E
  N I G E R     E T A M
```

PUZZLE 17

```
. H A . A B I D E D . . B
L A D . B A N . A . M A .
O R . U . C H A M B E R .
B E H I N D . . T E A . L
E S E . D O . G . . T H E
. . A . A C C O U N T . Y
H . R A N K . D . O L D .
I M . C . . G . E . . B .
. A F F E C T I O N . G O
R O E . . . R N A . T O N
O . L . M O E . T R A D E
B E L I E V E . S A I L S
E T A . T A S K . . L Y .
```

PUZZLE 18

```
J E S U S . . C H R I S T
A D A N A . . H E A L T H
E G Y P T . . E M P I R E
L E P E R . A R . . K O .
. . . E R A S T U S . I N
F O R F I T . B E I N G .
I U S E M E . . A N G E R
. R E C E P T I O N . R E
. A C T N O W T H A T . .
I R U . T U E S . N O A H
S E T . T E N . D E N Y .
. . E A T . D O G . S E M
. . S O . . T O . . R N .
```

PUZZLE 19

```
D O N E . . H E R . K I M
. G E N E R A T I O N . A
M . W . . S A D . O A K .
E . D I R T . E M T . E .
. G O O D N E S S . S . S
N O . N O . N O . H . F .
A V . E L M . S E E . U P
P E N . O . . A . L . . .
. R . F U L F I L L I N G
I N . A A . I . N E O . .
. O F F E R I N G . A S A
R E A L . T . H . . S T .
S E R F . H A T E D . S .
```

PUZZLE 20

```
A A R O N I T E S . M I A . A
B A N . D O . A B E . . . U .
I . A M A L E K . A W A G . .
G O . B E . I . B . . D U . .
A B N E R . . S C E N E S . .
I . . A S A H E L . . S T . .
L . J A H . S . . . . . U . .
S W . A T H E N I A N S . . .
. E D O M . E G . . V . . . .
. I . . R O B . E L . . . . .
. B A M A H . . A N N A S . .
T E N S . A . C . . M I . . .
O . A S S Y R I A . D A N . .
```

PUZZLE 21

```
H I M S E L F . A B E . I
O N . E . M A D . A . U S
N . W E . . I . . T O P .
O V E R C O M E S . F . N
. . . E P A . A . F R O .
R A I N . P L E D G E . B
. H O E . R . A . R . L .
O I N T M E N T . V I L E
N T . U S . E . A N D . .
. . O F F S P R I N G . T
C A N . F I T S . . S E E
R Y E . S O . . L B . M A
Y E S . N U M B E R . M .
```

PUZZLE 22

```
. E A G L E . S E N I R .
O T H E O P H I L U S O F
M E . B O H A N . . . G O
E R N A M E . C A . B E L
G N U . R E E L . E L K .
A A . S O . D R A W . I S
. L A H M I . E R H I M .
. . B E E R A . M E N . .
E V E . R A S E . T E M A
B E L . S M E L L . R E D
A N . A M A R I A H . N A
L O R D A R . A D A M A H
. M E O N E . M E D E S .
```

PUZZLE 23

B		W	A	S		S	A	V	E	D		S
A	H	A		C	R	A	N	E		E	R	E
N	I	G	E	R		N		X		W	A	R
	M		R	I	N	D	S		I		I	V
V		S	A	B	B	A	T	H	S		D	A
A	A		E		L		S		N			
I	L	L		S		S	C	A	R	L	E	T
N	O	V	A		I		A		C	A	N	
	S	A	N	C	T	I	F	Y		Y		T
S	E	T			F	E	E				T	O
	S	I	G	H	T			S	L	E	E	P
I		O		O	A	T	H		E	L	S	
S	I	N	N	E	R		S	M	A	L	L	

PUZZLE 24

P	O	N	T	I	U	S	P	I	L	A	T	E
O	N	E		S	R	O		A	N	O	N	
P		A	S		S	A	N		T	O		
	G	R	A	S	P		P	A	D	R	E	S
	R		L	C		M	O		S	O		
S	A	L	V	A	T	I	O	N		N	E	T
I	D	E	A	L		S	N	O	W		N	O
N	E	A	T	E	S	T		W	O	R	D	S
		R	I	D	E		C	H	O	R	U	S
A	N	N	O		N		L	E	D		R	E
R	E	I	N		D	O	O	R		M	I	D
T	O	N		B	E		S	E	T	I	N	
S		G	O		R	O	E		A	G	O	

PUZZLE 25

K	N	O	W	L	E	D	G	E		T	I	E
	R		A	N	N	O		T	O	R	O	W
L	A	D	Y		D	O	R		W	I	N	E
	A		H		R	N		U		S		S
S	O	R	R	O	W	S		H	O	M	E	
E	A	T		L	A		B	Y		P		A
E	T		W	I	S	D	O	M		H	A	M
K		B	A	N		O	N	E		A	H	
	A	R	E		B		N		O			
I	O	N		S	P	I	R	I	T	U	A	L
B	A	D		S	A	D		T	O	N		Y
I	R	S			I	S		R				
D	S		S	O	N		O	M	N	I		

PUZZLE 26

O	B	A	D	I	A	H	S		J	O	B	S
I	O		A	T		E	A		O		O	
J	O	H	N		J		D	A	N	I	E	L
O	K		I	R	O	N		A	D	Z	E	
B		N	E	H	E	M	I	A	H		R	
	G	E	L		L		S		H	A	M	
N	O			C	A	R	T			A		
A		J	E	R	E	M	I	A	H		U	R
H	E		G	U	N		A	C	E	D		K
U		A		T	O		H	O	S	E	A	
M	I	C	A	H	S		N	E		M	E	
	T	Y		N						O	N	
M	O	S	E	S		J	U	D	G	E	S	

PUZZLE 27

K	I	N	D		N	E	T		B	A	R	N
I	D	E	A		O	N		B	I	O		
N	E		T	H	E		B	E		L	O	O
D	A	R	E		L		A	B		E		N
R		A	S	K		A	B	B	A		A	
E	A	T		B	A	B	E		F	A	M	E
D	M		A		L		P	A	G	E	S	
	A	B	O	V	E			R	E	N	T	
F		N	A	N		A	N					
A	R	I	S	E		B	C		B	A	L	D
R	I	S	E	S		O	A	R		L	E	E
M	O	E		S	I	K	A		S	O	N	
S	T		T	O		L	E	P	R	O	S	Y

PUZZLE 28

M		K	G		S	E	L	D	O	M		
E	M	A	I	L		U	N	D	O	N	E	
T	O		T	O		N	T			R	A	
	R	C		B	C			M	A	L	E	S
P	E	A	C	E		H		A	H	A		P
E		D	M		S	A	C	K		Y		S
E	N	D		H	A	M		E	D	O	M	
P	A	Y	S		F	A			R	U	I	N
		A	M	E	N		P	I	T	S		
O	L	L	I	E		P	E	P		T	B	
L	A	I	D		M	O	O	N		S	O	
E	O	N		H	A		N		A	N	O	N
	T	E	A	C	H	E	R		O	N	E	

108

PUZZLE 29

```
U . S P A R R O W S . A T
N T . E M I T . S O . N O
M O O N . C . S W O R D S
E O N . C H A P . T O . S
T . M A . . I S H O P . .
. S H E P H E R D S . I S
H E A T . E L I . A I N T
A R T . B R I T . Y . T O
R V . D U E S . E E . . O
P A N . F . . S P R E A D
. N E . F O E . I . V . U
. T A B E R N A C L E . P
A S T E R . T . S O N S
```

PUZZLE 30

```
M E R C I F U L . M A R E
E G . A C . S O . E A R N
. G A T E . A B N E R S .
. S S . A . . T O . . A
A . H . A B I B . A N E R
B E E T . I . O G . . . E
S T R E N G T H E N E D .
A . . D . A . . R O M A N
L O T . T I N . A M I N O
O G . C A L E B . . T I E
M . E . B . T A B . E L
. V O L S . . E V I L S
T H E R E F O R E . . T
```

PUZZLE 31

```
P I E C E . W A I L . W E
E . B A . P A S S O V E R
R A B B I . R T . A I . G
I S . L T . E . V . M
S A F E . H O R S E M E N
H . E . N O W . . S O R E
. P A L M S . D O . C D
N E S T . A D O . W H Y
W E T . A N O N . A . S
. V . R U N . K . S A T E
J E R U S A L E M . F O E
E . I I . S A Y . F A R M
S T O N E . D . T A R E S
```

PUZZLE 32

```
. A . N E I G H B O U R S
O N . U N T I E . X . N A
V T . M D . T . K . P A L
E . O B E D I E N C E . U
R O B E D . N . E . O A T
C . R . . O W . P I E
O F F E R I N G . O L D
M M . D O S . P R E . W
E . C . O R . W E B . T A
. P A R T A K E R . M A R
P I C O . E . T I M O R
S C H O O L . S A V E D
. K E D . S . S H O E S
```

PUZZLE 33

```
G I H O N . C . J U D A H
R N S . A . R I O . A D O
O F . M O L E C H . B A R
O R S . M . T E N S . M E
M O A B I T E S . I S . B
. N M . H . S . I N S
S T U . T A R S H I S H .
O . E T O N . W E R E . A
L . L A B A N . C A R D S
O G . I . . H . A . S
M I D I A N I T E S . B E
O V A . H I R A M . A I R
N E B O . B A N . T I N T
```

PUZZLE 34

```
A N . T E L L E T H . I T
T O D O . O N A . O N E
E N D O . E A . B A R . M
. E . T H A N K E D . U P
T . H O T . A R E O . E
H I E . . A N N . P I S
O L D . T E S T A M E N T
U . S . H A T . C A N
S I . T I R E . L . S O
A S P . C . R . E A C H
N . T O K E N . B . O N
D O . R E . . O L I V E
. T H O R N S . B E S E T
```

PUZZLE 35

```
H I M . A H . A L I V E .
. T E A S E . L A N . M E
A . A B U N D A N C E . .
B E N O . . . R C . M I A
R N . U . C A M E L . M C
O . O N E . . . O G . C .
A B I D E T H . A B O V E
D . L . E . L E D . . P .
. . . A F R A I D . A T .
B A B E L . O L K . M A .
. C A L L E D . E B B . B
I T S . O . U . Y E L L .
. S H O W N . P R A N C E
```

PUZZLE 36

```
P O . B C . M I R A C L E
O F F E R . O N . F A . A
I F . D A R N . N A D I R
S . . . M O T H E R . . .
O N . H . . H I E . O A T
N A T I O N S . D E A D .
. M E N . O . U . A T O M
N E A T . T . P A T H . O
. S R . A H . . B S . T V
N . S T A I R . L . A R E
A S . O . N . P E A C E .
P I . S A G E . . I R A N
. P A S T . D O . R E D .
```

PUZZLE 37

```
W O R S E . W A N T . W E
A R E . G E E S E . L A V
R . W A G E S . W O V E .
N W . A D . P . W A V E R
S A I L S . O A S E S . .
. R . K . W A T C H . . B
O F F E R A . . E D . . E
F A I R E R . W I D O W S
. R R . T H E N . S H E .
W E E K S . M A N . T E T
E . . W H O L E . . A S .
R A . T A O . T R O U T .
E . W O N T . H . N T . .
```

PUZZLE 38

```
H U L L . H O U S E . M A
U S E . H E M S . A G E D
G E T . E R R . D R U M .
E R . H A B I T A T I O N
. . . C A T S . N H L . O
C . A I . H E . S T A R .
H A L L O W E D . . L B .
I L L S . W A S . M E O W
. M E T S . L . H A S T E
. S R O . . E R A . S H E
M . N O . R A R E . E D .
E . T E A M . I D . A R E
N O . S T A N D . A N . R
```

PUZZLE 39

```
. C I A . H O . B E . .
F A T S . I F . S U P E R
A S . A M . O F O T H N I
I S A . A O N A N . R O N
T I N A N D I N . P A S S
H A A N D O F . I R T H E
. . Z A I R . A S I A . .
I M A G E . U P A C H O R
T I R E . E L O I E L O I
A T E . A M A S A . O D E
B E N A M M I T H E . L I
O S E T . O I L . L I E N
R I S E . R I E . A S S .
```

PUZZLE 40

```
A P E . A B O V E . J O Y
G E N T L E N E S S . U R
A N D E S . E X P E C T S
I C O N . O D E . W E S .
N E W . B R I D E . D I P
. . . T R E E . S P A D E
L O V E I S . B A R R E N
A H I A N . B L U E . . .
M I A . G A I U S . C L C
. O L D . S S R . B O I L
B A S M A T H . A O R T A
U N . G E O G R A P H Y .
S S W . O R P A H . S E S
```

PUZZLE 41

I	S	A	I	A	H		I	S	R	A	E	L
M	A	R	T	H	A		N	O	A	H	T	O
A	L		S	A	M		V	A	N		H	I
G	U	R		Z	O	B	A	H		I	N	N
E	T	A	M		R	E	D		I	T	A	S
	E	W	E	S		E	K	R	O	N		
		D	I	E		R	O	O				
	E	V	E	N	T			A	N	T	S	
E	N	O	S		E	A	R		S	A	L	A
R	A	W		O	R	I	O	N		B	E	L
E	N		A	N	N		C	E	O		W	O
C	H	A	S	E	A		K	A	R	T	A	N
H	E	S	A	I	L		S	H	E	O	N	E

PUZZLE 42

W	O	R	D		L	A	D		A	B	I	B
A	B	I	A		E	H	I		D	A	M	E
R	E	D	N	O	T		M	A	D	M	E	N
	Y	I	E	L	D		O	R	I	O	N	
M	E	N		D	O	I	N	G		T	I	M
E	D	G	E		N	A	U	G	H	T	Y	
			A	G	E		H	E	N			
B	E	A	R	E	S	T			U	N	N	I
E	N	D		R	A	I	S	E		E	A	T
	D	O	D	A	I		A	H	I	A	H	
G	E	R	A	R	A		B	I	L	H	A	N
A	T	A	T		S	I	T		A	T	T	O
O	H	M	E		I	R	A		I	O	H	I

PUZZLE 43

S	T	E	A	D			D	E	M	O	N	
E	A	T	S		A	R	M		M	A	N	E
V	I	A		A	L	E	U	T		D	E	A
E	L	L		R	A	I	S	E		E	R	R
N	S		K		E			S	S			
		A	S	C	E	N	D	S				
	B	E	L		O	N	O		P	L	Y	
		O	B	S	E	R	V	E				
H	E		T	O		A	D		A	P		
O	L	E		G	R	E	A	T		A	D	O
M	O	P		S	O	R	T	S		R	E	E
E	P	I	C		B	E	E		M	A	P	S
R	E	S	T	S			H	U	M	T	Y	

PUZZLE 44

		I	A	M	B		C	A	S	E		
D	A	N	G	E	R		C	R	E	A	T	E
E	N	T	E	R		C		M	A	T	E	R
A	N			E	D	S				N	A	
D	A		E	L	M		I	M	A		T	S
			F	E	B		L	E	T			
S	H		F	E	R	V	E	N	T		A	L
P	A	C	E		A		N		R	A	M	A
A	L	E	C		C		C		I	T	E	M
R	E	N	T		E	V	E		B	O	N	E
	T	U	E		I		S	U	N			
A	B	R	A	M	S		P	E	T	E	R	S
	E	L		S			S	E	E	D		

PUZZLE 45

A	L	M		C	R	A	B		T	R	E	E
L	I	I		H	E	R	E		H	E	R	D
M	E	N		O	A	T	S		A	M	I	A
A	N	G	E	L	S		T	E	M	P	E	R
		N	E	O		O	R	A				
C	A	V	E	R	N		W	A	R	M	E	R
A	R	E						O	V	A		
B	E	T	H	E	L		I	S	A	I	A	H
		E	R	E		S	H	E				
M	A	K	I	N	G		R	A	C	H	E	L
A	B	I	S		A	R	A	M		A	B	E
A	I	N	T		T	E	E	M		T	A	V
L	A	G	S		E	U	L	A		E	L	I

PUZZLE 46

S	T	R	E	N	G	T	H		A	D	A	M
U	S	A		I	R	O	D	E		I	C	E
M	A	N	A	G	E		D	W	E	L	L	
M	R		S	H	E	M		I	E		E	A
E		I	T	K	E	P	T		M	A	N	
R	A	I	N		M	A			N	O		
	G	O		T	A	B	L	E		I		M
B	E	T	A		D	E	E	R		A	S	A
A	D	A	M		I	R	S		R	E	D	
O		E	G	O		T	U	B	A		O	
B	A	R	N		S	H	I	P		A	N	
A	C	T		A		A	N	O	I	N	T	
B	E		A	L	L	M	E	N		A	E	C

PUZZLE 47

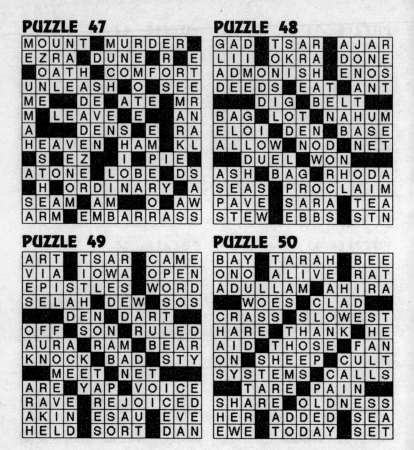

```
M O U N T   M U R D E R
E Z R A   D U N E   R   E
  O A T H   C O M F O R T
U N L E A S H   O   S E E
M E     D E   A T E   M R
M   L E A V E   E     A N
A     D E N S   E   R A
H E A V E N   H A M   K L
  S   E Z     I   P I E
A T O N E   L O B E   D S
  H   O R D I N A R Y   A
S E A M   A M   O   A W
A R M   E M B A R R A S S
```

PUZZLE 48

```
G A D   T S A R   A J A R
L I I   O K R A   D O N E
A D M O N I S H   E N O S
D E E D S   E A T   A N T
    D I G   B E L T
B A G   L O T   N A H U M
E L O I   D E N   B A S E
A L L O W   N O D   N E T
  D U E L   W O N
A S H   B A G   R H O D A
S E A S   P R O C L A I M
P A V E   S A R A   T E A
S T E W   E B B S   S T N
```

PUZZLE 49

```
A R T   T S A R   C A M E
V I A   I O W A   O P E N
E P I S T L E S   W O R D
S E L A H   D E W   S O S
    D E N   D A R T
O F F   S O N   R U L E D
A U R A   R A M   B E A R
K N O C K   B A D   S T Y
  M E E T   N E T
A R E   Y A P   V O I C E
R A V E   R E J O I C E D
A K I N   E S A U   E V E
H E L D   S O R T   D A N
```

PUZZLE 50

```
B A Y   T A R A H   B E E
O N O   A L I V E   R A T
A D U L L A M   A H I R A
    W O E S   C L A D
C R A S S   S L O W E S T
H A R E   T H A N K   H E
A I D   T H O S E   F A N
O N   S H E E P   C U L T
S Y S T E M S   C A L L S
    T A R E   P A I N
S H A R E   O L D N E S S
H E R   A D D E D   S E A
E W E   T O D A Y   S E T
```

Bible Crosswords

Collection #2

Compiled and Edited
by *Toni Sortor*

A Barbour Book

Bible
Crosswords

Collection #2

PUZZLE 1

Evelyn Boyington

ACROSS CLUES

1. Look _____ new heavens and a new earth. (2 Pet. 3:13)
4. I will _____ thee: on the third day. (2 Kgs. 20:5)
8. Health resorts.
12. My days _____ like a shadow. (Ps. 102:11)
13. Enter _____ his gates with thanksgiving. (Ps. 100:4)
14. We have seen his star in the _____. (Matt. 2:2)
15. I will destroy this _____. (Mark 14:58)
17. _____ no man any thing. (Rom. 13:8)
19. A greeting.
20. To hurt.
21. We _____ great plainness of speech. (2 Cor. 3:12)
22. He _____ to meet them. (Gen. 18:2)
23. A narrow cut.
25. Voice of _____ crying in the wilderness. (Matt. 3:3)
26. With _____ life will I satisfy him. (Ps. 91:16)
27. An _____ of oil for an ephah. (Ezek. 45:24)
28. I saw thee under the _____ tree. (John 1:50)
29. Arise, take up thy _____. (Matt. 9:6)
30. What think _____ of Christ? (Matt. 22:42)
31. We were _____ of God to be put in trust. (1 Thes. 2:4)
33. Chemical symbol for radium.
35. Hear my _____, O God. (Ps. 61:1)
36. Thou shalt _____ about thee. (Job 11:18)
37. Babylon is taken, _____ is confounded. (Jer. 50:2)
38. O Lord, _____ shall I say! (Josh. 7:8)
40. Height (abbr.).
41. He moveth his _____ like a cedar. (Job 40:17)

42. Even as a _____ gathereth her chickens. (Matt. 23:37)
43. Not willing that _____ should perish. (2 Pet. 3:9)
44. I would thou wert cold or _____. (Rev. 3:15)
45. A piece (abbr.).
46. Wheat beard.
47. _____ and built up in him. (Col. 2:7)
50. The high places also of _____. (Hosea 10:8)
52. The children of _____ of Hezekiah. (Ezra 2:16)
54. _____ up for yourselves treasures in heaven. (Matt. 6:20)
55. An examination.
56. Gaddiel the son of _____. (Num. 13:10)
57. How long will it be _____ thou be quiet? (Jer. 47:6)

DOWN CLUES

1. Liberal soul shall be made _____. (Prov. 11:25)
2. Raw metal.
3. My joy might _____ in you. (John 15:11)
4. Every mountain and _____ shall be brought low. (Luke 3:5)
5. Compass point.
6. Marvel not _____ this. (John 5:28)
7. _____ thy shoe from off thy foot. (Josh. 5:15)
8. Whereas I was blind, now I _____. (John 9:25)
9. Dad.
10. Ain, Remmon, and Ether, and _____. (Josh. 19:7)
11. O death, where is thy _____? (1 Cor. 15:55)
16. Brought me up also out of an horrible _____. (Ps. 40:2)
18. _____ are the children of God. (Rom. 8:16)
21. Christ died for the _____. (Rom. 5:6)
22. Moses took the _____ of God in his hand. (Ex. 4:20)
23. Timid.
24. I will _____ with my fathers. (Gen. 47:30)

4

25. An horn of _____. (1 Kgs. 1:39)
26. The Lord _____ me. (Gen. 24:27)
28. For then would I _____ away. (Ps. 55:6)
29. Therefore shall he _____ in harvest. (Prov. 20:4)
31. Thou _____ the Son of God. (John 1:49)
32. Powers of thinking.
33. Shimei and _____, and the mighty men. (1 Kgs. 1:8)
34. The Lord is good to _____. (Ps. 145:9)
35. How _____ these things be? (John 3:9)
37. The Lord mighty in _____. (Ps. 24:8)
38. Sowed tares among the _____. (Matt. 13:25)

39. The first of your dough for an _____ offering. (Num. 15:20)
40. And led Him away to _____ first. (John 18:13)
41. Ye take _____ much upon you. (Num. 16:3)
43. A sound of sympathy.
44. The sons of Lotan; _____, and Homam. (1 Chron. 1:39)
46. Go to the _____, thou sluggard. (Prov. 6:6)
47. The Lord dried up the water of the _____ sea. (Josh 2:10)
48. Give _____ to my words. (Ps. 5:1)
49. A solution for coloring.
51. Suffix used in forming plurals.
53. Peace _____ him that is far off. (Isa. 57:19)

5

PUZZLE 2

Helen Walter

ACROSS CLUES

1. Garden of _____.
5. Wander.
8. He is of _____; ask him. (John 9:21)
11. And the _____ and the morning were the first day. (Gen. 1:5)
12. The first man.
13. The first woman.
14. Pare.
16. Doctor (abbr.).
17. Director (abbr.).
19. Grass.
21. This _____ in remembrance of me. (Luke 22:19)
23. Lands surrounded by water.
26. Make broader.
28. Day and night shall not _____. (Gen. 8:22)
29. Chicago transportation.
31. What hast thou _____? (Gen. 4:10)
32. Spelling (abbr.).
33. Ye shall not eat of every _____ of the garden? (Gen 3:1)
35. Old Testament (abbr.).
36. Naomi's daughter-in-law. (Ruth 1:4)
37. Relatives.
40. Son of Adam and Eve.
41. _____ shall not eat of it. (Gen. 3:3)
42. Let _____ make man. (Gen. 1:26)
44. Hear the word of God, and _____ it. (Luke 8:21)
45. Vase.
47. Naked.
48. Either/_____.
49. I will make of thee a _____ nation. (Gen. 12:2)

52. To be in poor health.
54. And it was _____. (Gen. 1:7)
56. Deed.
57. North Atlantic Treaty Organization (abbr.).
60. _____ thou not the oppressor. (Prov. 3:31)
61. As of fire, and it sat upon_____ of them. (Acts 2:3)
62. Thou shalt _____ eat of it. (Gen. 2:17)

DOWN CLUES

2. Plan.
3. Be ye lift up, ye _____ doors. (Ps.24:7)
4. Compass direction.
5. Rend.
6. And they shall be _____ flesh. (Gen. 2:24)
7. That in the _____ to come. (Eph. 2:7)
8. Total.
9. And the Lord God planted a _____. (Gen. 2:8)
10. Printer's measure.
13. Decree.
15. Both _____ and high. (Ps. 49:2)
18. Love _____ another. (John 15:17)
20. And I _____ eat. (Gen. 3:12)
22. There is none good but _____. (Matt. 19:17)
24. Child shall play on the hole of the _____. (Isa. 11:8)
25. The _____ beguiled me. (Gen. 3:13)
27. Pier.
30. Meadow.
33. _____ me, and know my thoughts. (Ps. 139:23)
34. Lefthanded judge. (Judg. 3:15)
35. Paddle.

38. An _____ is nothing. (1 Cor. 8:4)
39. They have no rest day _____ night. (Rev. 14:11)
40. _____d is the ground for thy sake. (Gen. 3:17)
43. The _____ of the scornful. (Ps. 1:1)
46. Recreation (abbr.).
50. Beam.
51. I took the little book...and _____ it up. (Rev. 10:10)
53. Electrically charged atom.
55. Upon.
57. North Carolina (abbr.).
58. Exclamation.
59. _____ was very good. (Gen. 1:31)

PUZZLE 3

Helen Walter

ACROSS CLUES

1. Having _____ pieces of silver. (Luke 15:8)
4. I have found my sheep which was _____ (Luke 15:6)
7. Having a delicate open pattern.
11. A dried grape.
12. Enemy.
13. Vase.
14. I saw a _____ heaven. (Rev. 21:1)
16. Pieces of silver.
18. Direction.
19. Abraham set seven _____ lambs. (Gen. 21:28)
20. Entice.
21. Musical note.
23. Have a high regard for.
26. Signal for help.
28. _____ and outs.
29. That thou doest, _____ quickly. (John 13:27)
30. Woman's name.
31. Entreats earnestly.

33. Jacob's daughter. (Gen. 30:21)
35. _____ me, O Lord, in thy righteousness. (Ps. 5:8)
36. And they _____ out. (Mark 6:12)
37. He saw the spirit of God descending like a _____. (Matt. 3:16)
39. Took possession.
42. Doctor.
46. Come _____ worship him. (Matt. 2:2)
47. Rock of _____.
48. California (abbr.).
49. _____ say, can you see?
51. Where _____ treasure is. (Matt. 6:21)
53. _____ a little while. (John 14:19)
54. Used for fishing.
55. Wandered.

DOWN CLUES

1. The judgments of the Lord are _____. (Ps. 19:9)
2. He that hath _____ to hear. (Mark 4:9)
3. Number of sheep safe in the fold. (Matt. 18:12)
4. Ending for fishing_____ or clothes_____.
5. In one direction only.
6. Toward.
8. Burning.
9. Ice cream _____.
10. Opposite of no.
15. Married.
16. Hold fast.
17. Us.
22. Individuality.
24. Stuck in the mud.
25. I am the _____ shepherd. (John 10:11)
26. Mother.
27. South American mountain range.
32. Like a grain of mustard _____. (Luke 13:19)
34. A garden tool.
38. I am Alpha and _____. (Rev. 1:8)
40. Animal home.
41. Arrow.
43. Frosted.
44. Domestic animal.
45. Thou art my beloved _____. (Luke 3:22)
50. _____ is not here. (Matt. 28:6)
52. Let _____ make man. (Gen. 1:26)
53. That _____ love one another. (John 13:34)

9

PUZZLE 4
Faith Wade

ACROSS CLUES

1. Filthy conversation of the _____.
   (2 Pet. 2:7)
4. Pekod, and Shoa, and _____.
   (Ezek. 23:23)
7. New Testament (abbr.).
9. His _____ is in the law. (Ps. 1:2)
11. _____ have we confidence toward
    God. (1 John 3:21)
15. Feline.
16. Be not, as the _____. (Matt. 6:16)
19. Hush.
20. When the wicked _____. (Prov.
    11:10)
21. Let _____ many servants.
    (1 Tim. 6:1)
22. _____ not among thorns. (Jer. 4:3)
24. The son of _____, which was the
    son of Mattathias. (Luke 3:26)
26. Gaddiel the son of _____.
    (Num. 13:10)
27. Compass direction.
29. Bath-sheba's first husband.
    (2 Sam. 11:3)
30. Not down.
31. Negative.
32. Joshua sent men from Jericho to
    _____. (Josh. 7:2)
33. Mister (abbr.).
34. Newspaper want _____.
35. Rachel and Leah's father. (Gen.
    29:10)
37. Lord, by thy _____. (Ps. 30:7)
39. By the hill of _____. (Judg. 7:1)
40. And ye are not your _____.
    (1 Cor. 6:19)
41. In _____ with God and men.
    (Luke 2:52; NAS)

43. Nathan... and Shimei, and _____.
    (1 Kgs. 1:8)
44. _____, and ye clothed me.
    (Matt. 25:36)
45. You and I.
46. Esau's color at birth. (Gen. 25:25)
47. Noah's boat.

DOWN CLUES

1. Every man _____ his weapons.
   (2 Chron. 23:7)
2. Short of Edwin.
3. They delivered them the _____.
   (Acts 16:4)
4. Javan, Elishah, and Tarshish,
   _____. (Gen. 10:4)
5. The kingdom of _____ in Bashan.
   (Deut. 3:4)
6. _____ was over the household.
   (1 Kgs. 4:6)
8. His dwelling among the _____.
   (Mark 5:3)
10. A lion's den.
12. Take a bunch of _____. (Ex. 12:22)
13. He made the _____ of gold.
    (Ex. 39:2)
14. Opposite of yes.
17. Computer Printer (abbr.).
18. Jacob's brother. (Gen. 25:2-26)
21. Benjamin's third child.
    (1 Chron. 8:1)
23. And there sat in a _____.
    (Acts 20:9)
25. Buy _____ and hewed stone.
    (2 Kgs. 12:12)
26. _____ the little children to come
    unto me. (Mark 10:14)
28. I am the _____. (John 14:6)
34. _____ it, pass not by it. (Prov. 4:15)
35. For God so _____. (John 3:16)
36. Of _____, the family of the
    Arodites. (Num. 26:17)

10

38. United Nations (abbr.).
39. Thou shall not _____ unto thee. (Ex. 20:4)
41. Not near.
42. _____, and it shall be given. (Matt. 7:7)
45. Abraham's hometown. (Gen. 11:31)

PUZZLE 5

Diana Rowland

ACROSS CLUES

1. He that earneth_____. (Hag. 1:6)
6. Let all _____ that seek thee rejoice. (Ps. 40:16)
11. Thou shalt _____. (Ps. 102:13)
12. Eliab the son of _____. (Num. 2:7)
13. And I will walk _____ liberty. (Ps. 119:45)
14. He hath settled on his _____, _____ hath not. (Jer. 48:11; 2 words)
16. The ungodly are not _____. (Ps. 1:4)
18. Exist.
19. Ark of God came to _____...for there was _____ deadly... (1 Sam. 5:10, 11; 2 words)
20. On the east side of _____. (Num. 34:11)
21. _____ also the Jairite was _____ chief ruler. (2 Sam. 20:26; 2 words)
23. How great is the _____ of them! (Ps. 139:17)
24. Thou hast also turned the _____. (Ps. 89:43)
25. As for such as turn _____ unto. (Ps. 125:5)
27. More than twelve _____ of angels? (Matt. 26:53)
29. Who is a _____ but he that denieth. (1 John 2:22)
31. Thou art _____ _____ God that.... (Ps. 5:4; 2 words)
32. _____ will _____ his hand also in _____ sea. (Ps. 89:25; 3 words)
35. _____, so would we...them _____ say. (Ps. 35:25; 2 words)
38. And _____ out of the valley. (Ps. 60:6)
39. Lyric poem.
41. Beyond the tower of _____. (Gen. 35:21)
42. National Institutes of Health (abbr.).
43. Transgressions as _____...multitude, _____ did.... (Job 31:33, 34; 2 words)
45. Texas Instruments (abbr.).
46. I have given _____ unto the children. (Deut. 2:9)
47. Borders of Archi to _____. (Josh. 16:2)
48. Hewlett Packard (abbr.).
49. Unto thy father that _____ thee. (Prov. 23:22)
51. They that sow in _____. (Ps. 126:5)
53. And _____ the lamp of God...down _____ sleep. (1 Sam. 3:3; 2 words)
54. To _____ thee good at thy latter _____. (Deut 8:16; 2 words, reverse order)

DOWN CLUES

1. Beside the still _____. (Ps. 23:2)
2. Given _____ unto the children. (Deut. 2:9)
3. Of Brazillai the _____. (Ezra 2:61)
4. He called the name of the well _____. (Gen. 26:20)
5. Then shall the _____ be ashamed. (Micah 3:7)
6. Obey God rather _____ _____. (Acts 5:29; 2 words)
7. City of Sepharvaim, _____, and Ivah? (Is. 37:13)
8. God is my King of _____. (Ps. 74:12)
9. I am _____ troubled. (Ps. 77:4)
10. Lifted up as an _____ upon his land. (Zech. 9:16)
13. Of the course of _____. (Luke 1:5)
15. He restoreth my _____. (Ps. 23:3)
17. May fall by his strong _____. (Ps. 10:10)
20. Why make ye this _____, _____ weep? (Mark 5:39; 2 words)

22. What _____ thee now. (Is. 22:1)
24. And _____ taken...not any, _____ great. (1 Sam. 30:2; 2 words, reverse order)
26. The meek shall _____. (Ps. 22:26)
28. Called to _____ out into _____ place. (Heb. 11:8; 2 words)
30. A damsel came _____ hearken, named _____. (Acts 12:13; 2 words, reverse order)
32. Zophah, and _____, and Shelesh. (1 Chron. 7:35)
33. _____ also shall _____ a possession. (Num. 24:18; 2 words)

34. Beyond the tower of _____. (Gen. 35:21)
36. Quit of thine _____...words, _____ be it. (Josh. 2:20,21; 2 words)
37. Voyage, flight, or drive.
40. To speak in a theatrical manner.
43. Discovered _____ thy rebuke, O Lord, _____. (Ps. 18:15; 2 words)
44. _____ God:...of _____ strings. (Ps. 144:9; 2 words)
47. Mine _____ is as nothing. (Ps. 39:5)
50. The sons of Judah were _____. (Num. 26:19)
52. Rural Delivery (abbr.).

13

PUZZLE 6

Teresa Zeek

ACROSS CLUES

1. He was hidden in the bulrushes. (Ex. 2:3, 10)
5. Another name for Saul. (Acts 13:9)
8. _____ ye into all the world. (Mark 16:15)
10. There was no room in the _____. (Luke 2:7)
11. To rule _____ the day and ... night (Gen. 1:18)
13. _____. Even so, come, Lord Jesus. (Rev. 22:20)
15. Flashing _____ lights.
17. He _____ there an altar. (Gen. 33:20)
19. Stops nursing.
20. Masculine pronoun.
21. Suffix used to make a comparative word.
24. A very small quantity.
26. Prefix meaning "three."
27. Female deer.
29. The wicked have laid a _____ for me. (Ps. 119:110)
32. A set of three.
34. To be carried.
36. Scrooge says, "_____ humbug."
38. Minnesota (abbr.).
39. It was planted in a good _____. (Ezek. 17:8)
40. A swarm of _____. (Judg. 14:8)
41. Churning of milk bringeth forth _____. (Prov. 30:33)
43. Dominion over the fowl of the _____. (Gen. 1:26)
44. Support or brace.
46. Wipe your feet on our welcome _____.

48. Whoso keepeth the commandment shall _____ no evil thing. (Ec. 8:5)
49. Demonstration model (abbr.).
50. King of Moab. (Judg. 3:17)
53. Yellow tropical fruit.
56. God created the heaven and the _____. (Gen. 1:1)
57. Mary stayed with Elisabeth three _____. (Luke 1:56)

DOWN CLUES

1. Love the Lord with all thy heart,... soul, and..._____. (Matt. 22:37)
2. The Lord our God is _____ Lord. (Deut. 6:4)
3. Sins...as white as _____. (Isa. 1:18)
4. Even _____, come Lord Jesus. (Rev. 22:20)
5. The express image of his _____. (Heb. 1:3)
6. Blessed _____ the poor in spirit. (Matt. 5:3)
7. It is vain...to sit up _____. (Ps. 127:2)
8. The king of Debir, one; the king of _____. (Josh. 12:13)
9. Putting _____ the breastplate of faith and love. (1 Thes. 5:8)
12. Take me some _____. (Gen. 27:3)
14. "Jesus loves _____, this I know."
16. I will _____ leave thee. (Heb. 13:5)
18. Some trust in _____, and some in horses. (Ps. 20:7)
22. Christ has _____.
23. Advertisement (abbr.).
25. Saul of _____. (Acts 9:11)
28. Charity...toward each _____ aboundeth. (2 Thes. 1:3)
30. To revise.
31. _____, Father, all things are possible unto thee. (Mark 14:36)
33. I am (contraction).

The crossword grid is numbered with cells: 1, 2, 3, 4, 5, 6, 7, 8, 9 (row 1); 10, 11, 12, 13, 14 (row 2); 15, 16, 17, 18 (row 3); 19, 20, 21, 22 (row 4); 23, 24, 25, 26 (row 5); 27, 28, 29, 30 (row 6); 31, 32, 33, 34, 35 (row 7); 36, 37, 38, 39 (row 8); 40, 41, 42 (row 9); 43, 44, 45, 46, 47 (row 10); 48, 49 (row 11); 50, 51, 52, 53, 54, 55 (row 12); 56, 57 (row 13).

35. The _____ s shall melt with fervent heat. (2 Pet. 3:10)
37. The first three vowels.
41. Light_____.
42. Elkanah's home. (1 Sam. 2:11)
44. They went into one _____. (2 Kgs. 7:8)
45. Second tone of the diatonic scale.
47. Its waves thereof _____ themselves. (Jer. 5:22)

48. _____ God so loved the world. (John 3:16)
49. Rachel's maid, Bilhah's first son. (Gen. 30:6)
51. General Electric (abbr.).
52. Sixth tone of the diatonic scale.
54. I _____ THAT I AM. (Ex. 3:14)
55. Let _____ man deceive you. (2 Thes. 2:3)

PUZZLE 7

Janice Buhl

ACROSS CLUES

1. Are thou the _____ of the Jews? (Luke 23:3)
4. I am not _____ to destroy. (Matt. 5:17)
7. Do, re, me, _____.
9. _____ said unto Samuel, Go, lie down. (1 Sam. 3:9)
10. Abihail the son of _____. (1 Chron. 5:14)
11. Tuberculosis (abbr.).
13. She gave me of the tree, and I did _____. (Gen. 3:12)
14. Gold, silver, ivory, and _____ and peacocks. (1 Kgs. 10:22)
15. Full ears of corn in the _____ thereof. (2 Kgs. 4:42)
17. _____ king of Jarmuth. (Josh. 10:3)
19. Poured out my soul _____ the Lord. (1 Sam. 1:15)
21. The sons of Judah were _____ and Onan. (Num. 26:19)
23. The glory of the Lord shone _____ about them. (Luke 2:9)
24. Saint (abbr.).
26. Be as an _____ whose leaf fadeth. (Isa. 1:30)
27. Go _____ therefore. (Matt. 28:19)
28. _____ we love one another. (1 John 4:12)
29. Cut off his thumbs and his great _____. (Judg. 1:6)
31. And _____ came to pass. (Judg. 1:14)
33. Before the judgment of _____ of Christ. (Rom. 14:10)
36. Part in a play.
37. Take thou unto thee an iron _____. (Ezek. 4:3)
38. Your labour is not in _____. (1 Cor. 15:58)
39. It shall go _____ with him that is left. (Job 20:26)
40. Nothing.
41. Cain talked with _____ his brother. (Gen. 4:8)
43. _____ with joy receiveth it. (Matt. 13:20)
44. The _____, which they saw in the east. (Matt. 2:9)
47. Lo, the wicked _____ their bow. (Ps. 11:2)
49. Go to the _____, thou sluggard. (Prov. 6:6)
50. The beginning and the _____. (Rev. 22:13)
51. Noble poem.
52. So many _____ of voices. (1 Cor. 14:10)

DOWN CLUES

1. The Lord bless thee and _____ thee. (Num. 6:24)
2. _____ the Ahohite. (1 Chron. 11:29)
3. Wash thee with _____. (Jer. 2:22)
4. Ye cannot drink the _____ of the Lord. (1 Cor. 10:21)
5. They slew _____ upon the rock. (Judg. 7:25)
6. Thou shalt forget thy _____. (Job 11:16)
8. _____, and it shall be given you. (Luke 11:9)
10. Shem, _____, and Japheth. (Gen. 5:32)
11. _____ shalt deny me thrice. (Mark 14:30)
12. Did not our heart _____ within us? (Luke 24:32)

16

16. Him that for _____ and murder was cast into prison. (Luke 23:25)
18. Deborah _____, and went with Barak. (Judg. 4:9)
20. Until I make thy _____ thy foot stool. (Acts 2:35)
22. To _____ like a calf. (Ps. 29:6)
24. Long, narrow pieces.
25. Not lift up any iron _____ upon them. (Deut. 27:5)
30. Building wing.
32. Preparest a _____ before me (Ps. 23:5)

34. We have one father, _____ God. (John 8:41)
35. Is not _____ the Levite thy brother? (Ex. 4:14)
40. _____ the son of Ahitub. (2 Sam. 8:17)
41. Who _____ thou, Lord? (Acts 9:5)
42. Gaal the son of _____. (Judg. 9:26)
45. Convert skins to leather.
46. _____ it shall come to pass. (Ex. 4:9)
48. And the earth _____ without form. (Gen. 1:2)

17

PUZZLE 8

Janet Adkins

ACROSS CLUES

1. A sword is upon the liars; and they shall _____. (Jer. 50:36)
4. A little oil in a _____. (1 Kgs. 17:12)
8. The glory which thou gavest _____. (John 17:22)
10. Bringing gold, silver, ivory, and _____(s). (1 Kgs. 10:22)
11. I will _____ out my spirit unto you. (Prov. 1:23)
12. Calf meat.
14. Thou...hast _____ forth the people. (Ex. 15:13)
15. Sounds of hesitation.
16. Whose names are in the _____ of life. (Phil. 4:3)
17. They could not enter _____ because of unbelief. (Heb. 3:19)
18. True _____, help those women which laboured. (Phil. 4:3)
20. Even as a _____ gathereth her chickens. (Matt. 23:37; plural)
21. Roman numeral 6.
23. Like
24. Egyptian god.
26. Doth not _____ one of you on the sabbath loose his ox? (Luke 13:15)
28. One who installs or endows.
31. See thou tell _____ man. (Matt. 8:4)
32. As he thinketh in his heart _____ is _____. (Prov. 23:7; 2 words)
33. Grain.
35. Border state (abbr.).
37. Do all things without _____urings. (Phil. 2:14)
38. Short for Elizabeth.
40. Erie law enforcement agency.
41. Made you _____s to feed the church. (Acts 20:28, archaic)
43. They shall build houses and _____ it them. (Isa. 65:21)
45. Orderly.
46. Southwestern state (abbr.).
47. Yesterday (Spanish).
49. Route (abbr.).
50. Greek letter.
51. Ye shall be unto _____ a kingdom of priests. (Ex. 19:6)
52. And the king was _____. (Matt. 14:9)
53. The _____ head fell into the water. (2 Kgs. 6:5, alt. spelling)

DOWN CLUES

1. Surrealist artist.
2. Ye shall see heaven _____. (John 1:51)
3. Senator _____ Kennedy.
4. Wine bottle stoppers.
5. A type of trick.
6. Went forth with them from _____ of the Chaldees. (Gen. 11:31)
7. Man was created, did not _____.
8. Dangerous shark.
9. "Strength" (Heb.).
11. Unskillled worker.
13. Carried by the wind.
16. Let him _____ Anathema Marantha. (1 Cor. 16:22)
18. A thousand years in thy sight are but as _____. (Ps. 90:4; plural)
19. Yah_____.
20. Children of Ziha, the children of _____. (Neh. 7:46)
22. Publican...would not lift up so much as _____ eyes. (Luke 18:13)
24. Let us _____ together. (Isa. 1:18)

25. Thou _____ the man. (2 Sam. 12:7)
27. In whatsoever state I am, therewith to be _____. (Phil. 4:11)
29. System of naming things: _____clature.
30. I go unto Jerusalem _____ minister unto the saints. (Rom. 15:25)
34. Covet earnestly the _____ gifts. (1 Cor. 12:31)
36. Pertaining to the skin.
38. Rude child.
39. Symbol for tellurium.
42. Weird. (alt. spelling)
43. Belief system (suffix).
44. Mixed-up Elks Club.
48. Northern Pacific or B&O _____. (abbr.).
50. Former mate.

PUZZLE 9

Rebecca Souder

ACROSS CLUES

1. The patience of _____. (Jam. 5:11)
4. Messenger of God.
8. _____ so loved the world. (John 3:16)
10. Before.
11. There was _____ room for them. (Luke 2:7)
12. _____ be taxed with Mary. (Luke 2:5)
13. To place.
14. Mary's hometown. (Luke 1:26)
18. Exclamation of triumph.
19. The angel appeared to Joseph in a _____. (Matt. 1:20)
20. Son of Noah. (Gen. 6:10)
23. Valley where David fought Goliath. (1 Sam. 17:2)
25. Noah's second son.
28. Licenses Surgeon (abbr.).
31. Elizabeth (variation).
34. Pale.
37. About.
38. True.
40. Buzzing insect.
41. His _____ drew the third part of the stars. (Rev. 12:4)
43. Therefore, I _____ you. (Rom. 12:1 NIV)
44. Burnt offerings of _____. (Isa. 1:11)
45. District Attorney (abbr.).
46. Time in office.
47. And _____ came to pass. (Luke 1:41)
48. Mary's husband. (Matt. 1:20)
51. Life story (abbr.).
53. Rear Admiral (abbr.).
54. New (prefix).
56. _____, the angel of the Lord. (Luke 2:9)
57. Cyrenius was his governor. (Luke 2:2)
58. _____, and it shall be given. (Matt. 7:7)

DOWN CLUES

1. The Son of God.
2. Mine product.
3. He called the name of that place _____. (Gen. 28:19)
4. A prophetess. (Luke 2:36)
5. He built an ark.
6. Greek vowel.
7. The angel of the _____.
8. Entrance.
9. _____ to others. (Matt. 7:12 NIV)
15. Father of John. (Luke 1:59)
16. Make a mistake.
17. _____, thou that are highly favoured. (Luke 1:28)
21. _____ shall be called John. (Luke 1:60)
22. Every _____ that openeth the womb. (Luke 2:23)
24. Clue.
26. Cain's brother.
27. Come unto _____. (Matt. 11:28)
29. Melchizedek king of _____. (Gen. 14:18)
30. The angel _____. (Luke 1:26)
32. I am the way, the _____, and the life. (John 14:6)
33. It is good for us to be _____. (Matt. 17:4)
35. They sit in Moses' _____. (Matt. 23:2)
36. Touched the _____ of his garment. (Matt. 9:20)

Crossword grid with numbered cells:

Row 1: 1, 2, 3, [black], 4, 5, [white], 6, 7, [black], 8, [white], 9
Row 2: 10, [white], [white], [black], 11, [white], [black], 12, [white], [white], [white], [black], [white]
Row 3: 13, [white], [white], [black], 14, [white], 15, [white], [white], 16, [white], 17, [black]
Row 4: [white], [black], [white], [black], 18, [white], [white], [black], 19, [white], [white], [white], [white]
Row 5: 20, 21, [white], 22, [black], [white], [white], [black], [white], [black], [white], [white], [black]
Row 6: [black], 23, [white], [white], 24, [white], 25, 26, 27, [black], [white], 28, 29
Row 7: 30, [black], [white], 31, [white], [white], [white], [white], [white], 32, 33, [black], [white]
Row 8: 34, 35, 36, [white], [white], [black], 37, [white], [white], 38, [white], 39, [white]
Row 9: 40, [white], [white], [black], 41, 42, [white], [white], [black], 43, [white], [white], [white]
Row 10: 44, [white], [white], [white], [black], 45, [white], [white], [black], 46, [white], [white], [white]
Row 11: 47, [white], [white], [black], 48, [white], [white], 49, 50, [white], [white], [black], [white]
Row 12: [white], [black], 51, 52, [white], [black], [white], 53, [white], [white], 54, [white], 55
Row 13: 56, [white], [black], 57, [white], [white], [white], [white], [white], [black], 58, [white], [white]

39. Concurs.
42. Fuss.
48. Good tidings of great _____.
(Luke 2:10)
49. Historic period.
50. Cooking pot.
52. Unto you _____ born this day.
(Luke 2:11)
54. Not Available (abbr.).
55. All right.

PUZZLE 10

Rebecca Souder

ACROSS CLUES

1. With him on the sacred _____.
   (2 Pet. 1:18 NIV)
6. And to brotherly kindness, _____.
   (2 Pet. 1:7 NIV).
9. Absent (abbr.).
10. Division of Scripture.
11. _____, I am with you always.
    (Matt. 28:20)
12. Biblical beast used in the fields.
13. Our Savior _____ Christ.
16. Combining form meaning "having fruit."
18. Hebrew combining form for "God."
19. Thy word is a _____ unto my feet.
    (Ps. 119:105)
22. Draw out.
23. A more _____ word of prophecy.
    (2 Pet. 1:19)
25. Spoken.
26. Religion (abbr.).
27. Half of a kind of fly.
28. Not amateur.
29. A movie rating.
30. No prophecy of the _____ is of any private interpretation. (2 Pet. 1:20)
34. Jacob's first wife.
35. Pea's home.
36. Noah...a _____ of righteousness.
    (2 Pet. 2:5)
38. Lieutenant (abbr.).
39. _____ else.
40. Our Lord Jesus _____.
43. Received from God...honour and _____. (2 Pet. 1:17)
44. They are all gone _____. (Ps. 14:3)
46. Self.

48. Food regimen.
49. Thy _____ and thy staff. (Ps. 23:4)
50. From his old _____. (2 Pet. 1:9)
51. When _____ made known unto you.
    (2 Pet. 1:16)

DOWN CLUES

1. Were eyewitnesses of his _____.
   (2 Pet. 1:16)
2. A mark used in old manuscripts.
3. United States Ship (abbr.).
4. Indefinite article.
5. He, she, and _____.
6. Our _____ Jesus Christ.
7. There came such a _____ to him.
   (2 Pet. 1:17)
8. From the _____ glory. (2 Pet. 1:17)
11. The father of Eliasaph. (Num. 3:24)
14. Suffix meaning "small."
15. South America (abbr.).
17. Cleaned totally.
20. Land where Abraham offered Isaac. (Gen. 22:2)
21. For the _____ came not...by the will of man. (2 Pet. 1:21)
24. Reserve (abbr.).
28. Great and _____ promises.
    (2 Pet. 1:4)
29. Through faith...obtained _____.
    (Heb. 11:33)
31. Quahog is another word for a _____ m.
32. Direction.
33. If any of you do _____ from the truth. (Jam. 5:19)
36. The _____ and coming of our Lord.
    (2 Pet. 1:16)
37. Blood factor.
38. Company (British abbr.).
41. He prayed...that it might not _____.
    (Jam. 5:17)

42. Make all _____. (Mark 6:39)
43. Holy men of _____ spake. (2 Pet. 1:21)
45. Were_____witnesses. (2 Pet. 1:16)

47. _____ ye unto all the world. (Mark 16:15)
48. Roman numeral 501.

PUZZLE 11

Karen Kapferer

ACROSS CLUES

1. Behold, I shew you a _____.
   (1 Cor. 15:51)
6. He blessed Samuel. (1 Sam. 1:25)
8. Roe or hart.
9. Las Vegas (abbr.).
10. Tohu was the son of _____.
    (1 Sam. 1:1)
12. _____ killed his brother, Abel.
    (Gen. 4:8)
14. Negative.
15. Major airline (abbr.).
18. _____ out my transgressions.
    (Ps. 51:1)
19. A gift brought to Jesus. (Matt. 2:11)
21. City in Norway.
22. Someone looked up to or admired.
23. Royal Ambassador (abbr.).
24. _____omans, _____saiah,
    _____amentations.
26. Either/_____.
27. The _____ in heart shall be filled
    with his own ways. (Prov. 14:14)
32. He, _____, it.
33. City in Alaska.
34. Daniel, Isaiah, Amos, etc.
37. Who...had seen the grace of God,
    was _____. (Acts 11:23)
38. Before Abraham was, _____ _____.
    (John 8:58; 2 words)
39. Omri's son who became king.
    (1 Kgs. 16:29)
41. Win, lose, _____.
42. Ocean Pacific (abbr.).
43. Receive not the grace of God in
    _____. (2 Cor. 6:1)

46. This animal rebuked Balaam.
    (Num. 22:28)
47. To return to an earlier state.
48. Company (abbr.)
49. The _____ killeth, but the spirit
    giveth life. (2 Cor. 3:6)
50. The _____ shall rejoice. (Isa. 35:1)

DOWN CLUES

2. Ye _____, submit yourselves unto
   the elder. (1 Pet. 5:5)
3. Edward (abbr.).
4. The vail of the temple was _____.
   (Matt. 27:51)
5. You (biblical).
6. Speak _____ of no man. (Titus 3:2)
7. Not out.
9. The sleep of a _____ man is sweet.
   (Ec. 5:12; Am. spelling)
11. For your sakes he became _____.
    (2 Cor. 8:9)
13. Jesus healed the son of a _____.
    (John 4:46-50)
16. Tribulation _____ patience.
    (Rom. 5:3)
17. Whose mother was removed from
    being queen? (1 Kgs. 15:9-13)
20. A slow-moving tennis ball.
22. Institution for the sick.
25. Graven image.
28. Tree mentioned in Isaiah 44:14.
29. Less expensive.
30. A primary color.
31. Remember me when thou _____
    into thy kingdom. (Luke 23:42)
35. He...shall _____ up us also.
    (2 Cor. 4:14)
36. Thy faith hath _____ thee.
    (Luke 7:50)

40. Thou sowest...but _____ grain. (1 Cor. 15:37)
42. Iron.
44. It is.

45. I _____ that through ignorance ye did it. (Acts 3:17)
48. Credit (abbr.).

PUZZLE 12

Diana Rowland

ACROSS CLUES

1. _____ him in a manager. (Luke 2:7)
5. _____, the beloved physician. (Col. 4:14)
9. Standing afar _____...to me _____ sinner. (Luke 18:13; 2 words)
10. The name of the well _____. (Gen. 26:20)
11. And sold a _____ for wine. (Joel 3:3)
13. Will _____ rather say unto him. (Luke 17:8)
15. Beautician's wave.
18. The elder unto the elect _____. (2 John 1)
19. I _____ me men singers. (Ec. 2:8)
20. For every _____ is known by his own fruit. (Luke 6:44)
21. They marvelled _____ his answer. (Luke 20:26)
22. Come down _____ my child die. (John 4:49)
23. Many shall rejoice _____ his birth. (Luke 1:14)
24. I am _____ both to the Greeks. (Rom. 1:14)
28. _____ ye from him. (2 Sam. 11:15)
32. On the east side of _____. (Num. 34:11)
33. _____ the father of Abner. (1 Sam. 14:51)
34. Shelemiah the son of _____. (Jer. 36:26)
37. _____ the son of Jeroham. (1 Chron. 9:12)
40. So shall it _____ also in the days. (Luke 17:26)
41. His mother's name also was _____. (2 Kgs. 18:2)
43. _____ is not here, but is risen. (Luke 24:6)
44. Eloi, _____ lama sabachthani? (Mark 15:34)
47. _____, I say unto you. (Luke 7:26)
48. And Hushim, the sons of _____. (1 Chron. 7:12)
50. Behold the _____ of God. (John 1:29)
51. Love worketh no _____ to his neighbour. (Rom. 13:10)
52. The wicked _____ their bow. (Ps. 11:2)
53. Of _____, the family of the Eranites. (Num. 26:36)
55. Kish the son of _____. (2 Chron. 29:12)
57. Put a _____ on his hand. (Luke 15:22)
58. Every _____ at the feast of the passover. (Luke 2:41)

DOWN CLUES

1. Lo, the angel of the _____ came upon them. (Luke 2:9)
2. Of _____ great eagle, that she might _____. (Rev. 12:14; 2 words)
3. _____ thou be the Son of God. (Luke 4:3)
4. Is in _____ of eternal damnation. (Mark 3:29)
5. He wrote a _____ after this manner. (Acts 23:25)
6. He followeth not with _____. (Luke 9:49)
7. All these have I _____ from my youth up. (Luke 18:21)
8. Jamin, and _____. (1 Chron. 2:27)
11. He was exceeding _____. (Luke 23:8)
12. _____ _____ no pleasant bread. (Dan. 10:3; 2 words)
14. All that handle the _____. (Ezek. 27:29)
16. Wilt thou _____ it up in three days? (John 2:20)
17. That ye _____ withal it shall be. (Luke 6:38)

25. Cast the _____ away. (Matt. 13:48)
26. _____ them about thy neck. (Prov. 6:21)
27. But _____ thing is needful. (Luke 10:42)
29. Of his kingdom there shall be no _____. (Luke 1:33)
30. Hot beverage.
31. Jerimoth, and _____, five. (1 Chron. 7:7)
34. From the blood of _____ unto the blood. (Luke 11:51)
35. When _____ was dead. (1 Chron. 1:44)
36. _____ wait for him. (Luke 11:54)
37. Do to _____ and her king...shall ye take for _____ prey..._____ thee an ambush. (Josh. 8:2; 3 words)
38. Even as _____ _____ gathereth her chickens. (Matt. 23:37; 2 words)
39. There was there an _____ of many swine. (Luke 8:32)
42. I will punish _____ in Babylon. (Jer. 51:44)
45. Fill an _____ of it to be kept. (Ex. 16:32)
46. Zaccur, and _____. (1 Chron. 24:27)
48. The son of _____ was over the tribute. (1 Kgs. 4:6)
49. This is the _____. (Luke 20:14)
54. They might find _____ accusation. (Luke 6:7)
56. All shall _____ thine. (Luke 4:7)

27

PUZZLE 13

Evelyn M. Boyington

ACROSS CLUES

1. But _____ unto you. (Matt. 23:13)
4. A time to rend, and a time to _____. (Ec. 3:7)
7. The name of his city was _____. (1 Chron. 1:50)
10. The children of Aram; Uz, and _____. (Gen. 10:23)
11. Upon the great _____ of their right foot. (Ex. 29:20)
12. God...is _____ to deliver us. (Dan. 3:17)
14. Source.
16. You fathers, where _____ they? (Zech. 1:5)
17. _____ no violence to the stranger. (Jer. 22:3)
19. Eye hath not seen, nor _____ heard. (1 Cor. 2:9)
20. Fear and the _____, and the snare, are upon thee. (Isa. 24:17)
21. Ye have made it a _____ of thieves. (Mark 11:17)
22. Thou didst _____ on the Lord. (2 Chron. 16:8)
24. Golf score.
25. She bound the scarlet _____ in the window. (Josh. 2:21)
26. 4 in Roman numerals.
27. All they are brass, and _____, and iron. (Ezek. 22:18)
28. He _____ to meet him. (Gen. 29:13)
29. Joseph was a goodly _____. (Gen. 39:6)
32. _____ me, and be merciful unto me. (Ps. 26:11)
35. Edible grain.
36. Pronoun.
37. Why are _____ so fearful? (Mark 4:40)
38. My yoke is _____. (Matt. 11:30)
40. His eyes shall be _____ with wine. (Gen. 49:12)
41. Promises of God in him are yea, and in him _____. (2 Cor. 1:20)

43. How long will it be _____ thou be quiet? (Jer. 47:6)
44. _____ also, which went with Abram. (Gen. 13:5)
45. He maketh me to _____ down in green pastures. (Ps. 23:2)
46. Southern state (abbr.).
47. Their _____ calveth. (Job 21:10)
48. _____ smoke the ass. (Num. 22:23)
51. Early day.
53. Were there not _____ cleansed? (Luke 17:17)
54. Article.
55. Cereal grain.
56. The _____ number of them. (Num. 3:48)
57. Make us _____ together in heavenly places. (Eph. 2:6)

DOWN CLUES

1. _____ hath believed our report. (Isa. 53:1)
2. _____ Father which art in heaven. (Matt. 6:9)
3. _____ the Mahavite. (1 Chron. 11:46)
4. _____ up the gift of God. (2 Tim. 1:6)
5. Age.
6. When _____ were children. (Gal. 4:3)
7. The Lord taketh my _____ with them that help me. (Ps. 118:7)
8. Lincoln.
9. 49 in Roman numerals.
13. God planted a garden eastward in _____. (Gen. 2:8)
15. Respect to him that weareth the _____ clothing. (Jam. 2:3)
16. The birds of the _____ have nests. (Matt. 8:20)
18. Not _____ thing hath failed. (Josh. 23:14)
20. She took a _____, and poured them out. (2 Sam. 13:9)
21. Come and _____. (John 21:12)
22. Tear.
23. Adam called his wife's name _____. (Gen. 3:20)

28

Across/Down clues:

24. She fastened it with the _____. (Judg. 16:14)
25. There is a _____ here. (John 6:9)
27. Young child.
28. Peleg... begat _____. (Gen. 11:18)
30. I am the _____ of Sharon. (Song of Sol. 2:1)
31. Consider what I _____. (2 Tim. 2:7)
32. Thy _____ and thy staff they comfort me. (Ps. 23:4)
33. _____ hath not seen. (1 Cor. 2:9)
34. It is appointed unto _____ once to die. (Heb. 9:27)
36. It doth not _____ appear what we shall be. (1 John 3:2)
38. Lamprey.
39. Balak... hath brought me from _____. (Num. 23:7)

40. Put pure frankincense upon each _____. (Lev. 24:7)
41. To be troubled.
42. Neither desire thou his dainty _____. (Prov. 23:6)
44. Solitary.
45. Let the dry _____ appear. (Gen. 1:9)
47. Unto thee will I _____, O Lord. (Ps. 28:1)
48. David arose from off his _____. (2 Sam. 11:2)
49. _____ the son of Abdiel. (1 Chron. 5:15)
50. The angels of God _____ him. (Gen. 32:1)
52. Conjunction.
53. It is not for you _____ know. (Acts 1:7)

29

PUZZLE 14

Evelyn M. Boyington

ACROSS CLUES

1. Enemy.
4. _____ shalt thou serve. (Deut. 10:20)
7. Beno, and Shoham, and Zaccur, and _____. (1 Chron. 24:27)
11. All the rivers _____ into the sea. (Ec. 1:7)
12. Provoked the _____ One of Israel unto anger. (Is. 1:4)
13. The city had no _____ of the sun. (Rev. 21:23)
14. One who decrees.
16. Urn.
17. The Pharisees began to _____ him vehemently. (Luke 11:53)
18. Happenings.
20. Thou shalt not call her name Sarai, but _____. (Gen. 17:15)
22. Every one beareth _____s. (Song of Sol. 6:6)
23. Anab, and Eshtemoh, and _____. (Josh. 15:50)
24. The slothful man _____ not that which he took in hunting. (Prov. 12:27)
28. Unit of weight.
29. A distinct type.
30. Born.
31. Etched.
33. The bright and morning _____. (Rev. 22:16)
34. To whom be glory for _____. (Rom. 11:36)
35. Thou art _____. (Ps. 139:8)
36. Thou shalt not make unto thee any _____ image. (Ex. 20:4)
39. The fathers have eaten a _____ grape. (Jer. 31:29)
40. The desert shall rejoice, and blossom as the _____. (Is. 35:1)
41. The biology of heredity.
45. A thought.
46. Ages.
47. Until the day that _____ entered into the ark. (Luke 17:27)
48. Then bring _____. And he cast it into the pot. (2 Kgs. 4:41)
49. Till I shall _____ about it. (Luke 13:8)
50. Acquired.

DOWN CLUES

1. We have walked to and_____ through the earth. (Zech. 1:11)
2. _____ Father which art in heaven. (Matt. 6:9)
3. Ye have in heaven a better and an _____ substance. (Heb. 10:34)
4. Sharpening stone.
5. French island.
6. I come quickly; and _____ _____ is with me. (Rev. 22:12; 2 words)
7. _____ to themselves instruments of musick. (Amos 6:5)
8. Lima or snap.
9. They _____ not day and night. (Rev. 4:8)
10. March date.
12. For the Lord most _____ is terrible. (Ps. 47:2)
15. Esrom begat _____. (Matt. 1:3)
19. Clamp.
20. Satisfy.
21. And _____ they tell him of her. (Mark 1:30)
22. A liquid skin cleanser.
24. Hath greatly offended, and _____ himself upon them. (Ezek. 25:12)

Across/Down clues:

25. And _____ into the sepulchre, they saw a young man. (Mark 16:5)

26. _____ their claws in pieces. (Zech. 11:16)

27. Behold, _____ I am. (1 Sam. 12:3)

29. Wherefore God also _____ them up to uncleanness. (Rom. 1:24)

32. He to whom the Son will _____ him. (Luke 10:22)

33. The Lord _____ him in. (Gen. 7:16)

35. Thou sawest the feet and _____. (Dan. 2:41)

36. Forbidding.

37. Jehu _____ in a chariot. (2 Kgs. 9:16)

38. Am I _____ _____, or a whale? (Job 7:12; 2 words)

39. Catch.

42. Airport code to Erie, Pennsylvania.

43. Pigeon sound.

44. _____ thine house in order. (Isa. 38:1)

PUZZLE 15

Valerie Barrett

ACROSS CLUES

1. Joseph's firstborn. (Gen. 41:51)
10. Kings of armies did flee _____. (Ps. 68:12)
11. Then _____ my present. (Gen. 33:10)
14. _____ with her suburbs. (Josh. 21:32)
16. Cut off the ropes of the _____. (Acts 27:32)
17. Do they not _____ that device evil? (Prov. 14:22)
18. Gather a certain _____ every day. (Ex. 16:4)
20. Greatly _____ be praised. (Ps. 48:1)
21. Built there an altar, and called the place _____ beth-el. (Gen. 35:7)
22. Had devils long time, and _____ no clothes. (Luke 8:27)
25. Noah begat three sons, _____, Ham, and Japheth. (Gen. 6:10)
26. Puttest thy _____ in a rock. (Num. 24:21)
27. _____, every one that thirsteth. (Is. 55:1)
28. Judge me, O God, _____plead. (Ps. 43:1)
31. Shechem which is in the land of _____. (Gen. 33:18)
33. For the _____ that is in the land of Assyria. (Isa. 7:18)
34. Ye shall not _____ my face. (Gen. 43:3)
36. They _____ to and fro. (Ps. 107:27; past tense)
38. Thou art Simon the son of _____. (John 1:42)
40. Driven up and down in _____. (Acts 27:27)
42. As the _____, because he cheweth the cud. (Lev. 11:4)
44. Benjamin's _____ was five times. (Gen. 43:34)
45. Men shall _____ him out of his place. (Job 27:23)
46. _____ was concubine to Eliphaz. (Gen. 36:12)

DOWN CLUES

1. I will _____ thy seed to multiply. (Gen. 26:4)
2. Thou shalt set _____ unto the Lord. (Ex. 13:12)
3. There were _____ windows. (Ezek. 41:26)
4. To pass his _____, his strange act. (Isa. 28:21)
5. Israel went into the midst of the _____. (Ex. 14:22)
6. _____, Judah's firstborn. (Gen. 38:7)
7. Two men of the _____s strove. (Ex. 2:13)
8. An adder...that _____ the horse. (Gen. 49:17)
9. They shall _____ ashamed. (Hosea 4:19)
12. Having a live _____ in his hand. (Isa. 6:6)
13. Thou shalt not _____ of it. (Gen. 2:17)
15. The _____ of the children of Israel. (Ex. 28:9)
19. They shall call his name _____. (Matt. 1:23)
23. _____ unjust man is an abomination. (Prov. 29:27)

32

24. Cast them into the _____ _____. (Ex. 10:19)
25. And thou his _____, O Belshazzar. (Dan. 5:22)
27. Sons of Reuben: _____, and Phallu. (Gen. 46:9)
28. So _____ departed, as the Lord had spoken. (Gen. 12:4)
29. As though he _____ any thing. (Acts 17:25)
30. The roebuck, and the fallow _____(s). (Deut. 14:5)
32. The similitude of _____ transgression. (Rom. 5:14)
35. The children of Gad called the altar _____. (Josh. 22:34)
37. Whithersoever the governor _____eth. (Jam. 3:4)
39. Heber's wife took a _____ of the tent. (Judg. 4:21)
41. Cast down your slain _____. (Ezek. 6:4)
43. The abbreviation for the 17th book of the Old Testament.

PUZZLE 16

Valerie Barrett

ACROSS CLUES

1. The _____ said unto the younger. (Gen. 19:31)
7. The kingdom of _____ king of Bashan. (Num. 32:33)
9. He had _____ in the grave four days. (John 11:17)
10. A greeting.
11. Hear I _____ you, ye sons of Levi. (Num. 16:8)
13. A faithful _____ is health. (Prov. 13:17)
15. Nothing: _____ro.
16. Lord shall _____ to me another son. (Gen. 30:24)
17. _____ the son of Nathan. (2 Sam. 23:36)
18. With the _____ of the sword. (Gen. 34:26)
20. Bored a hole in the _____. (2 Kgs. 12:9)
21. Even _____ the tongue is a little member. (Jam. 3:5)
22. _____, the beloved physician. (Col. 4:14)
23. For, _____, the wicked bend their bow. (Ps. 11:2)
25. Blessed are ye that _____ beside all waters. (Isa. 32:20)
26. Achar, the troubler of _____. (1 Chron. 2:7)
30. Went forth to _____ into the land. (Gen. 12:5)
31. _____ that time the Lord said. (Deut. 10:1)
32. _____ the son of Kish. (1 Sam. 10:21)
34. Speak anything _____. (Dan. 3:29)
35. And _____ her brother said unto her. (2 Sam. 13:20)
40. The dove found _____ rest. (Gen. 8:9)
41. Filled with the _____ of the ointment. (John 12:3)
42. And if thy oblation _____ a meat offering. (Lev. 2:5)
43. _____ sinful nation. (Isa. 1:4)
45. Brought them unto _____ to see. (Gen. 2:19)
46. Which perished at _____dor. (Ps. 83:10)
47. An abbreviation for the third book before the New Testament; also an old, ugly woman.
48. _____ it in their hearts. (Jer. 31:33)
49. Offerings of the Lord made _____ fire. (Lev. 24:9)

DOWN CLUES

1. Their faces shall be as _____. (Isa. 13:8)
2. God said unto Moses. _____ _____. (Ex. 3:14)
3. They smote him under the fifth _____. (2 Sam. 4:6)
4. Shall this man be a _____ unto us. (Ex. 10:7)
5. Jemuel, and Jamin, and _____. (Gen. 46:10)
6. I will now put forth a _____ unto you. (Judg. 14:12)
7. Whether poor _____ rich. (Ruth 3:10)
8. Baldness is come upon _____. (Jer. 47:5)
11. I will break the _____ of your power. (Lev. 26:19)
12. Feathers with _____ gold. (Ps. 68:13)

1	2	3	4			5	6			7	8	
9						10			11			12
13				14							15	
				16				17				
18	19					20						
21			22							23		
						24		25				
26	27	28	29			30			31			
32				33								
34				35	36		37			38	39	
	40			41						42		
43	44			45					46			
47			48					49				

14. But _____ ministered before the Lord. (1 Sam. 2:18)

19. In his word _____ I hope. (Ps. 130:5)

23. One _____ for the Lord. (Lev. 16:8)

24. This great fire will _____ us. (Deut. 5:25)

25. As he was about to _____ into Syria. (Acts 20:3)

26. The vision of _____ the son of Amoz. (Isa. 1:1)

27. A shortened name for the ninth book of the Old Testament.

28. Let this _____ be under thy hand. (Isa. 3:6)

29. The Lord _____ will be a refuge. (Ps. 9:9)

33. Of Manasseh, _____ the son of Susi. (Num. 13:11)

36. And there went over a ferry _____. (2 Sam. 19:18)

37. It hath consumed _____ of Moab. (Num. 21:28)

38. My son, _____ my voice. (Gen. 27:8)

39. O ye sons of _____. (Ps. 4:2)

41. And all that handle the _____. (Ezek. 27:29)

44. _____: and he smelleth the battle afar off. (Job 39:25)

35

PUZZLE 17
Lee Esch

ACROSS CLUES

1. The Son of man is come to save that which was ____. (Matt. 18:11)
5. Let down your ____ for a draught. (Luke 5:4)
9. Low-ranking soldier (abbr.).
12. Take thine ____, eat, drink and be merry. (Luke 12:19)
13. Lengthy, lyrical poems.
14. River (Spanish).
15. Metric unit.
16. Speaks of.
18. Blueprints.
20. Takes to court.
21. Grinned.
24. Frosted.
26. Ties (one's shoes).
27. Monotony.
30. A city in Oklahoma.
31. Setting.
33. That from which metal is extracted.
34. I would that all ____ ____ even as I myself. (1 Cor. 7:7; 2 words)
36. Stolen waters are ____. (Prov. 9:17)
38. Not my will, but thine, be ____. (Luke 22:42)
39. Thunderous rains.
40. ____ Stravinsky.
42. Small unclean animal. (Lev. 11:29)
44. Highway directories.
46. David dwelt in the ____. (2 Sam. 5:9)
50. For ____ have sinned. (Rom 3:23)
51. The home of Salt Lake City.
52. He came ____ his own. (John 1:11)
53. Major football organization (abbr.).
54. Sandwich shop.
55. Sly, suggestive look.

DOWN CLUES

1. Make bare the ____. (Isa. 47:2)
2. Boat paddle.
3. Social Security Administration (abbr.).
4. For the ____ of God is holy. (1 Cor. 3:17)
5. Desert wanderer.
6. God planted a garden eastward in ____. (Gen. 2:8)
7. Stress.
8. Supersonic transport (abbr.).
9. The Lord...plentifully rewardeth the ____ ____. (Ps. 31:23; 2 words)
10. I am the ____, ye are the branches. (John 15:5)
11. The waves thereof ____ themselves. (Jer. 5:22)
17. ____ ____ men as trees, walking. (Mark 8:24)
19. Diminish.
21. Close hard.
22. The word was ____ flesh. (John 1:14)
23. ____ ____ ____ ____ things through Christ. (Phil 4:13; 4 words)
25. Peaks.
27. For the ____ that is in the land of Assyria. (Isa. 7:18)
28. A city in Utah.
29. New York team.
32. Incinerate.
35. In the beginning was the ____. (John 1:1)
37. Neither have I desired the ____ day. (Jer. 17:16)

39. Japanese fish dish.
40. Tehran is its capital.
41. Country club sport.
43. Gem.
45. Wet dirt.

47. For there is _____ God.
    (Mark 12:32)
48. A fixed path of travel (abbr.).
49. Rocky hilltop.

PUZZLE 18

Lee Esch

ACROSS CLUES

1. Legislator. (abbr.).
4. But now is Christ risen from the _____. (1 Cor. 15:20)
8. For a good man some would even _____ to die. (Rom. 5:7)
12. There is none good but _____. (Matt. 19:17)
13. The Pharisees began to _____ him vehemently. (Luke 11:53)
14. Esau's other name. (Gen. 25:30)
15. National Institutes of Health. (abbr.).
16. Break sharply and quickly.
17. How unsearchable are his judgments, and his ways _____ finding out. (Rom. 11:33)
18. Fifth book of the Old Testament.
21. If I _____ touch but his clothes. (Mark 5:28)
22. Chronic drunkard.
23. Thou canst not make one _____ white or black. (Matt. 5:36)
25. Ye have made it a _____ of thieves. (Mark 11:17)
26. Be thou cast into the _____. (Mark 11:23)
29. A king of Judah. (1 Kgs. 15:9)
30. Dignity or composure.
32. Vase.
33. Miles per hour. (abbr.).
34. The beginning and the _____. (Rev. 21:6)
35. Small quarrel.
36. And all things _____ of God. (2 Cor. 5:18)
37. Company executive. (abbr.).
38. Is not this _____, _____ _____ of Joseph? (John 6:42; 3 words)
43. 100 centavos.
44. Sight-seeing trip.
45. The number of whom is as the sand of the _____. (Rev. 20:8)
47. A custard or fruit-filled tart.
48. Ova.
49. _____ tide.
50. Hint.
51. Sit for a photo.
52. Female deer.

DOWN CLUES

1. He that hath the _____ hath life. (1 John 5:12)
2. A city in Oklahoma.
3. The 16th book of the Old Testament.
4. Layered with dirt.
5. Sea eagle.
6. Mount Sinai. (Gal. 4:25)
7. Removes from position of power.
8. RR station.
9. The first man.
10. Pinkish.
11. Emergency Medical Technician (abbr.).
19. United Arab Republic (abbr.).
20. Silver and gold have I _____. (Acts 3:6)
23. Noah's second son. (Gen. 5:32)
24. Snake.
25. Therefore _____ the Jews persecute Jesus. (John 5:16)
26. They _____ it had been a spirit. (Mark 6:49)
27. Time period.
28. Go to the _____, thou sluggard. (Prov. 6:6)
30. South American country.

31. Ballroom dance.
35. Female sibling (abbr.).
36. Behold, the man is become _____ _____ of us. (Gen. 3:22; 2 words)
37. Poem division.
38. Congeal.
39. Isaac's oldest son. (Gen. 27:1)

40. He was afraid _____ _____ thither. (Matt. 2:22; 2 words)
41. Embraces.
42. Mountain where Moses died. (Deut. 32:49,50)
43. Private First Class (abbr.).
46. Pres. Lincoln's name (abbr.).

PUZZLE 19

Kathy Johnson

ACROSS CLUES

1. The name the angel called him. (Luke 2:21)
6. She bore a son, and called his name _____. (Gen. 4:25)
10. Why, what _____ hath he done? (Mark 15:14)
11. _____ of Tarsus. (Acts 9:11)
12. Cossack leader.
15. In the song, Jesus is _____ging on my heart strings.
16. The shorter version of the name Joshua.
18. The ninth book of the Old Testament.
20. The prophets prophesy _____ in my name. (Jer. 14:14)
22. When they saw the _____, they rejoiced. (Matt. 2:10)
23. _____, Lord! God! (Jer. 4:10)
25. _____ is the kingdom of God. (Mark 4:26)

26. Written not with _____, but with the Spirit. (2 Cor. 3:3)
27. This man denied Jesus three times.
29. East central state (abbr.).
31. The abbreviation for aluminum.
33. The first three letters of the alphabet.
35. _____ handmaid bare unto Abraham. (Gen. 25:12)
38. This woman was given to her husband as a reward for conquering a city. (Judg. 1:12)
41. A rodent.
42. My _____ is at hand. (Matt. 26:18)
43. It's not a he or a she, it's an _____.
44. Cast ballet.
45. All unrighteousness is _____. (1 John 5:17)
46. And a certain woman named _____, a seller of purple. (Acts 16:14)
47. No man putteth _____ wine into old bottles. (Luke 5:37)

DOWN CLUES

1. And _____ bowed his head. (2 Chron. 20:18)
2. Adam's wife.
3. _____ on my right hand. (Heb. 1:13)
4. A city in southwest Germany.
5. The opposite of *yes*.
7. The seventeenth book in the Old Testament.
8. The nineteenth letter in the Greek alphabet.
9. Very big.
13. Cain's brother.
14. Found the _____ tied by the door. (Mark 11:4)
17. Prefix meaning "saliva."
19. Fed you with milk, and not with _____. (1 Cor. 3:2)
21. Cursed is the ground for thy _____. (Gen. 3:17)
22. Reaping that I did not _____. (Luke 19:22)
24. _____ is not here. (Luke 24:6)
28. _____ had stolen the images. (Gen. 31:19)
30. This woman was banished by a king. (Es. 1)
32. And when _____ saw it, he built an altar before it. (Ex. 32:5)
34. The man who killed Abel.
36. Ye that love the Lord, _____ evil. (Ps. 97:10)
37. A type of soup.
39. The abbreviation of *centimeter*.
40. First _____ kit.
42. Seventh note.

PUZZLE 20

Janet W. Adkins

ACROSS CLUES

1. _____-a-brac.
5. Type of lettuce.
8. Canadian Indian tribe.
12. Sons of Benjamin... Ehi and ___. (Gen. 46:21)
13. Mouth.
14. _____ avis; rarity.
15. Vapor (prefix).
16. Prominent sea (abbr.).
17. Company that tries harder.
18. The _____ of the righteous is only good. (Prov. 11:23)
20. And mine hand shall be upon the prophets...that _____ lies. (Ezek. 13:9)
22. West Coast state (abbr.).
23. Greek letter.
24. _____ of errors.
27. That ye might be partakers of the divine _____. (2 Pet. 1:4)
31. Onassis.
32. Uncooked.
33. Orthodontist's product.
37. Death, and mourning, and _____. (Rev. 18:8)
40. The name of the wicked shall _____. (Prov. 10:7)
41. Compass direction.
42. See that ye _____ not him that speaketh. (Heb. 12:25)
45. And I thank Christ Jesus our Lord, who hath _____(d) me. (1 Tim. 1:12)
49. Ammihud, the son of _____. (1 Chron. 9:4)
50. Priest's robe.
52. Platform.
53. Render therefore to all their _____. (Rom. 13:7)
54. Bad (prefix).
55. Margarine.
56. This (Spanish).
57. South by east (abbr.).
58. A thready fragment.

DOWN CLUES

1. Nail with a small head.
2. Learning by repetition.
3. Belief systems (suffix).
4. God made _____ among us, that the Gentiles...should hear the gospel. (Acts 15:7)
5. Thy cheeks are _____ with rows of jewels. (Son of Sol. 1:10)
6. Mine product.
7. To cause dejection.
8. Tie.
9. River in India.
10. Ireland.
11. Take thine _____, eat, drink. (Luke 12:19)
19. Radiation measure.
21. _____'s _____ boy!
24. The fourth part of a _____ of dove's dung. (2 Kgs. 6:25)
25. Hockey name Bobby _____.
26. _____ Farrow.
28. Geber the son of _____ was in the country of Gilead. (1 Kgs. 4:19)
29. His father saw him..._____, and fell on his neck. (Luke 15:20)
30. Poor man had nothing, save one little _____ lamb. (2 Sam. 12:3)
34. Ocean trip.
35. Greek goddess of the dawn.
36. Cooks vegetables.

37. Lift up the hands...and the _____ knees. (Heb. 12:12)
38. Girl's name.
39. A grassy field.
42. Past tense of *ride*.
43. Australian flightless birds.

44. They shall _____ themselves, and curse their king. (Is. 8:21)
46. Indonesian island.
47. Ye have eaten the fruit of _____. (Hosea 10:13)
48. Employee stock ownership plan.
51. Experiment room.

PUZZLE 21

Janet W. Adkins

ACROSS CLUES

1. Places of experiment.
5. It hath consumed _____ of Moab. (Num. 21:28)
7. Esau sold his birthright for _____.
11. Solomon's grandson. (1 Chron. 3:10)
12. Mother of Hezekiah. (2 Kgs. 18:2)
13. These ought ye to _____ done. (Matt. 23:23)
14. Woman's headwear.
16. And she [Shuah] conceived again and bore a son,..._____. (Gen. 38:4)
17. There remained two in the camp ...one was _____. (Num. 11:26)
18. Saul _____ his thousands, and David his ten thousands. (1 Sam. 29:5)
21. That escapeth from the sword of Jehu shall _____ slay. (1 Kgs. 19:17)
25. Military leader (abbr.).
28. For ye tithe mint and _____ and...herbs. (Luke 11:42)
30. Between (prefix).
31. Nicodemus...brought a mixture of myrrh and _____s. (John 19:39)
33. He that endureth to the _____ shall be saved. (Matt. 10:22)
35. V.P. Al _____.
36. Smallest.
38. And _____ orah a prophetess... judged Israel. (Judg. 4:4)
40. Ballet step (French).
41. Element.
43. Egg _____ yong.
45. Not with _____, as menpleasers. (Eph. 6:6)

50. Repetitive learning.
53. Not plural.
54. One thing on a list.
55. Telecommunications for the deaf (abbr.).
56. Optical device.
57. Puts on clothing.
58. Direction.
59. Soul, take thine _____. (Luke 12:19)

DOWN CLUES

1. And death and hell were cast unto the _____ of fire. (Rev. 20:14)
2. And the Lord had respect unto _____ and to his offering. (Gen. 4:4)
3. Their glory shall fly away like a _____. (Hosea 9:11)
4. Sons of Obed-edom..._____ the fourth. (1 Chron. 26:4)
5. Belonging to Abraham.
6. Firearm.
7. Displaying.
8. Sunbathe.
9. Madame Peron.
10. Cyst.
12. Joshua sent men from Jericho to _____. (Josh 7:2)
15. Head (abbr.).
19. Now the sons of _____ were sons of Belial. (1 Sam. 2:12)
20. Tribute to whom tribute is _____. (Rom. 13:7)
22. No man shall _____ me... (2 Cor. 11:10)
23. Greek goddess.
24. Greek god of war.
25. Young cow.
26. "Just as I am without one _____."
27. Turn over account (abbr.).

44

Down (clues shown)

29. Whose _____ is destruction. (Phil. 3:19)
32. Regards highly.
34. The Lord of hosts shall _____ them. (Zech. 9:15)
37. Plaything.
39. Bjorn _____.
42. Relaxes.
44. Egg or droplet.

46. A thousand shall fall at thy _____. (Ps. 91:7)
47. Outer pelvic bones.
48. Storage vessels.
49. Gaelic.
50. That he might _____ him out of their hands. (Gen. 37:22)
51. Relating to the ear (prefix).
52. Give it unto him which hath _____ talents. (Matt. 25:28)

PUZZLE 22

Janet W. Adkins

ACROSS CLUES

1. Where Paul addressed the Athenians. (Acts 17:22)
8. Dull.
12. Short for Abraham.
13. The sons of _____; Arah, Haniel, and Rezia. (1 Chron. 7:39)
14. Take thine _____ eat, drink, and be merry. (Luke 12:19)
15. To them which were in _____. (1 Sam. 30:29)
17. Father of Isaac.
19. Belonging to a righteous king. (1 Kgs. 15:11)
20. And the _____ went and called the child's mother. (Ex. 2:8)
21. Nickname of Hephzibah.
22. Girl's name.
23. How dogs drink.
26. America.
29. Sons of Onam...Shammai, and _____. (1 Chron. 2:28)
30. Shalt not abhor an _____. (Deut. 23:7)
34. And _____, and Abimael, and Sheba. (Gen. 10:28)
35. Uncommon.
36. Mouth.
37. School subject (abbr.).
38. Rocky hill.
41. Cease.
45. Killer whale.
46. Let him eat at _____. (1 Cor. 11:34)
47. The vision of _____. (Obad. 1:1)
51. Retired (abbr.).
52. Courageous man.
53. The Dalai _____.
55. He is of _____; ask him. (John 9:21)
56. For we have seen his _____ in the east. (Matt. 2:2)
57. And he conferred...with _____ the priest. (1 Kgs. 1:7)

DOWN CLUES

1. They could not drink the waters of _____. (Ex. 15:23)
2. Those that walk in pride he is able to _____. (Dan. 4:37)
3. Rejuvenated auto tire.
4. And the children of Aram; Uz, and _____. (Gen. 10:23)
5. Negative prefix.
6. Andean best of burden.
7. Jacob's father-in-law. (Gen. 28:1-2)
8. Though he were _____, yet shall he live. (John 11:25)
9. A cheer.
10. _____ took the silver. (1 Kgs. 15:18)
11. Bachelor of engineering of mines (abbr.).
16. Suppose.
18. _____ Tin Tin.
23. Type of retriever (abbr.).
24. Woman's name.
25. Buddy.
27. Yes (Spanish).
28. _____ the name of Jesus every knee should bow. (Phil. 2:10)
29. An oak...that pertained unto _____. (Judg. 6:11)
30. Before.
31. From _____ even to Beer-sheba. (Judg. 20:1)
32. Organization (abbr.).

33. Hoshea...sent messengers to _____ king of Egypt. (2 Kgs. 17:4)
38. Prefix meaning "three."
39. Florida city.
40. By faith the harlot _____ perished not. (Heb. 11:31)
42. Jewish holy book.
43. I am Alpha and _____. (Rev. 1:8)

44. Then Simon _____ having a sword drew it. (John 18:10)
45. Smell.
47. _____ and ahs.
48. Wager.
49. Sons of Jether; Jephunneh, and Pispah, and _____. (1 Chron. 7:38)
50. Sheep's cry.
54. Musical note.

47

PUZZLE 23

Janet W. Adkins

ACROSS CLUES

1. Headwear.
4. Girl's name.
8. Delete (typesetter's term).
12. Genetic material.
13. French city.
14. Black (poetic).
15. _____ and outs.
16. Leaving us an example, that ye should follow his _____s. (1 Pet. 2:21)
17. Englishman.
18. Get up and about.
20. To chant.
22. Mine _____ is as nothing before thee. (Ps. 39:5)
23. Dove's sound.
24. We remember...the melons,...leeks, and the _____. (Num. 11:5)
27. The king's chamberlains, Bigthan and _____. (Es. 2:21)
31. Kinsman (abbr.).
32. Dessert.
33. Do not interpretations _____ to God? (Gen. 40:8)
37. Thy _____ shall be to thy husband. (Gen. 3:16)
40. Civil Aeronautics Authority. (abbr.).
41. Historical period.
42. Wager.
45. Elevated train.
46. Unoccupied.
50. The sons of Mushi; Mahli, and _____. (1 Chron. 23:23)
52. Hawaiian welcome presents.
54. Neither/_____.
55. Capital of Peru.
56. It is appointed unto men _____ to die. (Heb. 9:27)
57. Power maker.
58. Yet will they _____ upon the Lord. (Micah 3:11)
59. Edgar Allan's kin.
60. Whom do men _____ that I the Son of man am?(Matt. 16:13)

DOWN CLUES

1. Manger.
2. Queen _____ furniture.
3. As the flower of the grass he shall _____ away. (Jam. 1:10)
4. Every man shall pitch with the _____ of their father's house. (Num. 2:2)
5. As vinegar upon _____ (pl.), so is he that singeth songs to a heavy heart. (Prov. 25:20)
6. Frozen water.
7. Describe.
8. I am _____ both to the Greeks and ...Barbarians. (Rom. 1:14)
9. River in Spain.
10. Cut of meat.
11. Between (prefix).
19. Chinese religion.
21. As the days of _____. (Matt. 24:37)
24. Sphere.
25. Born.
26. Love worketh no _____ to his neighbour. (Rom. 13:10)
28. Upon, over (prefix).
29. _____, we would see Jesus. (John 12:21)
30. Part of a giggle.
34. In the work cited.

1	2	3		4	5	6	7		8	9	10	11
12				13					14			
15				16					17			
18			19				20	21				
			22				23					
24	25	26					27			28	29	30
31										32		
33			34	35	36		37	38	39			
			40				41					
42	43	44		45			46			47	48	49
50			51		52	53				54		
55					56					57		
58					59					60		

35. Scottish *no.*
36. Horse's gait.
37. Graven by art and man's _____. (Acts 17:29)
38. Expunges.
39. Internal pouch.
42. A _____ and a pomegranate. (Ex. 39:26)
43. Singer _____ Gorme.

44. Son of Ishmael. (Gen. 25:13-15)
47. The _____ are a people not strong. (Prov. 30:25)
48. A suddenly bright star.
49. Salver.
51. The herd _____ violently down steep place. (Luke 8:33)
53. _____ch walked with God: and he was not (Gen. 5:24)

PUZZLE 24

Janet W. Adkins

ACROSS CLUES

1. Indian tribe of Peru.
5. Turned to the land of _____ l. (1 Sam. 13:17)
9. Fuel.
12. Fly away like a _____. (Hosea 9:11)
13. Unwanted plant.
14. Form of *to be.*
15. A bright thought.
16. "Praise Jehovah."
18. The sin of Judah is written with...the point of a _____. (Jer. 17:1)
19. Form of medicine.
20. Symbol for tantalum.
21. Lawyer (abbr.).
22. Travel chest.
24. And their coast was from...all the kingdom of _____. (Josh. 13:30)
25. Women's patriotic organization.
28. Against me do they devise my _____. (Ps. 41:7)
29. Uncle (Spanish).
30. Soccer great.
31. Shoe width.
32. "Strength" (Heb.).
33. Christmas song.
34. Thou _____ the man. (2 Sam. 12:7)
36. Unusual occurrence.
37. Amasa was a man's son, whose name was _____. (2 Sam. 17:25)
40. Belonging to Ali.
41. The Lord is my _____. (Ps. 23:1)
43. And he came and touched the _____. (Luke 7:14)
46. Meadow.
47. Opera solo.
48. Company insignia.
49. Ever (poetic).
50. Malt beverage.
51. And Seth lived a hundred and five years, and begat _____. (Gen. 5:6)

DOWN CLUES

1. In the same place.
2. Nests.
3. Therefore if any man be in Christ, he is a new _____. (2 Cor. 5:17)
4. As an _____ harder than flint have I made thy forehead. (Ezek. 3:9)
5. Large white birds.
6. Retained.
7. Of the sons of Bani...Maadi, Amram, and _____. (Ezra 10:34)
8. Skilled.
9. Early France.
10. Seed covering.
11. For he hath founded it upon the _____. (Ps. 24:2)
17. Put flame to the candle.
21. The house that was builded these many years _____. (Ezra 5:11)
22. Article.
23. Ye tithe mint and _____ and herbs. (Luke 11:42)
24. He shall pour _____ upon it. (Lev. 2:1)
25. I am in _____ daily, everyone mocketh me. (Jer. 20:7)
26. Great amount (2 words).
27. Because thou didst _____ on the Lord. (2 Chron. 16:8)
29. Asian holiday.
30. Lord, speakest thou this _____ unto us. (Luke 12:41)
33. The fourth part of a _____ of dove's dung. (2 Kgs. 6:25)
34. Arpeggio (abbr.).

35. I will make mention of _____ and Babylon. (Ps. 87:4)
36. Detection device.
37. When they had gone through the _____ unto Paphos. (Acts 13:6)
38. Give his angels charge over _____. (Ps. 91:11)
39. _____, O Israel: The Lord our God is one Lord. (Deut. 6:4)
40. Type of cheese.
42. Before.
44. The self.
45. Mrs. Jimmy Carter.

PUZZLE 25

ACROSS CLUES

1. First person pronoun.
2. An insect abundant in Palestine. (Prov. 6:6)
4. A basket of _____ fruit. (Amos 8:2)
8. A negative reply .
9. Teach thee in the way which thou shalt _____. (Ps. 32:8)
10. In regard to.
11. Hebrew prophet swallowed by a great fish.
13. He made the _____ also. (Gen. 1:16)
14. To exist; to live.
15. Which is Christ in you, the _____ of glory. (Col. 1:27)
18. United States of America (abbr.).
20. Thou shalt not make unto thee any _____ image. (Ex. 20:4)
22. Be _____ your sin will find you out. (Num. 32:23)
24. Mary... _____ at Jesus' feet. (Luke 10:39)
25. A coarse file.
27. An aquatic carnivorous animal with flippers.
30. An exclamation of surprise.
32. I am the _____ of Sharon. (Song of Sol. 2:1)
33. Associated Press (abbr.).
35. _____, I am with you always. (Matt. 28:20)
36. Sign of God's covenant with Noah.
41. A prefix meaning "not."
42. Innings Pitched (abbr.).
43. An early king of Edom. (Gen. 36:37)
44. No man is _____ of life. (Job. 24:22)
45. Fire that _____ between *the* cherubims. (Ezek. 10:7)
46. Rosemary's nickname.
47. Neuter pronoun.
48. Neither too good nor too bad.
50. Hath _____ man condemned thee. (John 8:10)
51. They...came down to _____. (Acts 16:8)
52. The garden where Adam and Eve lived. (Gen. 2:8)

DOWN CLUES

1. Belonging to me.
2. Popular middle name for girl.
3. Man who built the ark. (Gen. 6)
4. _____ our eyes wait upon the Lord. (Ps. 123:2)
5. A female parent.
6. To sin.
7. Rephah was his son, also _____. (1 Chron. 7:25)
11. God's son.
12. Pigs.
14. Vehicle for public conveyance of passengers.
16. We commune with God through _____.
17. Man did _____ angels' food. (Ps. 78:25)
19. Ye _____ a chosen generation. (1 Pet. 2:9)
21. Symbol for sodium.
23. First.
26. Sung by one person.
28. Ring.
29. To the seven churches which are in _____. (Rev. 1:4)
31. A dried grape. (1 Sam. 25:18)
34. The planet farthest from the sun.

37. Took away the sheep, and the oxen, and the _____. (1 Sam. 27:9)
38. Deborah was Rebekah's _____. (Gen. 35:8)
39. Without shedding of _____ is no remission. (Heb. 9:22)
40. Four-wheeled vehicle.
45. _____ will have all men to be saved. (1 Tim. 2:4)
49. Southeast (abbr.).

PUZZLE 26

Pamela Jensen

ACROSS CLUES

1. All things work together for _____. (Rom. 8:28)
5. Thou shalt be a _____. (Gen. 12:2)
12. Provoke not your children to _____. (Col. 3:21)
14. Capably.
15. The Lord _____ high is mightier. (Ps. 93:4)
16. And _____ her head. (2 Kgs. 9:30)
17. His deadly _____ was healed. (Rev. 13:3)
18. Weeded, cultivated.
20. National Recovery Administration (abbr.).
21. _____ the time appointed. (Gen. 18:14)
22. Ensign (abbr.).
23. He _____ is my rock. (Ps. 62:2)
25. A precious stone.
27. Royal Society (abbr.).
28. Vigor, strength.
29. For our lamps are _____ out. (Matt. 25:8)
30. Sent men from Jericho to _____. (Josh. 7:2)
31. Indicates three.
33. Earns, gains.
35. _____, thou art the Son of God. (John 1:49)
38. Turned into the _____ of summer. (Ps. 32:4)
40. Spirit of adoption, whereby we cry, _____. (Rom. 8:15)
41. Because thou didst _____ on the Lord. (2 Chron. 16:8)
42. A period of time.
43. Perhaps, possibly.
45. Let him _____. (Jam. 1:6)
47. Learn to _____ well. (Is. 1:17)
49. Shall we _____ with the sword? (Luke 22:49)
51. He that shall _____ unto the end. (Mark 13:13)
55. I _____ the door. (John 10:9)
56. Have _____ to righteousness. (Rom. 9:30)
57. The Lord stirred _____ the spirit. (Ezra 1:1)

DOWN CLUES

1. A _____ of sycamore fruit. (Amos 7:14)
2. Leeks, and the _____, and the garlick. (Num. 11:5)
3. Fabled giants.
4. But in _____ and in truth. (1 John 3:18)
6. Sin is the transgression of the _____. (1 John 3:4)
7. Horns of ivory and _____. (Ezek. 27:15)
8. To pronounce indistinctly.
9. I ever taught in the _____. (John 18:20)
10. Do thyself _____ harm. (Acts 16:28)
11. Strain at a _____. (Matt. 23:24)
13. Rural Delivery (abbr.).
19. An individual part of a whole.
21. A ligure, an agate, and an _____. (Ex. 39:12)
23. We live therefore, _____ die. (Rom. 14:8)
24. Butter in a _____ dish. (Judg. 5:25)
26. From Engedi even unto _____. (Ezek. 47:10)
28. A bracket on the ship's mast to support the trestle trees.
30. He said, _____, Father. (Mark. 14:36)

54

32. Symbol for element iridium.
34. Saint (abbr.).
36. He will bless the house of _____.
    (Ps. 115:12)
37. But whom say ye that _____ _____?
    (Mark 8:29; 2 words)
39. Minerals from which metals can be
    mined.
42. The garden of _____. (Joel 2:3)
44. Height times width.
46. _____ yourselves in the love of
    God. (Jude 21)
48. _____ it also in writing. (Ezra 1:1)
50. The nations are _____. (Jer. 51:7)
52. District Attorney (abbr.).
53. Right (abbr.).
54. And it shall come to pass _____ the
    last days. (Isa. 2:2)

55

PUZZLE 27

Pamela Jensen

ACROSS CLUES

1. _____, and be not afraid.
   (Matt. 17:7)
5. Be of good _____. (Isa. 41:6)
11. I will bless her, and _____ thee a son. (Gen. 17:16)
12. I will _____ all the families.
   (Jer. 1:15)
13. American Library Association.
   (abbr.).
14. Symbol for element rubidium.
15. Every man according to his _____.
   (Acts 11:29)
17. The kingdom of _____ in Bashan.
   (Josh. 13:12)
18. Salah begat _____. (Gen. 10:24)
19. Airport code for Tel Aviv/Jaffa, Israel.
20. British rank above a viscount and below a marquis.
21. Ex officio (abbr.).
22. A small, low islet of coral or sand.
24. Extravehiclular activity (abbr.).
26. Turn _____ unto me. (Zech. 1:3)
27. Minnesota (abbr.).
28. _____ shall offer it. (Lev. 1:3)
30. The _____ of the Lord. (John 12:38)
33. Capital of South Korea.
36. Play on the hole of the _____.
   (Is. 11:8)
39. And _____ is the way. (Matt. 7:14)
42. Daughters shall be _____. (Is. 60:4)
44. A company or group.
45. A group of five.
46. One _____ without blemish.
   (Num. 6:14)
47. Master of Arts (abbr.).
48. _____ shaddai, name of God.

49. Eleazar the son of _____.
   (2 Sam. 23:9)
50. Eight quarts.
51. For the sky is _____. (Matt. 16:2)
53. Actual Weight (abbr.).
54. Large open Eskimo boat.
56. I come to _____ thy will.
   (Heb. 10:9)
57. Monsignor (abbr.).
58. The Lord is _____ hand. (Joel 1:15)
59. The patience of _____. (Jam. 5:11)

DOWN CLUES

1. Make an _____ with me. (Is. 36:16)
2. A narrow strip of fabric.
3. Intravenous (abbr.).
4. _____ me...and know my heart.
   (Ps. 139:23)
5. Whosoever shall _____ on the name. (Acts 2:21)
6. In her mouth was an _____ leaf.
   (Gen. 8:11)
7. Ultimate (abbr.).
8. Associate in Arts (abbr.).
9. To him be _____. (Rev. 1:6)
10. He shall fly as an _____.
   (Jer. 48:40)
12. In the _____ of David. (Luke 2:4)
16. To Jerusalem every _____.
   (Luke 2:41)
23. Sixth century B.C. Greek author of fables.
25. Of more _____ than many sparrows. (Luke 12:7)
29. I will not _____ it. (Gen. 18:30)
31. Ye also have a _____ in heaven.
   (Col. 4:1)
32. _____ is the way. (Matt. 7:13)
34. One little _____ lamb.
   (2 Sam. 12:3)
35. To remove the contents.

56

37. _____ with that holy Spirit of prom-
    ise. (Eph. 1:13)
38. Doctor of Pedagogy (abbr.).
40. Sharp _____ of the mighty.
    (Ps. 120:4)
41. I have heard a _____ from the Lord.
    (Jer. 49:14)
43. Registered Nurse (abbr.).

47. All eat the same spiritual _____.
    (1 Cor. 10:3)
49. Seven days under the _____.
    (Lev. 22:27)
50. Airport code for Peoria, Illinois.
52. Female deer.
55. Now it came _____ pass.
    (Ruth 1:1)

PUZZLE 28

Pamela Jensen

ACROSS CLUES

1. Be ye kind one to another, _____.
   (Eph. 4:32)
12. O Lord, _____ me. (Ps. 6:2)
13. _____, thou art the Son of God.
    (John 1:49)
14. Battery size.
15. In Christ shall all be made _____.
    (1 Cor. 15:22)
17. National Basketball Association
    (abbr.).
18. Slippery.
19. A righteous man hateth _____.
    (Prov. 13:5)
21. The Hushathite slew _____.
    (2 Sam. 21:18)
23. Kentucky (abbr.).
25. Georgia (abbr.).
26. Enos, which was the son of _____.
    (Luke 3:38)
28. As the sand which is by the _____.
    (Heb. 11:12; 2 words)
30. Part of an ephah of barley _____.
    (Num. 5:15)
32. The prophet _____, David's seer.
    (2 Sam. 24:11)
33. Symbol for element thulium.
34. Veterans' Administration (abbr.).
36. God called the light _____.
    (Gen. 1:5)
37. And _____, and Migdal-el.
    (Josh. 19:38)
39. A single article.
41. Emergency Room (abbr.).
42. Cast the _____ on the right side.
    (John 21:6)
44. I will make of thee _____ great
    _____. (Gen. 12:2; 2 words)

46. _____ took Jeremiah. (Jer. 37:14)
49. Will set fire in _____. (Ezek. 30:14)
50. Should tell _____ man. (Luke 8:56)
51. Gone down in the _____.
    (2 Kgs. 20:11)
53. Ephesians (abbr.).
55. _____ will establish it for ever.
    (Ps. 48:8)
57. Make bare the _____. (Isa. 47:2)
58. District Attorney (abbr.).
59. _____ found a ship going to
    Tarshish. (Jonah 1:3)
60. Why will ye go with _____?
    (Ruth 1:11)
61. The bright and morning _____.
    (Rev. 22:16)
62. The _____ of the Lord. (Isa. 9:7)

DOWN CLUES

1. Magnify him with _____.
   (Ps. 69:30)
2. Long, snakelike fish.
3. She put her hand to the _____.
   (Judg. 5:26)
4. Delivery (abbr.).
5. Railroad (abbr.).
6. And they shall _____ upon him.
   (Isa. 22:24)
7. To fall back or recede.
8. Walk in pride he is able to _____.
   (Dan. 4:37)
9. Rhode Island (abbr.).
10. And peace have kissed _____ other.
    (Ps. 85:10)
11. The sun to rule by _____.
    (Ps. 136:8)
16. Isaac being _____ days old.
    (Gen. 21:4
18. And _____, and Penuel.
    (1 Chron. 8:25)
20. There is a son born to _____.
    (Ruth 4:17)

22. Atmosphere (abbr.).
24. A day, and a month, and a _____. (Rev. 9:15)
26. _____ men of honest report. (Acts 6:3)
27. A town in eastern England.
29. When _____-zede king of Jerusa-lem. (Josh 10:1)
31. He will bless the house of _____. (Ps. 115:12)
35. And they were all _____. (Luke 4:36)
38. Province of Saudi Arabia.

40. Symbol for element tantalum.
43. There were stings in their _____. (Rev. 9:10)
45. The _____ of Ethiopia shall not equal it. (Job 28:19)
47. They went up into an upper _____. (Acts 1:13)
48. A minute amount (Scot.).
52. Airport code for La Guardia, New York.
54. I will punish _____. (Jer. 51:44)
56. Delaware (abbr.).
59. Interjection expressing derision.

PUZZLE 29

Rebecca Souder

ACROSS CLUES

1. Brotherly _____. (2 Pet. 1:7)
8. Cuts of meat.
9. Grace and _____ be multiplied. (2 Pet. 1:2)
13. Through the _____ of him that hath called us. (2 Pet. 1:3)
16. Railcar (abbr.).
17. Jupiter's moon.
18. Overdose (abbr.).
19. Head doctor (abbr.).
21. Eschew evil, and do _____. (1 Pet. 3:11)
23. _____ the hart. . .(Psalm 42:1).
24. _____ and peace be multiplied. (2 Pet. 1:2)
27. Evil plan.
29. South America (abbr.).
30. That ye might be partakers of the _____ nature. (2 Pet. 1:4)
32. If these things be _____ you. (2 Pet. 1:8)
33. This is my beloved _____. (2 Pet. 1:17)
34. Poem.
35. Family group.
37. Greek letter.
38. Manuscript (abbr.).
39. And to knowledge _____. (2 Pet. 1:6)
41. Puerto Rico (abbr.).
42. Old style (abbr.).
43. Thou shalt make the _____ of the tabernacle. (Ex. 27:9)
46. Our _____ Jesus Christ.
50. Add to your faith _____. (2 Pet. 1:5)
51. _____, I am with you always. (Matt. 28:20)
52. Tin (symbol).
53. _____ _____ God gave unto them. (Acts 11:17 ASV; 2 words)
54. His divine _____ hath given unto us. (2 Pet. 1:3)

DOWN CLUES

2. Labor organization (abbr.).
3. Beloved, _____ are we the sons of God. (1 John 3:2)
4. Besides this, giving all _____, add to your faith virtue. (2 Pet. 1:5)
5. Direction.
6. Apocryphal book Esdras (abbr.).
7. Went quickly.
10. That in the _____ to come. . . (Ephesians 2:7)
11. Convict (abbr.).
12. For so an _____ shall be. (2 Pet. 1:11)
13. Into the everlasting _____. (2 Pet. 1:11)
14. That _____ prophecy of the scripture. (2 Pet. 1:20)
15. All things that pertain unto life and _____. (2 Pet. 1:3)
20. Doth also now _____ us. (1 Pet. 3:21)
22. Out of print (abbr.).
23. I fell _____ his feet as dead. (Rev. 1:17)
25. Eliminates.
26. 101 (Roman).
28. With him _____ the sacred mountain. (2 Pet. 1:18 NIV)
29. For _____ an entrance shall be. (2 Pet. 1:11)
31. Tree.
33. He was purged from his old _____s. (2 Pet. 1:9)
36. Military address.

37. Ma's mate.
39. Be established in the present _____. (2 Pet. 1:12)
40. I _____ you...to go and bear fruit. (John 15:16 NIV)
41. Sea _____.
43. Cost, insurance and freight (abbr.).
44. Regret.
45. Likened unto _____ virgins. (Matt. 25:1)
47. European mountain.
48. ___doo, African sorcery.
49. Royal Naval Reserve (abbr.).
50. 6 (Roman).

PUZZLE 30

Rebecca Souder

ACROSS CLUES

1. Greek letter.
3. Being the _____ of his glory. (Heb. 1:3)
11. One who inherits (2 words).
13. Greek monogram for Jesus.
14. Pint (abbr.).
15. And the... _____ of his person. (Heb. 1:3)
16. To whom shall we _____? (John. 6:68)
17. Either/_____.
18. Headquarters (abbr.).
19. New Hampshire.
20. _____ saith the Lord.
21. Kansas University.
22. New wine will _____ the bottles. (Luke. 5:37)
24. His servants _____ him. (John. 4:51)
25. That is (Latin abbr.).
26. French coin.

28. Thirty silver _____. (Matt. 26:15 NIV)
29. Greek vowel.
30. Better.
32. Comb. form meaning "wood."
33. _____ all things by the word of his power. (Heb. 1:3)
36. Thy throne, O God, _____ for ever. (Heb. 1:8)
37. A division of Scripture.
38. ...art my _____. (Heb. 1:5)
39. Grain or bread.
42. A more excellent _____ than they. (Heb. 1:4)
45. Greek porch.
46. Greek goddess.
47. Shew you a more _____ way. (1 Cor. 12:31)
49. Storekeeper (abbr.).
50. _____ hospitality one to another. (1 Pet. 4:9)
51. He that hath an _____ let him hear. (Rev. 2:7)
52. Kind of worshipers the Father _____. (Jn 4:23 NIV)
53. He looked for a _____. (Heb. 11:10)

DOWN CLUES

1. Ma's mate.
2. Hated _____. (Heb. 1:9)
3. Vegetables.
4. Loved _____. (Heb. 1:9)
5. Anger.
6. Right hand of the Majesty on _____. (Heb. 1:3)
7. _____ art my Son. (Heb. 1:5)
8. Nova Scotia (abbr.).
9. Hath in these last days _____ unto us. (Heb. 1:2)
10. Walks proudly.
12. His Majesty (abbr.).
18. Hemoglobin (abbr.).
20. The word of _____. (Jam. 1:18)
23. True.
24. Sent forth to _____ for them who shall be heirs of salvation. (Heb. 1:14)
27. Drink this ___. (1 Cor. 11:26)
28. Sitting upon...a _____. (Matt. 21:5)
29. And the _____...of his person. (Heb. 1:3)
31. Recipient.
34. Come nigh unto Damascus about _____. (Acts 22:6)
35. Dust...became _____. (Ex. 8:17 NIV)
40. My _____ is easy. (Matt. 11:30)
41. Emergency Service (abbr.).
43. The _____ is laid the root. (Matt. 3:10)
44. Master of Ceremonies (abbr.).
45. I will _____ thy son. (Ex. 4:23)
48. _____ there be light. (Gen. 1:3)
50. United Kingdom (abbr.).

PUZZLE 31

Connie Holman

ACROSS CLUES

1. Are they _____? (2 Cor. 11:22)
8. Pronoun for male.
10. There hath _____ temptation taken you. (1 Cor. 10:13)
11. Move laboriously.
12. A flattering mouth worketh _____. (Prov. 26:28)
13. Precious stone.
14. Athaliah the daughter of _____. (2 Chron. 22:2)
17. Second note of musical scale.
18. Good works for necessary _____. (Titus 3:14)
19. Death shall _____ from them. (Rev. 9:6)
20. Garment edge.
22. Opposite of came.
24. *Yes* in Spanish.
25. Selenium (abbr.).
26. His only _____ son. (John 3:16)
28. Work.
29. _____ the hart panteth. (Ps. 42:1)
30. Father.
32. Times when sun is farthest north or south in the ecliptic.
35. Do not set up any wooden _____ pole. (Deut. 16:21, NIV)
37. You.
38. _____ de Janeiro.
39. A tropical bird.
40. Three measures of barley for a _____. (Rev. 6:6)
42. I am ashamed and _____. (Ezra 9:6)
44. Yellowish green fruit.
46. _____ ye even so to them. (Matt. 7:12)

47. Too.
49. _____ him were all things created.) (Col. 1:16)
50. Belonging to a female.
51. Type of grain.
52. Pierces.
53. For we _____ his workmanship. (Eph. 2:10)

DOWN CLUES

1. Brings upon himself.
2. Therefore.
3. Silver, ivory, and _____. (1 Kings 10:22)
4. Type of shade tree. •
5. And, _____, I am with you. (Matt. 28:20)
6. Honoring false gods.
7. _____ Lanka.
8. All the _____ thereof shall be burned. (Micah 1:7)
9. Make thine _____ thy footstool. (Heb. 1:13)
13. Acquire.
15. An help _____ for him. (Gen. 2:18)
16. Veil of the temple was _____. (Mark 15:38)
21. Israel's female judge.
23. Apostle, and a _____ of the Gentiles. (2 Tim. 1:11)
26. _____ things of the world. (1 Cor. 1:28)
27. _____ in Bashan. (Deut. 4:43)
29. They were sawn _____. (Heb. 11:37)
30. At _____ westward. (1 Chron. 26:18)
31. Like _____ dove. (Hosea 7:11; 2 words)
33. Worth doing (2 words).
34. Very long time.

36. Built his _____ upon a rock. (Matt. 7:24)
41. Time long past.
43. _____ shall we ever be with the Lord. (1 Thes. 4:17)

45. Decline.
48. Location.
50. Expression of triumph.

1	2		3	4	5	6	7			8	9	10
11			12						13			
		14				15				16		
17	18					19			20	21		
22				23								
24		25		26				27				
						28						29
30	31		32			33						
34				35								
	36			37						38		
39			40						41		42	
		43				44		45				
46					47							

PUZZLE 32

Connie Holman

ACROSS CLUES

1. Thou shalt plant _____.
   (Deut. 28:39)
8. Standeth in _____ of thy word.
   (Ps. 119:161)
11. House _____ God. (Gen. 28:17)
12. More recent.
13. Once more; in a different way.
14. Scottish language.
16. Let your communication _____,
    Yea, yea. (Matt. 5:37)
17. Opposite of over.
19. Bays or coves.
22. Have _____ other gods before me.
    (Ex. 20:3)
23. Give to him that _____.
    (Matt. 5:42)
24. Characteristic.
27. Thou art _____ great. (Ps. 104:1)
28. Nothing more than.
30. Gather the _____ of Israel.
    (Ex. 3:16)
33. Stubborn.

34. More uncommon.
35. _____ lib.
36. Heavenly.
39. A time to rend, and a time to _____. (Ec. 3:7)
40. Nay.
41. My days _____ fulfilled. (Gen. 29:21)
43. Courtyard.
45. Trodden under foot of _____. (Matt. 5:13)
46. In the middle of.
47. The hearts of the people _____. (Josh. 7:5)

DOWN CLUES

1. One who works freely.
2. _____my people, which are called by my name. (2 Chron. 7:14)
3. In the wilderness of _____. (1 Sam. 24:1)
4. _____ of jubilee. (Lev. 27:17)
5. Stand in _____, and sin not. (Ps. 4:4)
6. Take pleasure in.
7. Neither eat nor _____. (Es. 4:16)
8. _____ angel of the Lord. (Luke 1:11)
9. Spider homes.
10. Save one little _____ lamb. (2 Sam. 12:3)
15. Cunning.
18. Thou, _____, thy son. (Ex. 20:10)
20. But the righteous into life _____. (Matt. 25:46)
21. Number of Noah's sons. (Gen 6:10)
25. Brother of Simon Peter.
26. Raging floods.
28. Small amount.
29. Breach for breach, _____ for _____. (Lev. 24:20)
31. Put it on a blue _____. (Ex 28:37)
32. Snakelike fish.
35. _____ home in the body. (2 Cor. 5:6)
37. Every bird of every _____. (Gen 7:14)
38. Eat of the _____ of life. (Rev 2:7)
39. Resort area; gym.
41. Quantity (abbr.).
42. The _____ of all things is at hand. (1 Pet. 4:7)
43. In the year of our Lord.
44. As for _____and my house. (Josh. 24:15)

PUZZLE 33

Connie Holman

ACROSS CLUES

1. Your _____ shall be desolate. (Ezek 6:4)
6. They had made themselves _____ to David. (1 Chron. 19:6)
11. Overshoe.
12. _____ and void.
13. Lose his life for my sake shall find _____. (Matt.16:25)
14. Affectedly shy.
16. Thicker parts at ends of side walls.
17. Being _____ freely by his grace. (Rom. 3:24)
20. _____, ego, superego.
21. _____ for me and my house. (Josh. 24:15)
22. Hoax.
24. Being _____ by the Holy Ghost. (Rom. 15:16)
28. _____ the son of Nun. (Num. 13:8)
29. Behold, all things are become _____. (2 Cor. 5:17)
30. Pass through the fire to _____. (2 Kgs. 23:10)
31. Anger.
33. Crack in a container.
34. Behind a vessel.
36. _____ the son of Abdiel. (1 Chron. 5:15)
38. A _____ of dragons. (Jer. 9:11)
40. Child.
41. With the same measure that ye _____. (Luke 6:38)
43. I _____ set my bow in the cloud. (Gen. 9:13)
44. Wing of building.
46. Primp.

48. _____ Syndrome.
50. For God _____ loved the world. (John 3:16)
51. Which is _____ in the scripture. (Dan. 10:21)
52. _____ gave his only begotten Son. (John 3:16)

DOWN CLUES

1. _____ the son of Jeroboam. (1 Kgs. 14:1)
2. Aquatic plant.
3. Light _____ rule the day. (Gen. 1:16)
4. I stand _____ the door. (Rev. 3:20)
5. Behold, it is a _____ people. (Ex. 32:9)
6. Potipherah priest of _____. (Gen. 46:20)
7. No room for them in the _____. (Luke 2:7)
8. There went _____ a decree from Caesar Augustus. (Luke 2:1)
9. I was by the river of _____. (Dan. 8:2)
10. Winter coasting vehicle.
14. Third note of musical scale.
15. Nahor's wife. (Gen. 11:29)
16. Have charge of, manage.
18. Scuffle.
19. They did all _____, and were filled. (Matt. 14:20)
23. Every 14 days.
25. Yet to come.
26. Able to reproduce.
27. Mend a stocking.
28. Limestone.
32. There were seven of _____ fire. (Rev. 4:5)
35. Second note of musical scale.

37. Great man.
39. I will not put my hook in thy _____. (2 Kgs. 19:28)
42. Even (contraction).
45. When ye pray, _____ not vain repetitions. (Matt. 6:7)
47. Thy servants have _____ pasture. (Gen. 47:4)
49. What?

PUZZLE 34

Teresa Zeek

ACROSS CLUES

1. Seek ye the Lord while he may be _____. (Isa. 55:6)
5. Go and _____ no more. (John 8:11)
8. In the beginning _____. (Gen. 1:1)
11. When we come to the _____. (Gen. 43:21)
12. In Gaza, in Gath, and in _____. (Josh. 11:22)
15. The second tone of the diatonic scale.
16. Cunning in knowledge, and understanding _____. (Dan. 1:4)
18. University of Iowa (abbr.).
19. Pennsylvania (abbr.).
20. Son of Canaan. (Gen. 10:15)
21. O come let us _____ Him.
22. God, who _____ sundry times. (Heb. 1:1)
23. And the tree of the field shall _____ her fruit. (Eze. 34:27)
24. An exclamation of relief.
25. Road (abbr.).
27. The power of _____ and Media. (Es. 1:3)
29. Heard me out of his holy hill. _____. (Ps. 3:4)
33. Another name for Mt. Sinai. (Deut. 4:10)
36. Christ _____ in me. (Gal. 2:20)
38. Thy will be _____ in earth. (Matt. 6:10)
39. White starchy grain.
40. It will _____(s) him to powder. (Luke 20:18)
42. Shall bake your bread in one _____. (Lev. 26:26)

43. Borrow money take _____ _____. (2 words)
45. Southeast (abbr.).
46. To day shalt thou _____ with me in paradise. (Luke 23:43)
47. Paul studied at the feet of _____. (Acts 22:3)
50. Who concerning the truth have _____. (2 Tim. 2:18)
52. In the beginning _____ the word. (John 1:1)
53. A well from which Jacob called Abner. (2 Sam. 3:26)
54. Baruch's father. (Jer. 32:12)

DOWN CLUES

1. I will make you _____ of men. (Mark 1:17)
2. It is appointed unto men _____ to die. (Heb. 9:27)
3. Endeavoring to keep the _____ of the Spirit. (Eph. 4:3)
4. A son of Jacob by Bilhah. (Gen. 30:5,6)
5. Whoso _____ man's blood, by man shall his blood be shed. (Gen. 9:6)
6. Identification (abbr.).
7. I will _____ you, and your little ones. (Gen. 50:21)
9. Naomi's daughter-in-law. (Ruth 1:14)
10. _____ is swallowed up in victory. (1 Cor. 15:54)
13. God shall wound the...hairy _____. (Ps. 68:21)
14. Blessed are the dead which _____ in the Lord. (Rev. 14:13)
17. One of the sons of Benjamin. (Gen. 46:21)
24. Moses' brother. (Ex. 4:14)

70

1	2	3		4		5	6	7		8	9	10
11				12	13				14		15	
16			17				18				19	
20					21						22	
		23								24		
25	26				27			28				
29		30	31	32			33			34	35	
	36				37			38				
39						40	41					
42				43	44					45		
46			47	48					49			
50		51				52						
	53					54						

26. The angel of the Lord encamps round about them that fear him, and _____ them. (Ps. 34:7 NKJV)

28. A nonmetallic chemical element used in medicine.

30. The third plague. (Ex. 8:16)

31. Still the enemy and the _____. (Ps. 8:2)

32. _____ restoreth my soul. (Ps. 23:3)

34. He shall be great unto the _____ of the earth. (Micah. 5:4)

35. I _____ you therefore, brethren. (Rom 12:1)

37. A group of people playing together.

39. Jonathan stripped himself of the _____. (1 Sam. 18:4)

40. One of the cities of refuge. (Deut. 4:43)

41. The Lord shall _____ him up. (Jam. 5:15)

44. It is written in the _____ of Moses. (1 Kgs. 2:3)

48. A woman's name.

49. A garland of flowers.

51. Rhode Island (abbr.).

PUZZLE 35

Teresa Zeek

ACROSS CLUES

1. Balaam's father. (Num. 22:5)
5. God the Father and in the _____ Jesus Christ. (1 Thes. 1:1)
9. _____ Lord bless thee. (Num. 6:24)
12. Mine _____ is kindled against them. (Hosea 8:5)
14. One of Caleb's sons. (1 Chron. 4:15)
16. A suffix used to form certain plurals.
17. I fell _____ his feet as dead. (Rev. 1:17)
18. Joshua sent men from Jericho to _____. (Josh. 7:2)
19. They removed from Jotbathah and encamped at _____. (Num. 33:34)
21. And _____ us not into temptation. (Matt. 6:13)
24. Hadad's father. (Gen. 36:35)
25. Nickname for Raymond.
26. King (French).
28. Wise men come from the _____. (Matt. 2:1)
31. The Lord is _____ indeed. (Luke 24:34)
33. A suffix meaning "devotion to."
34. Joab saw that the _____ of the battle was against him. (2 Sam. 10:9)
36. _____ therefore, having your loins girt about with truth. (Eph. 6:14)
38. Jesus wrote on the ground with his _____. (John 8:6)
40. _____ let the wickedness of the wicked come to an end. (Ps. 7:9)
41. _____ man cometh unto the Father, but by me. (John 14:6)
42. Identification (abbr.).
43. Every man having his _____ in his hand. (2 Chron. 23:10)
45. _____ good to them that hate you. (Matt. 5:44)
47. Jesus' name for Simon meaning "stone." (John 1:42)
49. Nickname for Donald.
51. If any of you do _____ from the truth. (Jam. 5:19)
52. And they put on him a purple _____. (John 19:2)
55. The unit of electromotive force.
57. Simon Peter's brother. (Matt. 4:18)
58. Aholibamah's mother. (Gen. 36:14)
59. The evening and the morning were the first _____. (Gen. 1:5)
60. The herd ran down a _____ place. (Luke 8:33)
61. Editors (abbr.).

DOWN CLUES

1. A son of Joel. (1 Chron. 5:5)
2. _____ into his gates with thanksgiving. (Ps. 100:4)
3. The King of Bashan. (Num. 21:33)
4. Preparing.
6. Bear ye _____ another's burdens. (Gal. 6:2)
7. Title interpreted as *Master*. (John 1:38)
8. For a good man some would even _____ to die. (Rom. 5:7)
10. The seven _____ are seven mountains. (Rev. 17:9)
11. One of Saul's sons, _____-baal. (1 Chron. 8:33)
13. Rhode Island (abbr.).
15. That women adorn themselves in _____ apparel. (1 Tim. 2:9)
20. Captain of the host of the King of Syria; leper. (2 Kgs. 5:1)
22. Moses' brother. (Ex. 4:14)
23. Blessed _____ the meek. (Matt. 5:5)

72

27. That no _____ of you be puffed up. (1 Cor. 4:6)
29. A little child (esp. a boy).
30. The _____ of a midwife. (Ex. 1:16)
32. As good _____ of the manifold grace of God. (1 Pet. 4:10)
33. Hammoleketh's son. (1 Chron. 7:18)
35. I will break in pieces the chariot and his _____. (Jer. 51:21)
37. Cain dwelt in the land of _____. (Gen. 4:16)
39. _____ ye thither unto us. (Neh. 4:20)
40. A style of abstract painting creat-
ing optical illusions.
44. A star that brightens intensely and then gradually dims.
46. Perform unto the Lord thine _____. (Matt. 5:33)
48. He departed into a mountain to _____. (Mark 6:46)
50. For _____ of us liveth to himself. (Rom. 14:7)
53. The Lord shall hiss...for the _____ that is in the land. (Isa. 7:18)
54. The poor man had nothing save one little _____ lamb. (2 Sam. 12:3)
56. There is a _____ here, which hath five barley loaves. (John 6:9)

73

PUZZLE 36

Teresa Zeek

ACROSS CLUES

1. What the children of Israel ate for forty years. (Ex. 16:35)
6. There hath _____ temptation taken you. (1 Cor. 10:13)
8. The firstborn of Isaac's twin sons. (Gen. 25:25)
11. Joel and Jehu's great-grandfather. (1 Chron. 4:35)
12. Shuah's second son. (Gen. 38:4)
14. Southern state (abbr.).
15. _____ and see that the Lord is good. (Ps. 34:8)
16. We were comforted over you in _____ our affliction. (1 Thes. 3:7)
17. The voice of _____ crying in the wilderness. (Matt. 3:3)
18. _____ for me and my house, we will serve the Lord. (Josh. 24:15)
19. _____ kingdom come. (Matt. 6:10)
20. Herod slew the children..._____ years old and under. (Matt. 2:16)
21. Even as a _____ gathereth her chickens under her wings. (Matt. 23:37)
23. The fourth tone of the diatonic scale.
24. A prophetess, the daughter of Panuel. (Luke 2:36)
26. A suffix forming the comparative degree.
27. God _____ forth his Son. (Gal. 4:4)
29. Mister (abbr.).
30. Moses _____ all the words of the Lord. (Ex. 24:4)
32. King of the Amalekites. (1 Sam. 15:8)
34. Street (abbr.).
35. One of the children of Shobal. (Gen. 36:23)
36. The well, Beer-lahai-roi, is between _____ and Bered. (Gen. 16:14)
38. And Zebadiah, and Arad, and _____. (1 Chron. 8:15)
39. I will punish _____ in Babylon. (Jer. 51:44)
40. At _____ time. (Matt. 12:1)
42. _____ though I walk through the valley. (Ps. 23:4)
44. Stingeth like _____ adder. (Prov. 23:32)
46. Nickname for Isaac.
47. _____, I am with you always. (Matt. 28:20)
49. Abihail was Mordecai's _____. (Es. 2:15)
51. To blend together.
52. These things I will that thou _____ constantly. (Titus 3:8)
54. From everlasting, and to everlasting. _____. (Ps. 41:13)
55. _____ ye then be risen with Christ. (Col. 3:1)
56. Ye call me _____ and Lord. (John 13:13)
57. Abraham...died in a good old _____. (Gen. 25:8)

DOWN CLUES

1. The apostle who was a tax collector. (Matt. 10:3)
2. Abijam's son. (1 Kgs. 15:8)
3. The first month. (Es. 3:7)
4. The fishermen...were washing their _____. (Luke 5:2)
5. A fermented drink.
6. _____ found grace in the eyes of the Lord. (Gen. 6:8)
7. The _____ wise God, be honour. (1 Tim. 1:17)
8. There is a woman that hath a familiar spirit at _____-dor. (1 Sam. 28:7)
9. David's firstborn. (2 Sam. 3:2)
10. _____ hospitality one to another. (1 Pet. 4:9)
13. Nickname for Albert.

17. He came unto his _____. (John 1:11)
19. A yellowish-brown color.
20. Six hundred shekels of gold went to one _____. (1 Kgs. 10:16)
22. They have _____ from the faith. (1 Tim. 6:10)
23. Suffer me that I may _____ the pillars. (Judg. 16:26)
25. The _____ of violence is in their hands. (Isa. 59:6)
27. They look and _____ upon me. (Ps. 22:17)
28. _____ up thy bed, and walk. (Matt. 9:6)
29. Thou art _____. (Acts. 12:15)
31. Children _____ your parents in the Lord. (Eph. 6:1)
33. Abda's grandfather. (Neh. 11:17)
34. There shall be as the _____ of an olive tree. (Isa. 24:13)
37. One of David's sons. (1 Chron. 3:5)
38. Shaphat's father. (1 Chron. 27:29)
41. Short for Texas.
43. A particular quality surrounding a person or thing.
45. He drew _____ to behold it. (Acts. 7:31)
48. Put _____ the old man with his deeds. (Col. 3:9)
50. Names (abbr.).
53. I am (contraction).

1	2	3	4	5			6	7	8		9	
10						11				12		
13					14							15
16						17						
	18				19				20			
21				22		23		24				
25	26	27	28			29			30		31	
32				33					34			
35					36		37	38		39		
40				41			42					
43			44		45					46	47	
		48					49		50			
	51					52						

PUZZLE 37

Joan F. Watt

ACROSS CLUES

1. When thou makest a feast, call the poor, the _____. (Luke 14:13)
6. He came unto his _____. (John 1:11)
9. Exist.
10. Set thine house in _____. (2 Kgs. 20:1)
11. Beam cross section.
13. Come upon.
14. Harbor.
16. In the way wherein I walked have they privily laid a _____ for me. (Ps. 142:3)
17. Year (abbr.).
18. Fermented beverage.
20. Loafer.
22. Encountered.
24. The men of Beth-el and _____. (Ezra 2:28)
25. Turn yourselves from your _____. (Ezek. 14:6)

76

29. See!
30. There shall come a _____ out of Jacob. (Num. 24:17)
32. Record.
33. Short for James.
34. First female.
35. Louse eggs.
36. Recedes.
39. Short for Albert.
40. Overhead transportation.
41. Roman numeral four.
42. A Hindu queen.
43. Governing assembly.
45. Greatest of them _____ to the least. (Jonah 3:5)
46. Note in musical scale.
48. The eye cannot say unto the hand, I have no _____ of thee. (1 Cor. 12:21)
49. Fuss.
51. Direction.
52. Wherewith one may _____ another. (Rom. 14:19)

DOWN CLUES

1. Mothers.
2. Space for sports event.
3. Perfect.
4. *Meter* in London.
5. Pertaining to Celts of Scotland.
6. We ought to _____ God. (Acts 5:29)
7. Come to me, all you who are _____ and burdened. (Matt. 11:28 NIV)
8. Short rest.
11. Part of verb *to be.*
12. Person of Moab.
15. Praise him with the _____ and dance. (Ps. 150:4)
19. For I know whom I have _____. (2 Tim. 1:12)
21. He was not that Light, but was sent to bear _____. (John 1:8)
23. Laid it in his own new _____. (Matt. 27:60)
24. Equally.
26. Give us day by day our _____ bread. (Luke 11:3)
27. Choose.
28. Course of study.
31. Assist.
37. Man shall not live by _____ alone. (Matt. 4:4)
38. Girl's name.
44. But ye have made it a _____ of thieves. (Matt. 21:13)
47. His mother marvelled _____ those things which were spoken of him. (Luke 2:33)
50. Coming from.

PUZZLE 38

Deborah Justice

ACROSS CLUES

1. Ahiam the son of _____.
   (2 Sam. 23:33)
6. _____, whose name was
   Belteshazzar. (Dan. 2:26)
10. She bare unto Amram _____ and
    Moses, and Miriam their sister.
    (Num. 26:59)
11. Bring _____ offering, and come
    into his courts. (Ps. 96:8)
12. Glass (abbr.).
13. Compete.
14. And they following _____ helped
    him. (1 Kgs. 1:7)
18. And _____, and Gibbethon, and
    Baalath. (Josh. 19:44)
19. I bear up the pillars of it. _____.
    (Ps. 75:3)
21. Confounded be all they that serve
    graven _____. (Ps. 97:7)
23. Negative.
24. Doctor of Dental Surgery (abbr.).
26. Created.
27. Salt Lake City is the capital.
28. Not applicable.
29. Daniel, _____, Joel.
32. If the _____ be on the fleece only.
    (Judg. 6:37)
35. Associate Press (abbr.).
36. In the twinkling of _____ eye.
    (1 Cor. 15:52)
37. There came two angels to _____.
    (Gen. 19:1)
40. Samantha (nickname).
42. A little water _____ _____ vessel.
    (1 Kgs. 17:10; 2 words)
43. A tool with a sharp blade.

45. And the lot fell upon _____.
    (Acts 1:26)
49. Pointed piece of metal.
51. A period of time.
52. Tensile strength (abbr.).
53. Crown (abbr.).
54. His father saw him, and had com-
    passion, and _____. (Luke 15:20)
55. The twentieth to _____.
    (1 Chron. 24:16)

DOWN CLUES

1. And to _____ that which was lost.
   (Luke 19:10)
2. And there followed _____ and fire.
   (Rev. 8:7)
3. The governor under _____ the king.
   (2 Cor. 11:32)
4. Nickname for Rosemary.
5. A people great, and many, and tall,
   as the _____s. (Deut. 2:10)
6. Why did _____ remain in ships?
   (Judg. 5:17)
7. Of mint and _____ and cummin.
   (Matt. 23:23)
8. _____ the son of Nathan.
   (2 Sam. 23:36)
9. _____ the son of Jaareoregim.
   (2 Sam. 21:19)
15. And _____, greet you. (Col. 4:14)
16. Jamin, and _____, and Jachin.
    (Ex. 6:15)
17. God's Son.
20. Sent unto _____ king of Hebron.
    (Josh. 10:3)
22. _____, Exodus, Leviticus.
25. To let fall.
29. A hand tool used for pounding or
    driving in.
30. Opposite of west.

31. _____ the daughter of Zibeon. (Gen. 36:2)
33. Gained victory.
34. _____ the mount of Olives. (Luke 22:39)
38. A time to mourn, and a time to _____. (Ec. 3:4)
39. Northern state.

41. Til thou hast paid the very last _____. (Luke 12:59)
44. Extra large (abbr.).
46. And Pispah, and _____. 2(1 Chron. 7:38)
47. Light yellowish brown color.
48. A type of tree.
50. Prepared an _____ to the saving of his house. (Heb. 11:7)

PUZZLE 39

Janet W. Adkins

ACROSS CLUES

1. God is _____ to graff them in again. (Rom. 11:23)
5. Arrest.
8. A light that shineth in a _____ place. (2 Pet. 1:19)
12. First king of Israel.
13. The self.
14. Great lake.
15. The sons of Appaim; _____. (1 Chron. 2:31)
16. Cat's hand.
17. Aromatic spice.
18. And _____, Hanan, Anan. (Neh. 10:26)
19. Tooth covering.
21. Then Jacob gave Esau bread and pottage of _____ tiles. (Gen. 25:34)
22. Let him _____ evil. (1 Pet. 3:11)
25. Become downcast.
29. Like the roaring of the _____. (Isa. 5:30)
30. *Much _____ About Nothing.*
31. Better...a man who controls his _____ than one who takes a city. (Prov. 16:32 NIV)
35. And I will give you _____s according to mine heart. (Jer. 3:15)
37. As the loving hind and the pleasant _____. (Prov. 5:19)
38. That we may _____ mercy, and find grace. (Heb. 4:16)
41. But I say unto you that ye _____ not evil. (Matt. 5:39)
45. _____ without ceasing. (1 Thes. 5:17)
46. Belonging to the King of Bashan. (Num. 21:33)

48. _____ was _____ son of Gad. (Gen. 46:16; 2 words)
49. Ireland.
50. Court, pursue.
51. Military standing.
52. Thou art _____, O Lord. (Ps. 119:151)
53. Negative prefix.
54. Angel (French).

DOWN CLUES

1. Continent.
2. Strike with a heavy blow.
3. For by the mounting up of _____ th with weeping. (Isa. 15:5)
4. Tishbite prophet. (1 Kgs. 17:1)
5. Relation of Lot to Abraham.
6. Turkish ruler.
7. Put on... _____ of mercies. (Col. 3:12)
8. For I will _____ of thee. (Job 38:3)
9. Esrom begat _____. (Matt. 1:3)
10. Chinese staple.
11. Main stem of a ship.
20. Teacher's organization.
22. Superlative ending.
23. We shall _____ him as he is. (1 John 3:2)
24. Machine part.
26. Dative (abbr.).
27. Former name of Tokyo.
28. The ungodly shall not stand in the judgment, _____ sinners in the congregation. (Ps. 1:5)
32. And the _____ of faith shall save the sick. (Jam. 5:15)
33. Not "a" or "u."
34. Fame.
35. Who being...the express image of his _____. (Heb. 1:3)
36. _____ fled away...to the tent of Jael. (Judg. 4:17)

38. Put him to an _____ shame. (Heb. 6:6)
39. Type of cheese.
40. Fictional plantation.
42. Neighbor of Iraq.

43. Is any merry? let him _____ psalms. (Jam. 5:13)
44. Arise, and _____ up thy bed and walk. (Mark 2:9)
47. Sticky substance.

PUZZLE 40

Janet W. Adkins

ACROSS CLUES

1. He _____ for apples.
5. Little drink.
8. The sons of Merari...Zaccur and _____. (1 Chron. 24:27)
12. Great amount (2 words).
13. Belonging to a girl.
14. Thou art _____, O Lord. (Ps. 119:151)
15. And a certain centurion's servant, who was _____ unto him, was sick. (Luke 7:2)
16. Indian dress.
17. From Shepham to Riblah on the east side of _____. (Num. 34:11)
19. The voice of the Lord divideth the _____ of fire. (Ps. 29:7)
21. For there is no work, nor _____ ...in the grave. (Ec. 9:10)
24. Good time.
25. Descendant of Eri. (Num. 26:16)
26. And Ahab told _____ all that Elijah had done. (1 Kgs. 19:1)
30. By faith _____ch was translated. (Heb. 11:5)
31. Pitch.
32. Eggs.
33. To _____ such an one unto Satan. (1 Cor. 5:5)
36. Accepted belief.
38. Teacher's organization.
39. Harsh.
40. Sought how they might take him by _____, and put him to death. (Mark 14:1)
43. Pod vegetable.
44. _____ avis: rarity.
45. Bringing gold and silver, ivory, and _____(s). (1 Kgs. 10:22)
47. Calendar entry.
51. What the little engine said (2 words).
52. Pasture.
53. And the Lord God planted a garden eastward in _____. (Gen. 2:8)
54. As the twig is _____, so grows the branch.
55. Noah entered the _____. (Gen. 7:7)
56. Foolish man built his house upon the _____. (Matt. 7:26)

DOWN CLUES

1. Cast the _____ away. (Matt. 13:48)
2. Bullfight cheer.
3. Feather scarf.
4. I am in a _____ betwixt two. (Phil. 1:23)
5. Let your light so _____ before men. (Matt. 5:16)
6. That is (Latin).
7. To offer for acceptance.
8. Mad.
9. First cast out the _____ out of thine own eye. (Matt. 7:5)
10. It is a _____ thing that the king requireth. (Dan. 2:11)
11. Spring flower.
18. Frozen water.
20. Bethel...was called _____ at the first. (Gen. 28:19)
21. Let us love...in _____ and in truth. (1 John 3:18)
22. Sea eagle.
23. String instrument.
26. Glass container.
27. This is now _____ of my bones. (Gen. 2:23)

28. So shall we _____ be with the Lord. (1 Thes. 4:17)
29. Not early.
31. Beverage.
34. There shall be no more thence an _____ of days. (Isa. 65:20)
35. Former serviceman/woman.
36. Golf peg.
37. Avoids.
39. Be swift to hear, slow to _____. (Jam. 1:19)
40. Away in a manger, no _____ for a bed.
41. And rejoiceth as a strong man to run a _____. (Ps. 19:5)
42. The children of Dishan...Uz, and _____. (Gen. 36:28)
45. In this manner.
46. Each.
48. Modern form of name of Lamech's wife. (Gen. 4:19)
49. _____ virgins; _____ lepers.
50. He that endureth to the _____ shall be saved. (Matt. 10:22)

PUZZLE 41

Janet W. Adkins

ACROSS CLUES

1. Tennis name Steffi _____.
5. Because their _____ is come unto me. (1 Sam. 9:16)
8. A Christmas carol.
12. Volcanic output.
13. Aaron and _____ stayed up his hands. (Ex. 17:12)
14. The people that followed _____ prevailed. (1 Kgs. 16:22)
15. City of Judah. (Josh. 15:32,50)
16. Sounds of questioning.
17. Blood vessel.
18. Practicer of divination.
20. From then until now.
21. The ungodly shall not stand in the judgment, _____ sinners in the congregation. (Ps. 1:5)
22. Facial twitch.
23. I counsel thee to buy of me gold tried in the _____. (Rev. 3:18)
26. Spake of his _____ which he should accomplish at Jerusalem. (Luke 9:31)
30. Blackbird.
31. Thieves _____ through and steal. (Matt. 6:19)
33. But I will not with ink and _____ write unto thee. (3 John 13)
34. Tambourines. (1 Sam. 18:6)
36. Went rapidly.
37. Compass direction.
38. Stadium cheer.
40. Sought how they might take him by _____. (Mark 14:1)
43. Taking away.
47. _____rn unto me, and I will return unto you. (Mal. 3:7)
48. Hawaiian dish.
49. Ye who sometimes _____ far off are made nigh. (Eph. 2:13)
50. Belonging to the mother of Hezekiah. (2 Kgs. 18:1,2)
51. The _____ shall not smite thee by day. (Ps. 121:6)
52. Sicilian volcano.
53. Stand open.
54. Possessive pronoun.
55. I am not worthy that thou shouldest enter under my _____. (Luke 7:6)

DOWN CLUES

1. A wise son maketh a _____ father. (Prov. 10:1)
2. Indian princess.
3. Tel _____.
4. There arose a mighty _____ in that land. (Luke 15:14)
5. Shall _____ up his wife which he hath taken. (Deut. 24:5)
6. German river.
7. Years. (abbr.).
8. New at an activity.
9. A sign of the future.
10. Norse explorer.
11. Thou shalt bind this _____ of scarlet thread in the window. (Josh 2:18)
19. Negative reply.
20. I was _____, and ye visited me. (Matt. 25:36)
22. Beverage.
23. All the _____ is the Lord's. (Lev. 3:16)
24. _____ _____ moment, in the twinkling of an eye. (1 Cor. 15:52; 2 words)
25. And the _____, which the Lord God had taken from man. (Gen. 2:22)

26. Desert (abbr.).
27. Appendix (abbr.).
28. Blessed are the pure in heart: for they shall _____ God. (Matt. 5:8)
29. From the beginning of the year even unto the _____ of the year. (Deut. 11:12)
31. Bring forth the _____ robe. (Luke 15:22)
32. Route (abbr.).
35. This evil people, which _____ to hear my words. (Jer. 13:10)
36. Light rain.
38. For the righteous God trieth the hearts and _____. (Ps. 7:9)
39. I _____ Alpha and Omega. (Rev. 1:8)
40. Jagged cliff.
41. And they slew the kings of Midian...Zur...Hur, and _____. (Num. 31:8)
42. Toppling over.
43. Drive out.
44. Turn down.
45. River in Italy.
46. His _____ also shall not wither. (Ps. 1:3)
48. Greek letter.

PUZZLE 42

Janet W. Adkins

ACROSS CLUES

1. Brought him to an _____. (Luke 10:34)
4. The house was filled with the _____ of the ointment. (John 12:3, Am. spelling)
8. Clip.
12. Deliver thyself as a _____ from the hunter. (Prov. 6:5)
13. This is now _____ of my bones. (Gen. 2:23)
14. Greek letter.
15. Of birds (prefix).
16. Very (French).
17. Went by plane.
18. Lunatic.
19. Again he _____ the same sacrifices. (Heb. 10:11 NIV)
21. Iowa (abbr.).
22. Rhode Island (abbr.).
23. We remember the leeks, and the _____. (Num. 11:5)
26. Leah was _____ eyed. (Gen. 29:17)
30. Teachers' organization.
31. And Bezaleel the son of _____. (Ex. 38:22)
32. God shall send them _____ delusion. (2 Thes. 2:11)
35. And John bare _____, saying, I saw the Spirit. (John 1:32)
37. Each (abbr.).
38. And she [Shuah] conceived, and bore a son; and he called his name _____. (Gen. 38:3)
39. I will not be an _____. (Isa. 3:7)
43. The disciples asked him again of the same _____. (Mark 10:10)

47. Naum, which was the son of _____. (Luke 3:25)
48. God (Spanish).
50. Then enquired he of them the hour be began to _____nd. (John 4:52)
51. The blind receive their sight, and the _____ walk. (Matt. 11:5)
52. Between (combining form).
53. 1/1000 inch.
54. Plutonium, arsenic (chem. symbols).
55. Scottish denials.
56. Isle in England.

DOWN CLUES

1. A duke of Edom. (Gen. 36:43)
2. Suddenly bright star.
3. No (German).
4. For whoso findeth me...shall _____ favour of the Lord. (Prov. 8:35)
5. Also called Tabitha. (Acts 9:36)
6. First number.
7. My strong habitation whereunto I may continually _____. (Ps. 71:3)
8. Spat.
9. Part in a play.
10. To do again and again: _____ate.
11. They shall give unto the priest the shoulder...and the _____(pl.). (Deut. 18:3)
20. Response of disgust (archaic).
23. Belonging to a son of Peleth. (Num. 16:1)
24. Let his _____ that he hath hid catch himself. (Ps. 35:8)
25. Adjective suffix.
27. A pair.
28. If any of you do _____ from the truth. (Jam. 5:19)
29. I will _____ evil beasts out of the land. (Lev. 26:6)

33. Born.
34. The Lord God planted a _____ eastward in Eden. (Gen. 2:8)
35. Distant.
36. Deletes.
39. My _____ cometh from the Lord. (Ps. 121:2)
40. Jacob's twin.
41. Woman's name.
42. Or if he finds lost property and _____ about it. (Lev. 6:3 NIV)
44. But the tongue can no man _____. (Jam. 3:8)
45. Man's name.
46. Because thou didst _____ on the Lord. (2 Chron 16:8)
49. For I am _____ _____ strait betwixt two. (Phil. 1:23; 2 words)

PUZZLE 43

Janet W. Adkins

ACROSS CLUES

1. And _____ things of the world ...hath God chosen. (1 Cor. 1:28)
5. He maketh me to _____ down in green pastures. (Ps. 23:2)
8. Redecorate.
12. Swiss mountains.
13. Intent.
14. Of _____ the family of the Arodites. (Num. 26:17)
15. To drive out.
16. Compete.
17. Nathaniel to his friends.
18. Scold severely.
20. King Solomon made a navy of ships...on the shore of the _____ _____. (1 Kgs. 9:26; 2 words)
22. Pitch.
23. Spanish *gold*.
24. She called his name _____: because I drew him out of the water. (Ex. 2:10)
27. As an _____ harder than flint have I made thy forehead. (Ezek. 3:9)
30. Rhode Island (abbr.).
31. Elevated trains.
32. Yes (Spanish).
33. I will incline mine ear to a _____ (Ps. 49:4)
36. A _____ of David.
38. National Rifle Association.
39. A son of Gad. (Gen. 46:16)
40. Who gave himself a _____ for all. (1 Tim. 2:6)
43. And the sons of Eliab; _____, and Dathan. (Num. 26:9)
47. Sufficient (archaic).
48. Money earned on account (abbr.).
50. _____torian: Roman bodyguard.
51. British princess.
52. Golf peg.
53. If a man die, shall he _____ again? (Job 14:14)
54. The young lions _____ after their prey. (Ps. 104:21)
55. First the blade, then the _____. (Mark 4:28)
56. Crisis: _____rgency.

DOWN CLUES

1. A cutting remark.
2. Medicinal plant.
3. Prod.
4. That he might know your _____, and comfort your hearts. (Col. 4:8)
5. Thou shalt also make a _____ of brass. (Ex. 30:18)
6. Roman numeral 3.
7. The hand of the Lord... smote them with _____. (1 Sam. 5:6)
8. Chosen in no specific pattern.
9. Historical periods.
10. A sword is upon the liars; and they shall _____. (Jer. 50:36)
11. Greek auditoriums.
19. British farewells.
21. Equal Rights Amendment.
25. Mouth.
26. _____, we would see Jesus. (John 12:21)
27. Pub drink.
28. _____ did that which was right in the eyes of the Lord. (1 Kgs. 15:11)
29. Nothing.
31. Inhabitnt of Elam.
34. A soft _____ turneth away wrath. (Prov. 15:1)
35. Sibling.
36. Earlier (prefix).

37. The _____ believeth every word. (Prov. 14:15)
39. He cannot _____ into the kingdom of God. (John 3:5)
40. Backward part.
41. _____ Domini.
42. Nickname for Wynona.
44. There stood up a priest with _____ and with Thummim. (Ezra 2:63)
45. Overhanging roof edge.
46. Southern Gen.: R.E._____.
49. Teachers' organization (abbr.).

PUZZLE 44

Glenn G. Luscher

ACROSS CLUES

1. A cake. (Ex. 16:31)
3. Mountain sheep. (Deut. 14:5)
8. A skiff.
9. A snake. (Ps. 140:3)
13. Trinitrotoluene (abbr.).
14. Portable steps.
16. An evening meal.
17. Perpetual. (Rom. 1:20)
19. Son of Zebulun. (Gen. 46:14)
20. Greek word signifying "the last." (Rev. 1:8)
22. Son of Appaim. (1 Chron. 2:31)
24. New Testament (abbr.).
26. Feminine case pronoun.
29. Builder of Nineveh. (Gen. 10:11)
31. Of the flesh. (Rom. 8:7)
32. Another name for father.
33. Truck driver's vehicle.
34. Not heavy.
35. Alternating current (abbr.).
36. Mexican painter Jose Clemente _____.

39. A promise. (Luke 1:73)
40. Same as tea cart.
44. Masculine pronoun.
45. Northwest Territory (abbr.).
46. Small ones.
47. Secret Service (abbr.).

DOWN CLUES

1. Sea monsters. (Gen. 1:21)
2. Food for animals.
3. Collapsible bed.
4. Used for gripping.
5. What you put on. (Prov. 7:10)
6. A furnace. (Ps. 21:9)
7. A net. (2 Tim. 2:26)
10. Fruit of the palm.
11. Where Og fought a battle.
    (Num. 21:33)
12. Cuts out. (Hosea 13:8)
15. Symbol for radium.
18. The grandmother of Timothy.
    (2 Tim. 1:5)
21. Those who are greedy eaters.
23. To set apart. (Ex. 40:9)
25. Gives instruction.
26. A book or roll. (Rev. 6:14)
27. John was clothed with camel's
    _____. (Mark 1:6)
28. Used to make alkaloids.
30. To hang loosely.
32. All her _____ are peace.
    (Prov. 3:17)
37. Buddhist sect developed in India.
38. A feline.
41. A preposition.
42. To move or proceed.
43. Old Testament (abbr.).

PUZZLE 45

Deborah Justice

ACROSS CLUES

1. _____, come forth, and flee. (Zech. 2:6)
3. _____, a prophetess. (Luke 2:36)
6. But a faithful man who can _____? (Prov. 20:6)
10. Alpha and _____. (Rev. 1:8)
12. To put into action.
14. Jacob's brother. (Gen. 27:6)
15. Bath-sheba's first husband. (2 Sam. 11:3)
16. Make thee _____ ark. (Gen. 6:14)
17. To make a mistake.
18. Spanish for *Yes.*
19. And the Lord shall _____ thee. (Is. 58:11)
20. Male parent (plural).
22. Short for Timothy.
23. And he went out to meet _____. (2 Chron. 15:2)
24. In no way.
25. A son of Benjamin. (Gen. 46:21)
26. _____ vera lotion.

28. A family's dwelling place.
29. Book between Jonah and Nahum (abbr.).
30. Missionary kid (abbr.).
31. Ex officio (abbr.).
32. For the Lord God is a _____. (Ps. 84:11)
34. This _____ that.
36. Not applicable (abbr.).
37. And love unto all the _____. (Eph. 1:15)
40. A brief sleep.
41. _____ ye therefore, and teach. (Matt. 28:19)
42. The howling thereof unto _____. (Isa. 15:8)
43. Come into the land of _____. (Lev. 14:34)
46. Jump on one foot.
47. No report (abbr.).
48. To express in words.
49. Opposite of 46 Down.
50. Strive to _____ in. (Luke 13:24)

DOWN CLUES

1. In my Father's _____. (John 14:2)
2. _____ to reign over Israel. (1 Kgs. 16:23)
3. Haman the _____(s). (Es. 8:3)
4. Jonah, Micah, _____.
5. And Dimonah, and _____. (Josh. 15:22)
6. _____ my sheep. (John 21:16)
7. That is to be ruler in _____. (Micah 5:2)
8. Box of ointment of spike_____. (Mark 14:3)
9. Dutch (abbr.).
11. Part of "Old MacDonald" chorus.
13. For my son _____. (Philemon 10).
21. It is time to _____ the Lord. (Hosea 10:12)
22. Thomas (nickname).
24. Midday.
25. Joshaviah, the sons of _____. (1 Chron. 11:46)
26. Movement.
27. To leave out.
28. Thus the _____ and the earth were finished. (Gen. 2:1)
33. Shemiramoth, and Jehiel, and _____. (1 Chron. 15:20)
35. Postpone.
38. Greek word meaning "love."
39. Thou art my _____. (Heb. 1:5)
43. A prefix meaning "jointly."
44. Go to the _____, thou sluggard. (Prov. 6:6)
45. We _____ going to attend church on Sunday.
46. _____ brought me up also out of a horrible pit. (Ps. 40:2)

PUZZLE 46

Glenn G. Luscher

ACROSS CLUES

1. Day of rest.
4. Adam was the first.
6. Southwest (abbr.).
7. Another name for Mother.
8. Stand fast in _____ spirit. (Phil. 1:27)
10. The strength of an _____. (Num. 23:22)
13. Nighttime movie.
15. A sleeping noise.
16. Saul's father. (1 Sam. 10:21)
18. Used for hearing.
20. Built rugged.
22. The _____ of wisdom is above rubies. (Job 28:18)
24. It _____ upon each of them. (Acts 2:3)
26. Automobile.
27. Cooling device.
28. Abraham's original name. (Gen. 17:5)
31. What rabbits do.

94

33. Uninvited picnic guest.
34. _____ the Arbite. (2 Sam. 23:35)
35. Another name for Father.
36. Road (abbr.).
38. Province of Asia Minor. (Acts 16:7)
40. With your _____ girded. (Ex. 12:11)
41. Frozen water.
43. Container used for cooking.
45. Move quickly.
46. Mary's sister. (Luke 10:38, 39)
47. A preposition.

DOWN CLUES

1. Peanut coverings.
2. Native of Tekoa. (Amos 1:1)
3. Tale or heavy thread.
4. Another name I call myself.
5. A conjunction.
6. Galilee is one.
9. Name of a Simeonite captain.
   (1 Chron. 4:42)

11. Without delay.
12. Lamech's son. (Gen. 5:28,29)
13. Extending far downward.
14. Unable to speak.
17. Exceedingly warm.
19. A bowlike curved line.
21. A city of Benjamin. (Josh. 21:17)
23. Collected agricultural product.
24. Name of Orphan Annie's dog.
25. Opposite of near.
27. One who raises livestock.
28. Son of Nadab. (1 Chron. 2:30)
29. One who speaks to cause injury.
    (1 Cor. 5:11)
30. A miry place. (Ezek. 47:11)
32. A mother or father.
37. A snake. (Job 20:16)
39. Male offspring.
42. California (abbr.).
44. Alcoholics Anonymous (abbr.).

PUZZLE 47

Debra Michaels

ACROSS CLUES

1. Birthplace of our Lord. (Matt. 2:1)
9. Ye know how that a good while _____. (Acts 15:7)
12. Maternal grandfather of King Josiah. (2 Kgs. 22:1)
13. Gamaliel, a _____ of the law. (Acts 5:34)
14. Original home of Abraham's family. (Gen. 11:28)
16. Kilogram (abbr.).
18. City destroyed by fire from heaven. (Gen. 19:24)
20. Her clothing is _____ and purple. (Prov. 31:22)
22. Let _____ esteem others better than themselves. (Phil. 2:3)
24. A plain in Babylon. (Dan. 3:1)
26. Cain asked, _____ I my brother's keeper? (Gen. 4:9)
27. Prepare a table for that _____. (Isa. 65:11)
28. Was in prison with Paul at Philippi. (Acts 16:25)
30. The lot is cast into the _____. (Prov. 16:33)
31. The Lord _____ is my strength. (Isa. 12:2)
33. God, who is _____ in mercy. (Eph. 2:4)
34. To wound with the teeth.
36. Two-wheeled vehicle used for travel and war. (Gen. 41:43)
39. Prefix meaning *in*.
40. Son of David. (2 Sam. 5:13-15)
44. Singular of the verb *have*.
46. Symbol for the chemical element barium.

48. Elder brother of Moses and Miriam. (Num. 26:59)
49. King of Bashan. (Num. 21:33)
50. Twig broom for sweeping. (Isa. 14:23)
53. Symbol for the chemical element chlorine.
54. Long period of time.
55. A sleeveless linen garment worn by priests. (Ex. 28:4)
56. Yard (abbr.).

DOWN CLUES

1. Disciples let Saul down by the wall in a _____. (Acts 9:25)
2. Nickname for Edward.
3. To make lace.
4. Greeting.
5. Los Angeles (abbr.).
6. Son of Bilhan. (1 Chron. 7:10)
7. Children of Gad called the altar _____, meaning witness. (Josh. 22:34)
8. A bushy head of hair.
9. The time is _____ hand. (Rev. 1:3)
10. Hungarian stew.
11. Oregon (abbr.).
15. Thy _____ and thy staff comfort me. (Ps. 23:4)
17. Bulb with a strong smell.
18. Atroth, _____, and Jaazer. (Num. 32:35)
19. Descendant of Mushi. (Num. 3:33)
20. Healing ointment.
21. Kilometer (abbr.).
23. Trainers in athletics.
25. To disturb the peace.
29. Alcoholics Anonymous.
32. Black.
35. Job's country. (Job 1:1)
37. Leniency shown to a guilty person.
38. Footwear.

41. Pennsylvania (abbr.).
42. Exclamation of derision.
43. How is the _____ become dim!
    (Lam. 4:1)
45. Past.
46. Insect.
47. Hooded venomous serpent.
    (Rom. 3:13)
51. Ohio (abbr.).
52. Missouri (abbr.).

PUZZLE 48

Janice A. Buhl

ACROSS CLUES

1. Moses stretched forth his hand over the _____. (Ex 14:27)
4. _____, a lamb stood on the mount Sion. (Rev. 14:1)
7. _____, holy, holy, Lord God Almighty. (Rev. 4:8)
10. Do they not _____ that devise evil? (Prov. 14:22)
11. I will bring thee unto _____ place. (Num. 23:27)
14. Ye shall not _____ the Lord. (Deut. 6:16)
16. The _____ out of the wood doth waste it. (Ps. 80:13)
17. Israel sighed by _____ of the bond age. (Ex. 2:23)
19. Give _____ unto the law. (Isa. 1:10)
21. Or a bright spot, white, and some what _____. (Lev. 13:19)
23. Children, _____ your parents. (Eph. 6:1)
25. Judah took a wife for _____ his firstborn. (Gen. 38:6)
26. Wound with a pointed weapon.
28. Fourth note in the musical scale.
29. _____, so would we have it. (Ps. 35:25)
30. He sent and signified it _____ his angel. (Rev. 1:1)
31. Do, Re, Mi, _____.
32. He turned and went away in a _____. (2 Kgs. 5:12)
35. Yet _____ they eat the passover. (2 Chron. 30:18)
37. And the man said unto _____, I am he. (1 Sam. 4:16)
39. Louisiana (abbr.).
40. _____ let not the Lord be angry. (Gen. 18:30)
42. If any man shall _____ unto these things. (Rev. 22:18)
44. The glory of the Lord shone round _____. (Luke 2:9)
47. And _____ came to pass. (Amos 7:2)
49. The best of them is as a _____. (Micah 7:4)
51. The scribes and the Pharisees began to _____ him vehemently. (Luke 11:53)
52. The book of the vision of _____ the Elkoshite. (Nahum 1:1)
54. Balaam the son of ___. (Micah 6:5)
56. Suffix meaning "to make" or "to become."
57. Strain at a _____, and swallow a camel. (Matt. 23:24)
58. Shall _____ away ungodliness from Jacob. (Rom 11:26)

DOWN CLUES

1. She bore a son, and called his name _____. (Gen. 4:25)
2. Sir, come down _____ my child die. (John 4:49)
3. _____ yourselves likewise with the same mind. (1 Pet. 4:1)
4. It is vain for you to rise up early, to sit up _____. (Ps. 127:2)
5. _____ the morrow they left the horsemen to go with him. (Acts 23:32)
6. So I _____ upon him, and slew him. (2 Sam. 1:10)
7. Then she arose with _____ daughters in law. (Ruth 1:6)
8. He struck it into the pan, _____ kettle. (1 Sam. 2:14)
9. In the second _____ of Darius. (Zech. 1:7)
12. And ye shall _____ the feast of unleavened bread. (Ex. 12:17)
13. Christ sitteth on the right _____ of God. (Col. 3:1)
15. O Lord God of hosts, hear my _____. (Ps. 84:8)
18. Into your hand _____ they delivered. (Gen. 9:2)
19. Established (abbr.).

20. _____ the son of Kolaiah.
    (Jer. 29:21)
22. Lord, that thou shalt call me _____.
    (Hosea 2:16)
23. I will offer it up for a burnt _____.
    (Judg. 11:31)
24. For he served _____, and wor-
    shipped him. (1 Kgs. 22:53)
27. Short for *good-bye*.
29. Anno Domini (abbr.).
33. I will cause an _____ of war to be
    heard. (Jer. 49:2)
34. Menahem the son of _____.
    (2 Kgs. 15:14)
36. Sarah heard it in the tent _____.
    (Gen. 18:10)
38. He did evil _____ the sight
    of the Lord. (1 Kgs. 22:52)

41. Were not the Ethiopians and the
    Lubims a _____ host?
    (2 Chron. 16:8)
43. I forgave thee all that _____.
    (Matt. 18:32)
45. Let them not fail to _____ the fat.
    (1 Sam. 2:16)
46. Sisera fled away on his feet to the
    _____. (Judg. 4:17)
48. Preserve hides.
49. _____ Jesus beheld them.
    (Matt. 19:26)
50. And _____ lived two and thirty
    years. (Gen. 11:20)
53. He saith among the trumpets,
    _____, ha. (Job. 39:25)
55. Who hath ascended up into heaven,
    _____ descended? (Prov.30:4)

99

PUZZLE 49

Mrs. Chester Vance Jr.

ACROSS CLUES

1. _____ I pray you. (Gen. 37:6)
4. King of _____, and Tidal. (Gen. 14:1)
7. _____ shall judge. (Gen. 49:16)
10. _____ of the Chaldees. (Gen. 15:7)
11. The king of _____. (Gen. 40:5)
12. Plane surface having bounds.
13. Alcoholics Anonymous (abbr.).
14. _____ light.
15. Who shall _____ thee. (Gen. 49:25)
17. A _____ of money. (Ex. 21:30)
19. _____, and Naphtali. (Ex. 1:4)
20. The hole of the _____. (Isa. 11:8)
21. Prepaid (abbr.).
24. Intensive care.
26. _____ of the house. (Gen. 43:19)
27. My _____ shall not go down. (Gen. 42:38)
29. Called their name _____. (Gen. 5:2)
32. Oklahoma (abbr.).
34. Red Cross (abbr.).
35. Gone six _____. (2 Sam. 6:13)
37. _____ wept. (Gen. 50:17)
39. Chief male character in story.
40. On top of.
41. _____ sinful nation. (Isa. 1:4)
42. Nickname of Deborah.
44. Skin or husk of grain.
46. Roman numeral for fifty.
47. East Indies (abbr.).
48. There was _____ water in it. (Gen. 37:24)
49. Poti-pherah, priest of _____. (Gen. 41:45)

51. But _____ Joseph's brother. (Gen. 42:4)
55. What he sayeth to you, _____. (Gen. 41:55)
56. English (abbr.).
57. These _____ words. (Gen. 44:6)

DOWN CLUES

1. _____ the Archite. (2 Sam. 15:32)
2. Descendant of Judah. (1 Chron. 4:21)
3. They do _____. (Ruth 2:9)
4. _____ were dim. (Gen. 27:1)
5. Low pressure.
6. Music term.
7. What will become of his _____. (Gen. 37:20)
8. Thousands and thousands of years (Eng. spelling).
9. Girl's name.
12. _____ it shall come to pass. (1 Sam. 2:36)
13. Swiss mountain.
16. The servant which is _____ from his master. (Deut. 23:15)
18. Put sackcloth _____ his loins. (Gen. 37:34)
22. Sink or drop down.
23. Measure equal to 1/12 of a foot.
25. Joseph's father. (Gen. 46:19)
28. Child that has lost his parents.
30. _____ stir him up. (Job. 41:10)
31. Dealt ye so ill with _____. (Gen. 43:6)
33. Kansas.
36. Judah spake unto him, _____, . . . (Gen. 43:3)
37. Patience of _____. (Jam. 5:11)
38. Give _____ to his commandments. (Ex. 15:26)
43. Place where his tent had _____. (Gen. 13:3)

44. _____ of the water. (Josh. 3:15)
45. There is _____ that can interpret it. (Gen. 41:15)
46. Ono, and _____. (1 Chron. 8:12)
50. Thy son's coat or _____. (Gen. 37:32)

51. Upon me _____ thy curse. (Gen. 27:13)
52. _____ one of us. (Gen. 3:22)
53. _____ and Pa.
54. Northeast.

PUZZLE 50

Mrs. Chester Vance Jr.

ACROSS CLUES

1. God of my master _____.
   (Gen. 24:42)
6. Thine only son _____. (Gen. 22:2)
10. Suffix indicating names in
    zoology.
12. Obstetrician (abbr.).
13. Idle chatter.
15. Even the men of _____. (Gen. 19:4)
17. Lifted up his _____. (Gen. 22:4)
19. Abbreviation for Micah.
20. Military cap.
23. Small deer.
25. Departed out of _____. (Gen. 12:4)
26. Vitamin _____.
27. Symbol for hydrogen.
28. Children by _____. (Gen. 16:2)
30. Lemon _____.
31. _____ the father of Lecah.
    (1 Chron. 4:21)
32. A spider: _____chnid.
33. Roman numeral for 201.

35. Pursued them unto _____. (Gen. 14:14)
37. Government issued.
39. Abram removed _____ tents. (Gen. 13:18)
40. Neither _____ thou any thing. (Gen. 22:12)
41. But _____ shall her name be. (Gen. 17:15)
43. Son of Haran. (Gen. 11:27)
44. Behind him a _____. (Gen. 22:13)
45. All that he _____. (Gen. 13:1)
47. Called the altar _____. (Josh. 22:34)
49. That I _____ bury my dead. (Gen. 23:4)
50. King of Salem. (Gen. 14:18)

DOWN CLUES

1. _____ of the Lord. (Gen. 22:15)
2. Abraham's daughter-in-law. (Gen. 24:67)
3. And Ishmael _____ son. (Gen. 17:25)
4. Bustle, fuss.
5. Assembled or created.
7. _____ shall thy seed be. (Gen. 15:5)

8. _____ and Phichol. (Gen. 21:22)
9. When he was _____. (Gen. 17:24)
11. *Ex officio.*
14. Expresses surprise or distress (Span.).
16. Get thee into the land of _____. (Gen. 22:2)
18. Dry, withered.
21. Dwelt in the wilderness of _____. (Gen. 21:21)
22. _____ the choice. (Gen. 23:6)
24. Twenty years _____. (Gen. 23:1)
27. _____ of Abram's cattle. (Gen. 13:7)
29. Sarai's handmaid. (Gen. 16:1)
34. Roman numeral for 101.
36. To make amends.
38. Abbreviation for Individual Retirement Account.
42. Behold, here I _____. (Gen. 22:1)
45. I _____ rather be a doorkeeper. (Ps. 84:10)
46. Yes (nautical).
48. Roman numeral for 600.
49. I

ANSWERS

PUZZLE 1

F	O	R		H	E	A	L		S	P	A	S
A	R	E		I	N	T	O		E	A	S	T
T	E	M	P	L	E		O	W	E		H	I
	A	I	L		U	S	E		R	A	N	
S	L	I	T		O	N	E		L	O	N	G
H	I	N		F	I	G		B	E	D		
Y	E		A	L	L	O	W	E	D		R	A
	C	R	Y		D	I	G		B	E	L	
W	H	A	T		A	L	T		T	A	I	L
H	E	N		A	N	Y		H	O	T		
E	A		A	W	N		R	O	O	T	E	D
A	V	E	N		A	T	E	R		L	A	Y
T	E	S	T		S	O	D	I		E	R	E

PUZZLE 2

E	D	E	N		R	O	A	M		A	G	E
	E	V	E	N	I	N	G		A	D	A	M
E	V	E		P	E	E	L		D	R		
D	I	R		O		S	O	D		D	O	
I	S	L	A	N	D	S		W	I	D	E	N
C	E	A	S	E		E	L		D	O	N	E
T		S	P		T	R	E	E		C		
	O	T		O	R	P	A	H		K	I	N
C	A	I	N		Y	E		U	S		D	O
U	R	N		R		N	U	D	E		O	R
R		G	R	E	A	T			A	I	L	
S	O		A	C	T		N	A	T	O		I
E	N	V	Y		E	A	C	H		N	O	T

PUZZLE 3

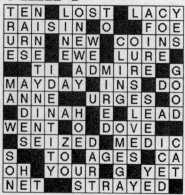

T	E	N		L	O	S	T		L	A	C	Y
R	A	I	S	I	N		O		F	O	E	
U	R	N		N	E	W		C	O	I	N	S
E	S	E		E	W	E		L	U	R	E	
		T	I		A	D	M	I	R	E		G
M	A	Y	D	A	Y		I	N	S		D	O
A	N	N	E			U	R	G	E	S		O
	D	I	N	A	H		E		L	E	A	D
W	E	N	T		O		D	O	V	E		
	S	E	I	Z	E	D		M	E	D	I	C
S			T	O		A	G	E	S		C	A
O	H		Y	O	U	R		G		Y	E	T
N	E	T			S	T	R	A	Y	E	D	

PUZZLE 4

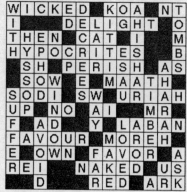

W	I	C	K	E	D		K	O	A		N	T
I				D	E	L	I	G	H	T		O
T	H	E	N		C	A	T		I			M
H	Y	P	O	C	R	I	T	E	S			B
	S	H		P	E	R	I	S	H		A	S
	S	O	W		E		M	A	A	T	H	
S	O	D	I		S	W		U	R	I	A	H
U	P		N	O		A	I			M	R	
F		A	D		Y		L	A	B	A	N	
F	A	V	O	U	R		M	O	R	E	H	
E		O	W	N		F	A	V	O	R		A
R	E	I			N	A	K	E	D		U	S
		D			R	E	D		A	R	K	

PUZZLE 5

PUZZLE 6

PUZZLE 7

PUZZLE 8

PUZZLE 9

PUZZLE 10

PUZZLE 11

```
M Y S T E R Y . . E L I
. O . D E E R . L V . N
Z U P H . N . C A I N .
. N O . T W A . B L O T
. G O L D . O S L O . B .
H E R O . R A . R I L .
O R . B A C K S L I D E R
S . C . S H E . N O M E
P R O P H E T S . G L A D
I A M . A H A B . N .
T I E . O P . V A I N . W
A S S . R E V E R T . C O
L E T T E R . D E S E R T
```

PUZZLE 12

```
. L A I D . L U K E .
. O F F A . E S E K .
G I R L . N O T . P E R M
L A D Y . G A T . T R E E
A T . . E R E . . A T
D E B T O R . R E T I R E
. A I N . . N E R .
A B D E E L . A D A I A H
B E . . A B I . . H E
E L O I . Y E A . A H E R
L A M B . I L L . B E N D
. E R A N . A B D I .
. R I N G . Y E A R .
```

PUZZLE 13

```
W O E . S E W . P A I .
H U L . T O E . A B L E
O R I G I N . A R E . D O
. E A R . P I T . D E N
R E L Y . P A R . L I N E
I V . T I N . R A N .
P E R S O N . R E D E E M
. O A T . Y O U . Y E
E A S Y . R E D . A M E N
E R E . L O T . L I E
L A . C O W . B A L A A M
. M O R N . T E N . T H E
. R Y E . O D D . S I T
```

PUZZLE 14

```
F O E . H I M . I B R I
R U N . H O L Y . N E E D
O R D A I N E R . V A S E
. U R G E . E V E N T S
S A R A H . T W I N .
A N I M . R O A S T E T H
T O N . G E N R E . N E E
E N G R A V E D . S T A R
. E V E R . T H E R E
G R A V E N . S O U R .
R O S E . G E N E T I C S
I D E A . E R A S . N O E
M E A L . D I G . G O T
```

PUZZLE 15

```
M A N A S S E H . B . B
A P A C E . R E C E I V E
K A R T A N . B O A T .
E R R . A . R A T E . E
. T O . M . E L . T . M
. W A R E . W . S H E M
. N E S T . H O . A
A N D . D . C A N A A N
B E E . S E E . N . D . U
R E E L E D . J O N A . E
A D R I A . M . C A M E L
M E S S . E . H I S S .
. D . T I M N A . L
```

PUZZLE 16

```
F I R S T B O R N . O G .
L A I N . H I . P R A Y
A M B A S S A D O R . Z E
M . R . A D D . I G A L
E D G E . M . L I D . L
S O . L U K E . E . L O
. E . C . S O W
I S R A E L . G O . A T
S A U L . G . N . I
A M I S S . A B S A L O M
I . N O . O D O U R . B E
A H . . A D A M . E N
H A G . W R I T E . B Y
```

PUZZLE 17

```
L O S T   N E T S   P V T
E A S E   O D E S   R I O
G R A M   M E N T I O N S
    P L A N S   S U E S
S M I L E D   I C E D
L A C E S   B O R E D O M
A D A   S C E N E   O R E
M E N W E R E   S W E E T
    D O N E   S T O R M S
I G O R   M O U S E
R O A D M A P S   F O R T
A L L   U T A H   U N T O
N F L   D E L I   L E E R
```

PUZZLE 18

```
S E N   D E A D   D A R E
O N E   U R G E   E D O M
N I H   S N A P   P A S T
  D E U T E R O N O M Y
    M A Y     S O T
H A I R   D E N   S E A
A S A   P O I S E   U R N
M P H   E N D   S P A T
    A R E     V I P
  J E S U S T H E S O N
P E S O   T O U R   S E A
F L A N   E G G S   E B B
C L U E   P O S E   D O E
```

PUZZLE 19

```
J E S U S   N   S E T H
E V I L   O   S A U L
H E T M A N   C   T U G
O   B   J O S H   E
S A M U E L   L I E S   S
H E L   S T A R   A
A A H   S O   L   I N K
P E T E R   W V   E
H   A L   A   A
A B C   C   S A R A H S
T   A C H S A H   R A T
  T I M E   I T   V O T E
S I N   L Y D I A   N E W
```

PUZZLE 20

```
B R I C   C O S   C R E E
R O S H   O R A   R A R A
A T M O   M E D   A V I S
D E S I R E   D I V I N E
    C A L   E T A
C O M E D Y   N A T U R E
A R I         R A W
B R A C E S   F A M I N E
    R O T   E N E
R E F U S E   E N A B L E
O M R I   A L B   D A I S
D U E S   M A L   O L E O
E S T E   S B E   W I S P
```

PUZZLE 21

```
L A B S   A R   S T E W
A B I A   A B I   H A V E
K E R C H I E F   O N A N
E L D A D   S L E W
    R   D   E L I S H A
C P T   R U E   I N T E R
A L O E   E N D   G O R E
L E A S T   D E B   P A S
F A C T O R   F O O
    E Y E S E R V I C E
R O T E   S I N G U L A R
I T E M   T D D   L E N S
D O N S   S E   E A S E
```

PUZZLE 22

```
M A R S H I L L   D R A B
A B E   U L L A   E A S E
R A C A L   A B R A H A M
A S A S   M A I D
H E P S   A N N   L A P
    U S A   J A D A
E D O M I T E S   O B A L
R A R E   O R A
E N G   T O R   S T O P
  O R C A   H O M E
O B A D I A H   B   R E T
H E R O   L A M A   A G E
S T A R   A B I A T H A R
```

PUZZLE 23

```
C A P   E N I D   D E L E
R N A   N I C E   E B O N
I N S   S T E P   B R I T
B E S T I R   I N T O N E
    A G E   C O O
O N I O N S   T E R E S H
R E L           P I E
B E L O N G   D E S I R E
    C A A   E R A
B E T   E L   V A C A N T
E D E R   L E I S   N O R
L I M A   O N C E   T V A
L E A N   P O E S   S A Y
```

PUZZLE 24

```
I N C A   S H U A   G A S
B I R D   W E E D   A R E
I D E A   A L L E L U I A
D I A M O N D   P I L L S
    T A   S   A T T
T R U N K   O G   D A R
H U R T   T I O   P E L E
E E E   E L   C A R O L
    A R T   R A R I T Y
I T H R A   B A B A S
S H E P H E R D   B I E R
L E A   A R I A   L O G O
E E R   B E E R   E N O S
```

PUZZLE 25

```
M E   A N T   S U M M E R
Y   N O   G O   O   R E
  J O N A H   S T A R S
B E   H O P E   H   H
U S A   G R A V E N   E
S U R E   S A T   R A S P
  S E A L   Y   A   O H
R   R O S E   S   L
A P   L O   R A I N B O W
I L   I P   S A U L   A
S U R E   W A S   R O   G
I T   S   H   E   S O S O
N O   T R O A S   E D E N
```

PUZZLE 26

```
G O O D   B L E S S I N G
A N G E R   A B L Y   O N
T I R E D   W O U N D   A
H O E D   U   N R A   A T
E N S   O N L Y   G E M
R S   B R I O   G O N E
E   A I   T R I   G E T S
R A B B I   D R O U G H T
  A B B A   L   R E L Y
E R A   M A Y B E   A S K
D O   P   R   S M I T E
E N D U R E   I   A M   E
N   A T T A I N E D   U P
```

PUZZLE 27

```
A R I S E   C O U R A G E
G I V E   C A L L   A L A
R B   A B I L I T Y   O G
E B E R   T L V   E A R L
E O   C A Y   E V A   Y E
M N   H E   D   A R M
E   B   S E O U L   A S P
N A R R O W   N U R S E D
T R O U P E   P E N T A D
  R A M   M A   E L
D O D O   P E C K   R E D
A W   U M I A K   T   D O
M S G R   A T   J O B   E
```

PUZZLE 28

```
T E N D E R H E A R T E D
H E A L   R A B B I   A A
A L I V E   N B A   I C Y
N   L Y I N G   S A P H
K Y   G A   S E T H   A
S E A S H O R E   M E A L
G A D   T M   V A   D A Y
I R O N   I T E M   E R
V   N E T   A N A T I O N
I R I J A H   Z O A N
N O   D I A L   E P H   B
G O D   L E G   D A   H E
  M E   S T A R   Z E A L
```

PUZZLE 29

```
K I N D N E S S
  L O I N S   P E A C E
K N O W L E D G E   G O N
I O   I   O D   E N T
N   S   G O O D   A S   R
G R A C E   P L O T   S A
D I V I N E   I N   S O N
O D E   C L A N   P I   C
M S   T E M P E R A N C E
    P R   O S       H
  C O U R T   S A V I O R
V I R T U E     L O   S N
I F T H E N     P O W E R
```

PUZZLE 30

```
P I   B R I G H T N E S S
A N H E I R   I H S   P T
  I M A G E   G O   O R
H Q   N H   T H U S   K U
B U R S T   R     M E T
  I E   E C U   C O I N S
E T A   O U T D O   N
X Y L   U P H O L D I N G
P   I S     N T   S O N
R Y E   N A M E   S T O A
E O S   E X C E L L E N T
S K   U S E     E A R   S
S E E K S   C I T Y
```

PUZZLE 31

```
I S R A E L I T E S   H E
N O   P L O D     R U I N
C   G E M   O M R I   R E
U S E S   F L E E   H E M
R   T   D   W E N T   S I
S E   B E G O T T E N   E
    L A B O R   A   A S
P A   S O L S T I C E S
A S H E R A H   T H O U
R I O   A N I   P E N N Y
B L U S H   P E A R   D O
A L S O   A   B Y   H E R
R Y E   S T A B S   A R E
```

PUZZLE 32

```
V I N E Y A R D S   A W E
O F   N E W E R   A N E W
L   G A E L I C     B E
U N D E R   I N L E T S
N O   D   A S K E T H
T R A I T   H   V E R Y
E   N   O   M E R E   E
E L D E R S   O R N E R Y
R A R E R   A D   A   E
  C E L E S T I A L   T
S E W   N O   C   A R E
P   A T R I U M   M E N
A M I D S T   M E L T E D
```

PUZZLE 33

```
A L T A R S   O D I O U S
B O O T   T   N   N U L L
I T   M I M   A N T A E
J U S T I F I E D   I D
A S   U   F L A M   B
H   S A N C T I F I E D
  O S H E A   N E W   A
  M O L E C H   I R E   R
L   L E A K   A S T E R N
A H I   D E N   T I K E
M E T E   D O   E L L   U
P R E E N   S   R E Y E S
S O   N O T E D     H E
```

PUZZLE 34

```
F O U N D   S I N   G O D
I N N   A S H D O D   R E
S C I E N C E   U I   P A
H E T H   A D O R E   A T
E   Y I E L D   I   A H H
R D     P E R S I A
S E L A H   T   H O R E B
  L I V E T H     D O N E
R I C E   E   G R I N D S
O V E N   A L O A N   S E
B E   G A M A L I E L   E
E R R E D   W A S   E   C
  S I R A H   N E R I A H
```

PUZZLE 35

```
B E O R   L O R D   T H E
A N G E R   N A A M   E S
A T   A I   E B R O N A H
L E A D   A   B E D A D
  R A Y   R O I   E A S T
O   R I S E N   I S M   A
F R O N T   E   S T A N D
F I N G E R   O H   N O
I D   W E A P O N   D O
C E P H A S   D O N   A
E R R   R O B E   V O L T
    A N D R E W   A H A H
D A Y   S T E E P   E D S
```

PUZZLE 36

```
M A N N A   N O   E S A U
A S I E L   O N A N   M S
T A S T E   A L L   O N E
T   A S   T H Y   T W O
H E N   F A     A N N A
E R   S E N T   M R   C
W R O T E   A G A G   S T
  E B A L   K A D E S H
A D E R   B E L   T H A T
D   Y E A   A N   I K E
L O   U N C L E   M I X
A F F I R M     A M E N
I F   M A S T E R   A G E
```

PUZZLE 37

```
M A I M E D   O W N   I S
O R D E R   I B E A M
M E E T S   S E A P O R T
S N A R E   Y R   A   I
  A L E   B   Y   B U M
W     M E T   A I   B
I D O L S   L O   S T A R
T A P E   J I M   E V E
N I T S   E B B S   A L
E L   S   I V   R A N I
S Y N O D   E V E N   L A
S   N E E D   A D O   T
  S W   N   E D I F Y
```

PUZZLE 38

```
S H A R A R   D A N I E L
A A R O N   A N   G L
V I E   A D O N I J A H
E L T E K E H   S E L A H
  A   I M A G E S   N O
D D S   M A D E   U T A H
  R   S   N   S   N A
H O S E A   D E W   T   M
A P   A N   S O D O M
M   S A M   I N A   A X
M A T T H I A S   N A I L
E R A   T S   C R N
R A N   J E H E Z E K E L
```

PUZZLE 39

```
A B L E   N A B   D A R K
S A U L   E G O   E R I E
I S H I   P A W   M A C E
A H I J A H   E N A M E L
    A   E   L E N
E S C H E W   S A D D E N
S E A       A D O
T E M P E R   P A S T O R
    R O E   E   I
O B T A I N   R E S I S T
P R A Y   O G S   E R I A
E I R E   W O O   R A N K
N E A R   N O N   A N G E
```

PUZZLE 40

```
B O B S   S I P   I B R I
A L O T   H E R   N E A R
D E A R   I   O   S A R I
    A I N   F L A M E S
D E V I C E   F U N
E R I T E   J E Z E B E L
E N O   T A R   O V A
D E L I V E R   T E N E T
    N E A   S E V E R E
C R A F T   P E A
R A R A   A P E   D A T E
I C A N   L E A   E D E N
B E N T   A R K   S A N D
```

PUZZLE 41

G	R	A	F		C	R	Y		N	O	E	L
L	A	V	A		H	U	R		O	M	R	I
A	N	I	M		E	H	S		V	E	I	N
D	I	V	I	N	E	R		S	I	N	C	E
			N	O	R		T	I	C			
F	I	R	E			D	E	C	E	A	S	E
A	N	I		B	R	E	A	K		P	E	N
T	A	B	R	E	T	S			S	P	E	D
			E	S	E		R	A	H			
C	R	A	F	T		R	E	M	O	V	A	L
R	E	T	U		P	O	I		W	E	R	E
A	B	I	S		S	U	N		E	T	N	A
G	A	P	E		I	T	S		R	O	O	F

PUZZLE 42

I	N	N		O	D	O	R		T	R	I	M
R	O	E		B	O	N	E		I	O	T	A
A	V	I		T	R	E	S		F	L	E	W
M	A	N	I	A	C		O	F	F	E	R	S
			I	A		R	I					
O	N	I	O	N	S		T	E	N	D	E	R
N	E	A							U	R	I	
S	T	R	O	N	G		R	E	C	O	R	D
			E	A		E	R					
H	E	A	L	E	R		M	A	T	T	E	R
E	S	L	I		D	I	O	S		A	M	E
L	A	M	E		E	N	T	E		M	I	L
P	U	A	S		N	A	E	S		E	L	Y

PUZZLE 43

B	A	S	E		L	I	E		R	E	D	O
A	L	P	S		A	I	M		A	R	O	D
R	O	U	T		V	I	E		N	A	T	E
B	E	R	A	T	E		R	E	D	S	E	A
			T	A	R		O	R	O			
M	O	S	E	S		A	D	A	M	A	N	T
	R	I		E	L	S		S	I			
P	A	R	A	B	L	E		P	S	A	L	M
			N	R	A		E	R	I			
R	A	N	S	O	M		N	E	M	U	E	L
E	N	O	W		I	N	T		P	R	A	E
A	N	N	E		T	E	E		L	I	V	E
R	O	A	R		E	A	R		E	M	E	

PUZZLE 44

W	A	F	E	R		C	H	A	M	O	I	S
H		O		B	O	A	T		V		N	
A	D	D	E	R		T	N	T		E		A
L	A	D	D	E	R		D	I	N	N	E	R
E	T	E	R	N	A	L		R			E	
S	E	R	E	D		O	M	E	G	A		
			I	S	H	I		L		N	T	
S	H	E		A	S	S	H	U	R		E	
C	A	R	N	A	L		A		T		P	A
R	I	G		L	I	G	H	T		A	C	
O	R	O	Z	C	O			O	A	T	H	
L		T	E	A	W	A	G	O	N		H	E
L		N	T		T	O	T	S		S	S	

PUZZLE 45

H	O		A	N	N	A		F	I	N	D
O	M	E	G	A		D	O		E	S	A	U
U	R	I	A	H		A	N		E	R	R	
S	I		G	U	I	D	E		D	A	D	S
E		T	I	M		A	S	A		E		E
	N	O	T		E	H	I		A	L	O	E
H	O	M	E		L		M	I	C		M	K
E	O		S	U	N		U		T		I	
A	N	D		N	A		S	A	I	N	T	S
V		E		N	A	P		G	O		O	
E	G	L	A	I	M		C	A	N	A	A	N
N		A			H	O	P		N	R		
S	A	Y		S	H	E		E	N	T	E	R

PUZZLE 46

S	U	N	D	A	Y		M	A	N		S	W
H			M	A		E		O	N	E		
U	N	I	C	O	R	N		D	R	E	A	M
C		N		S	N	O	R	E		A		U
K	I	S	H		A		E	A	R		T	
S		T	O	U	G	H		P	R	I	C	E
	S	A	T		E		F		C	A	R	
F	A	N		A	B	R	A	M		H	O	P
A	N	T		P	A	A	R	A	I		P	A
R	D		P		I		R		A		R	
M	Y	S	I	A		L	O	I	N	S		E
E		O		I	C	E		S		P	A	N
R	U	N		M	A	R	T	H	A		A	T

111

PUZZLE 47

```
B E T H L E H E M ▓ A G O
A D A I A H ▓ D O C T O R
S ▓ T ▓ U R ▓ P ▓ U ▓ ▓
K G ▓ S O D O M ▓ S I L K
E A C H ▓ D U R A ▓ A M ▓
T R O O P ▓ ▓ S I L A S ▓
▓ L A P ▓ J E H O V A H ▓
R I C H ▓ B I T E ▓ ▓ U ▓
▓ C H A R I O T ▓ M ▓ Z ▓
S ▓ E N ▓ N E P H E G ▓ ▓
H A S ▓ B A ▓ ▓ A A R O N
O G ▓ B E S O M ▓ ▓ C L ▓
E O N ▓ E P H O D ▓ Y D ▓
```

PUZZLE 48

```
S E A ▓ L O ▓ S ▓ H O L Y
E R R ▓ A N O T H E R ▓ E
T E M P T ▓ B O A R ▓ ▓ A
H ▓ R E A S O N ▓ E A R ▓
▓ ▓ A ▓ R E D D I S H ▓ ▓
O B E Y ▓ E R ▓ ▓ S T A B
F A ▓ E ▓ ▓ V ▓ A H ▓ B Y
F A ▓ R A G E ▓ D I D ▓ E
E L I ▓ L A ▓ ▓ ▓ O H ▓ ▓
R ▓ N ▓ A D D ▓ A B O U T
I T ▓ B R I E R ▓ U R G E
N A H U M ▓ B E O R ▓ E N
G N A T ▓ ▓ T U R N ▓ ▓ T
```

PUZZLE 49

```
H E A R ▓ E L A M ▓ D A N
U R ▓ E G Y P T ▓ A R E A
S ▓ A A ▓ E ▓ E ▓ N E O N
H E L P ▓ S U M ▓ D A N ▓
A S P ▓ ▓ P P D ▓ M ▓ I ▓
I C ▓ J ▓ D O O R ▓ S O N
▓ A D A M ▓ N ▓ O K ▓ R C
▓ P A C E S ▓ J O S E P H
H E R O ▓ A T O P ▓ A H ▓
▓ D E B B Y ▓ B ▓ B R A N
L ▓ ▓ E I ▓ ▓ R ▓ N O ▓
O N ▓ B E N J A M I N ▓ N
D O ▓ E N G ▓ S A M E ▓ E
```

PUZZLE 50

```
A B R A H A M ▓ I S A A C
N ▓ E ▓ I D A E ▓ O B ▓ I
G A B ▓ S O D O M ▓ I ▓ R
E Y E S ▓ E ▓ O ▓ M I C ▓
L ▓ K E P I ▓ R O E ▓ U ▓
▓ H A R A N ▓ P I L L ▓ M
H ▓ H E R ▓ H ▓ A D E ▓ C
E R ▓ A R A ▓ H ▓ C C I ▓
R ▓ D A N ▓ G I ▓ H I S ▓
D O ▓ T ▓ S A R A H ▓ ▓ E
M ▓ L O T ▓ R A M ▓ H A D
E D ▓ N ▓ D ▓ ▓ M A Y ▓ ▓
N ▓ M E L C H I Z E D E K
```

Bible Crosswords

Collection #3

Compiled and Edited
by *Toni Sortor*

A Barbour Book

Bible
Crosswords

Collection #3

Puzzle 1

Udena McKee

ACROSS CLUES

1. A receptacle made of bronze. (Ex. 30:18 NIV)
6. Political party.
10. _____ David prevailed over the Philistine. (1 Sam. 17:50)
11. _____ in a secret place. (1 Sam. 19:2)
12. Abram the _____. (Gen. 14:13)
14. Look not thou upon the wine when it is _____. (Prov. 23:31)
15. Whose son _____ stripling is. (1 Sam. 17:56)
17. Variant of "aeon".
19. African plant.
21. Take two _____ stones. (Ex. 28:9)
23. _____ no man any thing. (Rom. 13:8)
25. Do we, then, _____ify the law. (Rom. 3:31 NIV)
26. A king of Judah. (1 Kgs. 15:9)
27. Light of Israel shall _____ for a fire. (Isa. 10:17)
29. The calf and the _____ lion. (Isa. 11:6)
32. I am _____ and Omega. (Rev. 1:8)

4

34. An eagle's nest.
37. Storage place for crops.
38. Not beautiful.
39. Above him were _____s.
(Isa. 6:2 NIV)
41. The Lord was not _____.
(Num. 14:16)
43. He weighed the _____ of his
head. (2 Sam. 14:26)
44. Laid it in his own new _____.
(Matt. 27:60)
47. Winter melons with yellow rinds
and sweet flesh.
49. We have come from a _____.
country. (Josh. 9:6)
50. And they went _____ Joshua.
(Josh. 9:6)
52. A nourisher of thine _____ age.
(Ruth 4:15)
54. Seize, especially to arrest.
56. It is not in man that walketh to
_____ his steps. (Jer. 10:23)
57. Whosoever shall compel thee to
go a _____. (Matt. 5:41)

DOWN CLUES

1. Then released he _____ unto
them. (Matt. 27:26)
2. She again bore his brother
_____. (Gen. 4:2)
3. Ancient city. (Josh. 11:8)
4. Part of the psyche.
5. Casting a _____ into the sea.
(Matt. 4:18)
6. _____ he was set, his disciples
came. (Matt. 5:1)
7. _____ opened his mouth.
(Matt. 5:2)
8. Old world goat with large horns.
9. Gross (abbr.).
10. Direction.
13. Seth lived an hundred and five

years, and begot _____h.
(Gen. 5:6)
16. Jerusalem, the _____ city.
(Neh. 11:1)
18. There were those whosaid,
_____, our sons. (Neh. 5:2)
20. A marked feeling of well-being.
22. Send one of _____. (Gen. 42:16)
24. _____ of Egypt.
(Josh. 15:4 NIV)
26. That in the _____s to come.
(Eph. 2:7)
28. He departed thence and found
_____. (1 Kgs. 19:19)
30. And by our law he _____ to die.
(John 19:7)
31. With me there should be yea,
yea, and _____. (2 Cor. 1:17)
33. Beloved son, in whom I am well
_____. (Matt. 3:17)
35. Will a man _____ God?
(Mal. 3:8)
36. Adam called his wife's name
_____. (Gen. 3:20)
38. Yet will I not lift _____ my head.
(Job 10:15)
40. A bower covered with vines.
41. Neither shall thy name any more
be called _____. (Gen. 17:5)
42. _____ no fruit grow on thee
henceforward. (Matt. 21:19)
45. But are as the angels _____ God
in heaven. (Matt. 22:30)
46. No _____ was able to answer.
(Matt. 22:46)
47. He took the _____, and gave
thanks. (Matt. 26:27)
48. Alcoholic beverage.
51. They shall be _____ flesh.
(Gen. 2:24)
53. Direct current (abbr.).
55. Symbol for bismuth.

Puzzle 2

Udena McKee

ACROSS CLUES

1. If one went unto them from the _____. (Luke 16:30)
5. Sixth month of the Hebrew calendar. (Neh. 6:15)
8. Give tribute unto Caesar, or _____t? (Luke 20:22)
10. A rod of an _____ tree. (Jer. 1:11)
11. He made him to suck honey out of the _____. (Deut. 32:13)
14. A good _____ is rather to be chosen. (Prov. 22:1)
15. Satan. . .smote Job with sore _____. (Job. 2:7)
16. Month (abbr.).
17. American Medical Association (abbr.).
19. Vase or vessel.
21. The absence or reverse of.
23. God set them in the heaven to give _____. (Gen. 1:17)
25. _____ up thy strength. (Ps. 80:2)
28. Legislator (abbr.).
29. A favorite.
30. His enemy came and sowed _____s. (Matt. 13:25)
32. The shepherds who _____ my people. (Jer. 23:2 NIV)
35. Direction.
36. To give off or out.
37. A fine grit stone for sharpening.
38. Do you submit to _____ rules. (Col. 2:20 NIV)
39. And all the _____ of the land. (Lev. 27:30)
41. To find fault.
42. Behold, I send an angel before _____. (Ex. 23:20)

43. Wind direction.
45. _____ no man any thing. (Rom. 13:8)
48. There came two angels to _____. (Gen. 19:1)
52. _____ consider how great this man was. (Heb. 7:4)
53. Elkanah went to _____mah. (1 Sam. 2:11)
55. _____ your heart and not your garments. (Joel 2:13)
57. It shall bring forth _____ fruit. (Ezek. 47:12)
58. Condemned, especially to hell.

DOWN CLUES

1. Son of Bilhah and Jacob. (Gen. 35:25)
2. Chedorlaomer king of _____. (Gen. 14:1)
3. Descendants of Lot and his youngest daughter. (Gen. 19:38)
4. Female deer.
5. Wilderness of _____. (2 Kgs. 3:8)
6. Home of Abram. (Gen. 11:28)
7. Small or partial lobe.
9. At the beginning.
12. Home of Aquila and Priscilla. (Acts. 18:1-2)
13. Now make us a _____. (1 Sam. 8:5)
17. The weight thereof was _____ hundred and thirty. (Num. 7:13)
18. Arizona (abbr.).
20. Child shall play on the hole of the _____. (Isa. 11:8)
22. Either/_____.
24. Wife of Elkanah. (1 Sam. 1:2)
26. Do not _____. the Lord your God. (Deut. 6:16 NIV)
27. Fiber.

28. Third son of Adam and Eve. (Gen. 4:25)
30. To fasten or restrain.
31. Last _____.
33. Variant of aeon.
34. Degree (abbr.).
38. Iron sharpeneth _____. (Prov. 27:17)
40. I shall keep it unto the _____. (Ps. 119:33)
44. But I am a ____, and no man. (Ps. 22:6)

46. They also may without the word be _____. (1 Pet. 3:1)
47. Man had nothing, save one little _____ lamb. (2 Sam. 12:3)
49. Remember the days of _____. (Deut. 32:7)
50. Sons of God saw the daughters of _____. (Gen. 6:2)
51. Strange or different.
54. Morning time.
56. Nebraska (abbr.).

Puzzle 3

Udena McKee

ACROSS CLUES

1. Led the Israelites over the Jordan river. (Josh. 4:1)
6. Queen of the _____. (Matt. 12:42)
11. A crown of gold round _____. (Ex. 25:11)
12. Disciple and successor of Elijah. (1 Kgs. 19:16)
13. Marked with bands.
15. Part of the small intestine.
16. Overdraft (abbr.).
17. Born in his _____ house. (Gen. 14:14)
19. The _____es saw a man coming forth out of the city. (Judg. 1:24)
21. _____ thou return unto the ground. (Gen. 3:19)
22. Loose outer garment worn by ancient Romans.
23. He built there an altar, and called the place _____-bethel. (Gen. 35:7)
24. The Lord your God, _____ it is that fighteth for you. (Josh. 23:10)

8

25. Spiral or twisted form.
27. Who heard _____ words of God. (Num. 24:4)
29. Whoso putteth his trust in the Lord shall be _____. (Prov. 29:25)
31. _____ an earring of gold. (Prov. 25:12)
32. Los Angeles (abbr.).
34. Thus you _____ify the word of God. (Matt. 15:6 NIV)
36. One who excels.
37. If a man have long _____. (1 Cor. 11:14)
38. Past participle of lie.
40. The men of Bethel and _____. (Neh. 7:32)
42. Where golf ball is placed.
43. Give _____ this day. (Matt. 6:11)
45. City where the Philistines took the ark. (1 Sam. 5:1)
48. First home of Adam and Eve. (Gen. 2:8)
50. A native of Thailand.
52. What hast thou _____? (Gen. 4:10)
54. A good king of Judah. (2 Chron. 29:1)
55. A male cat.

DOWN CLUES

1. A dress or shirt ruffle.
2. Shortest book of the Old Testament.
3. Hannah prayed for a _____. (1 Sam. 1:11)
4. To crowd together.
5. Indian tribe from western U.S.

6. His _____ was in his hand. (1 Sam. 17:40)
7. Her mouth is smoother than _____. (Prov. 5:3)
8. _____ them to fasten the curtains. (Ex. 26:6 NIV)
9. _____ shall ye say to David. (1 Sam. 18:25)
10. Your steps will not be _____ (ed). (Prov. 4:12 NIV)
14. Where Joseph found his brothers. (Gen. 37:17)
18. Full of sorrow.
20. Jonadab told Amnon to pretend to be _____. (2 Sam. 13:5 NIV)
25. Symbol for calcium.
26. United States of America (abbr.).
28. Job's friend. (Job 2:11)
30. To fill with joy.
33. Symbol for argon.
35. Thou hast not _____ unto men, but unto God. (Acts. 5:4)
37. A tract of open land.
39. Your Father knoweth what things ye have _____ of. (Matt. 6:8)
40. Account of (abbr.).
41. Part of the psyche.
44. All of a man's ways _____ innocent to him. (Prov. 16:2 NIV)
46. _____ shall be called Woman. (Gen. 2:23)
47. Give me children, or else I _____. (Gen. 30:1)
49. That which was torn by beasts I brought _____ unto thee. (Gen. 31:39)
51. Mother.
53. Before them there were _____ such locusts. (Ex. 10:14)

Puzzle 4

Lee Esch

ACROSS CLUES

1. Silas' cellmate. (Acts. 16:25)
5. _____ aloud, spare not. (Isa. 58:1)
8. From whence come _____ and fightings among you? (Jam. 4:1)
12. Straight mark.
13. Grassy meadow.
14. Against (prefix).
15. Mine entrance.
16. Each (abbr.).
17. Fork prongs.
18. Longing.
19. Documents.
20. There is a _____ for the silver. (Job. 28:1)
22. Musical exercise.
26. All _____ _____ of God. (2 Cor. 5:18; 2 words)
30. Nothing.
31. Ritual.
32. Environmental watchdog (abbr.).
33. Buddies.
34. Before (poetic).
35. Acceptable (as a proposed law).
37. Grassy plant.
39. Carbonated beverage.
40. Renew _____ _____ spirit within me. (Ps. 51:10; 2 words)
43. Depot (abbr.).
46. The Spirit of the Lord God _____ _____ _____. . . (Isa. 61:1)
49. A Great Lakes state.
50. Thy _____ is like a tower of Lebanon. (Song of Sol. 7:4)
51. Golfer's requirement.
52. Display model (abbr.).
53. Raced.
54. A Great Lakes province (abbr.).
55. Biblical garden. (Gen. 2:8)

DOWN CLUES

1. Can _____ well on an instrument. (Ezek. 33:32)
2. Assistant.
3. Not welcomed.
4. _____ down your nets for a draught. (Luke 5:4)
5. Immediately his leprosy was _____. (Matt. 8:3)
6. Thou knewest that I _____ where I sowed not. (Matt 25:26)
7. Young adult (abbr.).
8. Beltline.
9. Feminine name.
10. A set path (abbr.).
11. Female sibling (abbr.).
17. Every good _____ bringeth forth good fruit. (Matt. 7:17)
19. Swine.
21. Compass direction.
23. Not embarrassed.
24. A seasoning herb.
25. Otherwise.
26. Three (Spanish).
27. The labourer is worthy of his _____. (Luke 10:7)
28. Military address (abbr.).
29. A police arrest record.
33. Cushion.
35. Air (prefix).
36. Child.
38. They _____ upon me with their mouths. (Ps. 22:13).

10

41. Reach hither thy hand, and thrust it _____ my side. (John 20:27)
42. Federal agents (for short).
44. Brethren, the _____ is short. (1 Cor. 7:29)
45. Twelve o'clock.

46. _____ and outs.
47. He it is to whom I shall give a _____. (John 13:26)
48. _____ hospitality one to another. (1 Pet. 4:9)
49. Poem.

Puzzle 5

Lee Esch

ACROSS CLUES

1. Arrived.
5. Bean counter (abbr.).
8. The trees of the field shall _____ their hands. (Isa. 55:12)
12. Will _____ _____ rob God? (Mal. 3:8; 2 words)
13. Hurl.
14. Assistant.
15. The _____ is clothed with strength. (Ps. 93:1)
16. Citizen of Tirane.
18. Food additive (abbr.).
19. Every _____ fled away. (Rev. 16:20)
20. Pointed tools.
22. Jesus Christ, the same yesterday, and _____, and for ever. (Heb. 13:8)
26. Ones who offer their services.
30. Compass direction.
31. Dry.
32. Farm organization for youth (abbr.).
33. Information.

34. 2000 pounds.
35. I lay down _____ _____ _____ the sheep. (John. 10:15; 3 words)
37. If thine _____ hunger, feed him. (Rom. 12:20)
39. _____ is good, save one. (Luke 18:19)
40. Prisoner.
43. Capture.
46. A Japanese island.
49. A city of Hawaii.
50. Hosea. (Rom. 9:25)
51. Abraham's burnt offering. (Gen. 22:13)
52. Aware of.
53. Purchases.
54. Before (poetic).
55. Selves.

DOWN CLUES

1. He maketh the storm a _____. (Ps. 107:29)
2. Old Testament prophet.
3. Imitation butter.
4. Alpha and Omega, the beginning and the _____. (Rev. 22:13)
5. Organize.
6. Survey.
7. Father God. (Mark 14:36)
8. I _____ _____ all things through Christ. (Phil. 4:13)
9. 52 (Roman numeral).
10. A city in Oklahoma.
11. My tongue is the _____ of a ready writer. (Ps. 45:1)
17. Insects.
19. Love worketh no _____. (Rom 13:10)
21. Marry.
23. Extremely loud.
24. Regarding (2 words).
25. Twelve months.
26. Do good to them that _____ you. (Matt. 5:44)
27. Press.
28. Major football organization (abbr.).
29. What things were _____ _____, _____ those I counted loss. (Phil. 3:7; 3 words)
33. Ye have made it a _____ of thieves. (Matt. 21:13)
35. Exotic pet bird.
36. Enemy.
38. Voice transmitters (informal).
41. He hath cast me into the _____. (Job 30:19)
42. Jewish month.
44. Singing part.
45. Sounds of disapproval.
46. Elf.
47. Oklahoma State University (abbr.)
48. Ye have taken away the _____ of knowledge. (Luke 11:52)
49. A garden tool.

Puzzle 6

Udena McKee

ACROSS CLUES

1. To crush.
4. The Spirit _____ truth.
   (1 John 5:6)
6. What all homes in the South have.
8. Wind direction.
10. _____ did that which was right.
    (1 Kgs. 15:11)
11. If I be _____, then my strength will go. (Judg. 16:17)
13. A Protestant denomination.
15. Land from which the Lord brought Abram. (Gen. 15:7)
16. Verse or rhyme.
18. A mental disorder.
20. Behold the _____ of God.
    (John 1:29)
21. _____ Moses lifted up the serpent. (John. 3:14)
22. The days that Adam lived were _____ hundred and thirty years.
(Gen. 5:5)
23. _____ else!
24. The mother of all living.
    (Gen. 3:20)
27. Fragrant shrub.
30. Location.
32. Seaman apprentice (abbr.).
34. Thou shalt make _____ covenant with them. (Ex. 23:32)
35. When the Lord smelled the pleasing _____.
    (Gen. 8:21 RSV)
36. Male cat.
37. Judah is a _____'s whelp.
    (Gen. 49:9)
39. Curve.

40. And when he had spit _____ his eyes. (Mark 8:23)
41. He _____ _____ meet them.
    (2 Sam. 10:5)
43. A particular thing (legal term).
44. King of Bashan. (Num. 21:33)
45. Seth lived _____ hundred and five years. (Gen. 5:6)
46. Drone.
47. Thou shalt have good _____.
    (Josh. 1:8)
48. Consumed.
49. So Absalom _____ the hearts of the men of Israel. (2 Sam. 15:6)
50. With regard to.
51. Golf peg.

DOWN CLUES

1. One who endangers success by meddling.
2. Ye shall be _____ gods.
   (Gen. 3:5)
3. Melchizedek, king of _____.
   (Gen. 14:18)
4. Abraham's son. (Gen. 16:11)
5. But Sarai was barren; _____ had no child. (Gen. 11:30)
6. Away, hence (archaic).
7. A hundred (comb. form).
9. How much less man, that is a _____? (Job. 25:6)
12. Football coach Parseghian.
14. Flower cluster.
15. Even those who by reason of _____ have their senses exercised. (Heb. 5:14)
17. Paddle for canoe.
19. Person who has access to confidential information.
25. But _____ covereth the mouth of the wicked. (Prov. 10:6)
26. Groups of animals.

14

28. Have ye _____ brother. (Gen. 43:7)
29. Bruise.
30. To weep with convulsive heaving.
31. An elementary child's flute.
32. This _____ unto the Lord. (Ex. 15:1)
33. Morning time.
36. Handyman's necessity.

38. And _____ the vine were three branches. (Gen. 40:10)
41. First king of Israelite nation. (1 Sam. 9:17)
42. Mantras.
47. _____ Joseph died, being a hundred and ten years old. (Gen. 50:26)
48. One (Scottish).

Puzzle 7

Janet W. Adkins

ACROSS CLUES

1. Bachelor (abbr.).
4. Limb.
7. Toi sent _____ his son. (2 Sam. 8:10)
12. Sea level (abbr.).
13. Gk. letter.
14. A land of oil _____, and honey. (Deut. 8:8)
15. Till there stood up a priest with Urim and _____. (Neh. 7:65)
17. Milk source.
18. Egyptian sun god.
19. And the angel took the _____. (Rev. 8:5)
21. Elf.
23. A _____ of the work. (James 1:25)
24. Ye _____ Antique Shoppe.
27. Extremely.
29. Direction.
30. Wing.
31. Fool.

16

33. Extra duty drill instructor.
35. Brown.
36. Added to a letter.
38. Man's name.
39. Ogle.
40. Sounds of laughter.
42. And Adam called his wife's name _____. (Gen. 3:20)
43. He leadeth me _____ the still waters. (Ps. 23:2)
45. That I will give you the rain of your land _____ his due season. (Deut. 11:14)
46. I will extend peace to her like a _____. (Isa. 66:12)
50. And took upon him the form of a _____. (Phil. 2:7)
52. By mouth.
53. A son of Gad. (Gen. 46:16)
54. Symbol for beryllium.
55. That he may dip the tip of his finger in _____. (Luke 16:24)
56. They shall say no more, The _____ of the covenant. (Jer. 3:16)

DOWN CLUES

2. For I am not _____ of the gospel of Christ. (Rom. 1:16)
3. Chartered Life Underwriter (abbr.).
4. Bearing weapons.
5. African animals.
6. Mother, look!
7. Journal (abbr.).
8. Ancient.
9. Make free, disencumber.
10. Hail.
11. Meridian (abbr.).
15. Not important.
16. Master of Ceremonies (abbr.).
20. Emergency room (abbr.).
22. Because of the _____ of evil men. (Job 35:12)
24. Margarine.
25. Long handled spoon.
26. Distinguished.
28. Second person possessive.
32. Tennessee (abbr.).
34. Practicer of divination.
36. The peace of God which _____ all understanding. (Phil. 4:7, modern sp.)
37. More bashful.
40. Blessed be _____ that cometh in the name of the Lord. (Ps. 118:26)
41. And we were driven up and down in _____. (Acts 27:27)
43. British (abbr.).
44. Electron volt (abbr.).
46. And the second _____ shall be an emerald, a sapphire, and a diamond. (Ex. 28:18)
47. And _____ also the Jairite was a chief ruler about David. (2 Sam. 20:26)
48. Large tub.
49. Eel (Old Eng.).
51. Arab cloak.

Puzzle 8

Janet W. Adkins

ACROSS CLUES

1. Monthly literature.
4. Delicate network fabric.
7. Of _____, the family of the Punites. (Num. 26:23)
10. Past.
11. Building wing.
12. _____ your affection on things above. (Col. 3:2)
13. Molding.
14. Among.
16. Tavern brew.
17. _____ _____ tells the story of King Saul.
20. A language of Southeast Asia.
21. That he may _____ upon you a blessing this day. (Ex. 32:29)
24. Radiation measure.
27. The sons of Elpaah...who built _____. (1 Chron. 8:12)
29. Prefix meaning "solid."
30. City of Judah. (Josh. 15:29)
32. Ye have not gone up into the _____s. (Ezek. 13:5)
34. Ireland.
35. _____ and Juliet.
37. Three.
39. Still.
40. Tie the score (2 words).
42. Now _____ was very old, and heard all that his sons did unto Israel. (1 Sam. 2:22)
44. A charmer...a wizard...a _____ All are an abomination. (Deut. 18:11, 12)
49. And the stork...the lapwing, and the _____. (Lev. 11:19)
51. Arizona Indian.
52. Therefore, hence.
53. Mother of all living.
54. Belonging to Mrs. Peron.
55. Stick for jumping.
56. Young man.
57. _____d died without children. (1 Chron. 2:30)
58. Troops (abbr.).

DOWN CLUES

1. The Wise Men.
2. Golden _____.
3. Whither thou _____, I will go. (Ruth 1:16)
4. Thou shalt destroy them that speak _____. (Ps. 5:6)
5. Woman's name.
6. They shall _____ up upon the houses. (Joel 2:9)
7. Praise him with the _____ and harp. (Ps. 150:3)
8. Sons of Bani. (Ezra 10:34)
9. Did eat.
13. About.
15. Render therefore to all their _____. (Rom. 13:7)
18. A Chinese religion.
19. Italian family; patrons of the Renaissance.
22. Nickname of Oriel.
23. Past tense of "go".
24. It is a _____ thing that the king requireth. (Dan. 2:11)
25. Black Sea arm.
26. Insane.
28. Grain.
31. Handwriting on the wall. (Dan. 5:25)
33. Basic proposition for an argument.
36. Settings of precious stones.
38. Longshoremen's union.

41. _____ me now...if I will not open you the windows of heaven. (Mal. 3:10)
43. Clumsy, unskilled.
45. Iridescent stone.
46. Farmer's produce.
47. Ova.
48. Kanga's child.
49. _____ boweth down. (Isa. 46:1)
50. And the king of Assyria brought men. . .from _____. (2 Kgs. 17:24)

Puzzle 9

Janet W. Adkins

ACROSS CLUES

1. Twelfth Hebrew alphabet letter.
5. Thou preparest a _____ before me. (Ps. 23:5)
9. Dad.
10. That (Spanish).
12. Joshua had taken _____ and utterly destroyed it. (Josh. 10:1)
14. Elder.
16. Wake up, O _____. (Eph. 5:14 NIV)
19. International unit (abbr.).
20. Tried.
22. Prior to.
23. New Testament.
24. Assert without proof.
25. The king will _____ him with great riches. (1 Sam. 17:25)
27. Intervals of two (prefix).
28. Nor the inhabitants of _____ and her towns. (Judg. 1:27)
29. To and _____.
30. Size.
31. Eldest son of Judah. (Gen. 38:3)
32. Roman number two.
33. Depot (abbr.).

20

35. Branches.
37. I _____ the Lord, and he heard me. (Ps. 34:4)
41. Compass direction.
43. And let his _____ that he hath hid catch himself. (Ps. 35:8)
44. _____ the Archite came to meet him. (2 Sam. 15:32)
45. Anno _____.
46. Plural suffix.
47. Ye _____ polluted bread. (Mal. 1:7)
49. "_____ Deum."
50. Added to a letter.
51. Southern general.
52. I stand _____ the door and knock. (Rev. 3:20)
54. Liquid measure (British).
55. I am. . .a _____ woman. (2 Sam. 14:5)

DOWN CLUES

2. News service.
3. Put his hand under the thigh of . . .his _____. (Gen. 24:9)
4. Signed over the property.
5. Type of dancer.
6. Balder.
7. Long Island (abbr.).

8. Like the earth which he hath _____ for ever. (Ps. 78:69)
11. Compass point.
13. We should pray for _____. (1 Tim. 2:2)
15. Any seem to be _____, and bridleth not his tongue. (Jam. 1:26)
17. Not a _____ to stand on.
18. Sea eagle.
19. Measure of increase.
21. Sea level.
26. In case.
33. Repress.
34. Peter, and _____ his brother. (Matt. 10:2)
36. Cuckoo.
38. Forgive _____ our debts. (Matt. 6:12)
39. Person of the Trinity, the Holy _____.
40. _____nium, silvery metallic element.
42. Ex. officio (abbr.).
48. Shoe width.
50. Greek letter.
52. Commercial message.
53. Who will have all men _____ be saved. (1 Tim. 2:4)

Puzzle 10
Janet W. Adkins

ACROSS CLUES

1. Lot sat in the _____ of Sodom. (Gen. 19:1)
5. Son of Shem. (Gen. 10:22)
9. Rehoboam sent _____ who was over the tribute. (1 Kgs. 12:18)
11. Where the altar is in an Eastern Church.
13. Person.
14. Sick people...taken with _____ diseases.(Matt. 4:24, modern sp.)
16. Elder son of Zeus.
17. Sanballat the _____. (Neh. 2:10)
18. Name prefix (Simon _____ Jonah).
19. Pertaining to an ecological sere.
20. Newspaper person (abbr.).
21. British thanks.
22. False god.
24. Hide thyself by the brook _____. (1 Kgs. 17:3)
28. _____ in me, and I in you. (John 15:4)
29. By the _____ of Babylon, there we sat down. (Ps. 137:1)
30. Fairy queen.
31. He was (Latin).
32. Civil Aeronautics Authority.
33. Put on strength, O _____ of the Lord. (Isa. 51:9)
36. Let his habitation be _____. (Acts 1:20)
39. Curved molding.
40. Neighbor of Iraq.
41. Snatches.

42. Vertical take off (abbr.).
43. When Sanballat...and _____ heard of it, it grieved them. (Neh. 2:10)
44. A curvy shape.
45. Norse god.

DOWN CLUES

1. Wife of Hosea. (Hosea 1:3)
2. Belonging to a son of Jether. (1 Chron. 7:38)
3. Sunbathe.
4. Printer's measure.
5. He laid the foundation thereof in _____ his firstborn. (1 Kgs. 16:34)
6. Edom _____ted from under the hand of Judah. (2 Kgs. 8:20)
7. So be it.
8. Seagoing prefix.
9. And _____ told Jezebel all that Elijah had done. (1 Kgs. 19:1)
10. He set it up in the plain of _____. (Dan. 3:1)
12. It is easier for a camel to go through the eye of a _____. (Matt. 19:24)
14. In the borders of _____ on the west. (Josh. 11:2)
15. Abraham...offered him...in the _____ of his son. (Gen. 22:13)
17. Warms.
19. Mix.
22. Business watchdog.
23. The king of _____ they took alive. (Josh. 8:23)
24. Give recognition.
25. For the labourer is worthy of his _____. (Luke 10:7)

26. Avoiding.
27. Short answers.
28. Motorists' club.
30. Woman's name.
32. Court (abbr.).
33. Once more.
34. Slew the kings of Midian...Zur...Hur, and _____. (Num. 31:8)
35. Network.
37. Southeast Asian country.
38. Is there any taste in the white of _____ egg? (Job 6:6)
39. NASA prefix.
41. In him is the love of _____ perfected. (1 John 2:5)
43. _____ visit the fatherless and widows. (Jam. 1:27)

Puzzle 11
Janet W. Adkins

ACROSS CLUES

1. Where she is nourished for a time, and _____. (Rev. 12:14)
5. I am. . .a _____ woman. (2 Sam. 14:5)
10. _____ and Thummim. (Ex. 28:30)
11. Father of Kish and Abner. (1 Chron. 26:28)
14. Grain storage building.
15. Scottish cap.
16. Jacob served _____ years for Rachel. (Gen. 29:20)
18. Edge.
19. Pull out the m_____ out of thine eye. (Matt. 7:4)
20. _____ in me, and I in you. (John 15:4)
21. Madame Peron.
22. Concerning.
23. Half an em.
24. For thine is the kingdom, the power, and the glory, _____, Amen (Matt. 6:13)

24

28. _____ did that which was right in the eyes of the Lord. (1 Kgs. 15:11)
29. Eldest son of Judah. (Gen. 38:3)
30. Chalice.
31. God shall _____ them. (Deut. 7:2)
34. Address word (abbr.).
36. Per (abbr.).
37. Exist.
38. Cubic (abbr.).
40. The ungodly shall not stand. . ._____ sinners in the congregation. (Ps. 1:5)
42. Moses said, Why _____ ye with me? (Ex. 17:2)
46. Sea eagle.
47. _____ boy!
48. So he bringeth them unto their desired _____. (Ps. 107:30)
49. Food from a tree.
50. _____ your heart, and not your garments. (Joel 2:13)
52. Then shall the kingdom of heaven be likened unto _____ virgins. (Matt. 25:1)
53. Legwear.
54. The _____ dwelt therein in times past. (Deut. 2:10)
55. Thou madest him a little _____ than the angels. (Heb. 2:7)

DOWN CLUES

1. Is under _____s. . .until the time appointed of the father.(Gal. 4:2)
2. Angry.
3. Silent actor.
4. Printer's measure.
6. Exists.
7. Dreadful.
8. In her mouth was an _____ leaf. (Gen. 8:11)
9. Out of man.
11. Bird's beak.
12. King of Midian. (Num. 31:8)
13. Scarlet.
16. The next day we arrived at _____s. (Acts 20:15)
17. Glacial snow.
24. The strangers shall _____ away. (Ps. 18:45)
25. Religion (abbr.).
26. A son of Gad. (Gen. 46:16)
27. It is a _____ thing that the king requireth. (Dan. 2:11)
32. Every.
33. Israel pitched beside _____-ezer. (1 Sam. 4:1)
34. The _____ is laid for him in the ground. (Job 18:10)
35. A symbol.
38. A little oil in a _____. (1 Kgs. 17:12)
39. Under (German).
41. Indian princess.
43. Headwear.
44. I have.
45. O king, he shall be cast into the _____ of lions. (Dan. 6:7)
46. Sufficient (arch).
51. Data management (abbr.).
53. _____ everyone that thirsteth. (Is. 55:1)

Puzzle 12

Joann Horn

ACROSS CLUES

1. To request earnestly.
6. Except ye _____, ye shall perish. (Luke 13:3)
11. What _____ thee, Hagar? (Gen. 21:17)
13. Daybreak.
14. To cook.
15. Talking horse.
16. Army Transport Service (abbr.).
18. The _____ of Kish. . .were lost. (1 Sam. 9:3)
19. Could.
21. Father of Jr.
23. As the _____ cometh out of the east. (Matt. 24:27)
25. Greeting.
26. Sackcloth and _____. (Luke 10:13)
28. Neither be _____ of other men's sins. (1 Tim. 5:22)
33. He _____ the more afraid. (John 19:8)
34. Disturb.
35. Middle French (abbr.).
37. Medicinal plant.
38. Person afflicted with sores.
40. The serpent beguiled me, and I did _____. (Gen. 3:13)
42. Avenge.
45. TV brand.
46. Ready for sudden action.
48. Thy disciples _____ and drink. (Luke 5:33)
50. Interject to express uncertainty.
51. Thy brother _____ against thee. (Luke 17:3)

DOWN CLUES

1. Moral story.
2. Children not accused of _____. (Titus 1:6)
3. Exclamation of sorrow.
4. Opposed to "no".
5. _____, thou that destroyed the temple. (Mark 15:29)
6. My joy might _____ in you. (John 15:11)
7. Having itching _____. (2 Tim. 4:3)
8. I _____ toward the mark. (Phil. 3:14)
9. The _____ shall serve the younger. (Rom. 9:12)
10. New York (abbr.).
12. Tea time (abbr.).
17. No room in the _____. (Luke 2:7)
19. He rode upon a _____. (Ps. 18:10)
20. Yesterday _____ the seventh hour. (John 4:52)
22. Holy _____. (Rom. 16:16)
24. Robes.
25. Cure.

27. Housewife (abbr.).
28. _____ the word. (2 Tim. 4:2)
29. Artery in the heart.
30. Lung disease.
31. Christ is _____. (Col. 3:11)
32. Guard.
34. Thither.
36. Day of the week (abbr.).

39. Keep thyself _____.
    (1 Tim. 5:22)
41. Mom.
43. Red or Dead.
44. Whereas thou _____ been
    forsaken and halted. (Isa. 60:15)
47. Lieutenant (abbr.).
49. Technical Sergeant (abbr.).

Puzzle 13

Jennifer Breeding

ACROSS CLUES

1. Mary's relation to Joseph.
4. O magnify the Lord with me, and let us exalt his name _____. (Ps. 34:3)
11. Trust _____ the Lord, and do good. (Ps. 37:3)
12. Appliance used for baking bread.
13. Nickname for Sarah's husband.
14. Thy rod and thy _____ they comfort me. (Ps. 23:4)
16. Ask, _____ it shall be given you. (Matt. 7:7)
17. Small Business Administration (abbr.).
18. They toil not, neither _____ they spin. (Matt. 6:28)
19. They shall mount up with the wings as _____. (Isa. 40:31)
21. Wile E. Coyote's mail order company.
22. What Jesus did for the 5,000 followers.

28

24. To refer to briefly or incidentally.
25. Shades of color.
27. _____ we walk by faith, not by sight. (2 Cor. 5:7)
28. Mr. _____.
29. Depend.
31. The glory of this _____ house shall be greater. (Haggai 2:9)
32. "O _____ Night."
33. Southeast (abbr.).
34. I will be _____ enemy unto thine enemies. (Ex. 23:22)
35. Receive the kingdom of God _____ a little child.(Mark 10:15)
36. He taketh away the first, that he may _____ the second. (Heb. 10:9)
41. Pollen loving insect.
43. _____, Fi, Fo, Fum.
44. Be _____ in the Lord. (Ps. 32:11)
46. The one and _____.
48. Is to hearing as a mirror is to seeing.
49. Parable of the _____ Talents. (Matt. 25:14)
50. For the Son of man is come to save that which was _____. (Matt. 18:11)
51. One Bobbsey sibling.

DOWN CLUES

1. For the Lord giveth _____. (Prov. 2:6)
2. "Come _____ My Heart, Lord Jesus."
3. Shall their unbelief make the faith of God without _____? (Rom. 3:3)
4. Glory _____ God in the highest. (Luke 2:14)
5. Egg shaped.
6. Parts of a chromosome that influence characteristics.
7. From the end of the heaven, and his circuit unto the _____ of it. (Ps. 19:6)
8. Let him make speed, and _____ his work. (Isa. 5:19)
9. _____ and flow.
10. Harvest.
15. Of whom the whole _____ in heaven and earth is named. (Eph. 3:15)
20. Geography (abbr.).
21. Heavenly being.
22. Two weeks.
23. Buck or doe.
25. Complete.
26. South Dakota (abbr.).
27. Do, Re, Mi _____.
29. Cain _____ up against Abel his brother. (Gen. 4:8)
30. Granny Clampett's homemade _____ soap.
31. Removable piece of a table top.
32. Convent attire.
33. Street (abbr.).
37. What Jacob's sons did to Joseph. (Gen. 37:27)
38. Edible red root.
39. Snail's pace.
40. Laughter.
42. Long period of time.
45. Daniel's temporary dwelling.
47. _____-yo.

Puzzle 14

Jennifer Breeding

ACROSS CLUES

1. For ye are all the _____ of God. (Gal. 3:26)
6. Trust in the Lord, and do _____. (Ps. 37:3)
9. _____ no evil; hear no evil; speak no evil.
10. For the eyes of the Lord are _____ the righteous. (1 Pet. 3:12)
12. Pull threads.
15. Behold, I send _____ Angel before thee. (Ex. 23:20)
16. Whoso trusteth _____ the Lord, happy is he. (Prov. 16:20)
17. Flaming.
18. "Where He _____ Me I Will Follow."
19. Now Abraham and Sarah were old and well stricken in _____. (Gen. 18:11)
21. He escaped the destruction of Sodom.
22. We.
23. Metal used to pave the streets in heaven.
24. Two x Four = _____.
27. Mentor to Samuel.
28. What shepherds do for the flock.
31. David did this to 20 Down.
32. A tingling that needs a scratch.
34. The foolish virgins forgot this. (Matt. 25:3)
36. Period of time between midnight and noon.
37. Language spoken by people of Ireland and Scotland.
39. The earth was without form, and _____. (Gen. 1:2)
42. The woman _____ the well.
43. So God created man in his own _____. (Gen. 1:27)
45. Tool for hitchhiking.
46. Homonym of "earn".
48. And _____ _____ go and prepare a place for you. (John 14:3; 2 words)
49. _____ are the pure in heart. (Matt. 5:8)
51. Sight, hearing, taste, smell, or touch.
52. One of 51 Across.

DOWN CLUES

1. Be of good _____. (Ps. 31:24)
2. Person of ancient Israel.
3. Covering of a tree limb.
4. Being forty days tempted of the _____. (Luke 4:2)
5. How is it that ye have _____ faith? (Mark 4:40)
6. First book of the Old Testament.
7. For better _____ worse.
8. Thickness, compactness.
11. Ye are of more _____ than many sparrows. (Matt. 10:31)
13. What running water does to soil.
14. _____ us therefore come boldly. (Heb. 4:16)
16. _____, ego, superego.
20. Bold Philistine.
25. It was meet that we should make merry, and be _____. (Luke 15:32)

26. Brother of Shem and Japheth. (Gen. 6:10)
28. Seamstress finger protector.
29. Sounds like "know".
30. Famines, and pestilences, and earthquakes, in _____ places. (Matt. 24:7)
33. What Zacchaeus does to the sycamore tree. (Luke 19:4)
35. _____, I am with you alway. (Matt. 28:20)

37. The opening to heaven.
38. West coast state (abbr.).
40. He _____ faithful and just. (1 John 1:9)
41. To determine the heaviness of.
44. Sudden, strong rush of air.
47. Device used by fishermen.
50. This _____ in remembrance of me. (Luke 22:19)

Puzzle 15

Jennifer Breeding

ACCROSS CLUES

1. _____ them that are rich in this world. (1 Tim. 6:17)
6. Gurgle.
10. Electrically charged atom.
11. Pungent scent.
13. Expend.
14. Temporary dwelling. (Ex. 33:10)
15. Happily.
16. Transit Authority (abbr.).
18. They went into the _____ of swine. (Matt. 8:32)
19. What Eve does to the fruit. (Gen. 3:13)
21. Earnest enthusiasm.
24. Ye see how _____ a letter I have written unto you. (Gal. 6:11)
26. The Lord my God will _____ my darkness. (Ps. 18:28)
30. Do not _____, my beloved brethren. (Jam. 1:16)

32. Thou shalt have _____ other gods before me. (Ex. 20:3)
33. Spoke.
34. Leah's relationship to Rachel.
36. Whosoever eateth leavened bread from the first day _____ the seventh day. (Ex. 12:15)
38. Nocturnal bird of prey.
39. Bachelor of Arts (abbr.).
40. Long _____ and far away.
41. Tender loving care (abbr.).
43. Rebuke not an _____, but intreat him as a father. (1 Tim. 5:1)
45. Unfreeze.
47. And the world passeth away, and the lust _____. (1 John 2:17)
49. Heavenly headpiece.
50. For anger resteth in the bosom _____ fools. (Ec. 7:9)
51. Snoopy.
53. Rocking _____.
56. Emergency Room (abbr.).
57. Refrigerator.

DOWN CLUES

1. And he went and joined himself to a _____ of that country. (Luke 15:15)
2. Weeder.
3. Yearly.
4. Let my people _____. (Ex. 5:1)
5. He do not whet the _____. (Ec. 10:10)
6. Harness for guiding a horse.
7. Let not the _____ rejoice, nor the seller mourn. (Ezek. 7:12)
8. Bachelor of Science (abbr.).
9. Serve in newness of spirit, and not in the oldness of the _____. (Rom. 7:6)
12. Paddle.
17. But as many _____ received him, to them gave he power. (John 1:12)
20. "Rock of _____, Cleft for Me."
22. Lest there be not _____ for us. (Matt. 25:9)
23. Itemize.
25. A soft _____ turneth away wrath. (Prov. 15:1)
27. The stride of a horse.
28. A small mountain peak.
29. Touchdown (abbr.).
31. To raise a child.
35. Against the law.
37. Belonging to the world's most famous boat builder.
39. _____ the mountains were brought forth. (Ps. 90:2)
40. Pay the penalty.
42. Chapter (abbr.).
44. Who by him _____ believe in God. (1 Pet. 1:21)
46. I am the _____, the truth, and the life. (John 14:6)
48. Every one.
52. _____ what shall a man give in exchange for his soul? (Matt. 16:26)
54. Greeting.
55. Illinois (abbr.).

Puzzle 16
Diana Rowland

ACROSS CLUES

1. Among all nations, for his _____. (Rom. 1:5)
5. Concerning his _____ Jesus Christ our Lord (Rom. 1:3)
8. _____ a servant of Jesus Christ. (Rom. 1:1)
12. Is become like the garden of _____. (Ezek. 36:35)
13. _____ deep sleep fell upon Abram; and, _____, an horror. (Gen. 15:12; 2 words)
14. Son of Helem. (1 Chron. 7:35)
15. The woman which hath _____ husband is bound. (Rom. 7:2)
16. For I _____ in the law of God. (Rom. 7:22)
19. And be not conformed _____ this world. (Rom. 12:2)
20. So they _____ both together. (John 20:4)
22. Favorite name for a dog.
23. Disk Operating System (abbr.).
24. For Christ _____ the end of the law. (Rom. 10:4)
26. And when he _____ with us at Assos. (Acts 20:14)
27. Who also were in Christ before _____. (Rom. 16:7)
28. They _____ fools. (Rom. 1:22)
31. I know both how to be _____. (Phil. 4:12)
35. And when king _____...And Israel vowed _____ vow. (Num. 21:1, 2; 2 words)
36. Drive out the inhabitants of _____. (Judg. 1:31)
37. Two _____ shall there be in one board. (Ex. 26:17)
39. _____ if _____ be found _____ his hand. (Ex. 21:16)
40. Who are _____ note among the apostles. (Rom. 16:7)
41. To point carefully.
43. Wert graffed _____ among them. (Rom. 11:17)
44. The night is _____ spent. (Rom. 13:12)

46. By a foolish nation I will _____ you. (Rom. 10:19)
48. For a voice declareth from _____. (Jer. 4:15)
51. So, as much _____ in me. (Rom. 1:15)
52. I have _____ my cause. (Job 13:18)
54. Do, Re, Mi, Fa, So, _____, Ti, Do.
55. He received the _____ of circumcision. (Rom. 4:11)
57. Put _____ stumbling block or _____ occasion. (Rom 14:13; 2 words)
58. And _____, and Tekoa. (2 Chron. 11:6)
60. Neither could any man _____ him. (Mark 5:4)
61. Then said _____, _____, I come. (Ps. 40:7; 2 words)
62. The rings, and _____ jewels. (Isa. 3:21)

DOWN CLUES

1. Let us draw _____ with a true heart. (Heb. 10:22)
2. _____, and Chelal, Benaiah. (Ezra 10:30)
3. But sin that dwelleth in _____. (Rom. 7:17)
4. And the _____ everlasting life. (Rom. 6:22)
5. And _____, had bought sweet spices. (Mark 16:1)
6. Being a wild _____ tree. (Rom. 11:17)
7. Make _____ friendship...and _____ snare to thy soul. (Prov. 22:24, 25; 3 words)
8. Out of the _____ wherein is no water. (Zech. 9:11)
9. I _____ a debtor. (Rom. 1:14)
10. Sing _____ thy name. (Rom. 15:9)
11. Country in Southeast Asia.
17. Sons of Judah. (Num. 26:19)
18. _____. _____. Haldeman, Nixon aide.
21. Prochorus, and _____, and Timon. (Acts 6:5)
23. Who shall _____ into the

34

deep? (Rom. 10:7)

25. Why is thy countenance
_____...but sorrow _____ heart.
(Neh. 2:2; 2 words)

27. Geuel the son of _____.
(Num. 13:15)

28. And the lapwing, and the _____.
(Deut. 14:18)

29. Sir, come down _____ my child
die. (John 4:49)

30. And thinkest thou this, O _____.
(Rom. 2:3)

32. I will break also the _____ of
Damascus. (Amos 1:5)

33. Naaman, _____, and Rosh.
(Gen. 46:21)

34. Nickname for Donald.

38. Above the _____ of the
seas...young men _____ spoiler
at noonday: _____have.
(Jer. 15:8) (3 words)

39. Mete it with an _____...had
_____ lack. (Ex. 16:18; 2 words)

42. Hattush, and _____, and Bariah.
(1 Chron. 3:22)

44. Stand _____ therefore in the
liberty. (Gal. 5:1)

45. The churches of _____ salute
you. (1 Cor. 16:19)

46. Thou art to pass over through
_____. (Deut. 2:18)

47. Do, _____, Mi.

49. And said, ._____, master!
(2 Kgs. 6:5)

50. For whosoever shall call upon the
_____ of the Lord. (Rom. 10:13)

52. So we, being many, are _____
body. (Rom. 12:5)

53. Into the _____ of lions. (Dan.6:7)

56. General Motors (abbr.).

59. No man dieth _____ himself.
(Rom. 14:7)

Puzzle 17

Martha Wall

ACROSS CLUES

1. _____ rather than choice gold. (Prov. 8:10)
10. Johns place of exile. (Rev. 1:9)
11. In addition.
12. Supplicate.
14. Divine radiance.
16. Leave.
17. Earthen vessel.
19. 502 (Roman numeral).
20. Like.
21. Entice.
22. Church official. (Titus 1:6 NIV)
24. Lair. (Ps. 10:9)
26. Shade trees.
30. Treasured jewel. (Ex. 28:18)
33. Consumed.
35. Adam's grandson. (Gen. 4:26)
36. Thus.
37. At once. (Mark 1:30)
39. Embalming ingredient. (John 19:40)
41. Sew.
43. Snake-like fish.

44. God answered by _____.
    (1 Kgs. 18:24)
45. Beauty's wondrous exchange.
    (Isa. 61:3)
46. Hemispherical structure.

DOWN CLUES

1. Solomon, and others.
2. Opposite directions (abbr.).
3. Ancient.
4. _____ are not of the night.
   (1 Thes. 5:5)
5. And (Latin).
6. Derogative name. (Ps. 22:16)
7. _____ bell. (Ex. 28:34)
8. Expression of dismay.
9. The _____ of the Lord run to
   and fro. (2 Chron. 16:9)
12. _____ goeth before destruction.
    (Prov. 16:18)
13. Clay's problem. (Jer. 18:4)

15. Medium for anointing. (Ex. 25:6)
17. The ungodly. . .scorneth _____.
    (Prov. 19:28)
18. Though they be _____ like
    crimson. (Isa. 1:18)
20. His _____ brought salvation.
    (Isa. 59:16)
23. Otherwise.
25. Extremities.
27. Contained evidence of theft.
    (Gen. 44:12)
28. Goliath, for one.
29. Precious stone. (Ex. 28:20)
31. Over and in contact.
32. Early shipbuilder. (Gen. 6:13-14)
34. Labored hard.
37. Generous invitation. (Matt. 7:7)
38. Canola and corn.
39. High elevation. (Gen. 14:6)
40. An oasis. (Ex. 15:27)
42. A signal.

Puzzle 18

Martha Wall

ACROSS CLUES

1. Compassionate. (Jam. 5:11)
6. Pleasant and mild.
12. Musical saga.
14. Mount. (Es. 6:8)
15. Inquisitive.
16. Behold.
18. _____ weigh the path. (Isa. 26:7)
19. Taken in adultery in the very
    _____. (John 8:4)
20. Seat of affection. (Phil. 1:7)
22. Eccentric joker.
23. Left hand (abbr.).
24. Introducing new angle.
    (Matt. 5:22)
25. Words of a talebearer _____ as
    wounds. (Prov. 26:22)
26. His banner over _____ was love.
    (Song of Sol. 2:4)
27. A memorial of _____.
    (Matt. 26:13)
29. For each.
30. Invitation to partake. (Isa. 55:1)
31. Herein is a marvelous _____.
    (John 9:30)
32. Hath translated _____ into the
    kingdom. (Col. 1:13)
34. High priest. (1 Sam. 1:9)
36. He that hath an _____. (Rev. 2:7)
39. Either.
41. This _____ thing I do.
    (Phil. 3:13)
43. Woman's name.
44. Any one of God's children.
    (abbr.)
45. In regard to.
46. Merrily.
48. There's more.
49. Goliath's hometown.
    (1 Sam. 17:4)
52. Part of clay, part of iron.
    (Dan. 2:41)
53. Pagan city. (Isa. 37:13)
54. Resound.
55. Friendly expression.
56. Where your treasure is, _____.
    (Matt. 6:21)
57. _____ of gold in pictures of
    silver. (Prov. 25:11)

DOWN CLUES

1. Levels of intonation.
2. Period.
3. Snug habitat. (Ps. 84:3)
4. Root out of _____ ground.
   (Isa. 53:2)
5. Each (abbr.).
7. Wordless question.
8. East of Eden. (Gen. 4:16)
9. Describing metal or mettle.
10. Takes for granted.
11. Often a treasured
    communication.
13. Satan's affirmative. (Gen. 3:1)
16. Place.
17. Historical time.
20. Feeling pain.
21. A great sadness.
24. Exist.
27. Gardening tool.
28. Reward: death. (Rom. 6:23)
29. To destroy them, and had cast
    _____. (Es. 9:24)
33. God does not _____. (Isa. 49:15)
35. Look.
37. Associate in Arts.
38. Scratches.
40. A measure to _____ even unto
    you. (2 Cor. 10:13)

42. If any man _____ of this bread.
 (John 6:51)
43. Beverage.
44. Not fresh.
47. A charged subatomic particle.
48. Their feet run to _____.
 (Prov. 1:16)

50. An article.
51. Aaron's resting place.
 (Num. 20:25)
53. An evil creature.
55. Spanish (abbr.).

Puzzle 19
Carol Stengel

ACROSS CLUES

1. A name of Christ. (Rev. 1:8)
7. _____ not ye against the Lord. (Num. 14:9)
11. We ought to _____ God rather than man. (Acts 5:29)
13. Why do the heathen _____? (Ps. 2:1)
14. Though they be _____ like crimson. (Isa. 1:18)
15. Shall I _____ of this disease? (2 Kings 8:8)
17. Many will _____ in that day. (Matt. 7:22)
19. Direction on the compass.
20. Academic degree (abbr.).
22. I will _____ my tabernacle among you. (Lev. 26:11)
23. He hath given _____ unto all men. (Acts 17:31)
26. Two men _____ up into the temple to pray. (Luke 18:10)
27. _____ of me. (Matt. 11:29)

40

30. A charge for a professional service.
31. Condescend.
33. Internal Revenue Service (abbr.).
35. Whom _____ ye that I am? (Luke 9:20)
36. _____ found grace in the eyes of the Lord. (Gen. 6:8)
37. Israel came by the way of the _____. (Num. 21:1)
41. In his favour is _____. (Ps. 30:5)
42. God doth _____ with man. (Deut. 5:24)
43. Abstain from all appearance of _____. (1 Thes. 5:22)

DOWN CLUES

1. _____ them that curse you. (Luke 6:28)
2. We beheld his _____.(John 1:14)
3. Seeth his brother have _____. (1 John 3:17)
4. Trust _____ the Lord with all thine heart. (Prov. 3:5)
5. Come boldly unto the throne of _____. (Heb. 4:16)
6. _____ that overcometh. (Rev. 3:5)
8. The self as distinguished from others.
9. Girl's name (abbr.).
10. Lead astray.
12. Ye will not believe, though it _____ told you. (Hab. 1:5)
13. Prefix meaning "again."
15. It _____ upon the earth forty days and nights. (Gen. 7:12)
16. _____ into his gates with thanksgiving. (Ps. 100:4)
18. How ye ought to _____ every man. (Col. 4:6)
20. A roll.
21. Many of them also which used curious _____ brought their books together. (Acts 19:19)
24. You are the God who _____ me. (Gen. 16:13 NIV)
25. Behold, he calleth _____. Mark 15:35)
28. Joseph was sold into _____. (Gen. 37:36)
29. Is there any taste in the white of _____ egg? (Job 6:6)
30. The whole body _____ joined together. (Eph. 4:16)
32. Used to form plurals.
34. He hath _____ every thing beautiful. (Ec. 3:11)
36. The kingdom of heaven is like a _____. (Matt. 13:47)
38. Suffix meaning "belongs to."
39. Old Testament name for God.
40. To glide on water or snow.

Puzzle 20

Lee Esch

ACROSS CLUES

1. Ruth's second husband. (Ruth 4:13)
5. Special attention (abbr.).
8. Donkey's cry.
12. He is _____ even to subdue all things. (Phil. 3:21)
13. Note of debt.
14. Citrus fruit.
15. Frog's cousin.
16. Paul's companion. (Acts 13:2)
18. Israeli Jew (abbr.).
19. Took care of.
20. But Peter followed him _____ off. (Matt. 26:58)
22. Concise; to the point.
26. Engraves.
30. He that hath an _____, let him hear. (Rev. 2:7)
31. Reserve Officers' Training Corps.
32. Assist.
33. Capital of Peru.
34. For there is _____ God. (1 Tim. 2:5)
35. Approximates.
37. Pertaining to Norwegians.
39. Become pale.
40. The blood of Jesus Christ... cleanseth us from _____ _____. (1 John 1:7)
43. British flyers (abbr.).
46. The Lord our _____ _____ _____ Lord. (Mark 12:29)
49. Tale.
50. The golden calf was one. (Acts 7:41)
51. Cereal grass (sing.).
52. We have seen his _____ in the east. (Matt. 2:2)
53. And straightway they forsook their _____. (Mark 1:18)
54. Speed measurement (abbr.).
55. Segment of time served.

DOWN CLUES

1. Body wash.
2. Woodwind instrument.
3. Gypsum.
4. The letter "Z" to a Britisher.
5. Lake _____ (Sea of Galilee).
6. Allow temporary possession.
7. Coagulated milk.
8. Knife part.
9. Eve was created from one.
10. Physicians group (abbr.).
11. Affirmative reply.
17. Let down your _____ for a draught. (Luke 5:4)
19. Roofing substance.
21. Government airwaves overseer (abbr.).
23. Repeat.
24. Jesus Christ, the _____ yesterday, and to day, and for ever. (Heb. 13:8)
25. Time periods.
26. He shall rule them with a rod of _____. (Rev. 2:27)
27. Unacceptable deed (informal).
28. Tiny portion.
29. Knowledge puffeth up, but charity _____. (1 Cor. 8:1)
33. Boy.
35. Slippery fish (plural).
36. What is _____, that thou art mindful of him? (Ps. 8:4)

38. Travels by water.
41. Cloth producer.
42. Break suddenly.
44. Mount Sinai. (Gal. 4:25)
45. Barn locale.

46. Cotton _____ (Eli Whitney invention).
47. Lengthy lyrical poem.
48. Speck.
49. Ultrafast airplane (abbr.).

Puzzle 21

Lee Esch

ACROSS CLUES

1. Mount _____; Moses died here. (Deut. 34:1)
5. He hath spread a _____ for my feet. (Lam. 1:13)
8. Mine entrance.
12. Above the top.
13. Boat paddle.
14. He _____ witness unto the truth. (John 5:33)
15. Gentle.
16. First one.
18. Samuel's mentor. (1 Sam. 3:1)
19. Still on the market.
20. We have seen his star in the _____. (Matt. 2:2)
22. Ancient Greek storyteller.
26. Returned to.
30. Time period.
31. Affirm.
32. Optimum (for short).
33. There shall come a _____ out of Jacob. (Num. 24:17)
34. Company top dog (abbr.).

44

35. Arguable.
37. _____ Oakley.
39. Why beholdest thou the _____ that is in thy brother's eye? (Matt. 7:3)
40. _____ yourselves therefore to God. (Jam. 4:7)
43. When thou wast under the _____ tree, I saw thee. (John 1:48)
46. From the beginning of the _____ God made them male and female. (Mark 10:6)
49. I saw the Spirit descending from heaven like a _____. (John 1:32)
50. Gasoline.
51. Digit.
52. To stuff.
53. Jail unit.
54. For Christ is the _____ of the law. (Rom. 10:4)
55. Part of the eye.

DOWN CLUES

1. Alaska city.
2. Why, what _____ hath he done? (Matt. 27:23)
3. _____ _____ the Lord Jesus Christ, and thou shalt be saved. (Acts 16:31; 2 words)
4. Fort _____; California army base.
5. Midday.
6. He that hath _____ to hear, let him hear. (Matt. 11:15)
7. Threesome.
8. _____ in me, and I in you. (John 15:4)
9. One of the 12 tribes of Israel.
10. Private old age fund (abbr.).
11. Far (prefix).
17. I will be _____ in the Lord. (Ps. 104:34)
19. Navy sailing vessel initials.
21. Atmosphere.
23. I have _____ _____ thee an open door. (Rev. 3:8; 2 words)
24. Spoken.
25. Peel.
26. A term of contempt. (Matt. 5:22)
27. Level.
28. Bill or check.
29. Tested.
33. I _____ daily with you teaching in the temple. (Matt. 26:55)
35. Written by Moses (abbr.).
36. Little fellow.
38. But Christ _____ _____, and in all. (Col. 3:11; 2 words)
41. Mouthful.
42. Nightlight.
44. _____ the Terrible.
45. Precious stones.
46. Cholorfluorocarbon (for short).
47. Feel regret.
48. Slippery fish.
49. 650 (Roman numeral).

The grid contains numbered cells: 1, 2, 3, 4, 5, 6, 7, 8, 9, 10, 11 / 12, 13, 14, 15 / 16, 17, 18 / 19, 20, 21, 22 / 23, 24, 25, 26 / 27, 28, 29, 30 / 31, 32, 33, 34, 35 / 36, 37, 38, 39 / 40, 41, 42, 43, 44 / 45, 46, 47, 48, 49 / 50, 51 / 52, 53, 54, 55 / 56, 57, 58

Puzzle 22

Judy Ellis

ACROSS CLUES

1. Because the enemy hath said against you, _____. (Ezek. 36:2)
4. 16th letter of the Greek alphabet.
6. Color.
12. _____ seed.
15. Also Hosah, of the children of Merari, had sons; _____ the chief. (1 Chron. 26:10)
16. _____ the son of Jair slew Lahmi. (1 Chron. 20:5)
17. A branch of the military (abbr.).
18. Paid (abbr.).
19. Doctor (abbr.).
20. I will even appoint over you terror, consumption, and the burning _____. (Lev. 26:16)
22. And when _____ defied Israel. (2 Sam. 21:21)
23. Pharaoh's daughter drew him up out of the water. (Ex. 2:5)
26. Hot or cold drink.
27. These things have I written unto

46

you concerning them that _____ you. (1 John 2:26)
28. Sons of Benjamin. (Gen. 46:21)
29. New Testament (abbr.).
31. He saith among the trumpets, _____. (Job 39:25)
32. The Lord is thy _____ upon thy right hand. (Ps. 121:5)
34. Crush.
36. If _____ be blameless, the husband of one wife. (Titus 1:6)
38. Have _____ weightier matters of the law. (Matt. 23:23)
40. And _____, Judah's firstborn, was wicked in the sight of the Lord. (Gen. 38:7)
42. Direction.
43. _____ not vain repetitions. (Matt. 6:7)
45. Determined to send _____ unto the brethren which dwelt in Judaea. (Acts 11:29)
49. South American grass.
50. A continual _____ given him of the king. (2 Kgs. 25:30)
52. Drink waters out of thine own _____. (Prov. 5:15)
53. Revise.
56. Her majesty (abbr.).
57. And in those days shall men _____ death. (Rev. 9:6)
58. After Joel, and before Obadiah.

DOWN CLUES

1. Prayer ending.
2. Child of Aram. (Gen. 10:23)
3. Publish in the palaces at _____. (Amos 3:9)
4. Cooking vessel.
5. The sixth captain for the sixth month was _____ the son of Ikkesh. (1 Chron. 27:9)
7. Isaac's eldest son.
8. Remember that thou in thy _____ receivedst thy good things. (Luke 16:25)
9. Lunar module (abbr.).
10. We are _____ and fatherless, our mothers are as widows. (Lam. 5:3)
11. Deep and _____.
13. Saul of _____.
14. Any of various nucleic acids.
21. Welcomes.
23. We would know therefore what these things _____. (Acts 17:20)
24. Bounce off.
25. Now the coat was without _____. (John 19:23)
27. _____, Meshach, and Abednego.
30. Thy lips are like a _____ of scarlet. (Song of Sol. 4:3)
33. Opposite of "live".
35. Went forth toward Geliloth, which is over against the going up of _____. (Josh. 18:17)
37. Screams.
39. Indian hut.
41. Having faithful children not accused of _____ or unruly. (Titus 1:6)
44. Spanish (abbr.).
46. And they came to _____, where were twelve wells of water. (Ex. 15:27)
47. Female sheep.
48. _____ ye well. (Acts 15:29)
51. Direction.
54. District attorney (abbr.).
55. Then Nebuchadnezzar came near _____ the mouth of the burning fiery furnace. (Dan. 3:26)

Puzzle 23

Janice Buhl

ACROSS CLUES

1. _____ shall not live by bread alone. (Matt. 4:4)
4. And the darkness he called _____. (Gen. 1:5)
9. My heart was _____ within me. (Ps. 39:3)
12. Mine _____ is as nothing before thee. (Ps. 39:5)
13. Let us go and serve _____ gods. (Deut. 13:13)
14. There was no room for them in the _____. (Luke 2:7)
15. Lo, I have given thee _____ dung. (Ezek. 4:15)
17. The _____ also dwelt in Seir. (Deut. 2:12)
19. On this side Jordan may be _____. (Num. 32:32)
20. Grace _____ unto you. (Rev. 1:4)
21. Los Angeles (abbr.).
23. Asa destroyed her _____, and burnt it. (1 Kgs. 15:13)
26. _____ unto me, and hear me. (Ps. 55:2)
29. And a river went out of _____ to water the garden. (Gen. 2:10)
31. When ye pray, _____ not vain repetitions. (Matt. 6:7)
33. I will _____ unto thy days fifteen years. (Isa. 38:5)
34. It _____ to him that was possessed with the devil. (Mark 5:16)
36. The young men of Aven and of _____-beseth. (Ezek. 30:17)
37. Hast thou eaten of the _____? (Gen. 3:11)
38. So that my feet did not _____. (2 Sam. 22:37)
40. Praise him for his mighty _____. (Ps. 150:2)
43. And he cast stones _____ David. (2 Sam. 16:6)
44. Thou shalt feed _____ people Israel. (2 Sam. 5:2)
45. Then led they Jesus from _____ unto the hall of judgment. (John 18:28)
47. Therefore shall he _____ in harvest. (Prov. 20:4)
48. He built even Bethlehem, and _____, and Tekoa. (2 Chron. 11:6)
49. _____ went and dwelt in her father's house. (Gen. 38:11)
52. And God said, Let there _____ light. (Gen. 1:3)
54. _____ made him a great feast. (Luke 5:29)
55. Went up to _____, and fetched a compass to Karkaa. (Josh. 15:3)
56. The name of the wicked shall _____. (Prov. 10:7)
57. Short for Emily.

DOWN CLUES

1. Geuel the son of _____. (Num. 13:15)
2. Hast thou not heard long _____? (2 Kgs. 19:25)
3. Behold, all things are become _____. (2 Cor. 5:17)
4. God is _____ respecter of persons. (Acts 10:34)
5. Whose name was _____ an Israelite. (2 Sam. 17:25)
6. Then Abraham gave up the _____. (Gen. 25:8)
7. Made he a woman, and brought _____ unto the man. (Gen. 2:22)
8. There is one _____ cut off from Israel. (Judg. 21:6)
9. Abraham lifted up _____ eyes. (Gen. 22:13)
10. Moses gave you _____ this side Jordan. (Josh. 1:14)

11. Tennessee (abbr.).
16. Neither shall the _____ of thy foot have rest. (Deut. 28:65)
18. And David sent out ten young _____. (1 Sam. 25:5)
22. I _____ no pleasant bread. (Dan. 10:3)
24. King David _____ unto the Lord. (1 Chron. 18:11)
25. The _____ number of them is to be redeemed. (Num. 3:48)
27. Saul abode in Gibeah under a _____. (1 Sam. 22:6)
28. Their ears are _____ of hearing. (Acts 28:27)
30. He will _____ suffer thy foot to be moved. (Ps. 121:3)
32. And daubed it with _____ and with pitch. (Ex. 2:3)

33. And he came _____, and drew near. (2 Sam. 18:25)
34. Abraham _____ Isaac. (1 Chron. 1:34)
35. Established (abbr.).
39. The wild goat, and the _____. (Deut. 14:5)
41. Aunt (Spanish).
42. Short for Samuel.
46. And the east border was the _____ sea. (Josh. 15:5)
47. And they filled them up to the _____. (John 2:7)
50. He shall be to _____ a son. (Heb. 1:5)
51. Avenue (abbr.).
53. Elmodam, which was the son of _____. (Luke 3:28)

49

Puzzle 24
Jeanne McDougall

ACROSS CLUES

1. Their _____ shall continue for ever. (Ps. 49:11)
5. They went up into an _____ room. (Acts 1:13)
9. There was no room for them in the _____. (Luke 2:7)
10. He kept him as the _____ of his eye. (Deut. 32:10)
11. Behold, it is a stiff _____ people. (Ex. 32:9)
14. Peter, Peter, pumpkin _____.
16. A cover, or top.
17. For we have seen his _____ in the east. (Matt. 2:2)
19. The _____ is the word of God. (Luke 8:11)
22. As they sailed he fell _____. (Luke 8:23)
25. Thou art not a _____ of the law. (Jam. 4:11)
28. A large vessel for dying quantities of fabric.

50

29. Sticky, yellowish sap from pine trees.
31. Resurrection Day.
34. Joshua, the son of _____. (Ex. 33:11)
35. Frequency Modulation (abbr.).
37. Under his _____ shalt thou trust. (Ps. 91:4)
39. Whosoever shall compel thee to go a _____. (Matt. 5:41)
41. The beginning and the _____. (Rev. 21:6)
42. _____ believed God. (Rom. 4:3)
45. The angel _____ was sent. (Luke 1:26)
46. Why do the heathen _____. (Ps. 2:1)
49. Measurement of the surface of a closed figure.
50. Precious stone.
51. Before Christ (abbr.).
52. Baby goats.
53. Learn first to shew _____ at him. (1 Tim. 5:4)

DOWN CLUES

1. He maketh my feet like _____ feet. (Ps. 18:33)
2. I and my father are _____. (John 10:30)
3. Your mother's brother.
4. Opposite of "happy."
5. Opposite of "down."
6. Whoso _____ God shall escape. (Ec. 7:26; modern spelling)
7. He had found one _____ of great price. (Matt.13:46)
8. The loving hind and pleasant _____. (Prov. 5:19)
12. Joking, teasing.
13. Edward's nickname.
15. Attentive.
18. Thank you in bank talk.
20. _____ and the morning were the first day. (Gen. 1:5)
21. _____ ye kind. (Eph. 4:32)
23. Adam's wife.
24. Incline thine _____ unto wisdom. (Prov. 2:2)
26. Opposite of "off".
27. Sports officials.
30. The Lord's Day.
32. Morning (abbr.).
33. Judah's daughter-in-law. (Gen. 38:11)
36. That which was spoken, by _____ the prophet. (Matt. 2:17)
37. You and I.
38. The name of Abram's wife was _____. (Gen. 11:29)
40. We are made in God's _____. (Gen. 1:27)
43. Flee as a _____ to your mountain. (Ps. 11:1)
44. Alabama (abbr.).
47. _____ thee behind me, Satan. (Luke 4:8)
48. Tuberculosis (abbr.).

Puzzle 25

Debra Michaels

ACROSS CLUES

1. Wood the ark was made of (Gen. 6:14)
6. A god in form of a dog-headed man. (2 Kgs. 17:31)
12. Town of northern Palestine. (Josh. 19:37)
13. A Benjamite. (Num. 1:11)
14. Northeast (abbr.).
15. One of David's guards. (2 Sam. 23:36)
17. Symbol for chemical element thulium.
18. A disease causing pain and swelling in muscles and joints.
21. Short for sister.
24. African fly.
25. Anger, wrath.
26. Hour (abbr.).
27. New Hampshire (abbr.).
28. Bread dipped in soup, milk, and other liquids. (Ruth 2:14)
29. Expressing disgust, impatience, relief.
30. Mother of King Hezekiah. (2 Kgs. 18:2)
32. Position of importance and honor among Hebrews. (Gen. 24:59)
34. The musical sound of bells.
37. Legal term meaning "the."
38. Mexican food served on a tortilla shell.
41. To attempt.
42. The North American reindeer.
43. A tool for breaking ground.

44. Where Samson slew the Philistines. (Judg. 15:9)
46. Symbol for chemical element chromium.
47. Frames of bars.
48. Through faith she received strength to conceive a child. (Heb. 11:11)
49. South America (abbr.).
50. Benjamin's son. (Gen. 46:21)
51. Wise men presented to Jesus gifts of gold, frankincense, and _____. (Matt. 2:11)

DOWN CLUES

1. First book of the Bible.
2. Greek word meaning "a song."
3. Public relations (abbr.).
4. A person legally entitled to succeed to property or rank.
5. One more than seven.
6. Nickel (abbr.).
7. A Judahite. (1 Chron. 4:3)
8. _____ ye holy: for I am the Lord your God. (Lev. 20:7)
9. A word called out to get attention.
10. Small insects. (Prov. 30:25)
11. A Levite and father of Joah. (2 Chron. 29:12)
13. An adhesive.
16. Principles determining beauty.
19. Mountain (abbr.).
20. Father of Abraham. (Gen. 11:27)
22. City of Naphtali. (Josh. 19:38)
23. Tomb. (Matt. 27:60)
27. Son of Cush. (1 Chron. 1:10)
29. Postscript (abbr.).

31. Daughter of Pharaoh.
(1 Chron. 4:18)
33. A Judahite. (1 Chron. 4:2)
34. The puma, or American panther.
35. I will life up mine _____ unto
the hills. (Ps. 121:1)

36. Extremely light wood.
39. Son of Terah. (Gen. 11:26)
40. County (abbr.).
45. Each (abbr.).

Puzzle 26

Diana Rowland

ACROSS CLUES

1. Therefore the law _____ slacked. (Hab. 1:4)
3. And _____ drove thence the three sons. (Josh. 15:14)
8. Eli, _____ sabachthani. (Matt. 27:46)
12. The Lord will not _____ good. (Zeph. 1:12)
13. As with the taker of _____. (Isa. 24:2)
14. Thither cause thy mighty _____. (Joel 3:11)
15. Teman, and _____, Zephi, and Gatam. (1 Chron. 1:36)
17. _____ Jones, financial company.
18. Thou hast had pity _____ the gourd. (Jonah 4:10)
19. Even to the _____ of them. (Jonah 3:5)
21. They that observe lying vanities _____. (Jonah 2:8)
25. They that _____ thy bread. (Obad. 7)
27. And be thou like a _____. (Song of Sol. 2:17)
28. _____ the second year of Darius. (Hag. 1:1)
29. And _____ not to Beer-sheba; for Gilgal shall surely _____. (Amos 5:5; 2 words)
32. What shall we _____ unto thee. (Jonah 1:11)
33. They shall lay hold _____ bow...against thee, _____ daughter of Zion. Jer. 6:23; 2 words)

54

34. Even _____, will judge between the _____ cattle. (Ezek. 34:20; 2 words)
35. Unto the _____ of the earth. (Micah 5:4)
36. And will _____ at all acquit the wicked. (Nahum 1:3)
37. For I _____ with you. (Hag. 2:4)
39. Came unto _____ unto _____ people. (Judg. 18:27; 2 words, reverse order)
41. _____ accept thy person? (Mal. 1:8)
42. Hast thou not heard long _____. (Isa. 37:26)
43. _____ have laid hands on their substance.(Obad 13)
44. Who _____ not daily.(Heb. 7:27)
47. He shall _____ with his teeth. (Ps. 112:10)
51. Behold, I _____ against thee. (Nahum 3:5)
52. Now the Lord _____ prepared a great fish. (Jonah 1:17)
54. The son of Naum, which was the son of _____. (Luke 3:25)
55. Call me _____. (Ruth 1:20)
57. _____ was a man subject to like passions. (Jam. 5:17)
59. It hath consumed _____ of Moab. (Num. 21:28)
60. As a man wipeth a _____. (2 Kgs. 21:13)
61. Whose soever sins ye _____. (John 20:23)
62. What do _____ imagine against the Lord? (Nahum 1:9)

DOWN CLUES
1. Mine _____ hath done them. (Isa. 48:5)
2. I have overthrown _____ of you. (Amos 4:11)
3. He whom thou _____ is cursed. (Num. 22:6)
4. For while they be folden together _____ thorns. (Nahum 1:10)
5. They of Persia and of _____. (Ezek. 27:10)
6. And _____, the firstborn _____ Judah. (1 Chron. 2:3; 2 words)
7. Yea, I am their _____. (Job 30:9)

8. And now, behold, I _____ thee this day. (Jer. 40:4)
9. There was one_____.(Luke 2:36)
10. And so is this nation before _____. (Hag. 2:14)
11. And his brightness was _____ the light. (Hab. 3:4)
16. Alcoholics Anonymous (abbr.).
20. Children's game.
22. Kanga's son in "Winnie the Pooh."
23. And I will appoint over them four _____. (Jer. 15:3)
24. Adam, Sheth, _____. (1 Chron. 1:1)
26. Go up _____ the mountain. (Hag. 1:8)
29. Duke Elah, duke _____. (Gen. 36:41)
30. For _____ the harvest. (Isa. 18:5)
31. And _____ on the east side. (Jonah 4:5)
33. She called his name Ben-_____. (Gen. 35:18)
35. Which is the _____ of our inheritance. (Eph. 1:14)
37. In his hand for very _____. (Zech. 8:4)
38. Plead with your _____. (Hosea 2:2)
39. This is _____ ephah that goeth forth. (Zech. 5:6)
40. Take some of the _____ of oil. (Lev. 14:15)
42. How shall I make thee as _____? (Hosea 11:8)
45. Stopped their _____. (Zech. 7:11)
46. Lest he _____ thee to the judge. (Luke 12:58)
48. The land is _____ the garden of Eden. (Joel 2:3)
49. Not spare continually to _____ the nations? (Hab. 1:17)
50. The priests thereof teach for _____. (Micah 3:11)
53. Mine eye also is _____. (Job 17:7)
55. Medical doctor (abbr.).
56. Howl, O Heshbon, for _____ is spoiled. (Jer. 49:3)
58. When the king of _____ saw it. (Josh. 8:14)

Puzzle 27

Jody Ellis

ACROSS CLUES

1. First book of New Testament.
7. In like manner also, that women _____ themselves in modest apparel. (1 Tim. 2:9)
12. Solomon's son was Rehoboam, _____ his son. (1 Chron. 3:10)
13. Alcoholics Anonymous (abbr.).
14. Train station.
15. Ice skating arena.
16. Unto _____, my own son in the faith. (1 Tim. 1:2)
18. Save Caleb the son of Jephunneh the _____. (Num. 32:12)
20. And Zanoah, and Engannim, Tappuah, and _____. (Josh. 15:34)
22. He left the _____ cloth, and fled from them naked. (Mark 14:52)
23. Grain storage place.
25. That the _____ men be sober. (Titus 2:2)
27. Artist's stand.
30. Upon the great _____ of his right foot. (Lev. 8:23)
32. Anger.
34. Facts.
35. For the lord is our judge, the Lord is our _____. (Isa. 33:22)
36. Doctor (abbr.).
37. Iowa (abbr.).
38. Executive order (abbr.).
39. A _____ without blemish. (1 Pet. 1:19)
42. Sow the fields, and _____ vineyards. (Ps. 107:37)
44. Tin symbol.
45. Imitate.
47. Yes (Spanish).
48. Teaspoon (abbr.).
50. Hammer.
51. Direction.
53. Latter-day Saints (abbr.).
54. Whereby the world that _____ was perished. (2 Pet. 3:6)

DOWN CLUES

1. Follows 1 across
2. _____ the Arbathite. (1 Chron. 11:32)
3. Tasting the most of tin.
4. When Joseph had _____ the body (Matt. 27:59)
5. For John the Baptist came neither _____ bread nor drinking wine. (Luke 7:33)
6. Or ministry, let us _____ on our ministering. (Rom. 12:7)
7. Why make ye this _____, and weep? (Mark 5:39)
8. But thou shalt utterly _____ it. (Deut. 7:26)
9. And Chepharhaammonai, and _____ and Gaba; twelve cities with their villages. (Josh. 18:24)
10. If ye fulfill the _____ law according to the scripture. (Jam. 2:8)
11. New Testament (abbr.).
17. Even out of the _____s of Gibeah. (Judg. 20:33)
19. Concerning _____, persecuting the church. (Phil. 3:6)
21. Let your _____ be known unto all men. (Phil. 4:5)
24. Thou _____ thy people like a flock. (Ps. 77:20)
26. Estimated Time of Arrival (abbr.).

28. Eleazar _____ son. (Ex. 6:25)
29. Though thou exalt thyself as the _____. (Obad. 4)
31. Princes shall come out of _____. (Ps. 68:31)
32. Four (Roman numeral).
33. He hath caused the arrows of his quiver to enter into my _____. (Lam. 3:13)

35. It is not for kings, O _____. (Prov. 31:4)
40. Ampere (abbr.).
41. Emitted blood.
43. Therefore also I have _____ him to the Lord. (1 Sam. 1:28)
46. Opposite of question (abbr.).
49. Ma and _____.
52. Inquiry (slang).

Puzzle 28

Pat Horning

ACROSS CLUES

1. We ought to ____ God rather than men. (Acts 5:29)
5. Son of Rachel. (Gen. 35:24)
11. Simon's wife's mother was taken with a great ____. (Luke 4:38)
12. Edible cereal grass.
13. Fa, so, ____.
14. Suffix indicating plural.
16. Odorous.
18. One of the twelve spies. (Num. 13:6)
20. And hath raised up ____ horn of salvation. (Luke 1:69)
21. Narrow beam of light.
23. Rod for billiards.
24. A time to rend, and a time to ____. (Ec. 3:7)
25. Pig pen.
27. Los Angeles (abbr.).
28. Large rodents.
30. Son of Jacob. (Gen. 30:13)
31. Change direction.
33. South Dakota (abbr.).

58

35. Give, and _____ shall be given unto you. (Luke 6:38)
36. Simple.
38. Light brown.
40. _____ unthankful lepers healed. (Luke 17:17)
41. Then shall the lame man _____. (Isa. 35:6)
43. Or if he shall ask an _____, will he offer him a scorpion? (Luke 11:12)
44. Cardiac Care Unit (abbr.).
46. Louisiana (abbr.).
47. North America (abbr.).
48. Put up thy sword into the _____. (John 18:11)
51. Average amount.
52. Reject.
54. Come ye yourselves _____ into a desert place. (Mark 6:31)
56. Loud.
57. Inner surface of the hand.

DOWN CLUES

1. Let us _____ the sacrifice of praise. (Heb. 13:15)
2. _____ ye holy; for I am holy. (1 Pet. 1:16)
3. In _____ _____ give thanks. (1 Thes. 5:18)
4. Expression of affirmation.
6. I put my hook in thy _____. (Isa. 37:29)
7. Merry gathering.
8. Already eaten.
9. Period of bad health.
10. Negative vote.
15. Pull.
17. But many that are first shall be _____. (Mark 10:31)
18. Cubic centimeter.
19. Purge out therefore the old _____. (1 Cor. 5:7)
22. And the Lord opened the mouth of the _____. (Num. 22:28)
26. Nevertheless.
29. Arkansas (abbr.).
30. _____ to the voice of my supplications. (Ps. 86:6)
32. Build.
34. To _____ from evil is understanding. (Job 28:28)
36. Remember his _____ no more. (Prov. 31:7)
37. Blessed is _____ that cometh in the name of the Lord. (Matt. 21:9)
39. Once more.
41. Halle_____jah.
42. Sound an _____ in my holy mountain. (Joel 2:1)
45. Roughen and redden.
48. Science (abbr.).
49. Owns.
50. Newspaper _____.
51. Comrade.
53. Do-Re-Mi-Fa-_____-La-Ti-Do.
55. Ma and _____.

Puzzle 29

Evelyn M. Boyington

ACROSS CLUES

1. To plop.
5. There is a _____ here, which hath five barley loaves. (John 6:9)
8. Joshua built an altar unto the Lord God of Israel in mount _____. (Josh. 8:30)
12. Then shall the _____ man leap as an hart. (Isa. 35:6)
13. Age.
14. A solo.
15. The high and lofty One that inhabiteth _____. (Isa. 57:15)
17. They passed through the _____ _____ea as by dry land. (Heb. 11:29)
18. Thick.
19. Spatter.
21. Indebted to.
24. Whatsoever ye shall _____ in my name, that will I do. (John 14:13)
25. Ship's direct steering.
28. Soon.
30. From the beginning of the year even unto the _____. (Deut. 11:12)
33. Where _____ the men which came into thee this night? (Gen. 19:5)
34. Let us lay _____ every weight. (Heb. 12:1)
35. Pekoe.
36. In a place where two ways _____. (Mark 11:4)
37. In the first year of Darius the _____. (Dan. 11:1)
38. The love of God is _____ abroad in our hearts. (Rom. 5:5)
39. _____ art thou, Lord? (Acts 9:5)
41. Revise.
43. _____ you this day whom ye will serve. (Josh. 24:15)
46. What thou _____, write in a book. (Rev. 1:11)
50. Gentleman (German).
51. Turn back thine hand as a grape _____ into the baskets. (Jer. 6:9)
54. Annoys.
55. Antelope.
56. Pro _____.
57. The smell of thy _____ like apples. (Song of Sol. 7:8)
58. Droop.
59. Break.

DOWN CLUES

1. They _____ before the men of Ai. (Josh. 7:4)
2. The Jews of _____ sought to stone thee. (John 11:8)
3. Sign.
4. There was not one feeble _____ among their tribes. (Ps. 105:37)
5. Hawaiian garland.
6. Where _____ thou? (Gen. 3:9)
7. All the _____ of my life. (Ps. 23:6)
8. British noblemen.
9. No man _____ it unto them. (Lam. 4:4)
10. Helps.
11. To whip.
16. I make all things _____. (Rev. 21:5)
20. Window glass.
22. Woe to them that are at _____ in Zion. (Amos 6:1)
23. Sly.

25. Eccentric wheel.
26. Unrefined rock.
27. They that weave _____ shall be
confounded. (Isa. 19:9)
29. The prophet of the Lord...whose
name was _____.(2 Chron. 28:9)
31. Born.
32. Mom and _____.
34. Minor prophet.
38. Cattle.
40. I saw, and behold a white _____.
(Rev. 6:2)
42. Adjective suffix.

43. Part of the face.
44. Champion.
45. As the partridge sitteth on _____.
(Jer. 17:11)
47. Of _____, the family of the
Eranites. (Num. 26:36)
48. Bristle.
49. A _____ for him in the way.
(Job 18:10)
52. American Newspaper
Association.
53. Pull.

61

Puzzle 30

Evelyn M. Boyington

ACROSS CLUES

1. I am the brother to dragons, and a companion to _____. (Job 30:29)
5. _____ the son of Abdiel. (1 Chron. 5:15)
8. Festive.
12. An invasion.
13. Leaned his hand on the wall, and a serpent _____ him. (Amos 5:19)
14. For this _____ is mount Sinai in Arabia. (Gal. 4:25)
15. But let him _____ in faith. (Jam. 1:6)
16. To marry.
17. Outer layer.
18. The man took a golden earring of half a _____ weight. (Gen. 24:22)
20. Trainee.
21. A brother offended is harder to be _____ than a strong city. (Prov. 18:19)
22. In that day when I _____ up my jewels. (Mal. 3:17)
23. The churches of _____ salute you. (1 Cor. 16:19)
25. Governing board.
28. Possesses.

29. The dogs came and licked his _____. (Luke 16:21)
30. Meadow.
32. Era.
34. Now the coat was without _____. (John 19:23)
35. For my yoke is _____. (Matt. 11:30)
36. A scarf.
37. Roller or ice.
39. Cooled.
42. Blaze.
43. Illuminated.
44. _____, Elah, and Naam. (1 Chron. 4:15)
45. Who shall _____ us away the stone? (Mark 16:3)
46. What _____eth thee, Hagar? (Gen. 21:17)
47. To break suddenly.
48. Children, _____ your parents in the Lord. (Eph. 6:1)
49. Yea, thou shalt _____ thy children's children. (Ps. 128:6)
50. To leer.

DOWN CLUES

1. Danish money.
2. _____ me, and I shall be whiter than snow. (Ps. 51:7)
3. Go, and do thou _____. (Luke 10:37)
4. Midwest state (abbr.).
5. _____ was a keeper of sheep. (Gen. 4:2)
6. In whom are _____ all the treasures of wisdom and knowledge. (Col. 2:3)
7. _____ is finished. (John 19:30)
8. God sent him forth from the _____ of Eden. (Gen. 3:23)
9. Terror, consumption, and the burning _____. (Lev. 26:16)
10. And it shall come to pass in the

_____ days. (Isa. 2:2)
11. Rabbi, thou _____ the Son of God. (John 1:49)
16. Blind, or broken, or maimed, of having a _____. (Lev. 22:22)
17. And they baked unleavened _____ of the dough. (Ex. 12:39)
19. All the Chaldeans, Pekod, and Shoa, and _____. (Ezek. 23:23)
20. Tricky.
22. A _____ heart doeth good like a medicine. (Prov. 17:22)
23. _____ sinful nation, a people laden with iniquity. (Isa. 1:4)
24. A pouch.
25. Who shall _____ him up. (Gen. 49:9)
26. Washing.
27. For all the promises of God in him are _____. (2 Cor. 1:20)
29. The last _____ of that man is worse. (Matt. 12:45)
31. I _____ become a fool (2 Cor. 12:11)
33. Almost.
34. This is my beloved _____, in whom I am well pleased. (Matt. 3:17)
36. The lapwing, and the _____. (Lev. 11:19)
37. A sloppy person.
38. Cabbage.
39. Yet they had a _____ for the mattocks. (1 Sam. 13:21)
40. Epochal.
41. To deceive.
42. I am full of tossings to and _____. (Job 7:4)
43. But wild beasts of the desert shall _____ there. (Isa. 13:21)
46. Even _____ Christ forgave you, so also do ye. (Col. 3:13)
47. Even _____, come, Lord Jesus. (Rev. 22:20)

Puzzle 31

Joann Horn

ACROSS CLUES

1. _____ as a grain of mustard seed. (Matt. 17:20)
5. I have _____ you with milk. (1 Cor. 3:2)
7. For _____ Jonas was three days and three nights. (Matt. 12:40)
9. Opposite of "young".
10. Heavenly messenger.
13. He is of _____; ask him. (John 9:21)
14. What foolish virgins forgot to take. (Matt. 25:3)
15. The lilies, they _____ not. (Matt. 6:28)
16. _____ that was washed to her wallowing. (2 Pet. 2:22)
17. Plural of "tooth".
19. They shall be one _____. (Gen. 2:24)
22. Inflict suffering.
25. Capable.
27. Unlearned and unstable _____. (2 Pet. 3:16)
28. Painful sore under skin.
30. Hollow-type grass.
32. The Lord is my _____, and I will not fear. (Heb. 13:6)
36. O _____ of little faith? (Matt. 6:30)
38. Number before seven.
39. Large body of water.
40. His heavens shall _____ down dew. (Deut. 33:28)
42. Whose hair is fallen off his head, he is _____. (Lev. 13:40)
43. _____ my soul from their destructions. (Ps. 35:17)
46. Be sick.
47. Man who preaches any other gospel. (Gal. 1:8)
49. Flightless bird.
50. Matthew (abbr.).
51. To stroke or caress.
52. Yours and mine.

DOWN CLUES

1. Twelve inches.
2. Foreigner.
3. They learn to be _____. (1 Tim. 5:13)
4. For whosoever _____, to him shall be given. (Matt. 13:12)
5. No _____ with works of darkness. (Eph. 5:11)
6. Election (abbr.).
7. Four days _____ I was fasting. (Acts 10:30)
8. Stitch.
11. Opposite of "yes".
12. The _____ of the Holy Ghost. (Acts 10:45)
13. Remainder of burnt wood.
18. Furniture we eat at.
20. To go astray.
21. An odour of a sweet _____. (Phil. 4:18)
23. New Testament (abbr.).
24. Children, _____ your parents. (Col. 3:20)
25. What we breathe.
26. Finish.

29. Swap.
31. I _____ all things for elect's sakes. (2 Tim. 2:10)
33. Exodus (abbr.).
34. _____ and hymns and spiritual songs. (Col. 3:16)
35. Snakelike fish.
37. Chosen of God.
38. For God _____ loved the world. (John 3:16)

41. I will give you _____. (Matt. 11:28)
42. A coffin.
43. Male sheep.
44. Southern state (abbr.).
45. Vessel for drinking.
48. Is it lawful to _____ good? (Mark 3:4)

Puzzle 32

Joann Horn

ACROSS CLUES

1. Scribes and Pharisees sit in Moses' _____. (Matt. 23:2)
5. Opposite of "thin."
9. _____ that cometh from above is above all. (John 3:31)
11. Window glass.
12. God had sworn with an _____ to him. (Acts 2:30)
13. Uncooked.
14. After the _____ of Melchizedek. (Ps. 110:4)
16. Seek things which are _____. (Col. 3:1)
18. Rip or pull apart.
20. The Lord is on my _____. (Ps. 118:6)
21. _____ shall a man give in exchange for his soul? (Matt. 16:26)
22. Did eat.
24. Tree of the olive family.
25. _____ than hell. (Job 11:8)
27. Spanish for "yes."

28. Word _____ God abideth in you. (1 John 2:14)
30. A male child.
31. To gain a victory.
32. Abstain from fleshly _____. (1 Pet. 2:11)
34. Sung in praise of God.
35. To kill.
38. How large a _____ I have written. (Gal. 6:11)
39. As a _____ doth gather her brood under her wings. (Luke 13:34)
40. Part of foot.
41. Let it be so.
43. A contract.
46. Agriculture (abbr.).
47. When he returned, he found them _____. (Mark 14:40)
48. God _____ loved the world. (John 3:16)
49. My yoke _____ easy, and my burden is light. (Matt. 11:30)
50. Type of bear.
51. Dwellings.

DOWN CLUES

1. Be found...without _____, and blameless. (2 Pet. 3:14)
2. Used for hearing.
3. To sit on my right hand _____ on my left. (Mark 10:40)
4. Plural of "tooth."
5. I go _____ prepare a place for you. (John 14:2)
6. Covering for head.
7. Baptism of John, was _____ from heaven? (Mark 11:30)
8. Discipline by punishment.
9. Thou shalt _____ treasure in heaven. (Mark 10:21)
10. Female sheep.
13. A staff or scepter.
15. Philip. . .heard him _____ the prophet Esaias. (Acts 8:30)
17. A coffin.
19. Took the little book. . .and _____ it up. (Rev. 10:10)
21. And Jesus said, _____ touched me? (Luke 8:45)
22. Sent to preach the gospel.
23. _____ with grace in your hearts to the Lord. (Col. 3:16)
24. Tossed about by waves.
26. Let each _____ other better than themselves. (Phil. 2:3)
27. Transgression.
29. They _____ away as an eagle toward heaven. (Prov. 23:5)
31. For their _____ shall not die. (Isa. 66:24)
33. Drowsy.
34. Chair, bench, or stool.
36. He that is _____ in. . .heaven is greater. (Matt. 11:11)
37. To fish with a hook.
40. Take ye _____, watch and pray. (Mark 13:33)
42. Sun rises here.
44. Primary color.
45. No way.
49. Opposite of "out."

Puzzle 33

Amy Rognlie

ACROSS CLUES

1. Matthew, Mark, Luke, _____.
5. Yet will I leave a _____. (Ezek. 6:8)
11. Jesus cried..., _____, Eloi, lama sabachthani? (Mark 15:34)
12. Sun (Spanish).
13. Ancient South American Indians.
14. Jesus...touched him, saying, I _____. (Matt. 8:3)
15. _____ yourselves unto God. (Rom. 6:13)
17. Jacob _____ pottage. (Gen. 25:29)
18. Mom.
19. Ye say that I cast out devils through _____. (Luke 11:18)
24. Under oaks and poplars and _____s. (Hosea 4:13)
27. North northeast (abbr.).
28. Thy name shall be called no more Jacob, but _____. (Gen. 32:28)
31. But _____ found grace in the eyes of the Lord. (Gen. 6:8)

68

34. Maine (abbr.).
35. Sharpen every man his _____.
    (1 Sam. 13:20)
36. _____ thy wife shall bear thee a
    son. (Gen. 17:19)
39. Give _____ to my words, O
    Lord. (Ps. 5:1)
41. Texas city: El _____.
42. Choose.
45. Joseph took them both, _____
    ...and Manasseh. (Gen. 48:13)
50. Butter substitute.
52. I beseech _____. (Phil. 4:2)
54. No scrip, no bread, no _____.
    (Mark 6:8)
55. A time to rend, and a time to
    _____. (Ec. 3:7)
56. Cow noise.

DOWN CLUES

1. Where is he that is born King of
    the _____? (Matt. 2:2)
2. A dish of many ingredients.
3. God will _____ thy right hand.
    (Isa. 41:13)
4. Nothing.
5. Ye are a chosen generation, a
    _____ priesthood. (1 Pet. 2:9)
6. The child did minister unto the
    Lord before _____.(1 Sam. 2:11)
7. Same as 4 down.
8. With; as well as.
9. North Carolina (abbr.).
10. Weed.
16. Thou hast been in _____ the
    garden of God. (Ezek. 28:13)

18. Myself.
20. Period of time.
21. Zinc (abbr.).
22. _____ the king of Syria was sick.
    (2 Kgs. 8:7)
23. The _____ out of the wood doth
    waste it. (Ps. 80:13)
25. A faithful witness will not
    _____. (Prov. 14:5)
26. Master of Science (abbr.).
29. They that sow in tears shall
    _____ in joy. (Ps. 126:5)
30. To obliterate.
32. All that handle the _____.
    (Ezek. 27:29)
33. _____ me, O Lord. (Jer. 17:14)
35. Southeast (abbr.).
37. Egyptian sun god.
38. (Love) always protects, always
    trusts, always _____.
    (1 Cor. 13:7 NIV)
40. Space.
43. Palestine Liberation Organization
    (abbr.).
44. There met him _____ men that
    were lepers. (Luke 17:12)
46. Color.
47. The second _____ shall be an
    emerald. (Ex. 28:18)
48. They departed from _____.
    (Num. 33:45)
49. Deceased Chinese leader, _____
    Tse-tung.
51. Old English (abbr.).
53. He had sent messengers to _____
    king of Egypt. (2 Kgs. 17:4)

Puzzle 34

Pamela Jensen

ACROSS CLUES

1. With _____, and with singing. (Neh. 12:27)
11. Sit on my right _____. (Heb. 1:13)
12. Go up to _____. (Josh. 8:1)
13. Let nothing _____. (Es. 6:10)
14. Shihon, and _____. (Josh. 19:19)
18. Tender loving care (abbr.).
19. Airport code for New Delhi, India.
20. Behold the _____ of the Lord. (Luke 1:38)
22. Kansas (abbr.).
24. Height (abbr.).
25. Standing room only (abbr.)
27. Shout for _____. (Ps. 65:13)
28. _____ will we sing. (Ps. 21:13)
30. His _____ begotten son. (Heb. 11:17)
32. _____ in peace. (Mark 5:34)
35. Airport code for Lisbon, Portugal.
37. Architectural-Engineering (abbr.).
38. Ibidem (abbr.).
39. Found young _____. (1 Sam. 9:11)
42. Verse (abbr.).
44. I have (contraction).
45. And _____ it up. (Rev. 10:10)
47. Month on Hebrew calendar.
49. To spread with a greasy substance.
51. The _____ leaped. (Luke 1:44)
53. Kill the _____. (Num. 35:27)
56. The angel _____. (Luke 1:26)
59. The _____ day. (Acts 25:6)
60. One _____ for all. (2 Cor. 5:14)
61. _____ king of Bashan. (Ps. 135:11)
62. Eleventh letter in Hebrew alphabet.

DOWN CLUES

1. Magnify him with _____. (Ps. 69:30)
2. Right _____ of fellowship. (Gal. 2:9)
3. Daughter of _____. (Gen. 36:2)
4. Airport code for New Delhi, India.
5. _____ thy wife shall bear thee a son. (Gen. 17:19)
6. _____ in the earth. (Gen. 6:4)
7. _____ we confess our sins. (1 John 1:9)
8. An holy _____. (1 Pet. 2:9)
9. To cover with a thin layer of gold.
10. Airport code for Salt Lake City, Utah.
15. _____ Lord God! (Ezek. 11:13)
16. Touchdown (abbr.).
17. Her Majesty's Ship (abbr.).
21. And he _____. (Mark 2:14)
23. Is _____ of the Spirit. (John 3:6)
26. Cereal grass.
29. Mount of _____. (John 8:1)
31. The first and the _____. (Rev. 22:13)
33. _____ your parents. (Eph. 6:1)
34. I _____ the Son of God. (Matt. 27:43)
36. A model of perfection.
40. To intend or direct.
41. Symbol for element sodium.

43. _____, we know. (John 3:2)
46. Heaven and the _____.
    (Gen. 1:1)
48. A _____ thing. (Dan. 2:11)
49. They shall _____ his face.
    (Rev. 22:4)

50. That could keep _____.
    (1 Chron. 12:38)
52. I _____ thee. (2 Kgs. 4:24)
54. _____, though I walk. (Ps. 23:4)
55. Expenses (abbr.).
57. Anno Domini (abbr.).
58. And _____ a voice. (Matt. 3:17)

Puzzle 35

Pamela Jensen

ACROSS CLUES

1. Jesus Christ the same _____. (Heb. 13:8)
9. The beginning and the _____. (Rev. 22:13)
12. _____ this day. (Ex. 12:17)
13. Seek to _____ in. (Luke 13:24)
15. To take away weapons.
16. The _____ which he promised. (Deut. 9:28)
18. Electrical engineer (abbr.).
19. At the _____ hand of God. (Rom. 8:34)
20. The people _____ _____ mind to work. (Neh. 4:6; 2 words)
22. The _____ of the sea. (Gen. 49:13)
25. They departed from _____. (Num. 33:45)
26. Money or goods given to poor, in love (singular).
27. _____ prophet. (Rev. 16:13)
28. A fig _____. (Mark 11:13)
29. Foot (abbr.).
31. Any three.

33. _____, I am with you.
    (Matt. 28:20)
35. Thunder and _____.
    (1 Sam. 12:17)
37. No room for them in the _____.
    (Luke 2:7)
38. The children of _____.
    (Ezra 2:57)
40. Unto the _____ down. (Ps. 50:1)
41. _____ Lord. (Ps. 120:2)
42. Let him be Anathema
    Maran-_____. (1 Cor. 16:22)
43. Hemoglobin (abbr.).
44. The _____ of the Lord.
    (2 Cor. 3:18)
47. "And sun" in Spanish.
48. Tailor (abbr.)
50. Prefix indicates "inside or
    "within."
51. I will _____ thee. (Gen. 22:17)
53. _____, Thou shalt love.
    (Rom. 13:9)
54. Glory and _____. (2 Pet. 1:3)

DOWN CLUES

1. Flee also _____ lusts.
   (2 Tim. 2:22)
2. East by north (abbr.).
3. Social Security Administration
   (abbr.).
4. The glory of the _____.
   (1 Cor. 15:40)

5. A weasel.
6. Revised Version (abbr.).
7. A territory of India.
8. Basic monetary unit of Japan.
9. Eastern time (abbr.).
10. The eye of a _____.(Matt. 19:24)
11. Nor to your _____. (Jer. 27:9)
14. Airport code for New Delhi,
    India.
17. Inclined upward.
21. Moses and _____. (Lev. 13:1)
23. Associate in Arts (abbr.).
24. Very low frequency (abbr.).
28. His ears shall _____. (Jer. 19:3)
30. Teachest _____. (Luke 20:21)
32. With a gold _____. (Jam. 2:2)
34. Grasses.
36. Not many _____ are called.
    (1 Cor. 1:26)
39. A unit of conductance, reciprocal
    to the ohm.
41. Airport code for O'Hare Field,
    Chicago, Illinois.
42. Sixteenth letter of Hebrew
    alphabet.
45. Multiply _____ the face of the
    earth. (Gen. 6:1)
46. My _____ is easy. (Matt. 11:30)
49. Revised Standard Version
    (abbr.).
51. Sky color (abbr).
52. Yes (Sp.).

Puzzle 36

Pamela Jensen

ACROSS CLUES

1. Your sins are _____.
   (1 John 2:12)
8. Ye shall be _____ indeed.
   (John 8:36)
12. _____ to pray. (Matt. 14:23)
13. I have _____ by experience.
    (Gen. 30:27)
14. Turnpike (abbr.).
15. South-southwest (abbr.).
16. River in Switzerland.
17. Thin cornmeal cake.
20. Tennessee (abbr.).
21. A weasel.
22. And _____ with her suburbs.
    (1 Chron. 6:75)
25. Right (abbr.).
26. The children of _____.(Jer. 2:16)
28. In the _____ of Jordan.
    (Mark 1:5)
30. Bone from the elbow to
    the wrist.
32. Set up our _____. (Ps. 20:5)
34. One _____, a prophetess.
    (Luke 2:36)
36. Cable News Network (abbr.).
37. Sixteenth letter in Greek
    alphabet.
38. They did eat _____. (Ex. 16:35)
40. The name of the well _____.
    (Gen. 26:20)
42. Symbol for element platinum.
43. Abraham and Sarah were _____.
    (Gen. 18:11)
44. The desert of _____.
    (Num. 27:14)
46. Symbol for element lithium.
47. From _____ lips. (Ps. 120:2)

49. King of the _____. (Matt. 2:2)
50. Symbol for element tin.
51. _____ of the Chaldees.
    (Gen. 11:28)
53. There was a continual _____
    given him of the king of
    Babylon. (Jer. 52:34)
55. With hands on the hips and
    elbows bowed outward.
56. Greek island.

DOWN CLUES

1. Peace from God the _____.
   (2 John 3)
2. We have therefore _____.
   (Gal. 6:10)
3. His sons were Ulam and _____.
   (1 Chron. 7:16)
4. Greece (abbr.).
5. _____ came to pass. (Josh. 1:1)
6. There is none _____. (Isa. 45:18)
7. He is a _____ creature.
   (2 Cor. 5:17)
8. Gold, and _____. (Matt. 2:11)
9. Ribonucleic acid (abbr.).
10. Poetic: ever.
11. Garden of _____. (Gen. 2:15)
15. A straw beehive.
18. And of sweet _____. (Ex. 30:23)
19. A small buffalo of Celebes and
    the Philippines.
20. _____ not to the right.
    (Prov. 4:27)
23. Frogs...into thine _____.
    (Ex. 8:3)
24. From the _____ even to the
    husk. (Num. 6:4)
27. Hemoglobin (abbr.).
29. Royal Society (abbr.).
31. Lane (abbr.).
33. They were _____. (Job 32:15)

34. The _____ of his eye. (Deut. 32:10)
35. Abraham was old, _____ well stricken. (Gen. 24:1)
39. _____ trees and precious stones. (2 Chron. 9:10)
41. Before rulers and _____. (Mark 13:9)

45. Archaic: certainly, assuredly.
48. I wrote them with _____. (Jer. 36:18)
52. Symbol for element rubidium.
54. Truck (abbr.).

Puzzle 37

Susan F. Weimer

ACROSS CLUES

1. The _____ that covereth the inwards. (Lev. 3:3)
3. Went to sojourn in the country of _____. (Ruth 1:1)
7. Jehu destroyed _____ out of Israel (2 Kgs. 10:28)
10. He placed _____ the east of the garden. (Gen. 3:24)
11. _____ also to save them to the uttermost. (Heb. 7:25)
12. Associated Press (abbr.).
13. Nor height, nor _____, nor any other. (Rom. 8:39)
16. The Lord sent _____ unto David. (2 Sam. 12:1)
17. Unto _____ the prophet the son of Amoz. (Isa. 37:2)
19. Short for "hello."
20. Bureau (abbr.).
21. Zimri, the son of _____, a prince. (Num. 25:14)

22. He shall send them a _____. (Isa. 19:20)
25. Her Highness (abbr.).
26. In thee shall all _____ be blessed. (Gal. 3:8)
27. An eagle stirreth up her _____. (Deut. 32:11)
28. Ye shall find the _____. (Luke 2:12)
31. Hi in the mirror.
32. Of fowls also of the _____. (Gen. 7:3)
33. In addition, also.
35. New Jersey (abbr.).
37. Nehemiah the son of _____. (Neh. 3:16)
39. Not on.
41. Being a wild _____ tree. (Rom. 11:17)
44. Though they be _____ like crimson. (Isa. 1:18)
46. Short for "good-bye."
47. The name of it called _____. (Gen. 11:9)
48. There was no room for them in the _____. (Luke 2:7)

DOWN CLUES

1. Shall the rich man _____ away. (Jam. 1:11)
2. Men _____ the bread of angels. (Ps. 78:25 NIV)
3. The three and twentieth to _____. (1 Chron. 25:30)
4. Obadiah (abbr.).
5. Alabama (abbr.).
6. These are their names: _____ in the hill country.(1 Kgs. 4:8 NIV)
7. David comforted _____ his wife. (2 Sam. 12:24)
8. The son of a Benjamite. (1 Sam. 9:1)
9. Heard them speak in his own _____. (Acts 2:6)
14. _____ then went out unto them. (John 18:29)
15. Tensile strength (abbr.).
18. Proud, _____, disobedient to their parents. (2 Tim. 3:2 NIV)
22. _____ them through thy truth. (John 17:17)
23. Seal up the _____ and prophecy. (Dan. 9:24)
24. To be upon.
29. Joshua had taken _____. (Josh. 10:1)
30. Because of unbelief they were _____ off. (Rom. 11:20)
34. _____ had six sons. (1 Chron. 9:44)
36. These three men, Noah, Daniel, and _____ were in it. (Ezek. 14:14)
37. Avenue (abbr.).
38. I have called by name Bezaleel the son of _____. (Ex. 31:2)
39. Obstetrics (abbr.).
40. Chemical symbol for iron.
42. The sixth tone of the diatonic scale.
43. Ibidem.
45. Daniel (abbr.).

Puzzle 38

Susan F. Weimer

ACROSS CLUES

1. To go away.
5. Citizens Band (abbr.).
7. _____, an apostle of Jesus Christ. (1 Pet. 1:1)
10. Blessed are the _____ in spirit. (Matt. 5:3)
11. Laker's home town.
12. Before noon.
13. A book of maps.
15. Breathed into his nostrils the _____ of life. (Gen. 2:7)
18. Prefix meaning "to do again."
19. I stand at the door, and _____. (Rev. 3:20)
21. Club used to strike a ball.
22. Because he _____ for you. (1 Pet. 5:7 NIV)
25. I will _____, and will deliver. (Isa. 46:4)
26. By the hearing of the _____. (Job 42:5)
28. Endured the _____, despising the shame. (Heb. 12:2)
30. He breaketh the bow, and cutteth the _____ in sunder. (Ps. 46:9)
32. My people hath been _____ sheep. (Jer. 50:6)
34. Near (abbr.).
35. Then he got into the _____. (Matt. 8:23 NIV)
36. Gather his _____ into the garner. (Matt. 3:12)
38. Not off.
39. Cheweth the _____, among the beasts. (Lev. 11:3)
41. An exclamation often used in cartoons.
43. An object used to stop up a hole.
45. A negative.
46. Fine, volcanic particles.
47. Escaped with the skin of my _____. (Job 19:20)

DOWN CLUES

1. A health resort.
2. Sweeter also than honey and the honey _____. (Ps. 19:10)
3. Account of (abbr.).
4. Every _____ which bringeth not forth good fruit. (Matt. 3:10)
6. A person who has had a _____. (John 13:10 NIV)
7. That were in the low _____ was Baalhanan. (1 Chron. 27:28)
8. We may _____ of the fruit. (Gen. 3:2)
9. A Sceptre shall _____ out of Israel. (Num. 24:17)
14. In the _____ thou shalt put the testimony. (Ex. 25:21)
16. A long-tailed rodent.
17. They that sow in _____. (Ps. 126:5)
19. Have the _____ of hell and of death. (Rev. 1:18)
20. Now ye are _____ through the word. (John 15:3)
21. That holy thing which shall _____ born. (Luke 1:35)
22. _____ lots upon my vesture. (Ps. 22:18)
23. Rural route (abbr.).
24. Having done any good _____ evil. (Rom. 9:11)

78

25. Sitteth not down first, and counteth the _____.(Luke 14:28)
27. Nor for the _____ that flieth by day. (Ps. 91:5)
28. Behold, he cometh with _____. (Rev. 1:7)
29. Wide is the gate and broad is the _____. (Matt. 7:13 NIV)
31. _____ that ye enter not into temptation. (Luke 22:40)

33. _____ unto God with the voice of triumph. (Ps. 47:1)
35. Before Christ.
37. The tabernacle of the _____ or the congregation. (Ex. 40:2)
40. Primate.
42. An exclamation of surprise.
44. General Electric (abbr.)

Puzzle 39

Susan F. Weimer

ACROSS CLUES

1. I would thou wert _____ or hot. (Rev. 3:15)
5. _____ us from evil. (Matt. 6:13)
11. _____ my voice. (Ex. 19:5)
12. _____ thou at my right hand. (Ps. 110:1)
13. Behold, _____ is the accepted time. (2 Cor. 6:2)
15. To make a hole.
17. Audiovisual (abbr.).
18. District Attorney (abbr.).
19. There is none righteous, _____ not one. (Rom. 3:10)
20. Not A, E, or O.
21. A sharp, shrill bark or yelp.
22. In the beginning _____. (Gen. 1:1)
23. He hath put a _____ song in my mouth. (Ps. 40:3)
26. Rejoice, and be exceeding _____. (Matt. 5:12)
28. The mountain of _____. (Deut. 34:1)

31. The ratio of the circumference of a circle to its diameter.
32. Whom Sarah bare to him, _____. (Gen. 21:3)
35. Prefix meaning "in."
36. Purple Heart (abbr.).
37. Bachelor of Arts (abbr.).
38. Unto one he gave five _____. (Matt. 25:15)
40. _____ that hath an ear. (Rev. 2:7)
41. Alabama (abbr.)
42. Not happy.
43. Football defensive lineman (abbr.).
44. They were not afraid of the king's _____. (Heb. 11:23 NIV)
47. Belly button.
48. The _____ of all evil. (1 Tim. 6:10)
49. Emergency Medical Service (abbr.).
50. The _____ of joy for mourning. (Isa. 61:3)

DOWN CLUES

1. There is therefore now no _____. (Rom. 8:1)
2. Obstetrician (abbr.).
3. For as many as are _____ by the Spirit. (Rom. 8:14)
4. As _____, and behold we live. (2 Cor. 6:9)
6. _____ said to Jacob, Feed me. (Gen. 25:30)
7. Lead them unto _____ fountains of waters. (Rev. 7:17)
8. And _____ repented the Lord that he had made man.(Gen. 6:6)
9. _____ thou not the oppressor. (Prov. 3:31)
10. Roseanna's nickname.
14. Jesus _____. (John 11:35)
16. None is _____, save one. (Luke 18:19)
24. Adah bare to Esau _____. (Gen. 36:4)
25. Have _____ their robes. (Rev. 7:14)
27. Doctor of Arts (abbr).
29. Unto all and upon all them that _____. (Rom. 3:22)
30. That they all may be _____. (John 17:21)
31. Delivered it from the _____ of corruption. (Isa. 38:17)
33. Whose name in the Hebrew tongue is _____. (Rev. 9:11)
34. I will _____ on the name of the Lord. (1 Kgs. 18:24)
39. In his hands the print of the _____. (John 20:25)
45. Democrat (abbr.).
46. Hew thee _____ tables of stone. (Deut. 10:1)

Puzzle 40

Beverly Barnes

ACROSS CLUES

1. By their _____ ye shall know them. (Matt. 7:20)
5. Jesus loves _____.
7. Lean _____ unto thine own understanding. (Prov. 3:5)
9. Bad grammar.
10. _____ are of God, little children. (1 John 4:4)
11. Intensive Care (abbr.).
12. The beginning and the _____. (Rev. 21:6)
14. A little _____ than the angels. (Heb. 2:7)
17. I will never leave _____. (Heb. 13:5)
20. Each (abbr.).
22. Delaware (abbr.).
23. I am meek and lowly in _____. (Matt. 11:29)
25. American Medical Association (abbr.).
27. Let thy words be _____. (Ec. 5:2)
28. Opposite of "brave."
29. Unto us a child is _____. (Isa. 9:6)
31. The head of the _____, the church. (Col. 1:18)
33. Postscript.
35. Opposite of "depart."
38. _____ be it.
39. A hot cereal, _____meal.
41. _____ him, and let him go. (John 11:44)
42. A bicycle's handle_____.
43. A little bird.
44. Missouri (abbr.).
45. Leave these out of your diet.
46. Cause thine _____ to hear. (Ps. 10:17)
47. A has_____.
49. A continent.
50. One who works in a bellfry.
52. Jesus saith unto her, Give me to _____. (John 4:7)
53. _____ evil with good. (Rom. 12:21)

DOWN CLUES

1. The just shall live by _____. (Gal. 3:11)
2. I will give thee hidden _____. (Isa. 45:3)
3. United Nations (abbr.)
4. _____ is finished. (John 19:30)
5. The Lord is _____ shepherd. (Ps. 23:1)
6. Moray _____.
7. If any man be in Christ, he is a _____ creature. (2 Cor. 5:17)
8. _____ stones at him. (2 Sam. 16:13)
13. Was _____, and is alive again. (Luke 15:24)
15. Ohio (abbr.).
16. God sent him forth from the garden of_____. (Gen. 3:23)
18. Charity...toward _____ other. (2 Thes. 1:3)
19. Period of time in history.
21. I _____ the way. (John 14:6)
24. The _____ of your faith. (1 Pet. 1:7)
26. Every perfect gift is from _____. (Jam. 1:17)
27. To cook in a skillet.
30. Musical poem.
31. Buffalo.

82

32. He will not fail thee, neither
_____ thee. (Deut. 31:8)
33. All _____ is given unto me.
(Matt. 28:18)
34. Abram took _____ his wife.
(Gen. 12:5)
36. Rule out (abbr.).
37. All Jews to depart from _____.
(Acts 18:2)
38. Silk and _____.

40. Sea bird.
42. Famous musician, Count _____.
45. Old MacDonald had one.
47. Nickname for Beverly.
48. Before (poetic).
51. _____ ye and teach all nations.
(Matt. 28:19)
52. _____ all to the glory of God.
(1 Cor. 10:31)

Puzzle 41

Faith Wade

ACROSS CLUES

1. Last book of the Bible.
9. A thing offered unto an _____. (1 Cor. 8:7)
10. Boaz and Ruth's son. (Ruth 4:21)
13. Cozbi, daughter of _____. (Num. 25:15)
14. Alpha and _____. (Rev. 1:8)
17. _____ and drink. (Acts 10:41)
18. _____ and Dimonah, and Adadah. (Josh. 15:22)
19. Sendeth _____ on the just and on the unjust. (Matt. 5:45)
21. A tenth part of the _____ (Num. 18:26)
24. _____ found grace. (Gen. 6:8)
26. The province of _____. (Dan. 8:2)
27. Dad.
29. _____ himself in water. (Num. 19:19)
31. Cast the _____. (John 21:6)
32. Who Cain murdered. (Gen. 4:8)

84

34. Linen _____. (1 Kings 10:28)
36. Not a she.
37. _____there be light. (Gen. 1:3)
39. _____ them about thy neck.
    (Prov. 6:21)
40. The beginning and the _____.
    (Rev. 22:13)
42. _____ Peter.
44. Symbol for nickel.
45. Papa and _____.
46. An _____ of the Lord.
    (Matt. 2:19)
49. Opposite of "out."
50. _____ I my brother's keeper?
    (Gen. 4:9)
51. Exalt his _____ together.
    (Ps. 34:3)
53. Shut the _____ mouths.
    (Dan. 6:22)
55. The number of lepers Jesus
    healed. (Luke 17:17)
56. What Gideon was checking for.
    (Judg. 6:37)
57. Children's teeth are set on
    _____. (Ezek. 18:2)

DOWN CLUES

1. One of these never touched
   Samson's head. (Judg. 16:17)
2. Mary was one. (Luke 1:27)
3. Edward's nickname.
4. God hates a proud _____.
   (Prov. 6:16, 17)
5. Under the shadow of the _____.
   (Ps. 91:1)

6. The feast of _____. (Ex. 34:22)
7. Negative.
8. Meadow.
11. Where Jesus was born.
12. Deuteronomy (abbr.).
15. Printer's measure
16. _____ the son of Abdiel.
    (1 Chron. 5:15)
20. Jesus healed his son. (John 4:46)
22. The _____Commandments.
23. Hast thou _____ of the tree?
    (Gen. 3:11)
25. Alcoholics Anonymous (abbr.).
27. Frying _____. (Lev. 7:9)
28. Jewish month.
30. Head covering.
33. They removed from _____
    (Num. 33:10)
35. North side of Bethemek, and
    _____. (Josh. 19:27)
38. Go ye in _____ all the world.
    (Mark 16:15)
41. He saw _____ smoke rising.
    (Gen. 19:28 NIV)
42. Identical.
43. I will praise thy _____.
    (Ps. 54:6)
45. Welcome _____.
47. _____ Testament.
48. God, that cannot _____.
    (Titus 1:2)
49. Suffix.
52. Newspaper.
54. Doctor of optometry. (abbr.)

Puzzle 42

Faith Wade

ACROSS CLUES

1. I am the _____ and the life. (John 11:25)
11. First garden.
12. Shiphi, the son of _____. (1 Chron. 4:37)
13. I stand _____ the door. (Rev. 3:20)
15. Ye do well that ye take _____. (2 Peter 1:19)
16. Abstain from _____ offered to idols. (Acts 15:29)
17. _____ not steal. (Mark 10:19)
18. Set in _____. (Titus 1:5)
19. Positive votes.
20. What you do at meals.
21. Short for Ezra.
221. Taxi _____.
23. A Hebrew refrain found often in Psalms. (Ps. 4:2)
26. Uncle's mate.
28. The captain's name. (Jer. 37:13)
30. His _____ are open unto their prayers. (1 Pet. 3:12)
31. Rosemary's nickname.
32. I am not come _____ destroy. (Matt. 5:17)
33. Benjamin's nickname.
34. Joseph's uncle. (Gen. 33:1, 2)
36. _____ thou not unto his words. (Prov. 30:6)
37. Allow.
38. They shall _____ comforted. (Matt. 5:4)
39. Pronoun.
40. A fool hath no delight _____ understanding. (Prov. 18:2)
41. The harvest is _____. (Joel 3:13)
42. Not fat.
45. New Hampshire (abbr.).
47. England (Abbr.).
48. A man shall _____ a pit. (Ex. 21:33)
49. Have no other _____ before me. (Ex. 20:3)

DOWN CLUES

1. Solomon's son. (1 Kgs. 11:43)
2. Mushi, Mahli, and _____. (1 Chron. 23:23)
3. The _____ is the Word of God. (Luke 8:11)
4. Be not children in _____. (1 Cor. 14:20)
5. Abraham's sacrifice.(Gen. 22:13)
6. Aaron's son. (Num. 3:32)
7. Bodies of _____. (Job 13:12)
8. Small children.
9. _____ and outs.
10. And she bare him _____. (Ex. 6:23)
14. Total (abbr.).
20. In lowliness of mind let _____ esteem others. (Phil. 2:3)
21. Elijah's companion. (2 Kgs. 2:11)
24. He that is an _____. (John 10:12)
25. Book of wisdom written by Solomon.
27. Help in time of _____. (Heb. 4:16)
29. Israel's favorite son. (Gen. 37:3)
33. _____ himself in water. (Num. 19:19)

35. _____ it up. (Rev. 10:10)
39. I will raise _____ up. (John 2:19)
43. Opposite of out
44. Edwin s nickname.
46. _____ forth into Galilee.
(John 1:43)

1	2	3	4	■	5	6	7	■	8	9	10	11
12				■	13			■	14			
15			16				■	17				
■		18				■	19	20				
21	22	23			■	24				■		■
25				■	26			■	27	28	29	
30			■	31			■	32				
33		34				■	35					
■		36			■	37						
38	39	40			■	41			■			
42			■	43	44			■	45	46	47	
48			■	49			■	50				
51			■	52			■	53				

Puzzle 43

Evelyn M. Boyington

ACROSS CLUES

1. In the beginning was the _____.
   (John 1:1)
5. I _____ rather be a doorkeeper.
   (Ps. 84:10)
8. Two of every _____ shalt thou
   bring into the ark. (Gen. 6:19)
12. One of the Great Lakes.
13. Come down _____ my child die.
   (John 4:49)
14. Between blood and blood,
    between _____ and plea.
    (Deut. 17:8)
15. God hath _____ the body
    together. (1 Cor. 12:24)
17. Thou shalt _____ this law before
    all Israel. (Deut. 31:11)
18. He loved them unto the _____.
    (John 13:1)
19. Figures of speech.
21. Signs, good or evil.
24. To glance at quickly.
25. Be ye _____ one to another.
    (Eph. 4:32)

88

26. He that sweareth to his own hurt, and _____ not. (Ps. 15:4)
30. Last book of the Bible (abbr.).
31. Blackboard or roofing tile.
32. Confederate commander.
33. In any place.
35. Russian emperor.
36. The very hairs of your _____ are all numbered. (Matt. 10:30)
37. Your fathers _____ are they? (Zech. 1:5)
38. Middle.
41. To hasten.
42. Entrance
43. Twirling.
48. He loved Rachel _____ than Leah. (Gen. 29:30)
49. Give _____ to my words. (Ps. 5:1)
50. Applaud.
51. I am alive for evermore, _____. (Rev. 1:18)
52. Tint
53. Electrocardiograms.

DOWN CLUES

1. They are _____ with the showers. (Job 24:8)
2. Unrefined mineral.
3. Edge.
4. Rely.
5. Thou shalt kill of thy _____. (Deut. 12:21)
6. They _____ all plain to him. (Prov. 8:9)
7. King David did _____ unto the Lord. (2 Sam. 8:11)
8. _____ up, O well. (Num. 21:17)
9. Butter substitute.
10. A quantity of paper.
11. Urchins.
16. Dashes.
20. Great _____.
21. Vegetable.
22. Manner.
23. Let not thine heart _____ sinners. (Prov. 23:17)
24. Broken pottery.
26. His leprosy was _____. (Matt. 8:3)
27. He is God; there is none _____ beside him. (Deut. 4:35)
28. His anger did _____ perpetually. (Amos 1:11)
29. _____ a little, and there a little. (Isa. 28:10)
31. Karite tree.
34. To bleach.
35. Thou shalt by no means come out _____. (Matt. 5:26)
37. That I may _____ Christ. (Phil. 3:8)
38. Mother.
39. Esau, who is _____. (Gen. 36:1)
40. Dreadful.
41. Weigh silver in the balance , and _____ a goldsmith. (Isa. 46:6)
44. For this cause _____ ye tribute also. (Rom. 13:6)
45. Kind, breed.
46. Old horse.
47. Gallons per second (abbr.).

Puzzle 44

Evelyn M. Boyington

ACROSS CLUES

1. Health resort
4. _____ them in pieces. (Micah 3:3)
8. Chemical symbols for calcium and francium.
12. Tamar was _____ wife. (Gen. 38:6)
13. Of the oaks...they made thine _____. (Ezek. 27:6)
14. Capital of Norway.
15. And the _____s grew. (Gen. 25:27)
16. American chemist.
17. Bachelor of Dramatic Arts (abbr. plural).
18. But _____, but as of God. (2 Cor. 2:17; 3 words)
21. The _____ and the Thummin. (Ex. 28:30)
22. Noggin.
23. And _____ lifted up his hand. (Lev. 9:22)
25. A thousand thousands (abbr.).

26. Upon the great _____ of their right foot. (Ex. 29:20)
29. The name of Abram's _____ was Sarai. (Gen. 11:29)
30. An ocean (abbr.).
31. Blessed be the Lord God of _____. (Gen. 9:26)
32. Greek letter.
33. Cast him into a _____. (Gen. 37:24)
34. Equals.
35. Jog.
37. Both low and high, _____ and poor, together. (Ps. 49:2)
38. God gave them the like gift _____. (Acts 11:17; 5 words)
43. Competes.
44. Take thine _____, eat, drink, and be merry. (Luke 12:19)
45. Our country.
46. _____ the son of Chelub. (1 Chron. 27:26)
47. Allowance.
48. And God _____ them in the firmament. (Gen. 1:17)
49. And God did _____. (Heb. 4:4)
50. Mixture.
51. Come down _____ my child die. (John 4:49)

DOWN CLUES

1. The kings of Sheba and _____ shall offer gifts. (Ps. 72:10)
2. Some athletes.
3. Be ye not _____. (Zech. 1:4; 3 words)
4. Behold, thy _____ Elisabeth. (Luke 1:36)
5. The third to _____. (1 Chron. 24:8)
6. Ram the first born, and Bunah, and _____. (1 Chron. 2:25)
7. Of the mind.
8. Hooded snake.
9. He...did evil in the sight of the Lord, _____ _____ _____ of Ahab. (2 Kgs 8:27; 4 words)
10. Level.
11. Blushing
19. Cleaving tool.
20. Snake-like fish.
23. Stand in _____, and sin not. (Ps. 4:4)
24. Little island.
25. A pad.
27. Above (poetic).
28. German river.
30. The Lord _____ them that fear him. (Ps. 103:13)
31. There rose up certain of the _____ of the Pharisees. (Acts 15:5)
33. Hull.
34. Gnasheth with his teeth and _____ away. (Mark 9:18)
36. When legislatures sit a second time.
37. Tricks.
38. Vow.
39. Bigness.
40. Son of Zerah. (1 Chron. 2:6)
41. Consumer.
42. Satisfy.

Puzzle 45

Janet Adkins

ACROSS CLUES

1. In _____ was there a voice heard. (Matt. 2:18)
5. And so forth.
8. Cut them with _____, and with harrows. (1 Chron. 20:3)
12. They called his name _____: he is the father of Jesse. (Ruth 4:17)
13. Standing Room Only (abbr.).
14. Equal.
15. Freezing point centigrade.
16. Greek "T".
17. House (Spanish).
18. Value of 15 cross.
20. To break camp.
24. To be (Spanish).
25. Then I will be an _____ unto thine enemies. (Ex. 23:22)
26. Matthew, sitting at the _____ of custom. (Matt. 9:9)
30. One (Scottish).
31. My _____ Sal.
32. Chinese Communist Party Chairman.
33. Found in _____ as a man, he humbled himself. (Phil. 2:8)
36. Summer T.V. fare.
38. By faith _____ch was translated. (Heb. 11:5)
39. Then I will set my face against that man and his _____. (Lev. 20:5)
40. I will _____ of thee. (Job 38:3)
43. Grain.
44. Tel _____.
45. Miss Farrow.
47. We stumble at _____ day. (Isa. 59:10)
51. Anger.
52. Put on strength, O _____ of the Lord. (Isa. 51:9)
53. _____ Timnah. (Gen. 36:40)
54. Ardor.
55. No (Scottish).
56. I am...the bright and morning _____. (Rev. 22:16)

DOWN CLUES

1. Woman's nickname.
2. Lincoln's nickname.
3. Mal de _____.
4. And _____ was over the tribute. (2 Sam. 20:24)
5. To bar legally.
6. _____ la la.
7. Pharisees and lawyers rejected the _____ of God. (Luke 7:30)
8. And thou shalt be _____, because there is hope. (Job 11:18)
9. His king shall be higher than _____. (Num. 24:7)
10. _____ me thoroughly from mine iniquity. (Ps. 51:2)
11. Thin strip of wood.
19. Atomic Energy Commission.
20. And the _____ hear. (Matt. 11:5)
21. Sicilian resort.
22. After "bees" and before "dees."
23. Belonging to me.
26. His father saw him,...and _____ and fell on his neck.(Luke 15:20)
27. The son of Omri, the son of _____. (1 Chron. 9:4)
28. _____, a servant of Jesus Christ. (Rom. 1:1)
29. Short for Anthony.
31. For a _____ _____ some would die. (Rom. 5:7; 2 words)

34. Joy shall be in _____ over one sinner that repenteth. (Luke 15:7)
35. There was no room for them in the _____. (Luke 2:7)
36. Sunbeam.
37. Improves.
39. Picture holder.
40. For a good man some would even _____ to die. (Rom. 5:7)

41. Not rendering _____ for evil. (1 Pet. 3:9)
42. Polish distance measure.
46. _____ an Ithrite. (2 Sam. 23:38)
48. Though our _____ward man perish. (2 Cor. 4:16)
49. Central European river.
50. Abner, the son of _____. (1 Sam. 14:50)

Puzzle 46

Janet Adkins

ACROSS CLUES

1. And next unto them repaired... _____ the Meronothite. (Neh. 3:7)
5. And in the twentieth year of Jeroboam king of Israel reigned _____ over Judah. (1 Kgs. 15:9)
8. Israeli leader Abba _____.
10. Dropped the first atomic bomb.
12. Pale.
13. Digraph.
14. My spirit shall not always _____ with man. (Gen. 6:3)
16. Rejoice not when thine _____ falleth. (Prov. 24:17)
18. Arabian prince.
19. Plural suffix.
20. Girl.
21. Place (abbr.).
22. Flies high.
24. He that is now called a Prophet was before time called a _____. (1 Sam. 9:9)
26. He that winneth souls is _____. (Prov. 11:30)

94

27. Bone (comb. form).
30. Every wise _____ buildeth her house. (Prov. 14:1)
32. _____ virgins, or lepers.
33. Norse god of thunder.
35. Captain of the "Nautilus."
36. Moses...came to the mountain of God, even to _____. (Ex. 3:1)
38. Continent (abbr.).
39. But there was none like unto _____...to work wickedness. (1 Kgs. 21:25)
43. Electron volt (abbr.).
44. Abstain from eating.
46. A swelling.
47. _____ a wise man, and he will love thee. (Prov. 9:8)
49. 365 days (abbr.).
50. The sun and the _____ were darkened. (Rev. 9:2)
51. The heathen _____, the kingdoms were moved.(Ps. 46:6)
52. Trieste liquid measure.
53. German article.
54. And _____ the priest...before the tabernacle...at Gibeon. (1 Chron. 16:39)

DOWN CLUES

1. As a _____ of gold in a swine's snout. (Prov. 11:22)
2. Are not _____ and Pharpar, rivers of Damascus, better? (2 Kgs. 5:12)
3. People of Denmark.
4. Poti-pherah priest of _____. (Gen. 41:45)
5. Those opposed.
6. No more death, neither _____, nor crying. (Rev. 21:4)
7. Mohammad _____.
9. Interjection.
10. Samantha Steven's Aunt _____erelda.
11. Reluctant.
13. _____ Cobb of baseball fame.
15. German city.
17. Woman's title of address.
18. A fundamental part.
21. A drudge, menial.
23. Island.
24. Compass point.
25. Incarnation of Vishnu.
27. He will hate the one and love the _____. (Matt. 6:24)
28. Pusher.
29. Craggy hill.
31. I will punish the multitude of _____. (Jer. 46:25)
34. Thou hast been my defence and _____. (Ps. 59:16)
37. His _____ had offended the ...king of Egypt. (Gen. 40:1)
39. Commercial.
40. Thy prayer is _____. (Luke 1:13)
41. Acid component of protein.
42. So _____ went down from mount Tabor. (Judg. 4:14)
45. Sediment (abbr.).
46. And she...bare a son; and he called his name _____. (Gen. 38:3)
48. They were so _____. (Jer. 24:2)
49. Hear this, all _____ people. (Ps. 49:1)
52. Digraph.

Puzzle 47

Janet Adkins

ACROSS CLUES

1. That he might _____ us alive. (Deut. 6:24)
6. Pitcher.
10. _____, which was the son of Seth. (Luke 3:38)
11. River in Bolivia.
12. Property agency.
15. O. T. book (abbr.).
17. Naval vessel designation.
18. Canadian Indian.
19. Where is _____ thy brother? (Gen. 4:9)
21. Till he should pay all that was _____ unto him. (Matt. 18:34)
22. Comes after em.
23. Celtic sea god.
24. Right to property.
25. Fr. article.
28. Yes (Spanish).
29. A word appearing in Psalms, 73 times.
31. Woman's title.
34. They could not enter ___ because of unbelief. (Heb. 3:19)
35. Minister's title.
36. Missing in Action.
38. Top of the head.
41. Academic degree.
42. Printer's measure.
44. Symbol for element tellurium.
45. Japanese sash.
46. Became captain over a _____. (1 Kgs. 11:24)
48. Put him to an _____ shame. (Heb. 6:6)
50. Northwest state (abbr.).
51. According to the prince of the power of the _____. (Eph. 2:2)
52. Now therefore _____ thyself what word I shall bring. (1 Chron. 21:12)
54. Full of _____, murder, debate. (Rom. 1:29)
56. As the loving hind and pleasant _____. (Prov. 5:19)
57. Sendeth _____ on the just and on the unjust. (Matt. 5:45)
58. Solomon reigned over all _____. (1 Kings 4:21)

DOWN CLUES

1. In a _____ of ground which Jacob bought. (Josh. 24:32)
2. But _____ died without children. (1 Chron. 2:30)
3. Within (comb form).
4. If ye fulfil the _____ law. (Jam. 2:8)
5. Competing against.
6. Wane.
7. Us.
8. Let him seek peace, and _____ it. (1 Pet. 3:11)
9. If ye then be _____ with Christ. (Col. 3:1)
13. Sea eagles.
14. _____, _____, I, O, U.
15. Possessive pronoun.
16. _____ Haig.
20. Egyptian pleasure god.
21. Double (prefix).
24. Top.
26. Compass point.
27. _____ shall be a serpent by the way. (Gen. 49:17)
28. Can faith _____ him? (Jam. 2:14)

96

30. Eternal life, which God, that can not _____. (Titus 1:2)

31. Northeast state.

32. I _____ Alpha and Omega. (Rev. 1:8)

33. A certain poor widow, threw in two _____. (Mark 12:42)

35. His father saw him...and _____ and fell on his neck. (Luke 15:20).

37. He found a certain man named _____. (Acts 9:33)

38. Ye shall receive _____.(Acts 1:8)

39. Are not _____ and Pharpar, rivers of Damascus, better? (2 Kgs. 5:12)

40. Musical note.

41. And Deborah said unto _____, Up; for this is the day. (Judg. 4:14)

43. All the city was _____ about them. (Ruth 1:19)

46. Occurring in intervals of two.

47. Mend socks.

49. Greek P.

51. _____ Rand.

53. Beware of _____s. (Phil. 3:2)

55. Roman numeral 6.

Puzzle 48

Janet Adkins

ACROSS CLUES

1. For God cannot be tempted with ____.(Jam. 1:13)
4. The voice of doves ____ing upon their breasts. (Nah. 2:7)
8. From (French).
10. Feather scarf.
11. Grow old.
12. Highest point.
14. He shall pour ____ upon it. (Lev. 2:1)
15. Prayer book (abbr.).
16. Father, forgive ____. (Luke 23:34)
17. North Dakota.
18. He that goeth about as a ____ revealeth secrets. (Prov. 20:19)
19. Let God be ____, but every man a liar. (Rom. 3:4)
20. Absence (abbr.).
22. Egyptian sun god.
23. He had sent messengers to ____ king of Egypt. (2 Kgs. 17:4)

25. Now the first lot came forth to Jehoiarib...the fourth to _____im. (1 Chron. 24:7, 8)
27. So can no _____ both yield salt water and fresh. (Jam. 3:12)
30. Citizens band radio.
31. Spanish aunts.
32. Prefix meaning "before."
33. Ye shall not fulfil the _____ of the flesh. (Gal. 5:16)
35. Liquified natural gas.
36. Then _____ and the other apostles answered, we ought to obey God. (Acts 5:29)
37. Steamer (abbr.).
38. Hubbub.
40. Before (poetic).
42. Each (abbr.).
44. It is a _____ thing that the king requireth. (Dan. 2:11)
45. Part of speech. (abbr.).
46. Naum, which was the son of _____. (Luke 3:25)
48. Return unto _____. (Mal. 3:7)
49. _____ boweth down. (Isa. 46:1)
50. What shall we _____? (Acts 2:37)
51. _____ women shall take hold of one man. (Isa. 4:1)
52. 3.14159.

DOWN CLUES

1. Black wood (poetic).
2. Faith is made _____.(Rom. 4:14)
3. Adjective suffix.
4. Thou preparest a _____ before me. (Ps. 23:5)
5. Symbol for the element silver.
6. Exist.
7. Belonging to a notable harlot.
8. Greek community.
9. Former.
13. And I will _____ them with the sword. (Jer. 29:18)
15. The name of his city was _____. (Gen. 36:39)
16. Beverage.
18. I am purposed that my mouth shall not _____. (Ps. 17:3)
19. Absent without permission.
21. Ship's stern.
23. Indian nobleman.
24. They were afraid both _____ and other. (Jer. 36:16)
26. Ye _____ days, and months. (Gal. 4:10)
28. Greases.
29. News service.
33. French article.
34. _____ clef.
36. Skin opening.
39. Condemn to everlasting punishment.
41. Receive him not, neither _____ him God speed. (2 John 10)
43. Tavern brew.
47. Roman numeral 4.
49. At intervals of two.

Puzzle 49

Janet Adkins

ACROSS CLUES

1. Massachusetts cape.
4. _____, a servant of Jesus. (Rom. 1:1)
8. Not only for wrath, but also for conscience _____. (Rom. 13:5)
12. Born.
13. "My people." (Hosea 2:1)
14. Ye shall see heaven _____ (John 1:51)
15. And _____ also the Jairite was chief ruler about David. (2 Sam. 20:26)
16. Rich soil.
17. Neither _____ your clothes. (Lev. 10:6)
18. He shall take other _____ and plaister the house. (Lev. 14:42; modern sp.)
20. Money earned on account (abbr.).
22. Play division.
23. I have made known _____ thee this day. (Prov. 22:19)
24. Their brethren of the second degree, Zechariah, _____. (1 Chron. 15:18)
27. We will come unto him and make our _____ with him. (John 14:23)
30. For as many as are _____ by the Spirit of God. (Rom. 8:14)
31. A son of Gad. (Gen. 46:16)
32. Horse mothers.
33. Man's nickname.
34. "Sing," past tense.
35. Anger.
36. The name of the wicked shall _____. (Prov. 10:7)
37. One was Bozez, and the name of the other _____.(1 Sam 14:4)

38. The captain of his host was Abner, the son of _____. (1 Sam. 14:50)
39. And (Latin).
40. Snake-like fish.
41. The king of Assyria brought men from..._____. (2 Kgs. 17:24)
42. God is our _____ and strength. (Ps. 46:1)
46. None is _____, save one. (Luke 18:19)
49. Englishman.
51. Roman numeral 54.
52. River in Yorkshire, England.
53. Narrow strip of wood.
54. Thoroughfare (abbr.).
55. Be ye therefore followers of God as _____ children. (Eph. 5:1)
56. Fencing sword.
57. Who will have all _____ to be saved. (1 Tim. 2:4)

DOWN CLUES

1. And Anab, and Eshtemoh, and _____. (Josh. 15:50)
2. Fiddled while Rome burned.
3. Thou art _____, O Lord. (Ps. 119:151)
4. As Peter was beneath in the _____. (Mark 14:66)
5. _____ize: arrange installment payments.
6. Hindu goddess of splendor.
7. Yea, they...tempted God, and _____ the Holy One of Israel. (Ps. 78:41)
8. Took unto them certain lewd fellows of the baser _____. (Acts 17:5)
9. Simian.
10. Knowledge.
11. Whose _____ is destruction. (Phil. 3:19)
19. Urchins.

21. And Cain went out...and dwelt in the land of _____. (Gen. 4:16)
24. Vegetable.
25. Sea eagle.
26. Draw _____ to God. (Jam. 4:8)
27. The children of _____, four hundred fifty four. (Ezra 2:15)
28. Thou wast naked and _____. (Ezek. 16:7)
29. Now an _____ is the tenth part of an ephah. (Ex. 16:36)
30. Wherefore, do ye..._____ the people from their work?(Ex. 5:4)
33. Of great reputation.
34. Individual character.
36. Last book of the Bible (abbr.).
37. Thou shalt not _____ a kid in his mother's milk. (Ex. 23:19)
40. Descendant of Eri.
41. And Zebadiah, and Arad, and _____. (1 Chron. 8:15)
43. And the sons of _____; Bedan. (1 Chron. 7:17)
44. The Lord God shall _____ unto him the throne of his father David. (Luke 1:32)
45. To seduce, if it were possible, _____ the elect. (Mark 13:22)
46. Jacob's seventh son.
47. Not "a" or "u".
48. Mouth
50. Modern music.

The crossword grid contains numbered cells: 1, 2, 3, 4, 5, 6, 7, 8, 9, 10, 11, 12, 13, 14, 15, 16, 17, 18, 19, 20, 21, 22, 23, 24, 25, 26, 27, 28, 29, 30, 31, 32, 33, 34, 35, 36, 37, 38, 39, 40, 41, 42, 43, 44, 45, 46, 47, 48, 49, 50, 51, 52, 53, 54, 55, 56, 57.

Puzzle 50

Keith Graham

ACROSS CLUES

1. Special worship event. (1 Cor. 10:21)
11. Number of Arabian nights (Roman numerals).
12. Whether therefore ye _____, or drink. (1 Cor. 10:31)
13. To gorge with water or deplete of money.
14. Therefore.
16. Nervous.
17. The Lord make his face _____ upon thee. (Num. 6:25)
18. Condition of Jesus' steed in Mark 11:2.
20. _____ the hart panteth after the water brooks. (Ps. 42:1)
21. Animal hide.
22. Shade tree.
23. Inclined territory.
25. Speaker's interjection of hesitation.
27. Mischievous one.

29. What 41 down is to God and man.
30. What shall be done in the _____? (Luke 23:31)
31. Elements used in 57 across.
34. That is (Latin abbr.).
35. _____, topaz, and the emerald. (Ezek. 28:13 NAS)
36. Rebuker of Balaam. (Num. 22:28)
37. A bishop must be...no _____. (Titus 1:7)
40. A portion of a circle.
42. This comprises most of the Bible (abbr.).
43. An bishop must be _____ to teach. (1 Tim. 3:2)
45. Said by many to be an ex-Christian nation (abbr.).
47. Children of the mind.
50. Gloves' companion.
51. _____ thou at my right hand. (Ps. 110:1)
52. Symbol for a precious metal.
53. Lawful.
56. Usually follows "tra" in tandem.
57. Another name for 1 across.

DOWN CLUES

1. When the ruler of the feast had _____ the water. (John 2:9)
2. Printer's measure.
3. What 41 down did in Eden.
4. Kingly.
5. Famine that was in the _____. (Gen. 26:1)
6. A thoroughfare or a holy one (abbr.).
7. They were to be poured out without the camp (Lev. 4:12)
8. Leviathan makes the deep do this. (Job 41:31)
9. Judas' mob came with these to arrest Jesus. (John 18:3)
10. _____ out a living.
15. See thou hurt not the _____ and wine! (Rev. 6:6)
17. Rate of travel.
19. An Arabian ruler.
23. Man is born unto trouble, as this flies upward. (Job 5:7)
24. Youthful equestrian's steed.
26. A grain.
28. Myself.
30. Track and field projectile.
31. Wager.
32. In _____ season we shall reap. (Gal. 6:9)
33. Neither shall they learn _____ any more (Isa. 2:4)
34. He saw the Lord, sitting up on a throne, high and lifted up. (Isa. 6:1)
38. Fish eggs.
39. The "boot" country.
40. Modern communications giant.
41. The adversary.
44. Deborah's kind of tree. (Judg. 4:5)
46. Farm structure.
48. The Dynamic _____.
49. Describes some wines.
54. _____ ye therefore. (Matt. 28:19)
55. Atop.

ANSWERS

Puzzle 1

```
B A S I N   W H I G   S O
A B I D E   H E B R E W
R E D   T H E   E O N   W
A L O E   O N Y X   O W E
B   N U L L   O   A S A
B E   P   Y O U N G   D
A L P H A   U   A E R I E
S I L O   U G L Y   O   V
  S E R A P H   A B L E
  H A I R   T O M B   E
C A S A B A   F A R   T O
U   E   O L D   N A B   N
P   D I R E C T   M I L E
```

Puzzle 2

```
D E A D   E L U L     N O
A L M O N D   R O C K   N
N A M E   O   B O I L S
  M O   A M A   U R N   E
A   N O N   Z   L I G H T
S T I R   R   S E N   A
P E T   T A R E   T E N D
  S E   E M I T   H O N E
I T S   T I T H E   N A G
R   T H E E   N W   H
O W E   E   S O D O M   O
N O W   R A   L   R E N D
  N E W   M   D A M N E D
```

Puzzle 3

```
J O S H U A   S O U T H
A B O U T   E L I S H A
B A N D E D   I L E U M
O D   D   O W N     S P I
T I L L   T O G A     E L
  A   E   H E   C U R L
T H E   S A F E   A S
    L A   N U L L   A C E
H A I R   L A I N
E   P   A I   T E E   U S
A S H D O D   E D E N   E
T H A I   M   D O N E
H E Z E K I A H   T O M
```

Puzzle 4

```
P A U L   C R Y   W A R S
L I N E   L E A   A N T I
A D I T   E A   T I N E S
Y E N   P A P E R S
    V E I N     E T U D E
T H I N G S A R E   N I L
R I T E   E P A   P A L S
E R E   A D O P T A B L E
S E D G E   S O D A
    A R I G H T   S T N
I S U P O N M E   O H I O
N O S E   T E E   D E M O
S P E D   O N T   E D E N
```

Puzzle 5

```
C A M E ■ C P A ■ C L A P
A M A N ■ L O B ■ A I D E
L O R D ■ A L B A N I A N
M S G ■ I S L A N D ■ ■
■ A W L S ■ ■ T O D A Y
H I R E L I N G S ■ E S E
A R I D ■ F F A ■ D A T A
T O N ■ M Y L I F E F O R
E N E M Y ■ ■ N O N E ■
■ ■ I N M A T E ■ N A B
H O K K A I D O ■ H I L O
O S E E ■ R A M ■ O N T O
B U Y S ■ E R E ■ E G O S
```

Puzzle 6

```
M A S H ■ I S ■ A C ■ S W
A S A ■ ■ S H A V E N ■ O
R ■ L U T H E R A N ■ U R
P O E M ■ M ■ A U T I S M
L A M B ■ A S ■ N I N E ■
O R ■ E V E ■ T ■ S ■ H
T ■ L I L A C ■ S I T E
■ S A ■ O ■ N O ■ O D O R
T O M ■ L I O N ■ B E N D
O N ■ S E N T T O ■ R E S
O G ■ A N ■ H U M ■ T
L ■ S U C C E S S ■ A T E
S T O L E ■ R E ■ T E E
```

Puzzle 7

```
B A C ■ A R M ■ J O R A M
■ S L ■ R H O ■ O L I V E
T H U M M I M ■ U D D E R
R A ■ C E N S E R ■ ■
I M P ■ D O E R ■ O L D E
V E R Y ■ S E ■ A L A ■ M
I D I O T ■ ■ E D D I
A ■ D U N ■ P S ■ O L I N
L E E R ■ H A H A ■ E V E
■ ■ B E S I D E ■ I N
R I V E R ■ S E R V A N T
O R A L ■ E R I ■ B E
W A T E R ■ S ■ A ■ A R K
```

Puzzle 8

```
■ M A G ■ L A C E ■ P U A
■ A G O ■ E L L ■ S E T
O G E E ■ A M I D ■ A L E
F I R S T S A M U E L ■
■ ■ T A I ■ B E S T O W
R A D ■ O N O ■ S T E R E
A Z E M ■ G A P ■ E R I N
R O M E O ■ T R I ■ Y E T
E V E N U P ■ E L I ■
■ N E C R O M A N C E R
B A T ■ H O P I ■ E R G O
E V E ■ E V A S ■ P O G O
L A D ■ S E L E ■ T P S
```

Puzzle 9

```
■ L A M E D ■ T A B L E ■
E ■ P A ■ E S A ■ A I ■ A
S R ■ S L E E P E R ■ I U
T E S T E D ■ P R E ■ N T
A L L E G E ■ E N R I C H
B I ■ R ■ D O R ■ F R O
L G ■ ■ ■ ■ ■ ■ E R
I I ■ ■ S T A ■ R A M I
S O U G H T ■ N E ■ N E T
H U S H A I ■ D O M I N I
E S ■ O F F E R ■ ■ T E
D ■ P S ■ L E E ■ A T ■ S
■ L I T R E ■ W I D O W ■
```

Puzzle 10

```
■ G A T E ■ A R A M ■
A D O R A M ■ B E M A ■ N
H U M A N ■ D I V E R S E
A R E S ■ H O R O N I T E
B A R ■ S E R A L ■ E D
■ ■ T A ■ M ■ B A A L
C H E R I T H ■ A B I D E
R I V E R S ■ M A B ■
E R A T ■ C A A ■ A R M
D E S O L A T E ■ O G E E
I ■ I R A N ■ G R A B S
T ■ V T O ■ T O B I A H
■ E S S ■ O D I N ■
```

Puzzle 11

```
T I M E S . . . W I D O W
U R I M . N E R . S I L O
T A M . S E V E N . R I M
O T E . A B I D E . E V A
R E . M . . . V . . E N .
. . . R O R E V E R . . .
. A S A . E R . . A M A .
. . D E L I V E R . . . .
S T E A . . B E . C U . .
N O R . C H I D E . E R N
A T A . H A V E N . N U T
R E N D . T E N . H O S E
E M I M S . . . L O W E R
```

Puzzle 12

```
P R A Y . A . R E P E N T
A I L E T H . E A R L Y .
R O A S T . . M R E D . .
A T S . I . A S S E S . .
B . C A N . I . S R . K
L I G H T N I N G . H I
E . E . . . A S H E S . .
. P A R T A K E R . W A S
T R O U B L E . M F . L .
H E R B . L E P E R . . .
E A T . M . P U N I S H .
R C A . A L E R T . E A T
E H . T R E S P A S S . .
```

Puzzle 13

```
W I F E . T O G E T H E R
I N . F . O V E N . A B E
S T A F F . A N D . S B A
D O . E A G L E S . T . P
O . A C M E . S . F E D .
M E N T I O N . T O N E S
. G . L . F O R . E D . .
. R E L Y . L A T T E R .
H O L Y . S E . A N . . .
A S . E S T A B L I S H .
B E E . E . F E . G L A D
I . O N L Y . E C H O . E
T E N . L O S T . T W I N
```

Puzzle 14

```
C H I L D R E N . G O O D
O . S E E . . O V E R . E
U N R A V E L . A N . I N
R . A F I R E . L E A D S
A G E . L O T . U S . . I
G O L D . D . . E I G H T
E L I . T E N D . S L A Y
. I T C H . O I L . A M .
G A E L I C . V O I D . W
A T . I M A G E . S . . E
T H U M B . U R N . I F I
E . B L E S S E D . . . G
S E N S E . T . T O U C H
```

Puzzle 15

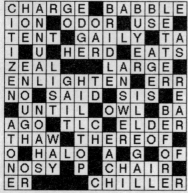

```
C H A R G E . B A B B L E
I O N . O D O R . U S E .
T E N T . G A I L Y . T A
I . U . H E R D . E A T S
Z E A L . . . L A R G E .
E N L I G H T E N . E R R
N O . S A I D . S I S . E
. U N T I L . O W L . B A
A G O . T L C . E L D E R
T H A W . T H E R E O F .
O . H A L O . A . G . O F
N O S Y . P . C H A I R .
E R . . C H I L L E R . .
```

Puzzle 16

```
N A M E . S O N . P A U L
E D E N . A L O . I M N A
A N . D E L I G H T . T O
R A N . R O V E R . D O S
. I S . M E T . M E . . .
B E C A M E . A B A S E D
A R A D A . . . A C C H O
T E N O N S . O R H E I N
. O F . A I M . I N . . .
F A R . A N G E R . D A N
A S . O R D E R E D . L A
S I G N . A A N . E T A M
T A M E . I L O . N O S E
```

Puzzle 17

```
K N O W L E D G E . C . E
I S L E . T O O . P R A Y
N . D . M . G L O R Y . E
G O . J A R . D I I . A S
S . L U R E . E L D E R .
. . D . D E N . E L M S .
. G . G . N . J . S . A .
D I A M O N D . A T E . C
. A . E N O S . S O . . K
A N O N . A . S P I C E S
S T I T C H . E E L . L .
K . L . U . F I R E . I .
. A S H E S . R . D O M E
```

Puzzle 18

```
T E N D E R . G E N I A L
O P E R A . Y . H O R S E
N O S Y . S E E . D O S T
A C T . H E A R T . N U T
L H . B U T . A R E . M E
S . H E R . S . A . P E R
. H O . T H I N G . U S .
F . E L I . N . E A R . I
O R . O N E . A D A . S T
R E . G A I L Y . E T C .
G A T H . T O E . I V A H
E C H O . . N . S M I L E
T H E R E . . A P P L E S
```

Puzzle 19

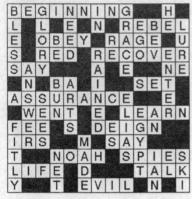

```
B E G I N N I N G . . H .
L . L . E . N . R E B E L
E . O B E Y . R A G E . U
S . R E D . R E C O V E R
S A Y . . A . E . . N E .
. N . B A . I . . S E T .
A S S U R A N C E . . E .
. W E N T . E . L E A R N
F E E . S . D E I G N . .
I R S . . M . S A Y . . .
T . . N O A H . S P I E S
L I F E . D . . T A L K .
Y . T . E V I L . N . I .
```

Puzzle 20

```
B O A Z . T L C . B R A Y
A B L E . I O U . L I M E
T O A D . B A R N A B A S
H E B . T E N D E D . . .
. . A F A R . . T E R S E
I N S C R I B E S . E A R
R O T C . A I D . L I M A
O N E . E S T I M A T E S
N O R S E . . F A D E . .
. . A L L S I N . R A F .
G O D I S O N E . S A G A
I D O L . O A T . S T A R
N E T S . M P H . T E R M
```

Puzzle 21

```
N E B O . N E T . A D I T
O V E R . O A R . B A R E
M I L D . O R I G I N A L
E L I . U N S O L D . . .
. . E A S T . . A E S O P
R E V I S I T E D . E R A
A V E R . M A X . S T A R
C E O . D E B A T A B L E
A N N I E . . M O T E . .
. . S U B M I T . . F I G
C R E A T I O N . D O V E
F U E L . T O E . C R A M
C E L L . E N D . L E N S
```

Puzzle 22

```
A H A . P I . Y E L L O W
M U S T A R D . S I M R I
E L H A N A N . A F . P D
N . D R . A G U E . H E .
. M O S E S . R . T E A .
S E D U C E . E H I . N T
H A . S H A D E . M A S H
A N Y . O M I T T E D . R
D . E R . E S E . U S E .
R E L I E F . . P A M P A
A L L O W A N C E . M . D
C I S T E R N . E D I T .
H M . . S E E K . A M O S
```

Puzzle 23

```
M A N   N I G H T   H O T
A G E   O T H E R   I N N
C O W S   H O R I M S
H   O U R S   B E   L A
I D O L   A T T E N D   T
  E D E N   R   U S E
A D D   O   B E F E L L
P I   T R E E   S L I P
A C T S   G   A T   M Y
C A I A P H A S   B E G
E T A M   T A M A R   A
  E   B E   L E V I   R
A D A R   R O T   E M   G
```

Puzzle 24

```
H O U S E S   U P P E R
I N N   A P P L E   O
N E C K E D   E A T E R
D   L I D   S T A R   A
S E E D   B   A S L E E P
  V   D O E R   E   V A T
R E S I N   E A S T E R
  N U N   F M   A   J
W I N G S   E   M I L E
E N D   A B R A H A M   R
  G A B R I E L   R A G E
T   Y   A R E A   G E M
B C   K I D S   P I E T Y
```

Puzzle 25

```
G O P H E R   N I B H A Z
E D R E I   G I D E O N I
N E   I G A L   B   T M
E   R H E U M A T I S M
S I S   T S E T S E   A
I R E   T   H R   N H
S O P   P H E W   A B I
  N U R S E   C H I M E
B   L E   T A C O   T R Y
A   C A R I B O U   H O E
L E H I   C R   G R I D S
S A R A   S A   A   A
A   E H I   M Y R R H
```

Puzzle 26

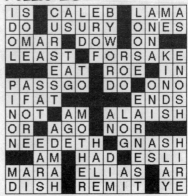

```
I S   C A L E B   L A M A
D O   U S U R Y   O N E S
O M A R   D O W   O N
L E A S T   F O R S A K E
    E A T   R O E   I N
P A S S G O   D O   O N O
I F A T       E N D S
N O T   A M   A L A I S H
O R   A G O   N O R
N E E D E T H   G N A S H
  A M   H A D   E S L I
M A R A   E L I A S   A R
D I S H   R E M I T   Y E
```

Puzzle 27

```
M A T T H E W   A D O R N
A B I A   A A   D E P O T
R I N K   T I M O T H Y
K E N E Z I T E   E N A M
  L I N E N   A   S I L O
L   E   A G E D   T   D
E A S E L   T O E   I R E
D A T A   L A W G I V E R
D R   G   E   Y   I A
E O   L A M B   P L A N T
S N   E M U L A T E   S I
T S P   P E E N   N E   O
  A   L D S   T H E N
```

Puzzle 28

```
O B E Y   B E N J A M I N
F E V E R   O A T   L A
F   E S   H   S M E L L Y
E   R   C A L E B   A N
R A Y   C U E   O   S E W
  S T Y   L A   R A T S
A S H E R   V E E R   S D
T   I T   M E R E   H   E
T A N   N I N E   L E A P
E G G   S   C C U   L A
N A   S H E A T H   P A R
D I S C A R D   A P A R T
  N O I S Y   P A L M
```

Puzzle 29

```
F L O P   L A D   E B A L
L A M E   E R A   A R I A
E T E R N I T Y   R E D S
D E N S E     S P L A S H
    O W E S   A S K
C O N N   A N O N   E N D
A R E   A S I D E   T E A
M E T   M E D E   S H E D
    W H O   E D I T
C H O O S E     S E E S T
H E R R   G A T H E R E R
I R K S   G N U   R A T A
N O S E   S A G   S N A P
```

Puzzle 30

```
O W L S   A H I   G A L A
R A I D   B I T   A G A R
A S K   W E D   C R U S T
S H E K E L   C A D E T
    W O N   M A K E
A S I A   R E G E N C Y
H A S   S O R E S   L E A
  C E N T U R Y   S E A M
    E A S Y   B O A
  S K A T E   F A N N E D
F L A R E   L I T   I R U
R O L L   A I L   S N A P
O B E Y   S E E   O G L E
```

Puzzle 31

```
F A I T H   F E D   A S
O L D   A N G E L   A G E
O I L   T O I L   S O W
T E E T H   F L E S H
  N   A     T O R M E N T
O   A B L E   W R E S T
B O I L   N   S   L   T
E   R E E D   H E L P E R
Y E   N   S I X   S E A
  L   D R O P   B A L D
R E S C U E   A I L   E
A C C U R S E D   E M U
M T   P E T   O U R S
```

Puzzle 32

```
S E A T   T H I C K   H E
P A N E   O A T H   R A W
O R D E R   I   A B O V E
T   T E A R   S I D E
    W H A T   A T E   S
A S H   D E E P E R   S I
W   O F   S O N   W I N
A   L U S T S   S O N G
S L A Y   L E T T E R   I
H E N   H E E L   A M E N
  A G R E E M E N T   A G
A S L E E P   S O   I S
  T E D D Y   T E N T S
```

Puzzle 33

```
J O H N   R E M N A N T
E L O I   S O L   I N C A
W I L L   Y I E L D   R
S O D   M A   D   E
    B E E L Z E B U B
E L M   R   N N E   O
  I S R A E L   N O A H
M E   E   R   S H A R E
  S A R A H   E A R   A
R   P A S O   D   L
O P T   E P H R A I M
O L E O   E U O D I A S
M O N E Y   S E W   M O O
```

Puzzle 34

```
T H A N K S G I V I N G S
H A N D   A I   F A I L
A N A H A R A T H   T L C
N D H   H A N D M A I D
K S   B   H T   S R O   R
S   J O Y   S O   O N L Y
G O   R   A   L I S   A E
I B   N   M A I D E N S
V E R   I V E   A T E
I Y A R   S M E A R   A
N   B A B E   S L A Y E R
G A B R I E L   N E X T
  D I E D   O G   K A P H
```

Puzzle 35

```
Y E S T E R D A Y █ E N D
O B S E R V E █ E N T E R
U N A R M █ L A N D █ E E
T █ R I G H T █ H A D A █
H A V E N █ I I M █ A L M
F A L S E █ L █ T R E E █
U █ F T █ R █ T R I O █ R
L O █ R A I N █ I N N █ S
█ A M I █ G O I N G █ O █
A T H A █ H B █ G L O R Y
Y S O L █ T L R █ E N D O
I █ █ B L E S S █ █ █ K █
N A M E L Y █ V I R T U E
```

Puzzle 36

```
F O R G I V E N █ F R E E
A P A R T █ L E A R N E D
T P K █ █ S S W █ A A R E
H O E C A K E █ T N █ █ N
E R M I N E █ H U K O K █
R T █ N O P H █ R I V E R
█ U L N A █ B A N N E R S
A N N A █ A █ M █ C N N █
P I █ M A N N A █ E S E K
P T █ O L D █ Z I N █ L I
L Y I N G █ J E W S █ S N
E █ N █ U R █ D I E T █ G
█ A K I M B O █ S █ K O S
```

Puzzle 37

```
F A T █ M O A B █ B A A L
A T █ A B L E █ A P █ A
D E P T H █ █ N A T H A N
E █ I S A I A H █ H I █ G
█ █ L █ Z █ B U █ S A L U
█ S A V I O U R █ H H █ A
N A T I O N S █ E █ █ G
█ N E S T █ I █ B A B E
█ C █ I H █ V █ A I R
█ T O O █ E █ A █ O
█ I █ N J █ A Z B U K
O F F █ O L I V E █ R E D
B Y E █ B A B E L █ I N N
```

Puzzle 38

```
S C A T █ C B █ P E T E R
P O O R █ A █ L A █ █ I
A M █ E █ T █ A T L A S
█ B R E A T H █ I █ R E
█ A █ E █ K N O C K █
B A T █ C A R E S █ L █ O
E █ C A R R Y █ E A R
█ C R O S S █ S P E A R
█ L O S T █ S █ R █ N R
B O A T █ W H E A T █ O N
C U D █ A █ O █ Y E O W
█ D █ P L U G █ N O
A S H █ E █ T E E T H
```

Puzzle 39

```
C O L D █ D E L I V E R █
O B E Y █ S I T █ N O W
N █ D I G █ A V █ V █ E
D A █ N O █ U I █ Y I P
E █ G O D █ N E W █ T
M █ D █ G L A D █
N E B O █ P I █ I S A A C
A █ E N █ I █ P H █ B A
T A L E N T S █ H E █ A L
I █ I █ A █ S A D █ D L
O █ E D I C T █ Z █ D
N A V E L █ W █ R O O T
█ E M S █ O I L █ N
```

Puzzle 40

```
F R U I T S █ M E █ N O T
A I N T █ █ Y E █ E █ H
I C █ E N D █ L O W E R
T H E E █ E A █ H █ D E
H E A R T █ A M A █ F E W
█ S C A R E D █ B O R N
█ H █ I █ B O D Y █ F
P S █ A R R I V E █ S O
O A T █ L O O S E █ B A R
W R E N █ M O █ F A T S
E A R █ B E E N █ A S I A
R I N G E R █ D R I N K
█ O V E R C O M E █ E
```

110

Puzzle 41

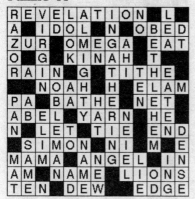

```
R E V E L A T I O N   L
A   I D O L   N   O B E D
Z U R   O M E G A   E A T
O   G   K I N A H   T
R A I N   G   T I T H E
  N O A H   H   E L A M
P A   B A T H E   N E T
A B E L   Y A R N   H E
N   L E T   T I E   E N D
  S I M O N   N I   M   E
M A M A   A N G E L   I N
A M   N A M E   L I O N S
T E N   D E W   E D G E
```

Puzzle 42

```
R E S U R R E C T I O N
E D E N   A L L O N   A T
H E E D   M E A T S   D O
O R D E R   A Y S   E A T
B   R   E Z   C A B
O   S E L A H   C   P
A U N T   I R I J A H   R
M   E A R S   R O   T O
  B E N   H   E S A U   V
  A D D   A   L E T   B E
I T   I N   R I P E   R
T H I N   E   N H   G   B
  E N G   D I G   G O D S
```

Puzzle 43

```
W O R D   H A D   S O R T
E R I E   E R E   P L E A
T E M P E R E D   R E A D
    E N D   I D I O M S
O M E N S   S C A N
K I N D   C H A N G E T H
R E V   S L A T E   L E E
A N Y W H E R E   T S A R
    H E A D   W H E R E
M E D I A N   H I E
A D I T   S P I N N I N G
M O R E   E A R   C L A P
A M E N   D Y E   E K G S
```

Puzzle 44

```
S P A   C H O P   C A F R
E R S   O A R S   O S L O
B O Y   U R E Y   B D A S
A S O F S I N C E R I T Y
    U R I M   H E A D
A A R O N   M I L   T O E
W I F E   P A C   S H E M
E T A   P I T   P E E R S
  T R O T   R I C H
A S H E D I D U N T O U S
V I E S   E A S E   U S A
E Z R I   T R E T   S E T
R E S T   H A S H   E R E
```

Puzzle 45

```
R A M A   E T C   S A W S
O B E D   S R O   E G A L
Z E R O   T A U   C A S A
    R   O   N A U G H T
D E C A M P   S E R
E N E M Y   R E C E I P T
A N E   G A L   M A O
F A S H I O N   R E R U N
    E N O   F A M I L Y
D E M A N D   R Y E
A V I V   M I A   N O O N
R I L E   A R M   D U K E
E L A N   N A E   S T A R
```

Puzzle 46

```
J A D O N     A S A
E B A N   O   E N O L A
W A N   T H   S T R I V E
E N E M Y   E M I R   E S
L A S S   P L   S O A R S
    S E E R   W I S E
O S T   W O M A N   T E N
T H O R   N E M O
H O R E B   N A   A H A B
E V   F A S T   E D E M A
R E B U K E   Y R   A I R
  R A G E D   E   O R N A
  D E R     Z A D O K
```

Puzzle 47

```
P R E S E R V E   E W E R
A   E N O S     B E N I
R E A L T Y   H A B   S S
C R E E   A B E L   D U E
E N   D   L E R   L I E N
L E S   D   S   S I
  S E L A H   M A D A M
    I N   R E V   M I A
P A T E   B A   E M   T E
O B I   B A N D   O P E N
W A   A I R   A D V I S E
E N V Y   A   R O E   A
R A I N   K I N G D O M S
```

Puzzle 48

```
E V I L   T A B E R   D E
B O A     A G E   A P E X
O I L   P B     T H E M
N D   T A L E B E A R E R
      T R U E   A B S
A   R A     S O   S E O R
F O U N T A I N     C B
T I A S   P R E   L U S T
  L N G   D   P E T E R
  S T R     A D O   E R E
B   E A   R A R E   V B
I   E S L I   M E   B E L
D O   S E V E N   P I   E
```

Puzzle 49

```
A N N   P A U L   S A K E
N E E   A M M I   O P E N
I R A   L O A M   R E N D
M O R T A R   I N T
    A C T   T O   B E N
A B O D E   L E D   E R I
D A M S   N E D   S A N G
I R E   R O T   S E N E H
N E R   E T   E E L
    A V A   R E F U G E
G O O D   B R I T   L I V
A I R E   L A T H   A V E
D E A R   E P E E   M E N
```

Puzzle 50

```
T H E L O R D S T A B L E
A   M I   E A T   S O A K
S O   E D G Y   S H I N E
T I E D   A S   P E L T
E L M   S L O P E S   E R
D   I M P   F O E   D R Y
  B R E A D A N D W I N E
I E   R U B Y   A S S
S T R I K E R   A R C   S
A   O T   A P T   U S A
I D E A S   H A T   S I T
A U   L E G A L   O   L A
H O L Y C O M M U N I O N
```

Bible
Crosswords

Collection #4

Compiled and Edited
by *Toni Sortor*

A Barbour Book

Bible
Crosswords

Collection #4

Puzzle 1

Lee Esch

ACROSS CLUES

1. There is no fear in _____. (1 John 4:18)
5. Depot (abbr.).
8. Jacob's brother.
12. Persia.
13. Slippery fish.
14. Outdoes.
15. Man.
16. Thy word is a _____ _____ my feet. (Ps. 119:105; 2 words)
18. Samuel's mentor.
19. It is I; be not _____. (John 6:20)
20. Plunges.
22. Ancient city of Edom.
26. Scent.
30. Embrace.
31. Car.
32. Cow's cry.
33. Yea, come, buy _____ and milk without money. (Isa. 55:1)
34. For to me to live is Christ, and to _____ is gain. (Phil. 1:21)

4

35. Thou hast been faithful over a
_____ _____, I will make thee
ruler over many.
(Matt. 25:21; 2 words)
37. Follow.
39. Sharp, distinctive flavor.
40. Water inlet for ships.
43. Distress call.
46. They _____ _____ leaves
together, and made themselves
aprons. (Gen. 3:7; 2 words)
49. _____ Town, South Africa.
50. Ended.
51. Ginger _____.
52. Region.
53. Sleepers.
54. Highways (abbr.).
55. And he spread abroad the _____
over the tabernacle. (Ex. 40:19)

DOWN CLUES

1. Citrus fruit.
2. Spoken.
3. Gives official sanction to.
4. Compass direction.
5. And his servant was healed in
the _____ hour. (Matt. 8:13)
6. Rend.
7. _____ Mater.
8. Musical exercise.
9. Truly this was the _____ of God.
(Matt. 27:54)
10. Be gentle unto all men, _____ to
teach, patient. (2 Tim. 2:24)

11. Troop entertainers (abbr.).
17. Hollow tube.
19. Yearly interest accrued (abbr.).
21. _____ _____ to prepare a place
for you. (John 14:2; 2 words)
23. And all _____ _____ of God.
(2 Cor. 5:18; 2 words)
24. Part of a ladder.
25. Unto him be glory...throughout
all _____. (Eph. 3:21)
26. Lose color.
27. The _____ of that house was
great. (Luke 6:49)
28. Behold, _____ is the day of
salvation. (2 Cor. 6:2)
29. Small country abodes.
33. Be victorious.
35. Therefore if thine enemy hunger,
_____ him. (Rom. 12:20)
36. Horse food.
38. Utilizers.
41. I will fetch my knowledge from
_____. (Job 36:3)
42. Untamed.
44. Some men's sins are _____
beforehand. (1 Tim. 5:24)
45. For we shall all stand before the
judgment _____ of Christ.
(Rom. 14:10)
46. Weep.
47. Adam's wife.
48. Marry.
49. Feline.

5

Puzzle 2

Lee Esch

ACROSS CLUES

1. He that soweth the good _____ is the Son of man. (Matt. 13:37)
5. A woman's short haircut.
8. Abound.
12. I looked, and behold a _____ horse. (Rev. 6:8)
13. Before (poetic).
14. Tear apart.
15. For _____ _____ the days that were before the flood. (Matt. 24:38; 2 words)
16. Not Jews.
18. Aves.
19. There shall be _____ _____ death. (Rev. 21:4; 2 words)
20. Mine entrance.
22. Decree.
26. Prepares for war.
30. Symbionese Liberation Army (for short).
31. Ye shall find a colt _____, whereon never man sat. (Mark 11:2)
32. And in those days he did _____ nothing. (Luke 4:2)
33. Pull along the ground.
34. _____ "King" Cole.
35. Provides insufficient wages.
37. Pale.
39. Evaluate.
40. Pacing with the clock.
43. Let the brother of _____ degree rejoice in that he is exalted. (Jam. 1:9)
46. Jacob's son by Rachel's maid. (Gen. 30:8)
49. Word with "ebb" or "neap."
50. Fabled monster.
51. _____ ye here, while shall I pray. (Mark 14:32)
52. Upon.
53. Behold, I stand at the _____, and knock. (Rev. 3:20)
54. To him was given the _____ of the bottomless pit. (Rev. 9:1)
55. Saucy; high spirited.

DOWN CLUES

1. Health resorts.
2. For we have seen his star in the _____. (Matt. 2:2)
3. John the Baptist's mother.
4. He lieth in wait secretly as a lion in his _____. (Ps. 10:9)
5. For God so loved the world, that he gave his only _____ Son. (John 3:16)
6. Utah city.
7. For there shall _____ _____ night there. (Rev. 21:25; 2 words)
8. Attempted.
9. Electric fish.
10. Compass direction.
11. Physicians (for short).
17. Three (Spanish).
19. Insect egg.
21. Mom's other half.
23. One of Moses' charges.
24. Hath not the potter power over the _____. (Rom. 9:21)
25. Labels.
26. Italian mountain.
27. Soldiers unaccounted for.
28. There is a _____ here, which hath five barley loaves. (John 6:9)
29. Endless time.
33. Station (abbr.).

35. Part of a whole.
36. Tattered cloth.
38. Anesthetic.
41. Conceal.
42. I say the truth in Christ, _____ _____ not. (Rom. 9:1; 2 words)
44. Fragrance.

45. Jesus _____. (John 11:35)
46. And Cain....dwelt in the land of _____. (Gen. 4:16)
47. Four days _____ I was fasting until this hour. (Acts 10:30)
48. Expert.
49. Strike gently.

7

Puzzle 3

Danny Carpenter

ACROSS CLUES

1. The only ____ Son. (John 1:18)
8. According to my ____est expectation and my hope. (Phil. 1:20)
11. Let the sea ____. (1 Chron. 16:32)
12. And the ____ was upon the earth forty days. (Gen. 7:12)
13. There was no room for them in the ____. (Lk. 2:7)
14. Not boy.
16. Four in Roman numerals.
17. Dull; grey; not colorful.
18. If a man for conscience toward God ____ grief. (1 Peter 2:19)
20. The highways ____ waste. (Isa. 33:8)
21. The Boston ____ party.
23. I ____, he is.
24. Either/____.
25. Eastern Standard Time (abbrev.).
26. Behold even to the ____, and it shineth not. (Job 25:5)
29. Even ____ Christ forgave you. (Col. 3:13)

8

30. The forty days before Easter.
32. Hath not the potter power over the ____. (Rom. 9:21)
34. " Much ____ About Nothing."
36. "____ ____ beautiful day in the neighborhood."
38. So he bringeth them unto their desired ____. (Ps. 107:30)
39. Swine ran violently down a ____ place into the sea. (Matt. 8:32)
40. "____ Maria."
41. United States (abbrev.).
42. I did cast them out as the ____ in the streets. (Ps. 18:42)
43. But we had the ____ of death in ourselves. (2 Cor. 1:9)
45. ____ each his own.
47. Let us ____ over unto the other side of the lake. (Lk. 8:22)
48. Choose one ____ the other.
49. And as ____ ____ lion; who shall rouse him up? (Gen. 49:9; 2 words)
51. Foe.
52. But the end is not ____. (Matt. 24:6)
53. Money paid to a doctor or lawyer.

DOWN CLUES

1. Able also to ____ the whole body. (Jam. 3:2)
2. Long period of time.
3. A male goose.
4. We shall live, and do this, ____ that. (Jam. 4:15)
5. Abiding in his tents according to their ____. (Num. 24:2)
6. The ____ of the wise. (Prov.18:15)
7. Large river in Africa.
9. ____ he thinketh in his heart, so is he. (Prov. 23:7)
10. Shall ____ hunger. (John 6:35)
14. The ____ of hell shall not prevail. (Matt. 16:18)
15. They are written for our ____. (1 Cor. 10:11)
16. If the ____ be blunt. (Ec. 10:10)
19. This is my ____ for ever. (Ex. 3:15)
22. "One Day ____ A Time."
27. A furry mammal.
28. They ____ to their brethren. (Neh. 10:29)
29. An affirmative vote.
30. ____, I am with you alway. (Matt. 28:20)
31. The trees...are full of ____. (Ps. 104:16)
32. To be discreet, ____, keepers at home. (Titus 2:5)
33. He will ____ the blood. (Deut. 32:43)
35. The house of Joseph sent to ____ Bethel. (Judg. 1:23)
37. ____ it therefore in your hearts. (Luke 21:14)
39. South Dakota (abbr.).
41. One (Sp.).
44. Arnold or Jones, for example.
46. A lyric poem.
49. Summer is now nigh ____ hand. (Luke 21:30)
50. The kingdom ____ his dear Son. (Col. 1:13)

Puzzle 4

Cheryl Kaiser

ACROSS CLUES

1. Man of great wisdom.
5. Heavenly being.
8. To view.
9. Regulations.
10. Trials.
12. _____ mountains...shall break... into singing. (Is. 55:12)
14. Primary.
17. Go ye, and tell that _____. (Luke 13:32)
19. Bride and _____.
20. Unto whomsoever _____ is given. (Luke 12:48)
23. Cut apart.
26. _____ of Sheba.
28. Father.
30. _____ Commandments.
31. "_____ the Cross" (hymn).
33. To long for.
34. Unbelievers.

DOWN CLUES

1. My God..hath _____ the lions' mouths. (Dan. 6:22)
2. Untruths.
3. One who relays messages.
4. My God shall supply all your _____. (Phil. 4:19)
5. Husband of Sarah.
6. The street of the city was pure _____. (Rev. 21:21)
7. Not first.
11. Tree.
13. This _____, and thou shalt live. (Luke 10:28)
15. White _____ snow.
16. The _____ is a little member. (Jam. 3:5)
18. Behold, I shew you a _____. (1 Cor. 15:51)
21. Because he first loved _____. (1 John 4:19)
22. I have sinned against _____, and before thee. (Luke 15:18)
24. To trouble.
25. To place.
27. Tidy, clean.
29. _____ of sorrows. (Isa. 53:3)
32. _____ ye holy. (1 Pet. 1:15)

Puzzle 5

Valerie Barrett

ACROSS CLUES

1. After threescore and two weeks shall _____ be cut off. (Dan. 9:26)
7. He sent him out of the _____ of Hebron. (Gen. 37:14)
11. _____ the Ahohite. (1 Chron. 11:29)
12. Sons of Shimei were, Jahath, _____. (1 Chron. 23:10)
15. And pursued them unto _____. (Gen. 14:14)
16. Behold, O mount _____. (Eze. 35:3)
17. The _____ of the Lord. (2 Kgs. 19:31)
18. Until it come _____ at your nostrils. (Num. 11:20)
19. Why is thy spirit so _____? (1 Kgs. 21:5)
20. When ye blow an _____. (Num. 10:5)
21. Mid-Atlantic State (abbr.).
22. They that handle the _____ of the writer. (Judg. 5:14)
24. And fast ye for _____. (Es. 4:16)
26. Every _____, whereon he lieth..., is unclean. (Lev. 15:4)
28. The trees of lign _____s which the Lord hath planted. (Num. 24:6)

32. Full _____ compassion.
(Ps. 112:4)
34. Consumption, and the burning
_____. (Lev. 26:16)
35. Now will we _____ worse with
thee. (Gen. 19:9)
36. Noah found _____ in the eyes of
the Lord. (Gen. 6:8)
38. With thy vine_____, and with
thy oliveyard. (Ex. 23:11)
39. Send forth their little _____ like
a flock. (Job 21:11)
41. The _____ shall plant, and shall
eat. (Jer. 31:5)
45. _____ wagons and four oxen.
(Num. 7:7)
48. Thou shalt _____ the Lord thy
God. (Deut. 6:5)
49. Even _____ will I certainly do
this. (1 Kgs. 1:30)
50. Fear was _____ every side.
(Ps. 31:13)
51. Good works for necessary
_____. (Titus 3:14)
53. O _____ of Sibmah, I will weep
for thee. (Jer. 48:32)
54. And she _____ them away.
(Josh. 2:21)
55. Vital juice in a tree.

DOWN CLUES

1. If thy father at all _____ me.
(1 Sam. 20:6)
2. Ezer, and _____. (1 Chron. 7:21)
3. The Lord _____ unto me.
(Jer. 1:7)
4. And said, I go, _____: and went
not. (Matt. 21:30)
5. Paltiel the son of _____.
(Num. 34:26)
6. _____ the Beth-elite build
Jericho. (1 Kgs. 16:34)
8. Why make ye this _____, and
weep? (Mark 5:39)

9. _____ him, all ye people.
(Rom. 15:11)
10. They which _____ in may see.
(Luke 8:16)
13. Sons of Caleb...; Iru, Elah,
and _____. (1 Chron. 4:15)
14. It hath been _____ of old time.
(Ec. 1:10)
22. Jacob held his _____ until they
were come. (Gen. 34:5)
23. Joined at the two _____ thereof.
(Ex. 28:7)
25. One that taketh a _____ by the
ears. (Prov. 26:17)
27. So _____ -hadad hearkened
unto king Asa. (1 Kgs. 15:20)
29. I am the _____ in my father's
house. (Judg. 6:15)
30. All that handle the _____, the
mariners. (Eze. 27:29)
31. The _____ of the congregation.
(Lev. 4:15)
33. By the breath of God _____ is
given. (Job 37:10)
37. Their throat is _____ open
sepulchre. (Ps. 5:9)
40. Zebulun shall dwell at the _____
of the sea. (Gen. 49:13)
41. And restore the over_____ unto
the man. (Lev. 25:27)
42. And thou _____ thy life.
(Judg. 18:25)
43. The swallow a _____ for herself.
(Ps. 84:3)
44. And take thee much _____.
(Jer. 2:22)
46. Out of the spoils _____ in
battles. (1 Chron. 26:27)
47. I took twelve men of you, _____
of a tribe. (Deut. 1:23)
52. If I be a master, where _____ my
fear? (Mal. 1:6)

Puzzle 6
Valerie Barrett

ACROSS CLUES

1. In his days the _____ revolted. (2 Chron. 21:8)
8. A pillar, which is in the king's _____. (2 Sam. 18:18)
12. The _____ are fallen unto me. (Ps. 16:6)
13. But put forth thine hand _____. (Job 1:11)
15. Hath not one _____ created us? (Mal. 2:10)
16. And Adam knew _____ his wife. (Gen. 4:1)
17. He shall _____ without instruction. (Prov. 5:23)
18. Any taste in the white of an _____? (Job 6:6)
19. Mibsam his son, _____ his son. (1 Chron. 4:25)
23. Make bare the _____. (Isa. 47:2)
24. Which perished at _____-dor. (Ps. 83:10)
25. For _____ of Zion shall go forth the law. (Isa. 2:3)
26. How we say "hath" today.
28. Where the birds make their _____. (Ps. 104:17)
30. And _____ came to pass. (1 Kgs. 16:11)
32. A raiser of _____es. (Dan. 11:20)
33. Our brother _____ is set at liberty. (Heb. 13:23)
36. And he _____ the burnt offering. (Lev. 9:12)
37. Do all the words of this _____. (Deut. 28:58)
38. Lord looked down from heaven _____ on the children. (Ps.14:2)
39. Taken a _____ of money with him. (Prov. 7:20)
40. Children of Aram; _____, and Hul. (Gen. 10:23)
41. _____, not so, my Lord. (Gen. 19:18)
43. I have been an _____ in a strange land. (Ex. 18:3)
45. To offer unto _____ in their due season. (Num. 28:2)
46. The words of _____ from the mouth of God. (2 Chron. 35:22)
48. Sibbechai the Hushathite slew _____. (2 Sam. 21:18)
50. To the chief Musician, _____-taschith. (Ps. 57:1)
51. An abbreviation for the book of Ruth.
52. You, _____ that one reign over you? (Judg. 9:2)
53. Noah builded an _____ unto the Lord. (Gen. 8:20)
55. A nation _____ out and trodden down. (Isa. 18:2)
56. After they were come to _____. (Acts 16:7)

DOWN CLUES

1. In bondage under the _____ of the world. (Gal. 4:3)
2. Whiles they _____ a lie unto thee. (Ezek. 21:29)
3. All their little _____, and their wives. (Gen. 34:29)
4. Hear _____ now therefore. (Prov. 5:7)
5. Saying, _____ this the city? (Lam. 2:15)
6. Unto the _____ of the eleventh year. (Jer. 1:3)
7. It was planted in a good _____. (Ezek. 17:8)
9. Mine _____ is as nothing before thee. (Ps. 39:5)
10. Trespass offering, and the _____ of oil. (Lev. 14:24)
11. By the two _____ was it coupled together. (Ex. 39:4)
14. The people _____ throughout their families. (Num. 11:10)
20. When the sun waxed _____.

(Ex. 16:21)

21. So he _____ do after the law. (Num. 6:21)

22. Hath required this _____ your hand. (Isa. 1:12)

26. The _____ appeareth, and the tender grass. (Prov. 27:25)

27. With the _____ to cut down. (Deut. 19:5; alt. sp.)

29. Have they not _____? (Judg. 5:30)

30. The groves and _____ shall not stand up. (Isa. 27:9)

31. As a thread of _____ is broken. (Judg. 16:9)

32. Of the _____ of the heart. (1 Chron. 29:18)

34. _____ the Ahohite. (1 Chron. 11:29)

35. On the wall of _____ he built much. (2 Chron. 27:3)

39. Become _____ upon the dry land. (Ex. 4:9)

41. The birth of Jesus Christ was _____ this wise. (Matt. 1:18)

42. But abide _____ fast by my maidens. (Ruth 2:8)

43. _____! it is made bright. (Ezek. 21:15)

44. Iru, Elah, and _____. (1 Chron. 4:15)

45. Call me not Naomi, call me _____. (Ruth 1:20)

47. Ye shall be _____ in pieces. (Dan. 2:5)

49. One of several layers.

54. Men of _____ smote of them. (Josh. 7:5)

15

Puzzle 7

Valerie Barrett

ACROSS CLUES

1. The Lord had a _____ in thy fathers. (Deut. 10:15)
7. Ye had turned _____ quickly. (Deut. 9:16)
11. And _____ shall be a possession. (Num. 24:18)
12. Gera, and Naaman, _____. (Gen. 46:21)
14. His ways _____ always grievous. (Ps. 10:5)
15. Gendereth to bondage, which is _____. (Gal. 4:24)
16. And _____ a proselyte of Antioch. (Acts 6:5)
17. Did they _____ to maintain the house of the Lord. (1 Chron. 26:27)
19. As it were an half _____ of land. (1 Sam. 14:14)
21. The borders of _____ on the west. (Josh. 11:2)
23. Or if he shall ask an _____, will he offer him a scorpion? (Luke 11:12)
26. Which perished at _____-dor. (Ps. 83:10)

16

27. Paul called one of the _____. (Acts 23:17)
32. The _____ of the Lord is clean. (Ps. 19:9)
33. Border of _____ the wilderness. (Josh. 15:1)
34. Fish of the _____. (Num. 11:22)
35. In the _____ which they hid. (Ps. 9:15)
37. Next unto him builded the _____ of Jericho. (Neh. 3:2)
40. Iru, _____, and Naam. (1 Chron. 4:15)
42. His _____ was a bedstead of iron. (Deut. 3:11)
46. The wicked are to _____ in wait. (Prov. 12:6)
47. _____ themselves from thee. (Deut. 7:20)
48. Stood in the _____ court. (Es. 5:1)
49. Children of Gad called the altar _____. (Josh. 22:34)
50. Joshua the son of _____. (Josh. 6:6)
51. A wild _____ used to the wilderness. (Jer. 2:24)

DOWN CLUES

1. Groanings of a _____ wounded man. (Ezek. 30:24)
2. The _____ of the sword. (Judg. 1:25)
3. Who daily _____eth us with benefits. (Ps. 68:19)
4. Zaccur the son of _____. (Neh. 3:2)
5. City of Sepharvaim, _____, and Ivah? (Isa. 37:13)
6. Ye seek, and _____ thou shalt come. (Deut. 12:5)
8. The sons of _____: Beth-lehem, and the Netophathites. (1 Chron. 2:54)
9. _____ also the Jairite was a chief. (2 Sam. 20:26)
10. Hast heard the _____ of the humble. (Ps. 10:17)
13. He casteth forth his _____ like morsels. (Ps. 147:17)
18. Couple the _____ together. (Ex. 26:6)
20. The _____ of the earth were afraid. (Isa. 41:5)
21. Being _____, we intreat. (1 Cor. 4:13)
22. Every _____ that goeth out. (Jer. 5:6)
24. The pelican, and the _____ eagle. (Lev. 11:18)
25. For it is _____ which worketh in you. (Phil. 2:13)
28. In _____ of the Chaldees. (Gen. 11:28)
29. Shalt have _____ other gods. (Deut. 5:7)
30. He smelled the _____ of his raiment. (Gen. 27:27)
31. Child shall play on the hole of the _____. (Isa. 11:8)
36. Two _____ of these smoking firebrands. (Isa. 7:4)
38. All the trees of _____. (Ezek. 31:16)
39. Even as a _____ gathereth. (Matt. 23:37)
41. _____ removed them, and begat Uzza. (1 Chron. 8:7)
42. And _____ them that they make them fringes. (Num. 15:38)
43. With silver, iron, _____, and lead. (Ezek. 27:12)
44. Offer _____ offering of the Lord. (Num. 9:7)
45. A _____ of robbers. (Jer. 7:11)
47. Which _____ told her not. (1 Kgs. 10:3)

Puzzle 8
Diana Rowland

ACROSS CLUES

1. God created the heaven and the _____. (Gen. 1:1)
6. The darkness he called _____. (Gen. 1:5)
11. Doth not even _____ itself teach you. (1 Cor. 11:14)
12. They had made themselves _____ to David. (1 Chron. 19:6)
14. For the kingdom of heaven is _____ hand. (Matt. 3:2)
15. And bring your youngest brother unto _____. (Gen. 42:34)
16. Darkness was upon the face _____ the deep. (Gen. 1:2)
17. The serpent beguiled _____, and I did eat. (Gen. 3:13)
18. Make Jerusalem _____, _____ a den of dragons. (Jer. 9:11; 2 words)
23. We are _____ men. (Gen. 42:31)
25. Called by name Bezaleel the son of _____. (Ex. 35:30)
26. Lot chose him all the _____ of Jordan. (Gen. 13:11)
28. Ninety years _____ and nine. (Gen. 17:1)
29. Multiple sclerosis (abbr.).
30. But where is the _____. (Gen. 22:7)
31. Give me children, _____ else I die. (Gen. 30:1)
33. Do, Re, Mi, Fa, So, La, _____, Do.
34. Abide ye here with the _____. (Gen. 22:5)
35. And _____ the lamp of God went out. (1 Sam. 3:3)
36. And, _____, Sarah thy wife shall have a son. (Gen. 18:10)
38. Postscript (abbr.).
39. Mathematics (abbr.).
40. Cajun state (abbr.).
42. When we came to the _____. (Gen. 43:21)
44. Zethan, and Tharshish, and _____. (1 Chron. 7:10)

47. Drive, park, or reverse.
49. We may _____ of the fruit of the trees. (Gen. 3:2)
50. Was like a weaver's _____. (2 Sam. 21:19)
51. And _____ went on his journeys. (Gen. 13:3)
52. Abram called _____ the name of the Lord. (Gen. 13:4)
54. Not a man left in _____ or Beth-el. (Josh. 8:17)
55. Postal abbreviation for Delaware.
56. Of Manasseh, _____ with her suburbs. (Josh. 21:25)
59. Which lieth _____ the south of _____. (Judg. 1:16; 2 words)
61. Like a _____ of fire in a sheaf. (Zech. 12:6)
62. If _____ find in Sodom..., _____ I will spare. (Gen. 18:26; 2 words)

DOWN CLUES

1. Among riotous _____ of flesh. (Prov. 23:20)
2. Behold, I am _____ the point to die. (Gen. 25:32)
3. The fat and the _____. (Ex. 29:22)
4. For his _____ unto the Lord _____ ram. (Lev. 5:15; 2 words)
5. Male and female created _____ them. (Gen. 1:27)
6. The waters shall _____ more become a flood. (Gen. 9:15)
7. _____ _____ set my bow in the cloud. (Gen. 9:13; 2 words)
8. Ask me never so much dowry and _____. (Gen. 34:12)
9. _____, every one that thirsteth. (Isa. 55:1)
10. What meaneth the noise of this _____? (1 Sam. 4:14)
11. The vision of _____ the Elkoshite. (Nahum 1:1)
13. Unto thy _____ will _____ give this land. (Gen. 12:7; 2 words)
19. And the king of _____ he hanged on a tree. (Josh. 8:29)
20. That ye do not your _____ before men. (Matt. 6:1)
21. Slang for "snatch" or "catch".

22. Prince Charles and Princess
    _____.

24. Abbreviation for book of
    Romans.

27. And to the east, and to the
    _____. (Gen. 28:14)

30. Also I shook my _____.
    (Neh. 5:13)

32. The sons of Eliezer were, _____
    the chief. (1 Chron. 23:17)

35. At the _____ of the garden of
    Eden. (Gen. 3:24)

36. Let there be _____. (Gen. 1:3)

37. To make _____ wise,...and did
    _____. (Gen. 3:6; 2 words)

39. Missing in Action (abbr.).

40. Of the Gershonites were, _____,
    and Shimei. (1 Chron. 23:7)

41. He _____ his trained servants.

(Gen. 14:14)

43. Not available (abbr.).

45. And there _____ put the man.
    (Gen. 2:8)

46. And _____ said unto me.
    (Gen. 24:40)

48. Let the sea _____.
    (1 Chron. 16:32)

53. National Council of Churches
    (abbr.).

54. Go to the _____, thou sluggard.
    (Prov. 6:6)

57. And he knew her again _____
    more. (Gen. 38:26)

58. Initials of Hubert Humphrey.

59. _____ heard thy voice..., and
    _____ was afraid.
    (Gen. 3:10; 2 words)

60. About (abbr.).

19

Puzzle 9

Diana Rowland

ACROSS CLUES

1. We have _____ his star in the east. (Matt. 2:2)
5. Upon the _____ of the rock. (Job 39:28)
9. Which have _____ the burden. (Matt. 20:12)
10. Pitched beside the well of _____. (Judg. 7:1)
12. Elmodam, which was the son of _____. (Luke 3:28)
13. Whose _____ was the sea. (Nahum 3:8)
15. The sons of Judah; _____, and Onan. (1 Chron. 2:3)
17. Large.
19. Even as a _____ cherisheth her children. (1 Thes. 2:7)
20. Federal Aviation Administration (abbr.).
21. From the blood of righteous _____. (Matt. 23:35)
23. But if thine _____ be evil. (Matt. 6:23)
24. Sickens.
25. The words of king _____. (Prov. 31:1)

27. Now there came a _____ over all the land. (Acts 7:11)
29. In the very _____. (John 8:4)
30. Of a truth thou _____ the Son of God. (Matt. 14:33)
31. And _____ the host _____. (Judg. 7:21; 2 words)
34. Laying up in _____ for themselves _____ good foundation. (1 Tim. 6:19; 2 words)
37. Cometh of the _____ of his patrimony. (Deut. 18:8)
38. She was of the _____ of twelve years. (Mark 5:42)
40. And they straightway left their _____. (Matt. 4:20)
41. A sons of Bela.. (1 Chron. 7:7)
42. And _____ even...they brought unto him _____ that were diseased. (Mark 1:32; 2 words)
44. Naaman, _____, and Rosh. (Gen. 46:21)
45. Attorney General (abbr.).
46. He shall come unto _____ the glory of Israel. (Micah 1:15)
48. Thou shalt love thy neighbour _____ thyself. (Matt. 19:19)
49. Into the mouth of the _____. (Nahum 3:12)
51. _____ the son of Kishi. (1 Chron. 6:44)
53. A greater than Jonas is _____. (Matt. 12:41)
54. Have ye not _____ what David did? (Matt. 12:3)

DOWN CLUES

1. Let your light _____ shine before men. (Matt. 5:16)
2. Ye do _____, not knowing the scriptures. (Matt. 22:29)
3. Ahira the son of _____. (Num. 10:27)
4. Son of Simeon. (1 Chron. 4:24)
5. Mine enemies _____ me sore. (Lam. 3:52)
6. And it is a _____ thing. (Dan. 2:11)

7. Blessed _____ thou, Simon Bar-jona. (Matt. 16:17)
8. _____ into the land of Israel. (Matt. 2:20)
9. They take a _____. (Amos 5:12)
11. Thus hath the Lord _____ with me. (Luke 1:25)
12. The curse upon mount _____. (Deut. 11:29)
14. Snoop into.
16. Be not _____ with thy mouth. (Ec. 5:2)
18. Ammiel the son of _____. (Num. 13:12)
20. And the two doors were of _____ _____. (1 Kgs. 6:34; 2 words)
22. Not given to filthy _____. (Titus 1:7)
24. His wife was of the daughters of _____. (Luke 1:5)
26. Estimated time of arrival (abbr.).
28. And did _____ the shewbread. (Matt. 12:4)
31. The churches of _____ salute you. (1 Cor. 16:19)
32. They gave _____ money unto the soldiers. (Matt. 28:12)
33. Doth not even _____ itself teach you. (1 Cor. 11:14)
34. Lydia, a _____ of purple. (Acts 16:14)
35. _____ the son of Kushaiah. (1 Chron. 15:17)
36. Thy will be done in earth, _____ it _____ in heaven. (Matt. 6:10; 2 words)
39. Western slang for "girl".
42. Arad, and _____. (1 Chron. 8:15)
43. The Jews of _____ sought to stone thee. (John 11:8)
46. I _____ no pleasant bread. (Dan. 10:3)
47. Health care degree.
50. Saying, _____, thou that destroyest the temple. (Mark 15:29)
52. Before Christ is BC; Anno Domini is _____.

Puzzle 10

Evelyn M. Boyington

ACROSS CLUES

1. And _____ Israel that were round about them fled. (Num. 16:34)
4. And _____ the son of Omri did evil. (1 Kgs. 16:30)
8. Have yet not read in the _____? (Matt. 12:5)
11. This is the _____ of the generations of Adam. (Gen. 5:1)
13. There shall not an _____ of him fall to the earth. (1 Kgs. 1:52)
14. Anger.
15. With long _____ will I satisfy him. (Ps. 91:16)
16. And they _____ him, and put on him a scarlet robe. (Matt. 27:28)
18. Grafted.
19. Come, _____ the place where the Lord lay. (Matt. 28:6)
20. Unsuitable.
24. Be not afraid of their _____. (Jer. 1:8)
28. Therefore called she his name _____. (Gen. 30:6)
30. Aim.
32. Alkali.
33. Ye tithe mint and _____ and all manner of herbs. (Luke 11:42)
34. He went and took _____ the daughter of Diblaim. (Hosea 1:3)
36. Ever (poetic).
37. Tax agency.
38. To wash.
39. He went out to meet _____. (2 Chron. 15:2)
40. Adhesive.
43. She scorneth the horse and his

_____. (Job 39:18)
45. The _____s are a people not strong. (Prov. 30:25)
47. Before (prefix).
50. Lift up a _____ against him. (Isa. 59:19)
55. Set me as a _____ upon thine heart. (Song of Sol. 8:6)
56. I am like an _____ of the desert. (Ps. 102:6)
57. Canal.
58. The son of Naum, which was the son of _____. (Luke 3:25)
59. _____ unto them that are wise in their own eyes. (Isa. 5:21)
60. College official.
61. The son of Arphaxad, which was the son of _____. (Luke 3:36)

DOWN CLUES

1. Our God whom we serve is _____ to deliver us. (Dan. 3:17)
2. Having your _____s girt about with truth. (Eph. 6:14)
3. The _____ of man shall be bowed down. (Isa. 2:17)
4. Exclamations.
5. "The Cat in the _____."
6. Put on.
7. Short.
8. The _____ of truth shall be established for ever. (Prov.12:19)
9. Your fathers, where _____ they? (Zech. 1:5)
10. Married.
12. Sharp.
17. Green vegetable.
21. Is there any taste in the white of an _____? (Job 6:6)
22. Go, wash in the _____ of Siloam. (John 9:7)
23. I love _____, my brother

Absalom's sister. (2 Sam. 13:4)
25. As it were the body of heaven in his _____. (Ex. 24:10)
26. I will lift up mine _____ unto the hills. (Ps. 121:1)
27. Antitoxin.
28. Dribble.
29. Invisible emanation.
31. The priests the sons of _____ shall come near. (Deut. 21:5)
35. Though they be _____ like crimson. (Isa. 1:18)
41. Light brown.
42. On the seventh day God _____ his work. (Gen. 2:2)
44. I will _____ me of mine adversaries. (Isa. 1:24)
46. The king arose, and _____ his garments. (2 Sam. 13:31)
48. We spend our years as a _____ that is told. (Ps. 90:9)
49. They took their journey from _____. (Ex. 16:1)
50. They that _____ in tears shall reap in joy. (Ps. 126:5)
51. For _____, saith he, shall be one flesh. (1 Cor. 6:16)
52. Brewed beverage.
53. Radioimmunoassay (abbr.).
54. Ye have made it a _____ of thieves. (Matt. 21:13)

23

Puzzle 11

Evelyn M. Boyington

ACROSS CLUES

1. The _____ was like a lion. (Dan. 7:4)
6. Thou shalt tread upon the lion and _____. (Ps. 91:13)
11. The Lord is risen _____. (Luke 24:34)
13. Recycled.
15. The children of Gad called the altar _____. (Josh. 22:34)
16. He hath cut _____ the cords of the wicked. (Ps. 129:4)
18. Trade union (abbr.).
19. _____ not your heart be troubled. (John 14:1)
21. Leah said, A _____ cometh. (Gen. 30:11)
22. Cozbi, the daughter of _____. (Num. 25:15)
23. They that _____ truly are his delight. (Prov. 12:22)
25. Incline thine _____ unto me. (Ps. 17:6)
26. Equalities.

27. A broken spirit _____ the bones. (Prov. 17:22)
29. Three times in a year did Solomon offer _____ offerings. (1 Kgs. 9:25)
30. Lest thou _____ thy foot against a stone. (Ps. 91:12)
31. He paid the _____ thereof. (Jonah 1:3)
32. Blouse.
34. I will restore _____ unto thee. (Jer. 30:17)
36. The _____ of the feet were part of iron. (Dan. 2:42)
37. Therefore called she his name _____. (Gen. 30:6)
38. _____, why persecutest thou me? (Acts 9:4)
40. The Lord _____ God shall deliver us. (2 Chron. 32:11)
41. They would come and take him by _____. (John 6:15)
43. Compass point.
44. Mind your _____ and Qs.
45. The Father _____ such to worship him. (John 4:23)
47. Southern state (abbr.).
48. Have their _____ exercised to discern both good and evil. (Heb. 5:14)
50. As they _____ he fell asleep. (Luke 8:23)
52. All the land which thou _____. (Gen. 13:15)
53. Masts.

DOWN CLUES
1. Let the _____ be joyful. (Ps. 96:12)
2. The Lord is risen _____. (Luke 24:34)
3. Ave.
4. The _____ and the waves roaring. (Luke 21:25)
5. Exam.
6. Zeal.
7. All the fountains of the great _____ broken up. (Gen. 7:11)
8. He set it up in the plain of _____a. (Dan. 3:1)
9. Plural ending.
10. _____ unto me; for I have redeemed thee. (Isa. 44:22)
12. Hath he not root in himself, but _____ for a while. (Matt.13:21)
14. None of the disciples _____ ask him. (John 21:12)
17. And _____ builded an altar unto the Lord. (Gen. 8:20)
20. Later.
22. The city Adam, that is beside _____. (Josh. 3:16)
24. All men are _____. (Ps. 116:11)
26. Knitting stitches.
28. Eastern Standard Time (abbr.).
29. Sheep's bleat.
31. Barriers.
32. Who _____ his ears from hearing of bloodshed. (Isa. 33:15 NKJ)
33. David made him _____ in the city of David. (1 Chron. 15:1)
34. Listen!
35. They shall not _____ nor thirst. (Isa. 49:10)
37. _____ thou well to be angry? (Jonah 4:4)
39. He _____ me beside the still waters. (Ps. 23:2 NKJ)
41. Charges.
42. Greek letters.
45. Compass point.
46. He smote them _____ and thigh. (Judg. 15:8)
49. Maine direction.
51. City on the west coast.

Puzzle 12

Debra Michaels

ACROSS CLUES

1. Musical instrument. (Dan. 3:5)
5. Large water bird. (Lev. 11:18)
11. A stroke with a whip.
12. A son of Cush. (Gen. 10:7)
13. In my Father's house _____ many mansions. (John 14:2)
14. Straight across a ship; abreast.
16. Wild animals or birds hunted.
17. Arkansas (abbr.).
18. _____ of Eden.
19. Pound (abbr.).
20. Ancient Thebes and capital of upper Egypt. (Nahum 3:8)
21. Delaware (abbr.).
23. Senior (abbr.).
26. Species of ox.
27. Moses' ark was made of this. (Ex. 2:3)
32. Double reed woodwind instrument.
33. God is _____present.
34. The pure in heart...shall _____ God. (Matt. 5:8)
35. Musical composition for two.
36. Set the table with these.
38. Certain days in the Roman calendar.
40. Yes.
41. Prefix meaning "two" or "double."
42. A close friend.
43. Tennessee (abbr.).
44. Right Reverend (abbr.).
46. I _____ unto the Lord with my voice. (Ps. 3:4)
48. Jot.
49. To meet the Lord in the _____. (1 Thes. 4:17)
51. Form of the word "air."
52. There _____ I in the midst of them. (Matt. 18:20)
53. Right (abbr.).
54. Poet Thomas.
55. To wash.

DOWN CLUES

1. Wild plant. (Job 8:11)
2. Gave Jacob his two daughters. (Gen. 29)
3. One who uses.
4. One of the apostles. (Matt. 10:3)
5. A thick pin.
6. Son of Shobal. (Gen. 36:23)
7. Favorite sacrifice. (Ex. 29:39)
8. California (abbr.).
9. A child of Dishan. (Gen. 36:28)
10. Roman emperor who persecuted Christians.
15. The _____...shall inherit the earth. (Matt. 5:5)
22. International Business Machines Corporation (abbr.).
23. Sister (abbr.).
24. Where moth and _____ doth corrupt. (Matt. 6:19)
25. Captain of Pharaoh's guard. (Gen. 37:36)
26. To sing with sudden changes in voice.
28. _____able; not forgivable.
29. Easter flower.
30. To Abraham and his _____ were the promises made. (Gal. 3:16)
31. To feel or show indecision.

33. Son of Kenaz. (Josh. 15:17)
37. In the air.
39. Irish father.
43. Waiter's necessity.

45. Pear-shaped tomato.
47. A period of time.
50. And God saw the light, that
_____ was good. (Gen. 1:4)

Puzzle 13

Debra Michaels

ACROSS CLUES

1. Strive to enter in at the strait _____. (Luke 13:24)
5. A crown.
10. A Christmas carol.
11. He leadeth me _____ the paths of righteousness. (Ps. 23:3)
12. Hesitating sound.
13. _____ whose stripes ye were healed. (1 Pet. 2:24)
14. The seventh month of the Jewish year.
15. Variety (abbr.).
17. Room (abbr.).
18. Train up a child in the way he should _____. (Prov. 22:6)
19. United States Mail (abbr.).
22. Sara's maid.
25. One tenth of one's income.
26. Blood classification system.
27. The children of _____. (Ezra 2:57)
29. To cut.
31. Clan.

28

33. Digit of the foot.
34. Place (abbr.).
35. Where the Beatitudes are found.
37. _____ save me for thy mercies' sake. (Ps. 6:4)
38. Between Beth-el and _____, on the west side of the city. (Josh. 8:12)
39. _____ children arise up, and call her blessed. (Prov. 31:28)
40. Queen who risked her life to save her people.
43. Nova Scotia (abbr.).
45. Right side (abbr.).
46. Second tone of a scale.
47. He that winneth souls is _____. (Prov. 11:30)
49. This is the day which the Lord hath _____. (Ps. 118:24)
50. The cow and the _____ shall feed. (Isa. 11:7)
52. The Lord is good _____ all. (Ps. 145:9)
53. South Dakota (abbr.).
54. David's close friend.
55. And _____ him that knocketh it shall be opened. (Matt. 7:8)

DOWN CLUES

1. A knot on the trunk of a tree.
2. Account of (abbr.).
3. The days of our years are three score years and _____. (Ps. 90:10)
4. The cousin of Mary.
5. Roman goddess. (Acts 19:27)
6. No room for them in the _____. (Luke 2:7)
7. Prayers, especially in private.
8. Equal Rights Amendment (abbr.).
9. But as for me and _____ house, we will serve the Lord. (Josh. 24:15)
16. Naomi's daughter-in-law.
20. They were told of the birth of Christ.
21. Whimper or whine.
22. Sell whatsoever thou _____, and give to the poor. (Mark 10:21)
23. Burrowing animals with pouched cheeks.
24. Symbol for element Radium.
28. Mountain (abbr.).
30. Doctors group (abbr.).
32. Concise.
36. A landmark on eastern boundary of Canaan. (Num: 34:11)
37. _____ how great is thy goodness. (Ps. 31:19)
40. A son of Gad. (Gen. 46:16)
41. Ye shall not _____ the Lord your God. (Deut. 6:16)
42. A bruised _____ shall he not break. (Matt. 12:20)
44. The little owl, and the great owl, and the _____. (Deut.14:16)
48. A retirement plan.
50. Billie Jo, Bobby Joe (abbr.).
51. A prefix meaning "early."
52. Symbol for element tantalum.

Puzzle 14

Janice A. Buhl

ACROSS CLUES

1. Thy master's son shall _____ bread. (2 Sam. 9:10)
4. Be _____ to do my commandments. (1 Chron. 28:7)
11. Is not this a _____ plucked out of the fire? (Zech. 3:2)
14. Be ye _____ as your fathers. (Zech. 1:4)
15. Stretch out thine hand over the _____. (Ex. 14:26)
16. Let us go and serve _____ gods. (Deut. 13:6)
17. Streets (abbr.).
18. And Jacob stole _____ unawares. (Gen. 31:20)
20. The first _____ was like a lion. (Rev. 4:7)
22. _____ gleaning grapes shall be left in it. (Isa. 17:6)
24. _____ you into your tents again. (Deut. 5:30)
26. I will _____ mine hand upon my mouth. (Job 40:4)
27. _____ the son of Abdiel. (1 Chron. 5:15)
29. As with the _____ of usury. (Isa. 24:2)
32. He shall eat _____ my table. (2 Sam. 9:11)
33. _____, inquire of Baal-zebub. (2 Kgs. 1:2)
35. His offering shall _____ of fine flour. (Lev. 2:1)
36. He moveth his _____ like a cedar. (Job 40:17)
39. And _____ went out, and wept bitterly. (Luke 22:62)
40. Zilpah _____ maid bare Jacob a son. (Gen. 30:10)
42. Have ye a father, _____ a brother? (Gen. 44:19)
43. I have _____ the ways of the Lord. (2 Sam. 22:22)
44. They took a _____, and opened them. (Judg. 3:25)
46. _____ the Ahohite. (1 Chron. 11:29)
47. I turned to see the voice that spake with _____. (Rev. 1:12)
48. Then I came to them of the captivity at _____-abib. (Ezek. 3:15)
49. The Egyptian had a _____ in his hand. (2 Sam. 23:21)
52. The children of Gad called the altar _____. (Josh. 22:34)
53. _____ him, and let him go. (John 11:44)
56. To be _____, and to be bakers. (1 Sam. 8:13)
58. The inhabitants of _____-dor and her towns. (Josh. 17:11)
59. French (abbr.).
60. Related.

DOWN CLUES

1. Horns of ivory and _____. (Ezek. 27:15)
2. Thou _____ a virtuous woman. (Ruth 3:11)
3. They departed from _____. (Num. 33:27)
5. Hearken unto me every _____ of you. (Mark 7:14)
6. There had been _____ rain in the land. (1 Kgs. 17:7)
7. The world also shall be _____. (1 Chron. 16:30)
8. If we _____ to commune with thee. (Job 4:2)
9. The wicked fall into their own _____. (Ps. 141:10)
10. He shall never _____ of death. (John 8:52)
12. Behold, all things are become _____. (2 Cor. 5:17)
13. Gather them in their _____. (Hab. 1:15)
19. Mine hour is not _____ come. (John 2:4)

21. The merchants of the _____ shall weep. (Rev. 18:11)
23. Out of the _____ came forth meat. (Judg. 14:14)
25. He asked for a writing _____. (Luke 1:63)
28. A son of Shemaiah. (1 Chron. 3:22)
30. They shall _____ the way of the Lord. (Gen. 18:19)
31. Joshua burnt _____. (Josh. 8:28)
32. I am appointed a preacher, and an _____. (2 Tim. 1:11)
34. Two _____ three witnesses. (Heb. 10:28)
37. _____, and it shall be given you. (Luke 11:9)
38. Thou takest up that thou _____ not down. (Luke 19:21)

41. To begin a fight.
43. Salute one another with an holy _____. (Rom. 16:16)
45. To the valley of Jiphthah-el toward the north side of Beth _____. (Josh. 19:27)
46. Love worketh no _____ to his neighbour. (Rom. 13:10)
50. Gym class.
51. And Isaac dwelt by the well Lahai-_____. (Gen. 25:11)
54. Love is the fulfilling _____ the law. (Rom 13:10)
55. To his own master he standeth _____ falleth. (Rom. 14:4)
57. Do ye look _____ things after the outward appearance? (2 Cor.10:7)

31

Puzzle 15

K. B. Liesner

ACROSS CLUES

1. Hosea's wife.
5. Herod...made an _____ unto them. (Acts 12:21)
11. Shall the _____ boast itself against him that heweth therewith? (Isa. 10:15)
12. A person from Ephesus.
14. The borrower is servant to the _____. (Prov. 22:7)
16. Greek god of music, poetry, and sunlight.
18. Noah builded _____ altar unto the Lord. (Gen. 8:20)
19. The Israelites had to _____ to living in the wilderness.
21. "Praise _____ the Lord."
22. Millimeter (abbr.).
23. Ninth letter of the Greek alphabet.
25. _____ _____ do all things through Christ which strengtheneth me. (Phil. 4:13; 2 words)
27. There was silence in heaven about the _____ of half an hour. (Rev. 8:1)
30. A city belonging to Simeon. (Josh. 19:7)

31. To repeat again.
32. Verse (abbr.).
33. Hiram's kingdom. (2 Sam. 5:11)
35. Get thee _____, Satan. (Matt. 4:10)
37. A city destroyed by the Israelites. (Josh. 8:21)
38. O come, let us _____ Him.
41. To judge.
43. Our good works are _____ without faith in God.
47. Josaphat's father. (Matt. 1:8)
48. A _____ of thieves.(Mark 11:17)
50. For whosoever will save his life shall _____ it. (Matt.16:25)
51. The first "marked man."
53. Put thou my tears into thy _____. (Ps. 56:8)
55. _____ them into the pot of pottage. (2 Kgs. 4:39)
56. I am; you are; he _____.
57. "A long, long way to run."

DOWN CLUES

1. Where Galatians come from.
2. Balak's offering. (Num. 22:40)
3. Adam, Isaac, Joseph, Paul, for example.
4. A bruised _____ shall he not break. (Isa. 42:3)
5. _____ that I had wings like a dove. (Ps. 55:6)
6. Attaches again.
7. The sucking child shall play on the hole of the _____. (Isa.11:8)
8. From the beginning of the crea_____. (Mark 10:6)
9. How the Israelites kept time: a sund_____.
10. Take now...thine _____ son Isaac. (Gen. 22:2)
13. I will _____ thee, O Lord, with my whole heart. (Ps. 9:1)
15. But he that believeth not shall be _____ed. (Mark 16:16)
17. Poetic form of "over".
20. Head of the Catholic church.
22. Thou shalt be a father of _____ nations. (Gen. 17:4)
24. Word after "heart," "stomach," and "head".
26. Lot dwelled in the _____ of the plain. (Gen. 13:12)
28. An incalculable amount of time.
29. Mother of Cain and Abel.
31. The color of the dragon having seven heads and ten horns. (Rev. 12:3)
34. Isaac's substitute. (Gen. 22:13)
36. What Jehoiada commanded set outside the temple gate. (2 Chron. 24:8)
37. Eve's husband.
39. Let us _____ with patience the race that is set before us. (Heb. 12:1)
40. _____ the hart panteth after the water. (Ps. 42:1)
42. Tongues like as of fire... sat upon _____ of them. (Acts 2:3)
44. _____, _____, lama sabachthani? (Mark 15:34; one word)
45. _____ wife, not exactly a "pillar" of the church.
46. Who his own _____ bare our sins. (1 Pet. 2:24)
48. Though I should _____ with thee. (Matt. 26:35)
49. For to this _____ Christ...died. (Rom. 14:9)
52. City given to Lot's children. (Deut. 2:9)
54. Abbreviation for 42 down.

Puzzle 16

Arlene Walker

ACROSS CLUES

1. _____ not. (Gen. 15:1)
5. Climbed up into a _____ tree. (Luke 19:4; modern sp.)
11. Storage under roof of a house.
13. _____ the right hand of God. (Rom. 8:34)
14. Cast the _____ on the right side. (John 21:6)
15. _____ unto God. (Rom. 6:11)
17. One little _____ lamb. (2 Sam. 12:3)
18. Three electrodes in an electron tube.
21. Good _____ bad. (2 Cor. 5:10)
22. _____ answered. (John 9:36)
24. Registered nurse (abbr.).
25. Shalt _____ in thine heart. (Rom. 10:9)
29. A woman's name.
30. Repulsive.
32. Drowsy.
34. Thou maintainest my _____. (Ps. 16:5)
35. He saith among the trumpets, _____. (Job 39:25)
36. Ribbed dress fabric.
38. Way of walking.
40. _____ in peace. (Acts 16:36)
41. As many _____ received him. (John 1:12)
43. Clever, cunning.
45. Mary hath chosen that good _____. (Luke 10:42)
47. My people are _____ to backsliding. (Hosea 11:7)
49. Bird providing sport and food.

51. Love worketh no _____. (Rom. 13:10)
53. One way to tie shoes.
55. The _____ of the valleys. (Song of Sol. 2:1)
56. _____ good unto all. (Gal. 6:10)

DOWN CLUES

1. _____ in that which is least. (Luke 16:10)
2. Suffix meaning "little."
3. Many shall rejoice _____ his birth. (Luke 1:14)
4. Rhode Island (abbr.).
6. Buried him in the _____. (Gen. 50:13)
7. Past tense of "eat".
8. Love _____ another. (1 John 4:7)
9. Put in other words.
10. Words of _____ life. (John 6:68)
12. Ungentlemanly.
16. Last Entry (abbr.).
19. In the case of.
20. My son, _____ my voice. (Gen. 27:8)
23. They shall _____ God. (Matt. 5:8)
25. Bacon, lettuce, and tomato (abbr.).
26. O.T. prophet who wrote about the Messiah.
27. Short for "elevated railway."
28. Short for "veterinarian."
29. Yes.
31. Purpose.
33. Prove validity of a will.
35. _____ are ye if ye do them. (John 13:17)
37. So _____eth my soul after thee, O God. (Ps. 42:1)
39. Journey.

42. Street (abbr.).

43. That we should _____ into Italy. (Acts 27:1)

44. They shall _____ as lions' whelps. (Jer. 51:38)

46. Large container for liquid.

48. Prefix.

50. _____ much the more. (Heb. 10:25)

52. Long Island (abbr.).

54. _____, I am with you alway. (Matt. 28:20)

Puzzle 17

Arlene Walker

ACROSS CLUES

1. God shall _____ them off.
   (Ps. 94:23)
4. If _____ man serve me.
   (John 12:26)
7. _____ the Lord. (Ex. 12:31)
11. Large monkeys.
13. Slippery fish.
15. Very Important Person (abbr.).

16. There is _____ beside me.
   (Isa. 45:6)
17. That thine eyes may be _____.
   (2 Chron. 6:20)
20. Printer's measures.
21. Chew the _____. (Deut. 14:7)
23. The _____ of perfectness.
   (Col. 3:14)
24. While the _____ was a
   preparing. (1 Pet. 3:20)
25. New, recent.
26. Attorney General (abbr.).
27. A _____ to be born. (Ec. 3:2)
29. Bushel (abbr.).

36

30. In the seventh year of his _____. (Es. 2:16)
33. Form of the word "root."
34. Short form of "umpire.}
36. An expert.
37. Ensign (abbr.).
38. A canopy of plant material.
41. From beginning to _____.
42. Northern sea duck.
44. He was _____ at that saying. (Mark 10:22)
46. Paddles used to row a boat.
47. Actual weight (abbr.).
48. Pronoun meaning "we".
49. Horsepower (abbr.).
50. The sower _____ the grain.
52. New England state (abbr.).
53. From the man's _____ God made a woman. (Gen. 2:22)
55. Seventh note of musical scale.
57. Below.
59. Go, return _____ to her mother's house. (Ruth 1:8)
60. Square (abbr.).
61. Adam _____ Eve.

DOWN CLUES

1. The sweet _____ from a far country. (Jer. 6:20)
2. Laid him on the altar _____ the wood. (Gen. 22:9)
3. Lord, thy pound hath gained _____ pounds. (Luke 19:16)
5. My God shall supply all your _____. (Phil. 4:19)
6. Go _____ into all the world. (Mark 16:15)

8. Lord _____ of the sabbath. (Matt. 12:8)
9. Outside layer of an orange.
10. Vice president (abbr.).
12. His _____ is with the righteous. (Prov. 3:32)
14. Lower part of the ear.
18. The _____ always with you. (Matt. 26:11)
19. Shew me a _____. (Judg. 6:17)
22. United Kingdom (abbr.).
24. Entertained.
25. Book of Israelites' wilderness wanderings.
26. He is of _____. (John 9:21)
27. Have _____ in heaven. (Mark 10:21)
28. Suffix which means "act" or "condition of."
29. Prickly seed case.
31. Each (abbr.).
32. Puts frosting on cake.
35. Full of deadly _____. (Jam. 3:8)
38. Take as one's own child.
39. Rural delivery (abbr.).
40. Worthy of his _____. (1 Tim. 5:18)
43. Direction of sunrise.
45. Largest continent.
47. Let all the people say, _____. (Ps. 106:48)
51. Marry.
54. Before Christ (abbr.).
56. Surely the Lord _____ in this place. (Gen. 28:16)
58. Interjection expressing triumph.

Puzzle 18

Arlene Walker

ACROSS CLUES

1. _____; for thy servant heareth. (1 Sam. 3:10)
8. Screech _____ also shall rest there. (Isa. 34:14)
10. They rose up in the morning _____. (1 Sam. 1:19)
11. I have given you every herb bearing _____. (Gen. 1:29)
13. Roll over (abbr.).
15. For example (abbr.).
16. _____ me, and know my thoughts. (Ps. 139:23)
18. Not accused of _____. (Titus 1:6)
19. Obituary (abbr.).
21. That I may _____ him out of sleep. (John 11:11)
23. Unto us a child is _____. (Isa. 9:6)
25. Her Majesty (abbr.).
26. Ye shall eat it in _____. (Ex. 12:11)
29. Flow out slowly.
31. Irish (abbr.).
32. Be _____ and of a good courage. (Josh. 1:9)
34. Written in the _____ of the book. (2 Chron. 24:27)
37. A _____ caught in a thicket. (Gen. 22:13)
40. Recorded.
41. Every _____ shall see him. (Rev. 1:7)
43. Bachelor of Arts (abbr.).
44. Creative works, skills.
45. Vote in favor.
46. Newborn child.
49. The going down of the _____. (Deut. 16:6)
51. Exclamation of disgust.
52. Singing or piloting a plane alone.
55. Give us a _____ in his holy place. (Ezra 9:8)
57. I _____ in the way of righteousness. (Prov. 8:20)
58. Laugh.

DOWN CLUES

1. When ye shall _____ for me. (Jer. 29:13)
2. Father.
3. Who can understand his _____? (Ps. 19:12)
4. A large amount.
5. Kentucky (abbr.).
6. Bachelor of Science (abbr.).
7. Great.
9. The men did the _____ faithfully. (2 Chron. 34:12)
12. Electrical engineer (abbr.).
14. Is any thing _____ hard for the Lord? (Gen. 18:14)
16. Short for Scottish cap.
17. 365 days.
20. Am I my _____ keeper? (Gen. 4:9)
22. _____ he shall appear. (1 John 3:2)
23. And _____ ye kind one to another. (Eph. 4:32)
24. Neither/_____.
27. If thou bring thy gift to the _____. (Matt. 5:23)
28. The _____ are gathered and burned. (Matt. 13:40)
30. Region, space.
33. Sound of roaring lion.

34. The Lord was my _____ (2 Sam. 22:19)
35. Choose.
36. Yard (abbr.).
38. We cry, _____, Father. (Rom. 8:15)
39. Perhaps.
42. _____ and old. (Josh. 6:21)

47. God is _____ to make him stand. (Rom. 14:4)
48. Sunshine state.
50. To constantly scold.
52. Salvation Army (abbr.).
53. Outside diameter (abbr.).
54. King of Bashan. (Ps. 136:20)
56. Illinois (abbr.).

Puzzle 19

Jonah and Sue Schrowang

ACROSS CLUES

1. The book after John.
4. The priests.
9. Greeting.
10. Pester.
12. Alpha and _____.
13. Negative response.
15. This man was eaten by worms. (Acts 12:21-23)
18. Before Christ.
20. Anno Domini.
21. God created the dry _____ on the third day.
22. Galatians is an Epistle of _____.
23. An offense against morals; sin.
24. Italian for "yes."
25. Peter saw this inthis vision in Acts 10.
29. And the tongue _____ a fire. (Jam. 3:6)
30. A teenager.
33. Whom _____ ye that I am? (Matt. 16:15)

35. This lady was King Xerxes' wife. (Esther 2, NIV)
36. Kitchen appliance.
38. Fourth letter in Greek alphabet.
40. First person pronoun.
42. _____ of the Chaldees. (Neh. 9:7)
43. Amusement.

DOWN CLUES

1. And laid their hands on the _____. (Acts 5:18)
2. Definite article.
3. Therefore the Lord himself shall give you a _____. (Isa. 7:14)
5. Adam's wife.
6. The virtuous woman is not _____. (Prov. 31)
7. Suffix.
8. They wore these in Bible times.
11. _____ ye therefore, and teach all nations.
14. Fifth month of the Hebrew calendar.
16. Rural Electrification Administration (abbr.).
17. And as it is appointed unto men _____ to die. (Heb. 9:27)
19. Then Philip went down to the city...and preached _____ unto them. (Acts 8:5)
22. Paul did this frequently.
23. Extraterrestrial.
26. The windows of _____ were opened. (Gen. 7:11)
27. Exodus (abbr.).
28. Thirteenth letter of the Greek alphabet.
29. Small island.
31. Metal-bearing mineral.
32. Strongest muscle in your body.
33. _____, pastors and teachers. (Eph. 4:11)
34. Know _____ that the Lord he is God. (Ps. 100:3)
37. Maiden name.
39. Measure equal to 252 gallons.
41. Mathematical symbol for "3.14."

Puzzle 20

Jesse and Sue Schrowang

ACROSS CLUES

1. God's Son.
4. First king of Israel.
8. Tribe of _____. (Num. 1:25)
9. Water vessel.
11. Shall dwell at the _____ of the sea. (Gen. 49:13)
12. And thou hast magnified thy _____. (Gen. 19:19)
14. Spanish for "yes."
15. In the twinkling of an _____. (1 Cor. 15:52)
16. Jesus is God's _____.
18. Substance used for washing.
21. Jacob's first son. (Gen. 29:32)
23. Each (abbr.).
24. Another word for "father."
25. You (KJV).
26. Gospel or Good _____.
28. For _____ have sinned. (Rom. 3:23)
29. Jesus cursed the fig _____. (Mark 11)
30. Used to pierce the side of Jesus.
33. _____ ye to the Lord. (Ex. 15:21)
35. Girl's name.
36. Whirlpool.
38. _____ upon the name of the Lord. (Zeph. 3:9)
41. Consider the lilies...they toil not, neither do they _____. (Matt. 6:28)
44. Long fish.
45. Tree of knowledge of good and _____. (Gen. 2:9)

46. Purpose.
47. Extraterrestrial (abbr.).

DOWN CLUES

1. _____ the Baptist.
2. Jesus is our _____.
3. He was manifested to take away our _____. (1 John 3:5)
4. _____ and Delilah.
5. Fruit drink.
6. "Peanuts" character.
7. Indefinite article.
10. Another spelling for a grain. (Ex. 9:32)
13. _____ shall be hid from mine eyes. (Hosea 13:14)
17. My sons, be not now _____. (2 Chron. 29:11)
18. Son of man _____ and saves that which was lost. (Luke 19:10)
19. Popular warm-weather sport.
20. Texas basketball team.
22. _____ the decree of the king. (Jonah 3:7)
23. Female lamb used in sacrifices.
27. Do they not _____ that devise evil? (Prov. 14:22)
31. State (abbr.).
32. Places in Joshua: _____-dor, _____-Haddah, _____-Hazor. (one word)
34. Garden.
37. Esther spake _____ again. (Es. 8:3)
39. _____ Maria (Hail Mary).
40. Past tense of "light."
42. The 16th letter of the Greek alphabet.
43. Opposite of "out."

Puzzle 21

Gladys Johnson

ACROSS CLUES

1. Woman who gleaned Boaz' fields.
4. I will _____ them from death. (Hosea 13:14)
7. Informal word for sibling.
9. A dueling sword.
11. One tenth of a dollar.
13. Organ of hearing.
14. To allow or permit.
15. Informal word for "mother."
17. The Holy Ghost shall come upon _____. (Luke 1:35)
19. Moses' father-in-law. (Ex. 18:5)
22. In the same manner.
24. To note maiden name.
25. Any monkey.
27. To walk proudly.
30. A metal of low strength.
32. Used in rowing.
33. A nephew of Abram. (Gen. 12:5)

34. Mary _____ the feet of Jesus. (John 12:3)
37. A chum.
39. To cast off.
40. A printing measure.
41. Second letter of Greek alphabet.
42. A mineral spring.
43. To become ragged.
45. And _____ bare Abram a son. (Gen. 16:15)
48. Introducing an alternative.
49. A negative vote.
50. Small child.
51. A heavenly messenger.

DOWN CLUES

1. To tear.
2. Not capable of any service.
3. A male.
4. And they parted his _____, and cast lots. (Luke 23:34)
5. Female deer.
6. The first mother.
7. And he _____ forth a raven. (Gen. 8:7)
8. Jesus had _____ from the grave.
10. Large shoe size.
12. A companion.
16. Emergency Room (abbr.).
18. A sound of triumph.
20. When _____ the king had heard these things. (Matt. 2:3)
21. A cereal grain.
23. A quality of character.
26. And delivered him to Pontius _____ the governor. (Matt. 27:2)
28. An instrument to aid in manual work.
29. A water vessel.
31. Thy word is a _____ unto my feet. (Ps. 119:105)
33. Forty days of fasting prior to Easter.
35. Captain of a floating zoo.
36. Rip or rend.
37. For each.
38. To dip a liquid.
41. A thick mass of ice.
42. Thou art my beloved _____. (Mark 1:11)
43. To make an edging.
44. Large measure of weight.
46. Position.
47. And Jethro said to Moses, _____ in peace. (Ex. 4:18)

Puzzle 22

Joan M. Jarzebinski

ACROSS CLUES

1. Sister of Lazarus. (John 11:2)
3. _____ seek ye first the kingdom of God. (Matt. 6:33)
6. But _____ ye first the kingdom of God. (Matt. 6:33)
9. I _____. (John 8:58)
10. _____ said, except a man be born again. (John 3:3)
12. Actual.
13. I _____ to prepare a place for you. (John 14:2)
14. In_____.
15. Charged particle.
17. Let both _____ together until the harvest. (Matt. 13:30)
18. Through faith unto _____. (1 Pet. 1:5)
20. Help for the alcoholic (abbr.).
22. _____ hath not seen, nor ear heard. (1 Cor. 2:9)
23. Eat.
24. He killed Goliath.
30. Whatsoever is not of faith is _____. (Rom. 14:23)
32. Precedes "one," "body," and "way."
33. They have beaten me, and I _____ it not. (Prov. 23:35)
35. _____ ye holy. (Lev. 20:7)
36. Not down but _____.
37. Father, Son, and Holy Ghost.

39. _____, now speakest thou plainly. (John 16:29)
40. Joy.
43. Let not your _____ be troubled. (John 14:1)
46. "Highway to _____," Michael Landon's show.
48. I love _____.
49. Landlord's income.

DOWN CLUES

1. See 1 across.
2. Morning.
3. My _____ Son. (Matt. 3:17)
4. We.
5. _____boat Annie.
7. Time without end.
8. The fear of the Lord is the beginning of _____. (Prov. 1:7)
10. Prison.
11. God _____ loved the world. (John 3:16)
16. No.
17. _____ is love. (1 John 4:8)
19. He invented the light bulb (initials).
21. Classified _____.
25. For we shall see him _____ he is. (1 John 3:2)
26. He will swallow up death in _____. (Isa. 25:8)
27. Not out.
28. "_____ Hymn of the Republic."
29. I am the way, the _____, and the life. (John 14:6)
31. _____ of lions. (Dan. 6:16)

33. Parable of the _____ tree. (Matt. 24:32)
34. I am the _____ of the world. (John 8:12)
35. Not _____ might. (Zech. 4:6)
38. 365 days.
39. Do, Re, Mi, Fa, So, _____.

41. Adam's mate.
42. Go to the _____, thou sluggard. (Prov. 6:6)
44. Former.
45. _____ God be the glory.
47. Printer's measure.

Puzzle 23

Cheryl Keiser

ACROSS CLUES

1. To glorify or honor.
5. Form by heating and hammering.
9. Her (opposite).
10. "Much _____ About Nothing."
11. Body part for hearing.
12. Anno Domini (abbr.).
13. Republican party (abbr.).
15. X-ray person (abbr.).
16. Railroad.
17. O Lord,..._____ me. (Jer. 15:15)
20. _____ unto others....
21. A Gadite. (1 Chron. 5:15)
22. Submit yourselves unto the _____. (1 Pet. 5:5)
25. Springs.
27. Sweet fluid made by bees.
30. Knock.
32. Come ____ with me. (1 Kgs. 13:7)
36. Do, Re, Mi, _____.
37. Nimble.
38. Persia.
39. Name given to Esau. (Gen. 32:3)

41. He that goeth forth..., bearing precious _____. (Ps. 126:6)
42. To be unwell.
43. There came a _____ over ...Egypt. (Acts 7:11)
46. Small amount.
47. Royal city of the Canaanites. (Josh. 17:11)
49. Unleavened bread in the tabernacle.
50. Single unit.

DOWN CLUES

1. Egyptian ruler.
2. To travel on.
3. I _____. (John 8:58)
4. In them did _____. (1 Pet. 1:11)
5. I will not _____ thy word. (Ps. 119:16)
6. With reference to (abbr.).
7. _____ of Eden.
8. For the _____ of the people. (Heb. 9:7)
10. Large monkey.

14. Amorite king. (Josh. 13:12)
18. This man's religion is _____. (Jam. 1:26)
19. What did you say?
23. City south of Jerusalem. (Josh. 10:3)
24. Princess _____.
26. Mountain range in Soviet Union.
28. Minor prophet.
29. Test.
30. In thy majesty _____. (Ps. 45:4)
31. Physical education (abbr.).
33. Metal-bearing rock.
34. Girl's name.
35. His name shall _____ for ever. (Ps. 72:17)
36. Extraordinary acts.
40. Ye _____ Country Inn.
43. Tap gently.
44. Now _____ we the sons of God. (1 John 3:2)
45. Theodore (nickname).
47. Blessed are they that _____ his commandments. (Rev. 22:14)
48. Off (opposite).

Puzzle 24

Pamela Jensen

ACROSS CLUES

1. _____, O isles, unto me. (Isa. 49:1)
6. Nor ear _____. (1 Cor. 2:9)
11. _____ one another. (1 Thes. 5:11)
12. Ten _____ of vineyard. (Isa. 5:10)
14. The _____ commandments. (Ex. 34:28)
15. Called the altar _____. (Josh. 22:34)
17. Joan of _____.
18. Connecticut (abbr.).
19. Tasmania (abbr.).
20. _____ be it. (Josh. 2:21)
21. Bow thine _____ to my understanding. (Prov. 5:1)
23. He called the name of that place Beth-_____. (Gen. 28:19)
24. But _____...receiveth us not. (3 John 9)
27. Agricultural (abbr.).
28. _____ to teach. (2 Tim. 2:24)
29. Each (abbr.).
31. Sign for Jesus.
32. Christ is the _____ of the church. (Eph. 5:23)
34. They which _____ in Asia. (Acts 19:10)
35. Scottish painter Sir Henry _____.
37. Electrical engineer (abbr.).
38. A _____ without blemish. (Lev. 5:15)
39. Local mean time (abbr.).
41. To give help.
42. Hebrews (abbr.).
44. Bowels did _____. (Gen. 43:30)
47. Errors excepted (abbr.).
48. Utah (abbr.).
49. Love one _____. (Rom. 13:8)
51. Dwell at _____. (Ps. 25:13)
53. Difficult experience that tests character.
54. God will _____ my soul. (Ps. 49:15)

DOWN CLUES

1. Written a _____ unto you. (Heb. 13:22)
2. Model of perfection.
3. Confess our _____. (1 John 1:9)
4. Territorial force (abbr.).
5. In his _____. (Ps. 18:24)
7. Give _____ to my prayer. (Ps. 55:1)
8. Good and _____ before God. (1 Tim. 5:4)
9. Railroad (abbr.).
10. A _____ from Caesar. (Luke 2:1)
13. Saint (abbr.).
16. Ye everlasting _____. (Ps. 24:7)
17. _____ believed God. (Jam. 2:23)
22. _____ Lord God! (Ezek. 11:13)
24. I...called _____ upon thee. (Ps. 88:9)
25. Fencing sword.
26. They were _____ asunder. (Heb. 11:37)
30. Stand in _____. (Ps. 4:4)
33. I was _____ with silence. (Ps. 39:2)
34. Thou shalt _____ me thrice. (Matt. 26:34)
35. Short for "radiation."
36. Right (abbr.).
38. Rhode Island (abbr.).
40. Kingdom of heaven is at _____. (Matt. 3:2)

41. American National Theatre and Academy (abbr.).
42. _____ healeth the broken. (Ps. 147:3)
43. A single article.
45. Incline thine _____ unto me. (Ps. 17:6)
46. My beloved is like a _____. (Song of Sol. 2:9)
47. They _____ in vision. (Isa. 28:7)
48. The _____ of edifying. (Eph. 4:29)
50. House of Lords (abbr.).
51. Mr. Sullivan.
52. Architectural-engineering (abbr.).

Puzzle 25

N. Teri Grottke

ACROSS CLUES

1. God told him to marry an unfaithful wife.
5. Law, ordinance. (Ex. 15:25)
10. Period of time.
11. Before Abraham was, _____ _____. (John 8:58; 2 words)
12. Judah's oldest son. (Gen. 38:3)
13. Proverbs king. (Prov. 31:1)
15. Nimrod's city. (Gen. 10:10)
18. David's successor. (1 Chron. 29:23)
20. Son of Boaz. (Ruth 4:21)
22. For this _____ is mount Sinai in Arabia. (Gal. 4:25)
24. Even of _____ my people is risen up. (Micah 2:8)
25. Next to him repaired _____ the son of Jeshua. (Neh. 3:19)
26. Mom.
28. Muppim, and Huppim, and _____. (Gen. 46:21)
30. Fifth son of Jacob. (Gen. 30:6)
32. The prophet to Hezekiah. (2 Kgs. 20:14)

35. A servant of Saul. (2 Sam. 9:9)
36. "A note to follow so."
37. Hewers of wood and _____s of water. (Josh. 9:23)
40. I _____ hath sent me. (Ex. 3:14)
42. Then the Spirit came upon _____. (1 Chron. 12:18)
44. If ye believe not that I am _____. (John 8:24)
45. Samuel's mentor. (1 Sam. 3:1)
47. King of Bashan. (Num. 21:33)
48. And _____ called the light Day. (Gen. 1:5)
49. And he built _____ in the wilderness. (2 Chron. 8:4)
51. A musical Levite. (1 Chron. 15:18)
52. An enlisted man.
54. Postscript (abbr.).
55. He shewed himself alive after his _____. (Acts 1:3)

DOWN CLUES

1. A greeting.
2. Oregon (abbr.).
3. He anointed David king over Israel. (1 Sam. 16:13)
4. Large monkeys. (1 Kgs. 10:22)
5. Spanish "yes."
6. _____ and Hermon shall rejoice in thy name. (Ps. 89:12)
7. _____, and Shema, and Moladah. (Josh. 15:26)
8. Telephone (abbr.).
9. _____...was wicked in the sight of the Lord. (Gen. 38:7)

14. But to do justly, and to _____ mercy. (Micah 6:8)
16. David's great-grandfather. (Ruth 4:21,22)
17. The fishers shall stand upon it from _____. (Ezek. 47:10)
19. Either/_____.
21. He defeated Goliath. (1 Sam. 17:49)
23. Went down unto _____. (Josh. 18:18)
25. Education (abbr.).
26. Type of grain. (Ezek. 4:9)
27. Solomon's great grandson. (1 Ch. 3:10)
29. Like two young _____ that are twins. (Song of Sol. 4:5)
31. But by my _____ Jehovah was I not known. (Ex. 6:3)
33. Son of Jether. (1 Chron. 7:38)
34. And _____ communed with them. (Gen. 34:8)
38. Shall be astonished, and _____ his head. (Jer. 18:16)
39. Violent outbursts of temper.
41. Covers.
43. Electrically charged particles.
46. The lot is cast into the _____. (Prov. 16:33)
50. _____/OFF.
51. Bachelor of Arts.
52. Shall the shadow _____ forward ten degrees. (2 Kgs. 20:9)
53. Being warned of God _____ a dream. (Matt. 2:12)

Puzzle 26

Marge Lifto

ACROSS CLUES

1. Thou shalt not muzzle the _____. (1 Tim. 5:18)
2. To put on a garment.
5. _____ of me, and I shall give thee. (Ps. 2:8)
8. Washington, _____.
10. Set the city on _____. (Josh. 8:19)
11. The wicked _____ their bow. (Ps. 11:2)
12. _____, the winter is past. (Sons of Sol. 2:11)
14. Why _____ we here? (2 Kgs. 7:3)
15. A time to be born, and a time to _____. (Ec. 3:2)
16. 40 (Roman numeral).
17. Mexican fare.
19. _____ with her suburbs. (1 Chron. 6:70)
21. A place to store coal.
22. An elevated track.
23. From whence cometh my _____. (Ps. 121:1)
24. I will break also the _____ of Damascus. (Amos 1:5)
25. Time in nothing _____. (Acts 17:21)
28. Biblical word for "wash."
31. The 7th Greek letter.
32. _____, lama sabachthani. (Matt. 27:46)
33. Subject for an essay.
35. Delivers a blow.
37. New Testament (abbr.).

38. I go _____ prepare a place for you. (John 14:2)
39. To begin.
42. Elimelech's wife. (Ruth 1:2)
45. _____ up and walk. (Luke 5:23)
47. In the year of our Lord (abbr.).
48. Where Christ was placed after His Crucifixion.
49. A heavenly garden.

DOWN CLUES

1. Thou anointest my head with _____. (Ps. 23:5)
2. Jesus had 12 _____. (Matt. 10:1)
3. Which maketh Arcturus, _____, and Pleiades. (Job 9:9)
4. They forsook their _____. (Mark 1:18)
5. Son of Shammua. (Neh. 11:17)
6. To fish a certain way.
7. Let us _____ before the Lord. (Ps. 95:6)
9. When they were come to the place, which is called _____. (Luke 23:33)
13. Old Testament (abbr.).
18. Having the ability.
20. _____, O Israel. (Zeph. 3:14)
24. To exist.
26. Limits to a certain amount.
27. As far as the _____ is from the west. (Ps. 103:12)
28. _____ some evil take me. (Gen. 19:19)
29. The _____ tree shall flourish. (Ec. 12:5)
30. Seven (Roman numeral).
34. The sun waxed _____. (Ex. 16:21)
36. A shade tree.

39. _____ on the right hand of God. (Mark 16:19)
40. Put on strength, O _____ of the Lord. (Isa. 51:9)
41. Adam lost one for Eve.

43. Not young.
44. Hotel.
46. For example (abbr.).
47. I _____ the bread of life. (John 6:35)

Puzzle 27

Bethany Keeny

ACROSS CLUES

1. The _____ our God will we serve. (Josh. 24:24)
4. The Lord smelled a sweet _____. (Gen. 8:21)
10. _____ they can save thee. (Jer. 2:28)
11. Any _____ thing shall not be eaten. (Lev. 7:19)
13. Tennessee (abbr.).
14. This _____ that.
15. Miscellaneous (abbr.).
16. _____ if he shall ask an egg. (Luke 11:12)
17. And shall _____ thee on a tree. (Gen. 40:19)
19. To cut.
20. I give _____ of all that I possess. (Luke 18:12)
23. _____ thou at my right hand. (Ps. 110:1)
24. "_____ Night, Holy Night."

26. _____ that men would praise the Lord. (Ps. 107:31)
27. Charity suffereth long, and _____ kind. (1 Cor. 13:4)
29. Jacob married _____ after the first seven years of work. (Gen. 29:23)
30. Very slow to move.
31. Smote him with the _____ of their hands. (Matt. 26:67)
33. Delaware (abbr.).
34. Is _____ for the kingdom of God. (Luke 9:62)
35. Opposite of "out."
36. _____ the Lion.
37. And Huppim, the children of _____. (1 Chron. 7:12)
38. _____ the high priest, and Caiaphas. (Acts 4:6)
40. Home of the Andes mountains.
41. Opposite of "wrong."
43. God caused a deep _____ to fall upon Adam. (Gen. 2:21)
44. To pester.
46. Dead _____.
48. Second note of the musical scale.
49. And I will raise _____ against thee. (Isa. 29:3)

DOWN CLUES

1. Neither do men _____ a candle. (Matt. 5:15)
2. Ye are the light _____ the world. (Matt. 5:14)
3. For the land, nor yet for the _____. (Luke 14:35)
4. South Carolina (abbr.).
5. Do not your _____ before men. (Matt. 6:1)
6. The _____ of the temple was rent. (Luke 23:45)
7. A body of water in the desert.
8. But ye have an _____ from the Holy One. (1 John 2:20)
9. Is God _____ who taketh vengeance? (Rom. 3:5)
12. North Dakota (abbr.).
13. Paul was told _____ go _____ Macedonia. (one word)
14. Go to the _____s, thou sluggard. (Prov. 6:6)
18. Joshua sent men from Jericho to _____. (Josh. 7:2)
21. The _____ shall melt with fervent heat. (2 Pet. 3:10)
22. The waters called he _____. (Gen. 1:10)
25. New Hampshire (abbr.).
26. And laid the wood in _____. (Gen. 22:9)
28. I will pour out my _____ unto you. (Prov. 1:23)
30. There was no room in the _____.
32. Did eat _____ thine own table. (2 Sam. 19:28)
34. I am like a green _____ tree. (Hosea 14:8)
35. John was exiled to the _____ of Patmos. (Rev. 1:9)
36. Jesus healed ten, but only one _____ thanked him. (Luke 17:12-17)
38. Of their shame that say _____, aha. (Ps. 70:3)
39. _____ the hart panteth. (Ps. 42:1)
40. Mexican money.
42. Precious jewel.
45. A suffix used to show comparison.
47. _____ her feet he bowed. (Judg. 5:27)

Puzzle 28 (NIV)

Janet Hopper

ACROSS CLUES

1. Slayer of Goliath.
   (1 Sam. 17:49)
5. Moses' successor. (Deut. 34:9)
10. Prayer ending.
11. Ark builder. (Gen. 6)
12. Zirconium (abbr.).
13. Joab heard this in the city.
    (1 Kgs. 1:41-45)
15. Husband of Sarah. (Gen. 17:15)
17. Moslem faith.
18. Isaac caught the _____ of his clothes. (Gen. 27:27)
19. Pharaoh of Egypt. (2 Kgs. 23:29)
20. God.
21. Organ mentioned in preparing offerings. (Lev. 3:4)
24. Saul's height compared with others. (1 Sam. 9:2)
26. Spanish affirmative.
27. The Lord lifts the needy from the _____ heap. (1 Sam. 2:8)
29. The priest's robe had bells and pomegranates around its _____. (Ex. 39:26)
30. The _____ of the prophet Isaiah was handed to Jesus. (Luke 4:17)
33. Favorite children's game.
34. King of Persia. (Ezra 4:5)
37. God to Moses: I _____.(Ex.3:14)
39. The evil spirit goes through _____ places seeking rest. (Matt. 12:43)
41. In the _____ that King Uzziah died. (Isa. 6:1)
42. Spanish for "river."
43. Number who did not give Jesus thanks. (Luke 17:17)

44. Those who cling to worthless _____ forfeit...grace. (Jonah 2:8)
46. Whatever you _____, work at it with all your heart. (Col.3:23)
47. He who works his land will have _____ food. (Prov. 12:11)
50. Ezra had devoted himself to the _____...of the Law. (Ezra 7:10)
51. He who _____ fantasies lacks judgment. (Prov. 12:11)

DOWN CLUES

1. His diet consisted of only vegetables and water. (Dan. 1:12)
2. One of the shepherds of Tekoa. (Amos 1:1)
3. Moses put this over his face. (2 Cor. 3:13)
4. David feigned to be this. (1 Sam. 21:13)
5. Old Testament man known for his patience.
6. The disciples were straining at these. (Mark 6:48)
7. Israel had participated in _____ prostitution. (Jer. 13:27)
8. Son of Joktan. (Gen. 10:27)
9. Gold jewelry offered to the Lord. (Num. 31:50)
11. Owned vineyard coveted by King Ahab. (1 Kgs. 21:2)
14. The fourth jewel decorating the foundation of heaven's wall. (Rev. 21:19)
16. Brother of Shomer. (1 Chron. 7:35)
22. Judas _____, betrayer of Jesus. (Matt. 26:14)
23. The _____ will be with child. (Matt. 1:23)

25. Left hand (abbr.).

28. Abraham took the knife to _____ his son. (Gen. 22:10)

30. The house of the righteous _____ firm. (Prov. 12:7)

31. Central Intelligence Agency (abbr.).

32. The rich will _____ at the misery coming them. (Jam. 5:1)

35. One must keep a tight _____ on the tongue. (Jam. 1:26)

36. Husband of Bathsheba. (2 Sam. 11:3)

38. Raised by the daughter of Pharaoh. (Ex. 2:10)

40. Herod thought John the Baptist had returned from being this. (Matt. 14:2)

42. Envy _____ the bones. (Prov. 14:30)

45. Genetic material.

48. Beside.

49. Washington, _____.

Puzzle 29

Karen Bush

ACROSS CLUES

1. He shall send his _____ before thee. (Gen. 24:7)
5. Three strands intertwined, typically hair.
10. For every head shall be _____. (Jer. 48:37)
11. A toothed wheel.
12. I and my Father are _____. (John 10:30)
13. Like a high wall in his own _____. (Prov. 18:11 NAS)
15. Children of Israel _____ the house of the Lord. (1 Kgs. 8:63)
16. A young person.
18. The kingdom of heaven is like unto a _____. (Matt. 13:47)
19. Plural of 18 across.
20. Shall he _____ in harvest. (Prov. 20:4)
22. Love of _____ is the root of all evil. (1 Tim. 6:10)
25. Behold, the _____ is become as one of us. (Gen. 3:22)

26. An expression of acknowledgment.
27. Abbreviation for a washroom.
28. _____ he went and took Gomer. (Hosea 1:3)
29. And _____ and Abihu. (Lev. 10:1)
31. Our fathers did eat manna in the _____. (John 6:31)
33. River in Lebanon.
35. Put on the _____ of light. (Rom. 13:12 NAS)
38. Suitable for a king.
40. _____ prophet is accepted in his own country. (Luke 4:24)
41. Even as a _____ tree casteth. (Rev. 6:13)
43. Genuine.
44. To write specifications.
46. And there appeared _____ angel. (Luke 22:43)
47. Nickname for Theodore.
48. Book of the Bible following Joel.
49. Flushes with water.
50. Crafty.

DOWN CLUES

1. Who shall _____ in thy tabernacle? (Ps.15:1)
2. How excellent is thy _____! (Ps. 8:1)
3. A wise son maketh a _____ father. (Prov. 10:1)
4. Border.
5. _____ your plowshares. (Joel 3:10)
6. To value.
7. Excessively dry.
8. Immediately you will find a _____. (Matt. 21:2 NAS)

9. Blessed is he who _____. (Rev. 1:3 NAS)
11. Ye blind guides, which strain at a _____. (Matt. 23:24)
14. From the breath of God _____ is made. (Job 37:10 NAS)
17. For _____ was dry upon the fleece only. (Judg. 6:40)
19. I _____ knew you. (Matt. 7:23)
20. Take the prophets of _____. (1 Kgs. 18:40)
21. Opposite of "beginning."
23. Bravo!
24. Of or relating to the nose.
25. Symbol for manganese.
26. Sing, _____ _____, thou that didst not bear. (Isa. 54:1; 2 words)
28. Shall not leave in thee one _____ upon another. (Luke 19:44)
30. But _____ the end it shall speak. (Hab. 2:3)
31. If a man shall _____ _____ pit. (Ex. 21:33; 2 words)
32. Ream (abbr.).
34. God shall supply all your _____. (Phil. 4:19 NAS)
36. And the other seed fell on _____ soil. (Luke 8:6 NAS)
37. From a great distance.
39. _____ master! For it was borrowed. (2 Kgs. 6:5)
42. When they couch _____ their dens. (Job 38:40)
44. For they neither _____ nor reap. (Luke 12:24)
45. Greek letter following chi.
47. Tone following La.

Puzzle 30

Glen G. Luscher

ACROSS CLUES

1. But ye shall receive _____. (Acts 1:8)
5. A son of Midian. (Gen. 25:4)
10. _____ the voice of the Lord. (Deut. 27:10)
11. We shall not all _____. (1 Cor. 15:51)
12. The Word was _____ flesh. (John 1:14)
13. My sins are not _____ from thee. (Ps. 69:5)
14. Son of Enoch. (Gen. 4:18)
16. Plural (abbr.).
17. Adina was his son. (1 Chron. 11:42)
19. Whosoever shall _____ the will of God. (Mark 3:35)
21. Imitation.
22. Great grandson of Asher. (1 Chron. 7:32)
24. Ruth's husband.
25. To gather.
28. Capital of Italy.
29. Father of Salathiel. (Luke 3:27)
32. An adversary.
34. Under the _____ they were gathered. (Job 30:7)
36. Type of palm.
37. He is faithful and just _____ forgive us. (1 John 1:9)
39. He _____ him, and said to him. (2 Kgs. 10:15)
40. He saith among the trumpets, _____. (Job 39:25)
41. Shechem's father. (Gen. 34:2)
43. Bartimaeus..._____ by the highway. (Mark 10:46)
44. Ephraim's grandson. (Num. 26:35-36)
45. Bring thee a _____ heifer. (Num. 19:2)
46. _____ on this side, and _____ on that side. (Josh 8:22; one word)

DOWN CLUES

1. The _____ of her strength shall cease. (Ezek. 30:18)
2. A son of Joktan. (Gen. 10:28)
3. With this ring, I thee _____.
4. Blessed are the _____ which see. (Luke 10:23)
5. Name of Shedeur's son. (Num. 7:30)
6. A lever operated by the foot.
7. _____ shall save his people. (Matt. 1:21)
8. Ye are our _____. (2 Cor. 3:2)
9. Son of Hillel. (Judg. 12:13)
11. Son of Harim. (Ezra 10:31)
15. Women _____ themselves in modest apparel. (1 Tim. 2:9)
18. She touched the _____ of his garment. (Matt. 9:20)
20. Son of Mahli. (1 Chron. 6:46)
22. For it is _____ cut off. (Ps. 90:10)
23. David's older brother. (1 Chron. 2:15)
24. Neither left they any to _____. (Josh. 11:14)
25. And all her _____ men were bound. (Nahum 3:10)
26. A covered coach.
27. Who gave himself a ransom for _____. (1 Tim. 2:6)

30. His seed shall _____ for ever.
(Ps. 89:36)
31. In his _____ shall stand up a vile
person. (Dan. 11:21)
33. Two days, or a month, or a
_____. (Num. 9:22)
35. Short for Theodore.

38. A paddle.
39. Thou art my beloved _____.
(Luke 3:22)
40. Noah's son. (Gen. 5:32)
42. Another name for mother.
43. His sickness was _____ sore.
(1 Kgs. 17:17)

63

1	2	3	4		5	6	7	8	9		10	11
12					13						14	
15					16				17	18		
19			20				21					
		22				23						24
25		26				27			28			
29					30							
		31		32				33		34		
35	36			37		38	39	40		41		
42			43		44		45		46			
47		48						49				
50				51		52		53				
	54				55							

Puzzle 31

Glenn G. Luscher

ACROSS CLUES

1. In the uttermost parts of the _____. (Num. 11:1)
5. A son of Shemaiah. (1 Chron. 3:22)
10. And she said, Yea, for _____ much. (Acts 5:8)
12. A son of Eliphaz. (Gen. 36:11)
13. The legs of the _____ are not equal. (Prov. 26:7)
14. Used before a noun.

15. Speck.
16. And ye shall eat the _____ of the land. (Gen. 45:18)
17. A _____bearer revealeth secrets. (Prov. 11:13)
19. But love ye your _____. (Luke 6:35)
21. Where moth and _____ doth corrupt. (Matt. 6:19)
22. Paul sent him into Macedonia. (Acts 19:22)
26. The 12th month of the Jewish sacred year. (Es. 3:7)
27. A son of Shashak.(1 Chron 8:22)
29. Youngest son of Jesse.
30. A son of Joktan. (Gen. 10:29)

64

31. Extraterrestrial (abbr.).
32. Desired _____ him letters to Damascus. (Acts 9:2)
33. I will divide Shechem, and _____ out. (Ps. 108:7)
35. The last one.
38. As a thread of _____ is broken. (Judg. 16:9)
41. Why is thy spirit so _____? (1 Kgs. 21:5)
42. The word of the Lord _____ with him. (2 Kgs 3:12)
43. A drink made from leaves.
45. To open before him the two leaved _____. (Isa. 45:1)
47. Mountain city of Judah. (Josh. 15:52)
49. His clothes shall be _____. (Lev. 13:45)
50. In _____ season we shall reap. (Gal. 6:9)
51. Will men take a _____. (Ezek. 15:3)
53. When they _____ in at the gates. (Ezek. 44:17)
54. Abraham set seven _____ lambs. (Gen. 21:28)
55. Neither shall he...eat _____ grapes. (Num. 6:3)

DOWN CLUES

1. _____ near, ye nations, to hear. (Isa. 34:1)
2. Why seek ye the living _____ the dead? (Luke 24:5)
3. Companion.
4. Take no thought...neither do ye _____. (Mark 13:11)
6. A sea of _____ mingled with fire. (Rev. 15:2)
7. No man _____ fruit of thee hereafter. (Mark 11:14)
8. God said unto Moses, I _____. (Ex. 3:14)
9. Son of Dedan. (Gen. 25:3)
10. No fountain both yield _____ water and fresh. (Jam. 3:12)
11. Be not ignorant of this _____ thing. (2 Pet. 3:8)
16. I will not _____ what man shall do. (Heb. 13:6)
18. Let him be _____ the younger. (Luke 22:26)
20. Son of Enoch. (Gen. 4:18)
21. Can the _____ grow up without mire? (Job 8:11)
23. Put it upon the _____ of the right ear. (Lev. 14:25)
24. Until they have _____ all my harvest. (Ruth 2:21)
25. The churches...were _____. (Acts 9:31)
26. Inhabitant from the plain of _____. (Amos 1:5)
28. _____ yourselves before the Lord. (1 Sam. 10:19)
30. I punished them _____. (Acts 26:11)
34. Ye have _____ that the Lord is gracious. (1Pet. 2:3)
36. Her _____ in her flesh be blood. (Lev. 15:19)
37. Rejoice ye in that day, and _____. (Luke 6:23)
39. Defeated king of Bashan. (Deu. 3:3)
40. Cast forth the _____. (Jonah 1:5)
44. City northwest of Judah. (Josh. 15:50)
46. He sat in the _____ door in the heat. (Gen. 18:1)
48. _____ down the tree. (Dan. 4:14)
52. Negative reply.

Puzzle 32

Janet W. Adkins

ACROSS CLUES

1. Dance step.
4. David took an _____, and played with his hand. (1 Sam. 16:23)
8. The reeds and _____s shall wither. (Isa. 19:6)
12. Indian tribe.
13. Unusual person or thing.
14. Recently deceased.
15. The liberal soul shall be made _____.(Prov. 11:25)
16. Insect parts.
17. The day cometh, that shall burn as an _____. (Mal. 4:1)
18. The worlds were _____ by the word of God. (Heb. 11:3)
20. Yet the _____ man is renewed day by day. (2 Cor. 4:16)
22. Compass direction.
23. For we shall _____ him as he is. (1 John 3:2)
24. To them that are sanctified in Christ Jesus, called to be _____. (1 Cor. 1:2)
27. He which converteth the sinner from the _____ of his way. (James 5:20; plural)
31. Flawed merchandise (abbr).
32. Residence (abbr.).
33. Thou art _____ , O Lord. (Ps. 119:151; comparative)
37. I thank Christ Jesus our Lord, who hath _____d me. (1 Tim.1:12)
40. Anger.
41. That the light shall _____ be clear. (Zech. 14:6)
42. And his feet shall stand in that day upon the mount of _____. (Zech. 14:4)

45. _____ not yourselves, but rather give place unto wrath. (Rom. 12:19)
49. Fetch olive branches, and _____ branches. (Neh. 8:15)
50. River flowing to the North Sea.
52. Math branch (abbr.).
53. Arabian prince.
54. _____ and void.
55. May (French).
56. Nevertheless at thy word I will let down the _____. (Luke 5:5)
57. Very (French).
58. Belonging to the talking horse.

DOWN CLUES

1. Knowledge _____eth up. (1 Cor. 8:1)
2. _____oth, and Dibon. (Num. 32:3)
3. Bristles.
4. Provide things _____ in the sight of all men. (Rom. 12:17)
5. Positively charged electrodes.
6. Quit work at 65 (abbr.).
7. I shall yet _____ him for the help of his countenance. (Ps. 42:5)
8. All the goodliness thereof is as the _____ of the field. (Isa. 40:6)
9. Volcano output.
10. The children of _____ of Hezekiah. (Neh. 7:21)
11. Masculine/feminine class (abbr.).
19. _____ of high degree are a lie. (Ps. 62:9)
21. The captain of his host was Abner, the son of _____. (1 Sam.14:50)
24. Be ye angry, and _____ not. (Eph. 4:26)

66

25. Blessed _____ the merciful. (Matt. 5:7)
26. _____ the Ithrite. (1 Chron. 11:40)
28. Sphere.
29. Kin (abbr.).
30. Compass direction.
34. I will extend peace to her like a _____. (Isa. 66:12)
35. Before.
36. To feel bitter.
37. I thank Christ Jesus our Lord, who hath _____d me. (1 Tim.1:12)
38. Long prose narratives.
39. Did eat.
42. His ears are _____ unto their cry. (Ps. 34:15)
43. And the people shall be as the burnings of _____. (Isa. 33:12)
44. First letter of a name (abbr.).
46. Call his _____ Jezreel. (Hos.1:4)
47. Let us be _____ and rejoice. (Rev. 19:7)
48. Protection.
51. Persian tribe member.

Puzzle 33

Janet W. Adkins

ACROSS CLUES

1. Yes (Spanish).
3. Hit sharply.
6. The promise made of none _____. (Rom. 4:14)
11. I _____ thee by God, that thou torment me not. (Mark 5:7)
12. Chinese pagoda.
13. Howl, O Heshbon, for _____ is spoiled. (Jer. 49:3)
14. French article.
15. With (German).
16. 60 minutes (pl.; abbr.).
17. Sierra Leone (abbr.).
19. The angel of the Lord appeared unto him in a _____. (Matt.1:20)
21. GA capital (abbr.).
22. Frog's kin.
25. No room for them in the _____. (Luke 2:7)
26. Heap.
27. A woman that hath a familiar spirit at _____. (1 Sam. 28:7)
29. Who made me a judge or a _____ over you? (Luke 12:14)
31. In the _____(pl.) of the book it is written of me. (Heb.10:7)

68

33. Dip thy morsel in the _____.
(Ruth 2:14)
36. The name of the Lord is a strong
_____. (Prov. 18:10)
40. _____, which was the son of
Seth. (Luke 3:38)
41. The 13th letter of the Hebrew
alphabet.
43. If ye shall ask any thing in my
_____, I will do it. (John 14:14)
44. Serving (abbr.).
45. So Hiram gave Solomon _____
trees. (1 Kgs. 5:10)
47. Continent (abbr.).
48. Light brown.
49. God, which hath not turned away
my prayer, _____ his mercy
from me. (Ps. 66:20)
51. Symbol for gold.
52. The children of Gad called the
altar _____. (Josh. 22:34)
53. How terrible _____ thou in thy
works! (Ps. 66:3)
54. Watching thereunto with
all...supplication for all _____.
(Eph. 6:18)
55. So he that getteth riches...shall
_____ them. (Jer. 17:11)
56. _____ (Kookie) Byrnes.
57. Shoe width.

DOWN CLUES

1. All the saints _____ you.
(2 Cor. 13:13)
2. Chemical suffix.
3. Alcoholic drink.
4. Dry.
5. Lab culture dish.
6. The month _____, which is the
seventh month. (1 Kgs. 8:2)
7. They...went their ways, one to
his _____, another to his

merchandise. (Matt. 22:5)
8. Foreign Agricultural Service
(abbr.).
9. He...entered into the _____, and
told Paul. (Acts 23:16)
10. Cain was a _____ of the ground.
(Gen. 4:2)
18. He...feigned himself _____ in
their hands. (1 Sam. 21:13)
20. Who for the joy that was set
before him _____ the cross.
(Heb. 12:2)
21. _____ and abet.
23. Poti-pherah priest of _____.
(Gen. 41:45)
24. The fourth part of a cab of _____
dung. (2 Kgs. 6:25)
26. River of Eden. (Gen. 2:11)
28. Receipt of goods (abbr.).
30. Animal doctor.
32. That ye shall weep and _____.
(John 16:20)
33. Giving honour unto the wife, as
unto the weaker _____.
(1 Pet. 3:7)
34. Whom thou wouldest not let
Israel _____. (2 Chron. 20:10)
35. Egg drink.
37. And my wrath shall _____ hot.
(Ex. 22:24)
38. Printer's measure.
39. Because they _____ to do
judgment. (Prov. 21:7)
42. Minister's residence.
45. Lord, dost thou not _____?
(Luke 10:40)
46. Whither have ye made a _____
to day? (1 Sam. 27:10)
48. The 23rd letter of the Hebrew
alphabet.
50. I will _____ evil beasts out of
the land. (Lev. 26:6)
51. Did eat.

Puzzle 34

Janet W. Adkins

ACROSS CLUES

1. Trademark.
5. Roman household god.
8. They put on him a purple _____. (John 19:2)
12. Jezebel said to _____, Arise, take possession of the vineyard of Naboth. (1 Kgs. 21:15)
13. Indian tribe.
14. Toward the coast of Edom southward were Kabzeel, and _____. (Josh. 15:21)
15. He shall also bring him to the door, or unto the door _____. (Ex. 21:6)
16. Machine part.
17. Chinese Communist leader.
18. Is not _____ on the Levite thy brother? (Ex. 4:14)
20. Put forth too much effort.
22. A wrathful man stirreth up _____. (Prov. 15:18)
25. Contend.
26. Places where David himself and his men were wont to _____. (1 Sam. 30:31)
27. There sat women weeping for _____. (Ezek. 8:14)
30. Alas.
31. One book of a series (abbr.).
32. Type of grass (Biblical sp.).
34. And let all the angels of God _____ him. (Heb. 1:6)
37. Therefore have I set my face like a _____. (Isa. 50:7)
39. European Economic Community.
40. As men enter a into city wherein is made a _____. (Ezek. 26:10)
41. There shall be no more thence an _____ of days. (Isa. 65:20)
44. Same sort as "i" and "u".
45. "Do," third person.
46. Mouth.
48. Use not _____ repetitions. (Matt. 6:7)
52. Holy Roman Emperor (962-973).
53. Mrs. Jimmy Carter.
54. To be (French).
55. Yet will they _____ upon the Lord. (Micah 3:11)
56. When there were _____ three months to the harvest. (Amos 4:7)
57. Know that it is _____, even at the doors. (Matt. 24:33)

DOWN CLUES

1. Separate those who _____ the water...like a dog. (Judg. 7:5 NIV)
2. Interjection.
3. Fuel.
4. So run, that ye may _____. (1 Cor. 9:24)
5. Not greedy of filthy _____. (1 Tim. 3:8)
6. Indonesian.
7. Taking away.
8. That he might _____ us from all iniquity. (Titus 2:14)
9. River to the Baltic Sea.
10. And they _____ their tongues like their bow for lies. (Jer. 9:3)
11. Therefore.
19. Stern of a ship.
21. Zest.
22. Study to _____ thyself approved. (2 Tim. 2:15; modern sp.)
23. Mexican food.
24. German river.

27. The veil of the temple was rent in twain from the _____ to the bottom. (Matt. 27:51)
28. And when _____h was come unto him, David demanded of him. (2 Sam. 11:7)
29. White metal.
31. Them that had gotten the _____ over the beast. (Rev. 15:2)
33. Biblical suffix.
35. They should rest yet for a little _____. (Rev. 6:11)
36. As a __ ___ gathereth her chickens. (Matt. 23:37)
37. Is a vanity tossed to and _____. (Prov. 21:6)
38. Beware of the _____ of the Pharisees. (Matt. 16:6)
40. Set him on his own _____. (Luke 10:34)
41. The golden calf.
42. Short letter.
43. Type of cheese.
47. Deliver thyself as a _____ from the hand of the hunter. (Prov. 6:5)
49. Did eat.
50. _____ the Ithrite. (1 Chron. 11:40)
51. And _____ begat Kish. (1 Chron. 8:33)

71

1	2	3		4	5	6	7		8	9	10	11
12				13					14			
15			16						17			
18						19		20				
			21		22		23				24	25
26	27	28		29		30		31				
32			33		34		35		36			
37				38		39		40		41		
42					43		44		45			
		46				47		48		49	50	51
52	53				54		55					
56					57					58		
59					60					61		

Puzzle 35

Janet W. Adkins

ACROSS CLUES

1. Separate those who _____ the water...like a dog. (Judg. 7:5 NIV)
4. _____ fast that which is good. (1 Thes. 5:21)
8. Kaffir warrior.
12. Nigerian Negro.
13. Away from the wind.
14. Woman's name.
15. So can no _____ both yield salt water and fresh. (Jam. 3:12)
17. A family name.
18. But is under _____s and governors. (Gal. 4:2)
19. _____, I have somewhat to say unto thee. (Luke 7:40)
21. In the morning the _____ lay round about the host. (Ex.16:13)
23. Then the _____ of the house shall be brought unto the judges. (Ex. 22:8)
26. And _____ begat Kish. (1 Chron. 8:33)

29. Cast into the _____ of lions. (Dan. 6:7)
31. O _____, where is thy sting? (1 Cor. 15:55)
32. Hereafter ye shall see heaven _____. (John 1:51)
34. Noise.
36. A certain Pharisee besought him to _____ with him. (Luke 11:37)
37. The _____ threw him to the ground. (Luke 9:42 NIV)
39. Mazel.
41. No (Scottish).
42. Thou shalt not _____ a kid in his mother s milk. (Ex. 23:19)
44. Securities and Exchange Commission (abbr.).
46. Shopping meccas.
48. They were counted worthy to suffer _____ for his name. (Acts 5:41)
52. Virginia Senator.
54. I beseech thee for my son _____. (Philemon 10)
56. By faith _____ offered unto God a more excellent sacrifice. (Heb. 11:4)
57. Glacial snow field.
58. Oven.
59. Thy feet are sunk in the _____. (Jer. 38:22)
60. _____ not the sayings of the prophecy of this book. (Rev. 22:10)
61. We shall _____ him as he is. (1 John 3:2)

DOWN CLUES

1. Wherefore _____ up the hands which hang down. (Heb. 12:12)
2. Father (Arabic).
3. Sulk.
4. Hostility.
5. Woman s name.
6. Hawaiian gifts of greeting.
7. Jeans fabric.
8. Carnal ordinances, _____ on them. (Heb. 9:10)
9. Say unto this _____, Remove hence. (Matt. 17:20)
10. Persona non grata (abbr.).
11. Biblical name ending.
16. And Cain went...and dwelt in the land of _____. (Gen. 4:16)
20. I am not _____, most noble Festus. (Acts 26:25)
22. Marry.
24. Sicilian volcano.
25. Korean president.
26. Dozes.
27. Fencing sword.
28. _____ now thy Creator. (Ec. 12:1)
30. Insect.
33. Having a reputation.
35. Refusal (pl.).
38. National Hockey League. (abbr.).
40. I am like a broken _____. (Ps. 31:12)
43. Belonging to the father of Bashemath. (Gen. 26:34)
45. Greek letter.
47. Dagger.
49. The words of _____, who was among the herdmen. (Amos 1:1)
50. I _____ on the work of thy hands. (Ps. 143:5)
51. This (Spanish).
52. Abraham went and took the _____, and offered him up. (Gen. 22:13)
53. Japanese sash.
55. Form of Eve.

Puzzle 36

Janet W. Adkins

ACROSS CLUES

1. They took them wives of the women of _____. (Ruth 1:4)
5. Expression of disgust.
8. We have seen his _____ in the east. (Matt. 2:2)
12. Domed projection of a church.
13. Because there was no room for them in the _____. (Luke 2:7)
14. _____ and see the works of God. (Ps. 66:5)
15. Doth the eagle...make her _____ on high? (Job 39:27)
16. There is a cup, and the wine is _____. (Ps. 75:8)
17. Curved moldings.
18. Leaders (abbr.).
20. From his shoulders and ____ he was higher. (1 Sam. 9:2)
22. Let us go...three days' journey into the _____. (Ex. 5:3)
25. Belonging to Egyptian sun god.
26. And _____ thine heart to understanding. (Prov. 2:2)
27. My tongue is the __-__ of a ready writer. (Ps. 45:1)
28. Bore his _____ through with a thorn? (Job 41:2)
31. Tumeric.
32. Why is thy spirit so _____? (1 Kgs. 21:5)
33. In the manner of.
34. Evening (poetic).
35. Make lace.
36. The children of..._____. (Neh. 7:47)
38. Machine part.
39. But out of a branch of her roots shall one stand up in his _____. (Dan. 11:7)

40. And the cart came into the field of _____. (1 Sam. 6:14)
43. Insect egg.
44. Jesus cried with a loud voice, saying, _____. (Mark 15:34)
45. Route (abbr.).
47. He...saw others standing _____ in the marketplace. (Matt. 20:3)
51. And have the keys of _____. (Rev. 1:18)
52. _____ _____ he that liveth, and was dead. (Rev 1:18; 2 words)
53. Whither have ye made a _____ to day? (1 Sam. 27:10)
54. Preowned.
55. Is _____ merry? let him sing. (Jam. 5:13)
56. Even unto the _____ of the year. (Deut. 11:12; plural)

DOWN CLUES

1. Will a _____ rob God?(Mal. 3:8)
2. Unlock (poetic).
3. Thy King cometh unto thee: ...riding upon an _____. (Zech. 9:9)
4. _____: but the name of that city was called Luz. (Gen. 28:19)
5. But seek ye _____ the kingdom of God. (Matt. 6:33)
6. Chemical suffix.
7. Who for the joy that was set before him _____ the cross. (Heb 12:2)
8. Flat-bottomed boats.
9. Roman attire.
10. Of U.S. origin (abbr.).
11. A crown...upon his head, and a _____ in his right hand. (Matt. 27:29)
19. And will make Ninevah... _____ like a wilderness. (Zeph. 2:13)

21. Temple vessel: fire _____.
22. For a good man some would even _____ to die. (Rom. 5:7)
23. Fencing sword.
24. Meted out heaven with the _____. (Isa. 40:12)
27. Butter serving unit.
28. And the sons of Onam were, Shammai, and _____. (1 Chron. 2:28)
29. Large quantity (2 words).
30. Opposite of "wax."
32. Then Philip went down to the city of _____, and preached Christ unto them. (Acts 8:5)
35. Greek T.
36. Greek letter.
37. Clothing.
38. Unto us a _____ is born. (Isa. 9:6)
39. Because mine _____ doth not triumph over me. (Ps. 41:11)
40. _____ the Antothite. (1 Chron. 12:3)
41. Corrida cheers.
42. Smote Job...from the _____ of his foot. (Job 2:7)
46. Sunbathe.
48. Put on.
49. Boy.
50. Eight kings of England.

75

Puzzle 37

Judy Ellis

ACROSS CLUES

1. Old Testament book.
12. A son of Shobal. (1 Chron. 1:40)
13. And an hundred sheep, beside harts, and _____. (1 Kgs. 4:23)
15. Veterans' Administration (abbr.).
16. Sailor.
17. Route (abbr.).
18. Twelve months (abbr.).
19. Son of Amoz (abbr.). (2 Kgs. 19:20)
21. Little island.
23. And Eshton begat..._____. (1 Chron. 4:12)
24. _____, and Dumah, and Eshean. (Josh. 15:52)
26. Direction.
27. Old Testament book (2 parts).
33. Branch office (abbr.).
34. United Artists (abbr.).
35. Yet he cheweth not the cud; he is _____. (Lev. 11:7)
36. And he said, _____, it is yet high day. (Gen. 29:7)

76

37. Zacchaeus climbed up into a _____ comore tree. (Luke 19:4)
38. And Ashur the father of _____ had two wives. (1 Chron. 4:5)
39. The throne of _____ and of the Lamb. (Rev. 22:3)
40. Women's Army Corp (abbr.).
42. One who swears to an affidavit.
45. And _____ the daughter of Leah. (Gen. 34:1)
47. Crass.
48. The children of _____, and Hushim, the sons of Aher. (1 Chron. 7:12)
49. And if any man will _____ thee at the law. (Matt. 5:40)
52. Sweet drinks, made from limes or lemons.
53. Fifth Old Testament book.

DOWN CLUES

1. Third Old Testament book.
2. Every one that is proud, and _____ him. (Job 40:11)
3. Pa's mate.
4. Elevated railroad.
5. Illness on Amtrak.
6. Great trunk that carries blood.
7. Tellurium (symbol).
8. Son of Merari. (1 Chron. 24:27)
9. Seven angels came _____ of the temple. (Rev. 15:6)
10. Raleigh is the capital (abbr.).
11. Fair weather: for the _____ is red. (Matt. 16:2)
14. "Mr." in Spanish (abbr.).
16. Light brown.
20. Hushim was his son. (1 Chron. 7:12)
22. Sir, come down _____ my child die. (John 4:49)
24. Association (abbr.).
25. Blood analysis (2 words).
26. And I saw as it were a _____ of glass. (Rev. 15:2)
28. Out of order.
29. Because they called thee an _____, saying, This is Zion. (Jer. 30:17)
30. Direction.
31. As free, and not using your liberty for a _____ of maliciousness. (1 Pet. 2:16, modern sp.)
32. For ye shall be as an oak whose _____ fadeth. (Isa. 1:30)
33. Not a brunette.
39. Flashy.
41. Behold, I send _____ Angel before thee. (Ex. 23:20)
43. Fire control (abbr.).
44. Duke Magdiel, duke _____. (1 Chron. 1:54)
45. Alexander the coppersmith _____ me much evil. (2 Tim. 4:14)
46. Shade.
50. Son of Judah. (Gen. 38:6)
51. Called to be _____ apostle. (Rom. 1:1)

Puzzle 38

Judy Ellis

ACROSS CLUES

2. She _____ me of the tree, and I did eat. (Gen. 3:12)
4. For all the prophets and the law prophesied until _____. (Matt. 11:13)
7. He that sacrificeth unto any god, save _____ the Lord only. (Exo. 22:20)
9. _____, let that night be solitary. (Job 3:7)
11. _____ Saul also among the prophets? (1 Sam. 10:12)
12. They that received tribute money came _____ Peter. (Matt.17:24)
13. The Lord will lighten my _____. (2 Sam. 22:29)
17. The God of my mercy shall prevent _____. (Ps. 59:10)
18. Love worketh no _____ to his neighbour. (Rom. 13:10)
20. And this is the promise that he hath promised us, even eternal _____. (1 John 2:25)
22. Where there is _____ vision, the people perish. (Prov. 29:18)
24. Thou shall not _____ false witness against thy neighbour. (Ex. 20:16)
26. He planteth an _____, and the rain doth nourish it. (Isa. 44:14)
27. Ma's companion.
28. Upon the great _____ of his right foot. (Lev. 8:23)
31. _____ that thou didst not lay these things to thy heart. (Isa. 47:7)
32. And _____ that believed came. (Acts 19:18)
34. That Christ cometh _____ the seed of David. (John 7:42)
36. Continue in prayer, and watch in the _____ with thanksgiving.

(Col. 4:2)
38. And whether it be cow or _____, ye shall not kill it. (Lev. 22:28)
39. Father, _____ thy hands I commend my spirit.(Luke 23:46)
42. The children of Gad called the altar _____. (Josh. 22:34)
43. Prove all _____; hold fast that which is good. (1 Thes. 5:21)
45. _____ the day of the Lord is near. (Joel 3:14)
47. United Nations (abbr.).
48. I _____ the way, the truth, and the life. (John 14:6)
49. Tennessee (abbr.).
51. So soon as I shall _____ how it will go with me. (Phil. 2:23)
52. Ye know that our record is _____. (3 John 12)
53. And all that handle the _____, the mariners. (Ezek. 27:29)

DOWN CLUES

1. _____ Paul cried with a loud voice, saying, Do thyself no harm. (Acts 16:28)
2. And we know that we are of _____. (1 John 5:19)
3. Moose.
5. That he might be revealed in _____ time. (2 Thes. 2:6)
6. Nova Scotia (abbr.).
8. We accept it...most _____ Felix. (Acts 24:3)
10. And they cried out all at _____. (Luke 23:18)
14. Then _____ those virgins arose, and trimmed their lamps. (Matt. 25:7)
15. Therefore ye _____ of Jacob are not consumed. (Mal. 3:6)
16. If I _____ witness of myself, my witness is not true. (John 5:31)
18. In the same place (abbr.).
19. The lot is cast into the _____. (Prov. 16:33)

78

21. And he reigned over all the kings _____ the river. (2 Chron. 9:26)
23. _____ that my people had hearkened unto me. (Ps. 81:13)
25. Whosoever shall say to his brother, _____. (Matt. 5:22)
29. Each (abbr.).
30. Their _____ and strength unto the beast. (Rev. 17:13)
31. And Tychicus have I _____ to Ephesus. (2 Tim. 4:12)
33. For they know _____ the way of the Lord. (Jer. 5:4)
35. When they that _____ them saw what was done, they fled. (Luke 8:34)

36. And the city had no need of the sun...to. (Rev. 21:23)
37. For I through the law, am dead to the law, that I _____ live unto God. (Gal. 2:19)
40. If ye shall ask any thing in my _____, I will do it. (John 14:14)
41. Why do we and the Pharisees fast _____? (Matt. 9:14)
44. Shade.
46. Lod, and _____, the valley of craftsmen. (Neh. 11:35)
48. Gold (symbol).
50. For do I now persuade men, _____ God? (Gal 1:10)

79

Puzzle 39

Pamela Jensen

ACROSS CLUES

1. The _____ of Jesus. (John 2:1)
6. The _____ loveth the Son. (John 3:35)
12. After the _____ of Melchisedec. (Heb. 7:17)
13. Rejoice at his _____. (Luke 1:14)
14. Raised _____ from the dead. (Rom. 6:4)
15. Long-tailed rodent.
17. The _____ of the tabernacle. (Ex. 38:20)
18. National Hockey League (abbr.).
20. South America (abbr.).
21. I will _____ unto thy days. (2 Kgs. 20:6)
22. As many _____ received him. (John 1:12)
23. Disciple named _____. (Acts 9:36)
26. Electroencephalogram (abbr.).
28. Come to _____ end. (Ps. 7:9)
29. Very large picture on a wall.

31. Under the fifth _____.
(2 Sam. 2:23)
33. This _____ the day which the
Lord hath made. (Ps. 118:24)
34. Manuscript (abbr.).
35. Six on a _____. (Lev. 24:6)
37. A _____ out of the stem of Jesse.
(Isa. 11:1)
38. Symbol for holmium.
39. _____ thy neighbour.
(Lev. 19:18)
40. Symbol for lawrencium.
41. Sin no _____. (John 8:11)
43. Birds of the air have _____.
(Luke 9:58)
45. Took the _____ of Elijah.
(2 Kgs. 2:14)
47. Deuteronomy (abbr.).
48. _____ not kill. (Jam. 2:11)
49. _____ be with you. (1 Pet. 5:14)
50. Rising up _____. (Jer. 29:19)
54. Could _____ stones.
(Judg. 20:16)
56. _____ up the tabernacle.
(Ex. 26:30)
57. Fathers did _____ manna.
(John 6:49)
58. Yea be yea; and your _____.
(Jam. 5:12)
59. _____ heard of your faith.
(Eph. 1:15)

DOWN CLUES

1. Come, and let us go up to the
_____ of the Lord. (Mic. 4:2)
2. We are _____ and fatherless.
(Lam. 5:3)
3. Touchdown (abbr.).
4. _____ name was Elisabeth.
(Luke 1:5)
5. Timotheus and _____.
(Acts 19:22)
7. _____ in me, and I in you.
(John 15:4)
8. Material used to kindle fires.
9. Hours (abbr.).
10. Eastern time (abbr.).
11. The son of _____. (Luke 3:27)
16. Asian goatlike mammal.
17. Short for Papa.
19. Pound (abbr.).
24. The King eternal, _____.
(1 Tim. 1:17)
25. Lord spake unto Moses and to
_____. (Lev. 15:1)
27. Boys and _____. (Zech. 8:5)
30. I have _____ you. (Mal. 1:2)
32. Set my _____ in the cloud.
(Gen. 9:13)
36. As for the _____ border.
(Num. 34:6)
38. An _____ and good heart.
(Luke 8:15)
41. Representation of a region.
42. The popular name of Rodrigo
Diaz (2 words).
44. That our _____ may be full.
(2 John 12)
46. Poetic for "even."
48. Dealer (abbr.).
51. Actor's Equity Association
(abbr.).
52. A beam of visible light.
53. Both of you and _____.
(Rom. 1:12)
55. Genesis (abbr.).
59. Which _____ have set before
thee. (Deut. 30:1)

Puzzle 40

Pamela Jensen

ACROSS CLUES

1. Your _____ Father will also forgive. (Matt. 6:14)
8. Multitude of the heavenly _____. (Luke 2:13)
12. Descended to _____. (Josh. 18:16)
13. _____ to your faith. (2 Pet. 1:5)
14. Symbol for silver.
15. Wire gauge (abbr.).
16. Here I _____. (Gen. 22:1)
18. _____ his feet. (Ex. 4:25)
19. The _____ that is set before us. (Heb. 12:1)
20. American Medical Association (abbr.).
21. Airport code for Birmingham, England.
22. Tennessee (abbr.).
23. Elisha came to _____. (2 Kgs. 8:7)
27. _____ greater joy. (3 John 4)
29. Fast ye for _____. (Es. 4:16)
30. Woman having _____ pieces of silver. (Luke 15:8)
31. Let there _____ light. (Gen. 1:3)
32. He saw a _____ tree. (Matt. 21:19)
33. I will make him _____ help meet. (Gen. 2:18)
34. The _____ shall serve the younger. (Rom. 9:12)
36. _____ I my brother's keeper? (Gen. 4:9)
37. Battalion (abbr.).
38. Every man that asketh you _____ _____ of the hope. (1 Pet.3:15; 2 words)

40. _____ to do well. (Isa. 1:17)
42. Symbol for tin.
43. Wyoming (abbr.).
44. The _____ Light. (John 1:9)
46. It is _____. (Matt. 4:7)
49. Indicates 100.
51. Symbol for nickel.
53. South America (abbr.).
54. Armies together for _____. (1 Sam. 28:1)
57. Army Transport Service (abbr.).
58. Symbol for sodium.
59. Russian river that flows into Arctic Ocean.

DOWN CLUES

1. I the Lord search the _____. (Jer. 17:10)
2. Zanoah, and _____. (Josh. 15:34)
3. Symbol for argon.
4. _____ unto the mighty God. (Ps. 132:2)
5. The white of an _____. (Job 6:6)
6. Symbol for neon.
7. South American mammal known for its soft, fleecy wool.
9. Have sworn _____. (Ezek. 21:23)
10. Special delivery (abbr.).
11. Total digestible nutrients (abbr.).
17. A _____ in heaven. (Col. 4:1)
18. _____ in goodness and truth. (Ex. 34:6)
20. Peace be with you all. _____. (Rom. 15:33)
24. Look from the top of _____. (Song of Sol. 4:8)
25. Also _____ bodies. (1 Cor. 15:40)
26. So _____ numbered them. (Num. 1:19)

82

28. _____ the king of Bashan.
(Deut. 3:1)
31. The _____ cattle. (Gen. 30:32)
32. _____ cometh by hearing.
(Rom. 10:17)
35. Symbol for einsteinium.
37. Dark red bulbous root.
38. Administration for National
Recovery (abbr.).
39. New York (abbr.).
40. Demas, _____, my fellow-
labourers. (Philemon 24)
41. Right Worth (abbr.).
45. Sabbath of _____. (Lev. 23:3)
47. Information (short for).
48. _____ a child is known.
(Prov. 20:11)
50. In thine _____ eyes. (Prov. 3:7)
52. Paper and _____. (2 John 12)
55. Associate in Arts (abbr.).
56. Symbol for rhenium.

Puzzle 41

Evelyn Boyington

ACROSS CLUES

1. Upon the _____ of it thou shalt make pomegranates. (Ex. 28:33)
4. The troops of _____ looked. (Job 6:19)
8. Let us go to the _____. (1 Sam. 9:9)
12. Stand in _____, and sin not. (Ps. 4:4)
13. Of _____, the family of the Eranites. (Num. 26:36)
14. The devil threw him down, and _____ him. (Luke 9:42)
15. About.
16. Leave out.
17. Wise men.
18. _____ for thy life; look not behind thee. (Gen. 19:17)
20. The soldiers led him away into the _____. (Mark 15:16)
21. _____ thou the man that spakest unto the woman? (Judg. 13:11)
22. Charity never _____. (1 Cor. 13:8)
25. Thou shalt make his _____ to receive his ashes. (Ex. 27:3)
27. Gathered it, and ground it in _____. (Num. 11:8)
28. Sun god.
29. _____, even the ancient high places are ours. (Ezek. 36:2)

30. Sword handles.
31. Ye shall speak into the _____.
    (1 Cor. 14:9)
32. Note of the musical scale.
33. Actualities.
34. No man shall _____ me of this
    boasting. (2 Cor. 11:10)
35. They...encamped at _____.
    (Num. 33:34)
37. Copy.
38. The children of _____, seven
    hundred seventy and five.
    (Ezra 2:5)
39. Thorns and _____ are in the way
    of the froward. (Prov. 22:5)
42. He bringeth them unto their
    desired _____. (Ps. 107:30)
44. They that _____ upon the Lord
    shall renew their strength.
    (Isa. 40:31)
45. If God _____ loved us, we ought
    also to love one another.
    (1 John 4:11)
46. Angers.
47. Girl's name.
48. Give _____ to his
    commandments. (Ex. 15:26)
49. A slight hollow.
50. Crew.
51. A word spoken in _____ season.
    (Prov. 15:23)

DOWN CLUES

1. And the _____, because he
   cheweth the cud. (Lev. 11:6)
2. Following the _____ great with
   young. (Ps. 78:71)
3. And ye will not come to _____.
   (John 5:40)
4. Thou shalt not _____ the Lord
   thy God. (Matt. 4:7)
5. Canal.
6. Pad.
7. For _____ angel went down.
   (John 5:4)
8. _____ for all manner of beasts.
   (2 Chron. 32:28)
9. As swift as the _____ flieth.

(Deut. 28:49)
10. How long will it be _____ thou
    be quiet? (Jer. 47:6)
11. Matter: law.
16. Wherein shall go no galley with
    _____. (Isa. 33:21)
17. Glides.
19. There was a marriage in _____
    of Galilee. (John 2:1)
20. Stops.
22. Washed away the _____.
    (Isa. 4:4)
23. Group of three.
24. Praise the Lord with _____.
    (Ps. 33:2)
25. Behold a _____ horse. (Rev. 6:8)
26. And _____ the son of Omri did
    evil. (1 Kgs. 16:30)
27. Prophet to Jotham, Ahaz, and
    Hezekiah. (Micah 1:1)
30. Into the chamber of the sons of
    _____. (Jer. 35:4)
31. The children of _____ of
    Hezekiah. (Ezra 2:16)
33. David departed, and came into
    the _____ of Hareth.
    (1 Sam. 22:5)
34. He _____ on the ground.
    (John 9:6)
36. He sent forth a _____. (Gen. 8:7)
37. Shechem, and Likhi, and _____.
    (1 Chron. 7:19)
39. Heber, which was the son of
    _____. (Luke 3:35)
40. _____ was a cunning hunter.
    (Gen. 25:27)
41. Famine waxed _____ in the land
    of Egypt. (Gen. 41:56)
42. A city that is set on an hill can
    not be _____. (Matt. 5:14)
43. Her sins, which _____ many.
    (Luke 7:47)
44. _____ unto them that call evil
    good. (Isa. 5:20)
47. Arise, _____ shall teach!
    (Hab. 2:19)
48. The children of Gad called the
    altar _____. (Josh. 22:34)

Puzzle 42

Evelyn Boyington

ACROSS CLUES

1. Whether it be _____ or ewe, ye shall not kill it. (Lev. 22:28)
4. A strong _____ from the enemy. (Ps. 61:3)
9. Thy god, O _____, liveth. (Amos 8:14)
12. Stand in _____, and sin not. (Ps. 4:4)
13. Representative.
14. The wheat and the _____ were not smitten. (Ex. 9:32)
15. _____ is the man that trusteth in him. (Ps. 34:8)
17. No man _____d for my soul. (Ps. 142:4)
18. Piece out.
19. Led him unto the _____ of the hill. (Luke 4:29)
21. Jonah was gone down into the _____ of the ship. (Jonah 1:5)
24. I sat down and wept, and _____. (Neh. 1:4)
27. In the beginning was the _____. (John 1:1)
28. And Jacob _____ a vow. (Gen. 28:20)
29. Thy servants are _____ spies. (Gen. 42:11)
30. Not willing that _____ should perish. (2 Pet. 3:9)
31. All thy house shall be _____. (Acts 11:14)
32. I took the little book...and _____ it up. (Rev. 10:10)
33. Greek letter.
34. What _____ thee, O thou sea? (Ps. 114:5)
35. Poems.
36. The whirlwind shall _____ them. (Isa. 41:16)
38. Sound of contempt.
39. Bring forth the _____ robe. (Luke 15:22)
40. Given to hospitality, _____ to teach. (1 Tim. 3:2)
41. When thou wentest out of _____. (Judg. 5:4)
43. Fed.
47. Giants dwelt therein in _____ time. (Deut. 2:20)
48. Cast him into _____ darkness. (Matt. 22:13)
50. Unrefined mineral.
51. A time to be born, and a time to _____. (Ec. 3:2)
52. If I come again, I will not _____. (2 Cor. 13:2)
53. And I saw a _____ heaven. (Rev. 21:1)

DOWN CLUES

1. The fourth part of a _____. (2 Kgs. 6:25)
2. I am like an _____ of the desert. (Ps. 102:6)
3. Tiny.
4. Fulfil your works, your daily _____. (Ex. 5:13)
5. Molding.
6. Married.
7. _____ passant. (French)
8. Direction (abbr.).
9. He is _____ away of his own lust. (Jam. 1:14)
10. The birds of the _____ have nests. (Matt. 8:20)
11. Born.
16. Thy _____ shall be great. (Job 5:25)
17. Ever the silver _____ be loosed. (Ec. 12:6)
19. They _____ the knee before him. (Matt. 27:29)
20. Regretted.
21. Trades.
22. Pertaining to a charged particle.
23. I will _____ up thy rivers. (Isa. 44:27)

24. A pestilent fellow, and a _____ of sedition. (Acts 24:5)
25. _____ into his gates with thanksgiving. (Ps. 100:4)
26. What _____ thou here, Elijah? (1 Kgs. 19:9)
28. Manservant.
31. Perches.
32. Why make ye this _____, and weep? (Mark 5:39)
34. The children of _____ of Hezekiah. (Neh. 7:21)
35. He goeth _____ _____ meet the armed men. (Job 39:21; 2 words)
37. Who can _____ in the fierceness of his anger? (Nahum 1:6)
38. Seed.
40. Clown.
41. And Jacob _____ pottage. (Gen. 25:29)
42. Samuel ministered unto the Lord before _____. (1 Sam. 3:1)
43. Depot (abbr.).
44. Not (prefix).
45. How long will it be _____ thou be quiet? (Jer. 47:6)
46. Like a cloud of _____ in the heat of harvest. (Isa. 18:4)
48. Bone (prefix).
49. The thorns grew _____, and choked it. (Mark 4:7)

Puzzle 43

Helen Walter

ACROSS CLUES

1. Thou shalt call his _____ Jesus. (Matt. 1:21)
5. They shall call his name _____. (Matt. 1:23)
11. Revises.
13. A cry of pain.
14. Avenue (abbr.).
15. His name shall be called _____. (Isa. 9:6)
18. Married.
19. Rhode Island (abbr.).
20. The meek shall _____ and be satisfied. (Ps. 22:26)
21. Good, better, _____.
23. Soon.
28. Characteristic.
30. King of Tyre. (1 Kgs. 5:1)
31. Be of good _____. (Acts 23:11)
33. Purpose.
34. South Carolina (abbr.).
35. Damaged.
37. And, _____, the angel of the Lord came upon them. (Luke 2:9)

38. Estimated time of arrival (abbr.).
39. Aramaic "son of."
40. Greek letter.
41. Egg-shaped.
43. On all sides.
45. Cure.
46. Rim.
47. Serpent.
48. Extra sensory perception (abbr.).
50. Light (abbr.).
51. I will _____ up mine eyes. (Ps. 121:1)
52. The _____ of a trumpet. (Ps. 47:5)

DOWN CLUES

1. Sing unto him a _____ song. (Ps. 33:3)
2. "Come, let us _____ Him."
3. Pastor.
4. Estimated time of departure (abbr.).
6. My _____ shall speak of wisdom. (Ps. 49:3)
7. A tool.
8. United Auto Workers (abbr.).
9. _____ Father, The Prince of Peace. (Isa. 9:6)
10. But if ye be _____ of the Spirit. (Gal. 5:18)
12. Southeast (abbr.).
16. Musical note.
17. When they _____, I will not hear. (Jer. 14:12)
21. Composer of organ music.
22. Ye that _____ at his word. (Isa. 66:5)
24. Buckeye state.
25. Edge.
26. Transpose (abbr.).
27. Young Men's Christian Association (abbr.).
29. Region.
32. The _____ is the end of the world. (Matt. 13:39)
33. Continually.
36. Cart.
38. Left-handed man. (Judg. 3:15)
40. Edgar Allen _____.
41. Spoken.
42. Unit of electrical current.
44. Whatsoever ye do in word or _____. (Col. 3:17)
48. _____cetera.
49. Postscript (abbr.).

Puzzle 44

Lee Esch

ACROSS CLUES

1. There is no fear in _____. (1 John 4:18).
5. 1/60 of a minute (abbr.).
8. Ripe harvest.
12. ...the number of whom _____ _____ the sand of the sea. (Rev. 20:8; two words)
13. No man can serve _____ masters. (Matt. 6:24).
14. Top-notch.
15. Somersault.
16. Lord, _____ me when thou comest into thy kingdom. (Luke 23:42)
18. Eternity.
19. Degrade.
20. But what things were _____ to me, those I counted loss for Christ. (Phil. 3:7)
22. Silly fellow.
26. Salvation _____ unto the Lord. (Psa. 3:8)
30. Digit.
31. In a frenzy (var.).
32. Three (prefix).
33. Study to _____ thyself approved unto God. (2 Tim. 2:15)
34. Title of address.
35. My flesh also _____ _____ in hope. (Psa. 16:9; two words)
37. Fashion.
39. Let God be true, but every man a _____. (Rom. 3:4).
40. Arch.
43. Land of _____ (Cain's home).
46. One who plays the market.
49. John _____ witness of him.

(John 1:15)
50. For I was an hungered, and ye gave me _____. (Matt. 25:35).
51. In time past.
52. Will _____ _____ rob God? (Mal. 3:8; two words).
53. Teach me thy way, O Lord, and lead me in a plain _____. (Psa. 27:11)
54. British flyers (for short).
55. Becomes semisolid.

DOWN CLUES

1. For whosoever will save his _____ shall lose it. (Matt. 16:25).
2. Norwegian city.
3. Let nothing be done through strife or _____. (Phil. 2:3)
4. Sixth sense (for short).
5. ...the _____ of sin is the law. (1 Cor. 15:56)
6. Pitcher.
7. Unconscious state.
8. It is easier for a _____ to go through the eye of a needle... (Matt. 19:24)
9. Thou shalt not defraud thy neighbour, neither _____ him. (Lev. 19:13)
10. The Lord our God is _____ Lord. (Deut. 6:4)
11. For each.
17. Engrave.
19. Container.
21. First rate.
23. ...for there is none _____ _____...Whereby we must be saved. (Acts 4:12; two words)
24. Troubles.
25. Salamander.
26. Singing part.

27. Send forth.
28. Time period.
29. ...but Cain was a _____ _____ the ground. (Gen. 4:2)
33. Spanish Mrs. (for short).
35. Congressmen (abbr.)
36. The _____ of truth shall be established for ever (Pro. 12:19).
38. He _____ in wait secretly as a lion in his den. (Psa. 10:9).
41. ...for we have seen his _____ in the east, and are come to worship him. (Matt. 2:2)
42. Ancient Roman garment.
44. Spoken.
45. Lairs.
46. Demon.
47. Teacher's organization (for short).
48. Tub.
49. He hath taken a _____ of money with him. (Pro. 7:20)

Puzzle 45

Helen Walter

ACROSS CLUES

1. Ark builder.
4. The ark rested...upon the mountains of _____. (Gen. 8:4)
9. How long _____ ye between two opinions? (1 Kgs. 18:21)
10. Creative work.
11. I _____ the Lord thy God. (Deut. 5:6)
13. A bit of news or information.
15. And _____ came to pass. (Gen. 8:13)
16. Also known as (abbr.).
17. He sent forth a _____. (Gen. 8:8)
19. Possesses.
21. Metropolitan (abbr.).
22. One hundred years.
24. Confined.
25. South Carolina (abbr.).
26. For a good man some would even _____ to die. (Rom. 5:7)
27. A metal container.
28. A son of Noah. (Gen. 5:32)
30. Hotel.

31. Out of print (abbr.).
32. Junior (abbr.).
33. Eastern Standard Time (abbr.).
34. A musical play.
35. Michigan (abbr.).
36. Wood that the ark was made of.
39. Pronoun (abbr.).
41. Medicine acting as a sedative.
44. _____ is more precious than rubies. (Prov. 3:15)
45. Under_____ (below).
46. Hannah's son.
49. He shall be like a _____ planted by the rivers. (Ps. 1:3)
50. And the flood was _____ days upon the earth. (Gen. 7:17)
51. Fuel.
52. Bring up, raise.
53. Sound expressing doubt or surprise.

DOWN CLUES

1. North America (abbr.).
2. In her mouth was an _____ leaf. (Gen. 8:11)
3. _____ unto me, and hear me. (Ps. 55:2)
5. Save for a _____ day.
6. _____ and crafts.
7. Route (abbr.).
8. Thine iniquity is _____ away. (Isa. 6:7)
9. Possessed.
12. _____-of-fact.
14. Blessed are they that _____. (Matt. 5:4)
16. These things saith the _____. (Rev. 3:14)
18. There is none _____ of stumbling in him. (1 John 2:10)
20. Small songbird.
23. Drive too closely.
24. Used to write on.
25. Son of Noah.
27. Deal with problems.
29. Mountain (abbr.).
32. Son of Noah.
34. Exclamation.
37. Different in nature or kind.
38. Physical education (abbr.).
40. Depend.
42. Domesticated animals.
43. Let God be true, but every man a l_____. (Rom. 3:4)
44. Make your calling and election _____. (2 Pet. 1:10)
47. Africa (abbr.).
48. Nickname for Aaron's brother?

Puzzle 46

Helen Walter

ACROSS CLUES

1. _____ is the man. (Ps. 1:1)
7. Of the same quantity.
11. Why do the heathen _____. (Ps. 2:1)
12. They shall deceive the _____ elect. (Matt. 24:24)
14. _____ brought forth her first-born son. (Luke 2:7)
15. Object of worship.
16. _____ into his gates with thanksgiving. (Ps. 100:4)
18. A bird of the _____. (Ec. 10:20)
20. The ungodly are not _____. (Ps. 1:4)
22. Why _____ I mourning? (Ps. 43:2)
24. He is our _____ and our shield. (Ps. 33:20)
26. Make thy face to shine _____ thy servant. (Ps. 31:16)
29. Veterans' Administration (abbr.).
31. Under the shadow of the _____. (Ps. 91:1)
33. Let go.
35. _____ word is a lamp unto my feet. (Ps. 119:105)
36. Thy right hand, and thine _____. (Ps. 44:3)
37. Italic (abbr.).
39. Associated Press (abbr.).
40. Indian garment.
42. Thou shalt have none _____ gods before me. (Deut. 5:7)
45. Printer's measure.
47. Commander of Saul's army. (1 Sam. 17:55)
48. Came down.
49. August (abbr.).
50. Psalm writer.
52. Total.
54. Precious stone.
56. Army _____ hall.
57. Arise, O Lord; _____ me. (Ps. 3:7)
58. _____ are his people. (Ps.100:3)

DOWN CLUES

1. They shall still _____ forth fruit. (Ps. 92:14)
2. Young boy.
3. Id, _____, superego.
4. Hebrew word in some Psalms.
5. His mercy is _____. (Ps. 100:5)
6. Animal home.
7. Our _____ wait upon the Lord. (Ps. 123:2)
8. ...the glory which shall be revealed in _____. (Ro. 8:18)
9. Word of contentment.
10. _____ God arise. (Ps. 68:1)
13. Route (abbr.).
17. Not smooth.
19. That is.
21. The ungodly shall _____ stand. (Ps. 1:5)
23. Above.
25. _____ bargain.
27. Physician (abbr.).
28. New York (abbr.).
30. Do not your _____ before men. (Matt. 6:1)
32. _____ is a good thing to give thanks. (Ps. 92:1)
33. Rejoiceth as a strong man to run a _____. (Ps. 19:5)
34. A large plane.
38. O _____, rebuke me not. (Ps. 38:1)

39. Barren.

41. Automobile Association of America (abbr.).

43. I _____ put my trust in the Lord God. (Ps. 73:28)

44. They came to _____. (Ex. 15:27)

46. It is he that hath _____ us. (Ps. 100:3)

51. Mine _____ is as nothing before thee. (Ps. 39:5)

52. I _____ troubled. (Ps. 38:6)

53. District supervisor (abbr.).

55. Judge _____, O God. (Ps. 43:1)

Puzzle 47

Helen Walter

ACROSS CLUES

1. Older son of Rachel.
6. Lo, my _____ arose. (Gen. 37:7)
10. A place for sacrifices.
11. The sun and the moon and eleven _____ made obeisance to me. (Gen. 37:9)
12. Twelve months.
13. Joseph's position in Egypt. (Gen. 39:4)
15. (Jacob) poured _____ upon the top of it. (Gen. 28:18)
16. Virginia (abbr.).
17. Greek letter.
19. Number on baseball team.
20. Figure _____.
22. The truth shall make you _____. (John 8:32)
23. Pharaoh took off his _____ from his hand. (Gen. 41:42)
25. The _____ of gladness. (Ps. 45:7)
27. Fear and _____ shall fall upon them. (Ex. 15:16)

29. Height (abbr.).
31. Colorado (abbr.).
32. There _____ none greater. (Gen. 39:9)
33. Consumed.
34. Road surface material.
36. Joseph dreamed _____ _____. (Gen. 37:5; 2 words)
38. _____ me in thy truth. (Ps. 25:5)
39. _____ a certain man found him. (Gen. 37:15)
41. Israel _____ Joseph more than all his children. (Gen. 37:3)
43. Trouble.
46. How...can I... _____ against God? (Gen. 39:9)
47. For example (abbr.).
48. Method of dyeing cloth.
50. Passage.
52. _____ Testament.
53. Delete.
54. Metropolitan (abbr.).

DOWN CLUES

1. Noisy bird.
2. Spread for bread.
3. Soiled.
4. Opposite of "later."
5. Pronoun (abbr.).
6. Make _____ paths for your feet. (Heb. 12:13)
7. Possesses.
8. Before.
9. Free from germs.
11. There came up out of the river _____ kine. (Gen. 41:18)
13. Run.
14. Rhode Island (abbr.).
18. Continent.
21. _____, every one that thirsteth. (Isa. 55:1)
24. Perfect model.
26. Nay, my _____, but to buy food. (Gen. 42:10)
28. Seven _____ came up in one stalk. (Gen. 41:22)
30. Biblical unit of money.
35. Rosy.
36. And he _____ no more. (Deut. 5:22)
37. Receiver of the ten commandments.
40. I will fasten him as a _____. (Isa. 22:23)
42. I am the _____, ye are the branches. (John 15:5)
44. Doctor of optometry (abbr.).
45. Each.
47. Keep me as the apple of the _____. (Ps. 17:8)
48. Toward.
49. Whence come _____? (Gen. 42:7)
51. Room (abbr.).

Puzzle 48

Lee Esch

ACROSS CLUES

1. And now abideth faith, _____, charity. (1 Cor. 13:13)
5. He is _____ the God of the dead. (Mark 12:27)
8. Jesus attended a wedding here.
12. So be it.
13. Physician's group (abbr.).
14. And he took one of his _____. (Gen. 2:21)
15. Behold, I _____ you forth as sheep in the midst of wolves. (Matt. 10:16)
16. The wife of Moses.
18. High explosive (for short).
19. And the Spirit of God moved upon the face of the _____. (Gen. 1:2)
20. Pitcher.
22. Bone (prefix).
26. He came to Jesus by night.
30. The sixth captain...was _____. (1 Chron. 27:9)
31. Having their conscience seared with a hot _____. (1 Tim. 4:2)
32. _____ Pan Alley.
33. Send out.
34. _____ Cruces, New Mexico.
35. Religious sect of Jesus' day.
37. _____ ye in at the strait gate. (Matt. 7:13)
39. Praise him for his mighty _____. (Ps. 150:2)
40. Experience again.
43. Female sibling (for short).
46. It is your Father's good _____ to give you the kingdom. (Luke 12:32)

49. For if we believe that Jesus died and _____ again. (1 Thes. 4:14)
50. Belonging to Adam's wife.
51. Feel ill.
52. Prophetic sign.
53. Floor covering.
54. Uncle Sam's sailing vessel (abbr.).
55. Undesirable plant.

DOWN CLUES

1. Thou _____ the words of eternal life. (John 6:68)
2. Sign.
3. The apostles received the Holy Ghost on this day.
4. For Christ is the _____ of the law. (Rom. 10:4)
5. Jesus' hometown.
6. Leave out.
7. Record.
8. For the preaching of the _____ is to them that perish foolishness. (1 Cor. 1:18)
9. Foxes have holes, and birds of the _____ have nests. (Luke 9:58)
10. National Basketball Association.
11. Common tree.
17. Aces (for short).
19. Marry.
21. Was victorious.
23. In the latter _____ _____ shall depart from the faith. (1 Tim. 4:1; 2 words)
24. A Great Lake.
25. Cereal grass (pl.).
26. Egyptian river.
27. It borders Iraq.
28. Soldier unaccounted for.
29. Solves a mystery.

33. Founded (abbr.).
35. Company overseer (abbr.).
36. He casteth forth his _____ like morsels. (Ps. 147:17)
38. Expunge.
41. Hawaiian feast.
42. Eye part.

44. _____ _____ men as trees, walking. (Mark 8:24)
45. Here I am; _____ me. (Isa. 6:8)
46. House cat.
47. 56 (Roman numeral).
48. Scaleless fish.
49. Propel a boat manually.

Puzzle 49

Pamela Jensen

ACROSS CLUES

1. To _____ the brokenhearted. (Luke 4:18)
4. Honour, and glory, and _____. (Rev. 5:12)
11. The hearing _____. (Prov. 20:12)
12. _____ it with the prayers. (Rev. 8:3)
13. The _____ to come. (Eph. 2:7)
15. Princes of Midian, _____. (Josh. 13:21)
16. Preach the word in _____. (Acts 16:6)
18. Lines (abbr.).
19. The son of _____. (1 Kgs. 4:9)
21. Doctor of Divinity (abbr.).
22. A _____ come from God. (John 3:2)
25. Airport code for Monte Carlo, Monaco.
27. Uz and _____. (Gen. 36:28)
28. _____ the beauty of the Lord. (Ps. 27:4)

31. To rid of excess by cutting.
32. Zechariah, _____.
    (1 Chron. 15:18)
33. Though they be _____ like
    crimson. (Isa. 1:18)
34. Japanese city.
35. Established church (abbr.).
36. The waters called he _____.
    (Gen. 1:10)
37. Biology: resembling a string of
    beads.
39. Mother.
40. She is thine _____. (Lev. 18:14)
43. Let us _____ before the Lord our
    maker. (Ps. 95:6)
46. To demand the restoration or
    return of.
48. Following the _____ great with
    young. (Ps. 78:71)
49. Turn ye unto _____. (Zech. 1:3)
50. Symbol for chlorine.
51. Scrap of cloth.
52. Known unto _____ the mystery.
    (Eph. 3:3)
53. _____; and he smelleth the battle.
    (Job 39:25)
54. _____ in peace. (Mark 5:34)

DOWN CLUES

1. I will restore _____ unto thee.
   (Jer. 30:17)
2. Fly as the _____. (Jer. 49:22)
3. Now these _____ thy servants.
   (Neh. 1:10)
5. A _____ of hospitality.
   (Titus 1:8)
6. One of a people of southern
   Nigeria.
7. Science fiction (abbr.).
8. I the Lord _____ the heart.
   (Jer. 17:10)
9. Internal Revenue Service (abbr.).
10. Let us be _____ and rejoice.
    (Rev. 19:7)
14. Offer up spiritual _____.
    (1 Pet. 2:5)
15. Garden of _____. (Gen. 2:15)
17. Idaho (abbr.).
20. To everlasting._____. (Ps. 41:13)
23. Holy garments for _____.
    (Ex. 28:2)
24. Sons of Pharez...Hezron and
    _____. (Gen. 46:12)
26. Weep no _____. (Isa. 30:19)
28. All things are _____ new.
    (2 Cor. 5:17)
29. Will increase in _____.
    (Prov. 9:9)
30. Doctor of Dental Science (abbr.).
31. Technical knockout (abbr.).
32. My cry came _____ him.
    (Ps. 18:6)
36. Witnessing both to _____ and
    great. (Acts 26:22)
37. God my _____. (Job 35:10)
38. Contraction for "I am."
41. United Artists (abbr.).
42. Symbol for thulium.
44. Northwest Airlines (abbr.).
45. Electroencephalogram (abbr.).
47. Circuit Court of Appeals (abbr.).
49. Every knee shall bow to _____.
    (Rom. 14:11)

Puzzle 50

Janet W. Adkins

ACROSS CLUES

1. Thou shalt _____ coals of fire on his head. (Rom. 12:20)
5. I must also see _____. (Acts 19:21)
9. They shall still bring forth fruit in _____ age. (Ps. 92:14)
12. Bearing.
13. Great god of love.
14. Spicknel.
15. And they slew the kings of Midian...Evi..Hur, and _____. (Num. 31:8)
16. Celebration.
17. Had compassion, and _____, and fell on his neck. (Luke 15:20)
18. West coast state.
20. Thou shalt destroy them that speak _____. (Ps. 5:6)
22. Howbeit _____ fled...to the tent of Jael. (Judg. 4:17)
25. Female saint (abbr.).
26. Explosive initials.
28. They could not _____ in because of unbelief. (Heb. 3:19)
32. Anglo-Saxon slave.
35. Only the gold...silver..._____. (Num. 31:22)
37. The _____ is fulfilled. (Mark 1:15)
38. Two hundred shekels of silver, and a _____ of gold. (Josh. 7:21)
40. Sun.
42. _____ Tin Tin.
43. Adherent to an ism.
45. And they departed into a _____ place. (Mark 6:32)
47. He died in a good old age, full of _____. (1 Chron. 29:28)
50. It hath consumed _____ of Moab. (Num. 21:28)
52. Yes (Spanish).
53. Undo (poetic).
54. Belonging to the priest. (1 Kgs. 1:7)
59. By way of.
60. And Ahab _____ Jezebel all that Elijah had done. (1 Kgs. 19:1)
61. _____: he is the father of Jesse, the father of David. (Ruth 4:17)
62. Put it upon the tip of the right _____ of Aaron. (Ex. 29:20)
63. Creator of Perry Mason.
64. Cast the _____(pl) on the right side of the ship. (John 21:6)

DOWN CLUES

1. Take Aaron and Eleazar...and bring them up unto mount _____. (Num. 20:25)
2. How long will it be _____ thou be quiet? (Jer. 47:6)
3. Priestly garment.
4. We have _____ with God through our Lord Jesus Christ. (Rom. 5:1)
5. Sports official.
6. City in Russia.
7. For the law was given by _____. (John 1:17)
8. That he might know your _____, and comfort your hearts. (Col. 4:8)
9. _____ the son of Michael. (1 Chron. 27:18)
10. Yet will they _____ upon the Lord. (Micah 3:11)
11. Thou shalt bake it with _____. (Ezek. 4:12)
19. O God, thou _____ my God. (Ps. 63:1)
21. He that receiveth me receiveth him that _____ me. (Matt.10:40)
22. I will _____ thee out of my mouth. (Rev. 3:16)
23. A foolish man...built his house upon the _____. (Matt. 7:26)

24. Go to the _____, thou sluggard. (Prov. 6:6)
27. "_____ the season to be jolly."
29. Bind the _____ of thine head upon thee. (Ezek. 24:17)
30. Arabian prince.
31. For he _____ Israel from the house of David. (2 Kgs. 17:21)
33. Direction (abbr.).
34. Protection.
36. And Cain went out...and dwelt in the land of _____. (Gen. 4:16)
39. Plural suffix.
41. Add thou not unto his words, _____ he reprove thee. (Prov. 30:6)
44. And the coast reacheth to _____.

(Josh. 19:22)
46. And Israel sent messengers unto _____ king of the Amorites. (Num. 21:21)
47. He sent forth a _____. (Gen. 8:8)
48. Of bees.
49. But into the second went the high priest alone once every _____. (Heb. 9:7)
51. A small brook.
54. Did eat.
55. Fruit drink.
56. Lincoln.
57. Retired (abbr.).
58. Students for a Democratic Society.

103

ANSWERS

Puzzle 1

```
LOVE  STA  ESAU
IRAN  EEL  TOPS
MALE  LAMPUNTO
ELI  AFRAID
   DIPS   PETRA
FRAGRANCE  HUG
AUTO  MOO  WINE
DIE  FEWTHINGS
ENSUE   TANG
    SEAWAY  SOS
SEWEDFIG  CAPE
OVER  ALE  AREA
BEDS  RDS  TENT
```

Puzzle 2

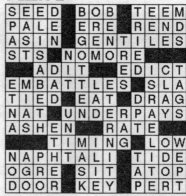

```
SEED  BOB  TEEM
PALE  ERE  REND
ASIN  GENTILES
STS  NOMORE
   ADIT   EDICT
EMBATTLES  SLA
TIED  EAT  DRAG
NAT  UNDERPAYS
ASHEN   RATE
    TIMING  LOW
NAPHTALI  TIDE
OGRE  SIT  ATOP
DOOR  KEY  PERT
```

Puzzle 3

```
BEGOTTEN  EARN
ROAR  RAINS  S E
INN  GIRL  A  IV
D  DRAB  ENDURE
LIE  TEA  AM  OR
E  R  EST  MOON
  C  AS   LENT  S
CLAY  ADO  ITSA
HAVEN  E  STEEP
AVE   US   DIRT
SENTENCE  O  TO
T  GO  OR  ANOLD
ENEMY  YET  FEE
```

Puzzle 4

```
SOLOMON  ANGEL
H  I  E  B  O  A
U  E  SEE  RULES
TESTS  D  A  D  T
   L  E  THE  D
   MAIN  T  A  FOX
M  S  GROOM
Y     E  N  MUCH
SEVER  G  S  S  E
T  E  QUEEN  PA
E  X  M  E  TEN  V
R     AT  B  A    E
YEARN  HEATHEN
```

Puzzle 5

M	E	S	S	I	A	H			V	A	L	E
I	L	A	I		Z	I	N	A		D	A	N
S	E	I	R		Z	E	A	L		O	U	T
S	A	D		A	L	A	R	M		D	E	
	D		P	E	N		M	E		R		
D		B	E	D		B		A	L	O	E	
O	F		A	G	U	E		D	E	A	L	
G	R	A	C	E		N		Y	A	R	D	
	O	N	E	S		H		S		E		
	S		P	L	A	N	T	E	R	S		
T	W	O		L	O	V	E		S	O		
	O	N		U	S	E	S		I		A	
V	I	N	E		S	E	N	T		S	A	P

Puzzle 6

E	D	O	M	I	T	E	S		D	A	L	E
L	I	N	E	S		N	O	W		G	O	D
E	V	E		D	I	E		E	G	G		
M	I	S	H	M	A		L	E	G		E	
E	N		O	U	T		P		H	A	S	
N	E	S	T	S		I	T		T	A	X	
T		P		T	I	M	O	T	H	Y		O
S	L	E	W		L	A	W		O		U	P
	D		B	A	G		U	Z		H		
O	H		A	L	I	E	N		G		M	E
N	E	C	H	O		S	A	P	H		A	L
	R	U		O	R		A	L	T	A	R	
M	E	T	E	D			M	Y	S	I	A	

Puzzle 7

D	E	L	I	G	H	T		A	S	I	D	E
E	D	O	M		E	H	I		A	R	E	
A	G	A	R		N	I	C	O	L	A	S	
D	E	D	I	C	A	T	E		M		I	
L		U		H			A	C	R	E		
Y		D	O	R		E	G	G		E	N	
	C	E	N	T	U	R	I	O	N	S		D
A		F	E	A	R		E	D	O	M		S
S	E	A		I		R		N	E	T		
P		M	E	N		H		E	L	A	H	
	B	E	D	S	T	E	A	D		L	I	E
H	I	D	E		I	N	N	E	R		L	
E	D		N	U	N		N		A	S	S	

Puzzle 8

	E	A	R	T	H		N	I	G	H	T	
N	A	T	U	R	E		O	D	I	O	U	S
A	T		M	E			O	F		M	E	
H	E	A	P	S	A	N	D		T	R	U	E
U	R	I		P	L	A	I	N		O	L	D
M	S		L	A	M	B		O	R		T	I
		A	S	S		E	R	E				
L	O		P	S		M	A	T	H		L	A
I	N	N		A	H	I	S	H	A	H	A	R
G	E	A	R		E	A	T		B	E	A	M
H	E		O	N			A	I		D	E	
T	A	N	A	C	H		I	N	A	R	A	D
	T	O	R	C	H		I	T	H	E	N	

Puzzle 9

	S	E	E	N		C	R	A	G			
	B	O	R	N	E		H	A	R	O	D	
E	R		R	A	M	P	A	R	T		E	R
B	I	G		N	U	R	S	E		F	A	A
A	B	E	L		E	Y	E		A	I	L	S
L	E	M	U	E	L		D	E	A	R	T	H
		A	C	T				A	R	T		
A	L	L	R	A	N		S	T	O	R	E	A
S	A	L	E		A	G	E		N	E	T	S
I	R	I		A	T	A	L	L		E	H	I
A	G		A	D	U	L	L	A	M		A	S
	E	A	T	E	R		E	T	H	A	N	
	H	E	R	E		R	E	A	D			

Puzzle 10

A	L	L		A	H	A	B		L	A	W	
B	O	O	K		H	A	I	R		I	R	E
L	I	F	E		S	T	R	I	P	P	E	D
E	N	T	E			S	E	E				
	I	N	E	P	T		F	A	C	E	S	
D	A	N		G	O	A	L		L	Y	E	
R	U	E		G	O	M	E	R		E	E	R
I	R	S		L	A	V	E		A	S	A	
P	A	S	T	E		R	I	D	E	R		
	A	N	T				A	N	T	E		
S	T	A	N	D	A	R	D		S	E	A	L
O	W	L		E	R	I	E		E	S	L	I
W	O	E		D	E	A	N		S	E	M	

Puzzle 11

```
F I R S T ■ A D D E R ■
I N D E E D ■ R E U S E D
E D ■ A S U N D E R ■ T U
L E T ■ T R O O P ■ Z U R
D E A L ■ E A R ■ P A R S
■ D R I E T H ■ B U R N T
■ D A S H ■ F A R E ■
S H I R T ■ H E A L T H
T O E S ■ D A N ■ S A U L
O U R ■ F O R C E ■ N N E
P S ■ S E E K E T H ■ G A
S E N S E S ■ S A I L E D
■ S E E S T ■ ■ S P A R S
```

Puzzle 12

```
F L U T E ■ P E L I C A N
L A S H ■ S E B A ■ A R E
A B E A M ■ G A M E ■ A R
G A R D E N ■ L B ■ N O
■ N ■ D E ■ I ■ S R ■
P ■ Y A K ■ B U L R U S H
O B O E ■ O M N I ■ S E E
T ■ D U E T ■ P L A T E S
I D E S ■ H ■ A Y E ■ D I
P A L ■ T N ■ R ■ R R ■ T
H ■ C R I E D ■ I O T A
A I R ■ A E R O ■ A M ■ T
R T ■ D Y L A N ■ L A V E
```

Puzzle 13

```
G A T E ■ D I A D E M ■ M
N O E L ■ I N ■ E R ■ B Y
A ■ N I S A N ■ V A R ■
R M ■ S ■ N ■ G O ■ U S M
L ■ H A G A R ■ T I T H E
■ A B O ■ A M I ■ H E W
A ■ S E P T ■ T O E ■ P L
M A T T H E W ■ N ■ O H
A I ■ H E R ■ E S T H E R
■ N S ■ R S ■ Z ■ E ■ R E
■ W I S E ■ B ■ M A D E
B E A R ■ T O ■ P ■ S D
J O N A T H A N ■ T O ■
```

Puzzle 14

```
E A T ■ C O N S T A N T ■
B R A N D ■ N O T ■ S E A
O T H E R ■ E ■ A ■ S T S
N ■ A W A Y ■ B E A S T
Y E T ■ G E T ■ L A Y ■ E
■ A H I ■ T A K E R ■ A
A T ■ G O ■ B E ■ T A I L
P E T E R ■ L E A H S ■ A
O R ■ A ■ K E P T ■ K E Y
S ■ I L A I ■ T ■ M E
T E L ■ S P E A R ■ E D
L ■ L O O S E ■ C O O K S
E N ■ F R ■ A K I N ■ T
```

Puzzle 15

```
G O M E R ■ O R A T I O N
A X E ■ E P H E S I A N
L E N D E R ■ A P O L L O
A N ■ A D A P T ■ N ■ Y E
T ■ M M ■ I O T A ■ ■ R
I C A N ■ S P A C E ■ E
A I N ■ R E E C H O ■ V S
■ T Y R E ■ ■ H E N C E
A I ■ A D O R E ■ H ■ A
D E E M ■ ■ U S E L E S S
A S A ■ D E N ■ L O S E
M ■ C A I N ■ B O T T L E
■ S H R E D ■ ■ I S ■ F A
```

Puzzle 16

```
F E A R ■ S Y C A M O R E
A T T I C ■ A T ■ N E T
I ■ ■ A L I V E ■ E W E
T R I O D E ■ E ■ ■ O R
H E ■ B ■ ■ S ■ R N
F ■ B E L I E V E ■ A D A
U G L Y ■ S L E E P Y ■ L
L O T ■ H A ■ T ■ R E P
■ A ■ G A I T ■ G O ■ A S
S L Y ■ P A R T ■ B E N T
A ■ E ■ P H E A S A N T
I L L ■ ■ Y ■ K N O T ■ L
L I L Y ■ ■ ■ K ■ E ■ D O
```

Puzzle 17

```
CUT ANY   SERVE
APES  EEL  VIP
NONE E OPEN  S
EN CUD  BOND I
   ARK NEO  AG
TIME BU  REIGN
ROUT  UMP  ACE
ENS  ARBOR E R
A END  EIDER E
SAD  OARS A AW
US  HP  SOWS MA
RIB TI  NETHER
EACH SQ D  AND
```

Puzzle 18

```
SPEAK B M  OWL
EARLY  SEED  O
A RO T EG  TRY
RIOT  OB AWAKE
C R BORN  HM A
HASTE  OOZE IR
  L A STRONG
STORY H N  RAM
TAPED  EYE  BA
ARTS  PRO BABY
Y   F SUN  BAH
  SOLO  NAIL A
LEAD  GIGGLE P
```

Puzzle 19

```
ACTS  LEVITES
P HI  V D  NAG
OMEGA E L   NO
S N A  HEROD
T O  BC  E AD
LAND  H  PAUL
E C ERROR   SI
SHEET  I A N
  E X IS YOUTH
SAY  ESTHER  E
OVEN  L  DELTA
ME  E E P   UR
ENTERTAINMENT
```

Puzzle 20

```
JESUS   SAUL A
O A I GAD URN
HAVEN  MERCY
N I SI S  EYE
  SON  SOAP  B
S REUBEN  E EA
PA G YE  NEWS
U ALL K  TREE
R I   SPEAR B
SING E ANN  A
  EDDY  CALL
SPIN EEL EVIL
 INTENT   ET
```

Puzzle 21

```
 RUTH  REDEEM
SIS E A O V A
EPEE DIME EAR
N LET MA E  I
THEE JETHRO S
 AS T NEE APE
 STRUT R TIN
 L OAR LOT L
ANOINTED  PAL
MOLT EN BETA
SPA  TATTERED
O HAGAR  OR E
NO TOT  ANGEL
```

Puzzle 22

```
MARY BUT  SEEK
AM  JESUS T N
R REAL GO E O
TO  ION  GROW
H SALVATION L
AA  EYE  DINE
 DAVID  B T D
T SIN D ANY G
R C FELT  BE
UP TRINITY Y
T LO G GLEE A
HEART  HEAVEN
 X YOU T RENT
```

Puzzle 23

```
P R A I S E   F O R G E
H I M   I   A D O   E A R
A D     G O P   R T   R R
R E V E N G E   G     D O
A   A H I     E L D E R
O   I   F O U N T A I N S
H O N E Y   R   C
  B   X   R A P   H O M E
F A   A G I L E   I R A N
E D O M   D     S E E D
A I L   D E A R T H   U
T A D   A   R   E   D O R
S H E W B R E A D   O N E
```

Puzzle 24

```
L I S T E N   H E A R D
E D I F Y       A C R E S
T E N   E D   A R C   C T
T A S   S O   B   E A R
E L   D I O T R E P H E S
R   A G R   A P T   E A
  A   I H S   H E A D   W
D W E L T   R A E B U R N
E E   Y   R A M   L M T
N   H   A I D   H E B   I
Y E A R N   E E     U T
  A N O T H E R   E A S E
O R D E A L   R E D E E M
```

Puzzle 25

```
H O S E A   S T A T U T E
E R A   P   I A M     E R
L E M U E L   B A B E L
L   U   S O L O M O N   O
O B E D   V   R   A G A R
  L A T E     E Z E R
M A   V     A R D   D A N
I S A I A H   O   Z I B A
L A   D R A W E R     A M
L   L   A M A S A I   H E
E L I     O G   G O D
T A D M O R   B E N   G I
  P S   N   P A S S I O N
```

Puzzle 26

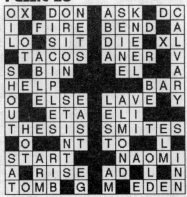

```
O X   D O N   A S K   D C
I   F I R E   B E N D   A
L O   S I T   D I E   X L
  T A C O S   A N E R   V
S   B I N     E L   A
H E L P       B A R
O   E L S E   L A V E   Y
U   E T A   E L I
T H E S I S   S M I T E S
  O   N T   T O   L
S T A R T     N A O M I
A   R I S E   A D   L   N
T O M B   G   M   E D E N
```

Puzzle 27

```
L O R D   S A V O U R   U
I F   U N C L E A N   T N
G   A N D   M I S C   O R
H A N G     S L I T   I
T I T H E S     S I T   G
  S I L E N T   O   O H
I S   L E A H   I N E R T
  P A L M S   N   D E
F I T   E   I N   L E O
I R   A N N A S   P E R U
R I G H T   S L E E P   S
  T E A S E   E   S E A
  M   R E   F O R T S
```

Puzzle 28

```
D A V I D   J O S H U A
A M E N   N O A H   Z R
N O I S E   A B R A H A M
I S L A M   B   S M E L L
E   N E C O   E L   E
L I V E R   T A L L E S T
  S I   A S H   H E M   S
S C R O L L   C   S   W
T A G   D A R I U S   A M
A R I D   Y E A R   R I O
N I N E   I   I D O L S
D O   A B U N D A N T   E
S T U D Y   C H A S E S
```

Puzzle 29

```
A N G E L   B R A I D   R
B A L D   G E A R   O N E
I M A G I N A T I O N   A
D E D I C A T E D   K I D
E     N E T       N E T S
  B E G     M O N E Y
M A N   O H   L A V   S O
N A D A B   D E S E R T
  L I T A N I   A R M O R
A   N   R E G A L     N O
F I G   R E A L   S P E C
A N   T E D   A M O S   K
R   R I N S E S   W I L Y
```

Puzzle 30

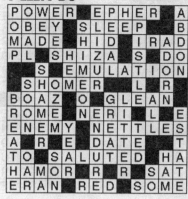

```
P O W E R   E P H E R   A
O B E Y   S L E E P     B
M A D E   H I D   I R A D
P L   S H I Z A   S   D O
    S   E M U L A T I O N
    S H O M E R     L   R
B O A Z   O   G L E A N
R O M E   N E R I   L   E
E N E M Y   N E T T L E S
A   R   E   D A T E     T
T O   S A L U T E D   H A
H A M O R   R   R   S A T
E R A N   R E D   S O M E
```

Puzzle 31

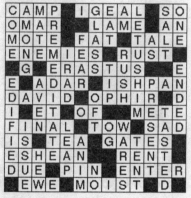

```
C A M P   I G E A L   S O
O M A R     L A M E   A N
M O T E   F A T   T A L E
E N E M I E S   R U S T
  G   E R A S T U S     E
E   A D A R   I S H P A N
D A V I D   O P H I R   D
I   E T   O F   M E T E
F I N A L   T O W   S A D
I S   T E A   G A T E S
E S H E A N   R E N T
D U E   P I N   E N T E R
  E W E   M O I S T   D
```

Puzzle 32

```
P A S   H A R P   F L A G
U T E   O N E R   L A T E
F A T   N O T A   O V E N
F R A M E D   I N W A R D
      E S E   S E E
S A I N T S   E R R O R S
I R R             R E S
N E A R E R   E N A B L E
      I R E   N O T
O L I V E S   A V E N G E
P I N E   E L B E   A L G
E M I R   N U L L   M A I
N E T   T R E S   E D S
```

Puzzle 33

```
S I   R A P   E F F E C T
A D J U R E   T A A   A I
L E   M I T   H R S   S L
U   M   D R E A M   A T L
T O A D   I N N   P I L E
E N D O R   D I V I D E R
    V O L U M E S
V I N E G A R   T O W E R
E N O S   M E M   N A M E
S V G   C E D A R   X   F
S A   T A N   N O R   A U
E D   A R T   S A I N T S
L E A V E   E D D   E E
```

Puzzle 34

```
L O G O   L A R   R O B E
A H A B   U T E   E D E R
P O S T   C A M   D E N G
      A A R   O V E R D O
S T R I F E   V I E
H A U N T   T A M M U Z
O C H   V O L   R I E
W O R S H I P   F L I N T
    E E C   B R E A C H
I N F A N T   E O A
D O E S   O R A   V A I N
O T T O   R O S   E T R E
L E A N   Y E T   N E A R
```

Puzzle 35

Puzzle 36

Puzzle 37

Puzzle 38

Puzzle 39

Puzzle 40

Puzzle 41

H	E	M		T	E	M	A		S	E	E	R
A	W	E		E	R	A	N		T	A	R	E
R	E		O	M	I	T		S	A	G	E	S
E	S	C	A	P	E		H	A	L	L		
		A	R	T		F	A	I	L	E	T	H
P	A	N	S		M	I	L	L	S		R	A
A	H	A		H	I	L	T	S		A	I	R
L	A		F	A	C	T	S		S	T	O	P
E	B	R	O	N	A	H		A	P	E		
		A	R	A	H		S	N	A	R	E	S
H	A	V	E	N		W	A	I	T		S	O
I	R	E	S		I	O	L	A		E	A	R
D	E	N	T		T	E	A	M		D	U	E

Puzzle 42

C	O	W		T	O	W	E	R		D	A	N
A	W	E		A	G	E	N	T		R	I	E
B	L	E	S	S	E	D		C	A	R	E	
			E	K	E		B	R	O	W		
S	I	D	E	S		M	O	U	R	N	E	D
W	O	R	D		V	O	W	E	D		N	O
A	N	Y		S	A	V	E	D		A	T	E
P	I		A	I	L	E	D		O	D	E	S
S	C	A	T	T	E	R		S	N	O	R	T
		B	E	S	T		A	P	T			
S	E	I	R			S	P	O	O	N	E	D
O	L	D		O	U	T	E	R		O	R	E
D	I	E		S	P	A	R	E		N	E	W

Puzzle 43

N	A	M	E		E	M	M	A	N	U	E	L
E	D	I	T	S		O	W		A	V	E	
W	O	N	D	E	R	F	U	L		W	E	D
	R	I		E	A	T				R		
B	E	S	T		S	H	O	R	T	L	Y	
A		T	R	A	I	T		H	I	R	A	M
C	H	E	E	R		A	I	M		S	C	
H	A	R	M	E	D		L	O		E	T	A
	R		B	A	R		W		P	H	I	
O	V	A	L		A		A	R	O	U	N	D
R	E	M	E	D	Y		Y		E	D	G	E
A	S	P			E	S	P			E		
L	T		L	I	F	T		S	O	U	N	D

Puzzle 44

L	O	V	E		S	E	C		C	R	O	P
I	S	A	S		T	W	O		A	O	N	E
F	L	I	P		R	E	M	E	M	B	E	R
E	O	N		B	E	R	A	T	E			
		G	A	I	N		C	L	O	W	N	
B	E	L	O	N	G	E	T	H		T	O	E
A	M	O	K		T	R	I		S	H	E	W
S	I	R		S	H	A	L	L	R	E	S	T
S	T	Y	L	E		L	I	A	R			
			I	N	S	T	E	P		N	O	D
I	N	V	E	S	T	O	R		B	A	R	E
M	E	A	T		A	G	O		A	M	A	N
P	A	T	H		R	A	F		G	E	L	S

Puzzle 45

	N	O	A	H		A	R	A	R	A	T	
H	A	L	T			A	R	T		A	M	
A		I	T	E	M		I	T		A	K	A
D	O	V	E		O	W	N	S		M	E	T
	C	E	N	T	U	R	Y		P	E	N	T
S	C		D	A	R	E		C	A	N		E
H	A	M		I	N	N		O	P		J	R
E	S	T		L		O	P	E	R	A		
M	I		G	O	P	H	E	R		P	R	
	O	P	I	A	T	E			S	H	E	
	N	E	A	T	H		S	A	M	U	E	L
	T	R	E	E			F	O	R	T	Y	
G	A	S		R	E	A	R		E	H		

Puzzle 46

B	L	E	S	S	E	D		E	Q	U	A	L
R	A	G	E		V	E	R	Y		S	H	E
I	D	O	L		E	N	T	E	R		T	
N		A	I	R		S	O		N			
G	O		H	E	L	P		U	P	O	N	
	V	A		A	L	M	I	G	H	T	Y	
R	E	L	E	A	S	E		T	H	Y		
A	R	M		I	T	A	L		A	P		
C		S	A	R	I		O	T	H	E	R	
E	M		A	B	N	E	R		A	L	I	T
	A		A	U	G		D	A	V	I	D	
A	D	D		S			G	E	M		M	
M	E	S	S		S	A	V	E		W	E	

111

Puzzle 47

J	O	S	E	P	H			S	H	E	A	F
A	L	T	A	R				S	T	A	R	S
Y	E	A	R		O	V	E	R	S	E	E	R
	O	I	L		P		V	A			P	I
A		N	I	N	E		E	I	G	H	T	
F	R	E	E		R	I	N	G		O	I	L
R		D	R	E	A	D		H	T		C	O
I	S			A	T	E		T	A	R		R
C		A	D	R	E	A	M		L	E	A	D
A	N	D		S		L	O	V	E	D		
	A	D	O		P		S	I	N		E	G
T	I	E	D	Y	E		E	N	T	R	Y	
O	L	D		E	R	A	S	E		M	E	T

Puzzle 48

H	O	P	E		N	O	T		C	A	N	A
A	M	E	N		A	M	A		R	I	B	S
S	E	N	D		Z	I	P	P	O	R	A	H
T	N	T		W	A	T	E	R	S			
		E	W	E	R			O	S	T	E	O
N	I	C	O	D	E	M	U	S		I	R	A
I	R	O	N		T	I	N		E	M	I	T
L	A	S		P	H	A	R	I	S	E	E	S
E	N	T	E	R			A	C	T	S		
			R	E	L	I	V	E		S	I	S
P	L	E	A	S	U	R	E		R	O	S	E
E	V	E	S		A	I	L		O	M	E	N
T	I	L	E		U	S	S		W	E	E	D

Puzzle 49

H	E	A	L		B	L	E	S	S	I	N	G
E	A	R				O	F	F	E	R		L
A	G	E	S		E	V	I		A	S	I	A
L	L		A		D	E	K	A	R		D	D
T	E	A	C	H	E	R		M	C	M		
H		A	R	A	N		B	E	H	O	L	D
	T	R	I	M		B	E	N		R	E	D
	K	O	F	U		E	C		S	E	A	S
M	O	N	I	L	I	F	O	R	M		R	
A		C		M	O	M		A	U	N	T	
K	N	E	E	L		R	E	C	L	A	I	M
E	W	E	S		M	E		C	L		N	
R	A	G		M	E		H	A			G	O

Puzzle 50

H	E	A	P		R	O	M	E		O	L	D
O	R	L	E		E	R	O	S		M	E	U
R	E	B	A		F	E	S	T		R	A	N
			C	A		L	E	A	S	I	N	G
S	I	S	E	R	A		S	T	E			
P		A		T	N	T		E	N	T	E	R
E	S	N	E		T	I	N		T	I	M	E
W	E	D	G	E		S	O	L		R	I	N
			I	S	T		D	E	S	E	R	T
D	A	Y	S		A	R		S	I			
O	P	E		A	B	I	A	T	H	A	R	S
V	I	A		T	O	L	D		O	B	E	D
E	A	R		E	R	L	E		N	E	T	S